D0847815

THE MAKING OF MODERN THEOLOGY
NINETEENTH- AND TWENTIETH-CENTURY TEXTS

This major series of theological texts is designed to introduce a new generation of readers—theological students, students of religion, professionals in ministry, and the interested general reader—to the writings of those Christian theologians who, since the beginning of the nineteenth century, have had a formative influence on the development of Christian theology.

Each volume in the series is intended to introduce the theologian, to trace the emergence of key or seminal ideas and insights, particularly within their social and historical context, and to show how they have contributed to the making of modern theology. The primary way in which this is done is by allowing the theologians chosen to address us in their own words.

There are three sections to each volume. The Introduction includes a short biography of the theologian, and an overview of his or her theology in relation to the texts which have been selected for study. The Selected Texts, the bulk of each volume, consist largely of substantial edited selections from the theologian's writings. Each text is also introduced with information about its origin and its significance. The guiding rule in making the selection of texts has been the question: In what way has this particular theologian contributed to the shaping of contemporary theology? A Select Bibliography provides guidance for those who wish to read further both in the primary literature and in secondary sources.

Series editor John W. de Gruchy is Professor of Christian Studies at the University of Cape Town, South Africa. He is the author of many works, including *Church Struggle in South Africa*, and *Theology and Ministry in Context and Crisis*.

Volumes in this series

1. *Friedrich Schleiermacher: Pioneer of Modern Theology*
2. *Rudolf Bultmann: Interpreting Faith for the Modern Era*
3. *Paul Tillich: Theologian of the Boundaries*
4. *Dietrich Bonhoeffer: Witness to Jesus Christ*
5. *Karl Barth: Theologian of Freedom*
6. *Reinhold Niebuhr: Theologian of Public Life*
7. *Karl Rahner: Theologian of the Graced Search for Meaning*
8. *Gustavo Gutiérrez: Essential Writings*

Gustavo Gutiérrez

BT
83.57
.G855213
1996

35235650

THE MAKING OF MODERN THEOLOGY

Nineteenth- and Twentieth-Century Texts
General Editor: John W. de Gruchy

GUSTAVO GUTIÉRREZ
Essential Writings

JAMES B. NICKOLOFF
Editor

Fortress Press
Minneapolis

GUSTAVO GUTIÉRREZ
Essential Writings
The Making of Modern Theology series

First Fortress Press edition 1996. Published in cooperation with Orbis Books. Copyright © 1996 Orbis Books. All rights reserved. Except for brief quotations in critical articles or reviews, no part of this book may be reproduced in any manner without prior written permission from the publishers. For permissions write to Orbis Books, P.O. Box 308, Maryknoll, NY 10545-0308 U.S.A.

Cover design: Neil Churcher
Cover photo: Courtesy of *La República,* Lima, Peru

Library of Congress Cataloging-in-Publication Data

Gutiérrez, Gustavo, 1928–
   [Selections. English. 1996]
   Essential writings / Gustavo Gutiérrez : edited by James B.
Nickoloff. — 1st Fortress Press ed.
       p. cm. — (The making of modern theology)
   Includes bibliographical references.
   ISBN 0-8006-3409-8 (alk. paper)
   1. Liberation theology. 2. Theology, Doctrinal. I. Nickoloff,
James B. II. Title III. Series.
BT83.57.G855213 1996
230'.2—dc20   96-34927
                                               CIP

The paper used in this publication meets the minimum requirements of American National Standard for Information Sciences—Permanence of Paper for Printed Library Materials, ANSI Z329.48-1984.

Manufactured in the U. S. A   AF 1-3409

01   00   99   98   97   96   1   2   3   4   5   6   7   8   9   10

CONTENTS

CONTENTS

PREFACE

The present selection from the writings of Gustavo Gutiérrez incorporates texts from all of his full-length theological monographs. It includes several articles from the Peruvian journal *Páginas* that have not before appeared in English translation, an opinion from the Lima daily *La República*, and the unedited texts of two public addresses (one from 1968, the other from 1993). The documents are organized thematically and, within each theme, chronologically. The aim is to acquaint the reader with the broad lines, finer points, and development over time of Gutiérrez's thought.

In Peru the prayer of thanksgiving that follows the communion rite of the mass often involves a number of people from the congregation who, one by one, express thanks for God's gifts. This truly communal *acción de gracias* reminds us that gratitude stands with protest and proclamation as a pillar of the church of the poor. The same must be said of the theology of liberation. Here I would like to acknowledge some of those who, by their generosity, have helped me in preparing this anthology and, in the process, revealed to me the liberating power of the gift of self.

Because the humble and believing builders of God's reign—the true inspirers of Gustavo Gutiérrez's theology—all too often remain anonymous in this world, the personal friendships with members of the parish community of Cristo Redentor in Rímac (Lima) that grew during the year and a half (1986–88) I lived, worked, and learned there represent a special gift. In truth I owe these friendships—and much more—to Gustavo Gutiérrez who, to the surprise of many outside Peru, has long served as pastor of that community. His gracious (and courageous) invitation to me to live and work with him allowed me to see how personal discipleship, pastoral ministry, exacting scholarship, and unconditional love stand behind his treatment of every theological problem. It is my hope that this anthology serves him, and the people he serves, well.

I want to thank Robert Ellsberg, editor-in-chief of Orbis Books, for selecting me to assemble these texts, and J. Michael West and Joe Bonyata of Fortress Press for coaching me through the process. Debts large and small are also owed to the staff at the Instituto Bartolomé de Las Casas-Rímac in Lima; to members of the Society of Jesus (Jesuits) of both New England and Peru; to the missioners of the Catholic Foreign Mission Society of America (Maryknoll) and in particular to Stephen P. Judd; and to my own teachers at the Weston (now Weston Jesuit) School of Theology in Cambridge, Massachusetts, the Jesuit

School of Theology at Berkeley, and the Graduate Theological Union in Berkeley, California.

I wish to acknowledge in a special way the support I have received from the College of the Holy Cross (Worcester, Massachusetts). This includes the keen interest taken in my work by friends and colleagues; the exceptional willingness of many students to struggle in mind and heart with the challenges posed by Gutiérrez's theology (and whose questions have made me grapple with the same); and the public commitment to justice as well as excellence made by the Administration and Board of Trustees of the College, especially John E. Brooks, S.J., former president of the College, in awarding the doctorate *honoris causa* to Gustavo Gutiérrez in 1994.

At the heart of Christian commitment, Gustavo Gutiérrez reminds us, stands the God who is the Friend of Life (Wis. 11:24-26). Faithful friends—to put it theologically—mediate the holy Friend's love; their support alone—to put it simply—makes it possible to complete a volume such as this one. It is my hope that Mary Ann Hinsdale; Grant B. Farquharson and Brian J. McMahon; Rose Gallagher; Barbara Paul; Thomas Martin; Dennis, Marsha, and Karl Johnson; and all of my large family can recognize their contributions here. I know that Robert D. McCleary will be able to.

EDITOR'S NOTE

While it has not been possible to review the translation of all the texts included in this volume, numerous alterations and sometimes substantial changes have been made in previously published material. Readers are urged, of course, to consult the original Spanish texts when possible.

INTRODUCTION

The unmistakable dynamism of the "theology of liberation" formulated by Gustavo Gutiérrez in the last third of the twentieth century is fundamentally simple to name: the twofold commitment he has made to the God of life in whom he believes and to his own people, the believing poor of Peru (and through them to all people). Yet as pastor, teacher, and theologian, he demonstrates that being "bound" to God and to others means in the final analysis being freed, freed from self-centered existence and freed for loving service. In places far from his home in Lima—never before considered a theological center of note—he has moved readers with his reflections on the mysteries of freedom and love. Yet that same distance from his world makes misunderstanding possible, as debates about liberation theology have demonstrated. The present volume offers a selection of representative texts which, it is hoped, will enable the reader to perceive the breadth and depth of Gutiérrez's radical challenge to late twentieth-century Christians. This Introduction to the texts seeks to assist the North Atlantic reader hear his challenge accurately. If Gutiérrez's theological conclusions are defective, as some have claimed, let him be held accountable; if his "re-reading" of the Christian message is on the mark, as many others believe, let us face it head on. In either case, not only is simple fairness to one of the twentieth century's most creative, yet controversial, theologians at stake. More importantly in the view of many, the Christian community's understanding and practice of the message of Christ and the church's very relationship to the God of "the least of the least,"[1] whose numbers grow daily, hang in the balance.

The potency of Gutiérrez's theological vision surely derives from the Pauline triad on which he takes his stand: faith, whose biblical opposite is fear; hope, which gives the lie to all false "realism"; and love, which alone can overcome sin and allow God to reign "on earth as in heaven." Genuine faith is nothing more (or less) than a courageous trust in "things unseen"; Christian faith means placing one's life in the care of the unseen God of Jesus Christ. Hope, which Gutiérrez carefully distinguishes from optimism, is rooted not in human powers but in God's promise and fidelity to that promise. Finally, deeds of love—and not words alone—give flesh to faith and hope. It should not surprise anyone at the close of the twentieth century that such faith, hope, and love meet resistance in many quarters.

Those who know the life and thought of Gustavo Gutiérrez best recognize the courage he shares with the people he has chosen to stand alongside, namely the despised and unimportant of the world who struggle to recover the life given them unconditionally by the Creator but stolen from them by others. Courage shapes Gutiérrez's practice and his theory; indeed, courage is required to link the two dialectically, as Gutiérrez suggests they must be. While fear silences tongues and paralyzes hands, faith and hope, cultivated with courage, loosen tongues to protest the outrages of history and animate hands to reshape that history. Gutiérrez is convinced that in God's plan courage will overcome fear.

FROM THE POOR OF PERU, FOR THE CHURCH OF CHRIST

Gustavo Gutiérrez's often decisive role[2] in national, regional, and international theological conversations and the recognition this has earned him around the world[3] have not made him forget his own origins. Born on June 8, 1928, Gutiérrez spent a humble childhood in Lima and, like many of his fellow Peruvians, knew the hardships of genuine poverty and illness as well as the joys of a loving family. A trying bout of osteomyelitis put him in bed from the age of twelve to eighteen, taught him what physical pain is, and turned him into an avid reader and a cultivator of close friendships. Among the topics of conversations with his precocious young friends were the Christian faith and the political situation of Peru. Perhaps the most important legacy of his childhood was an exceptional sensitivity to the physical, psychological, and spiritual suffering of others.

Gutiérrez began his higher studies at the University of San Marcos in Lima as a medical student with plans to become a psychiatrist. After three years, however, he decided to enter the seminary to prepare for ordination as a Catholic priest of the Archdiocese of Lima. Recognizing his brilliance as a student, some of his friends urged him to go to Europe, a plan his bishop accepted. From 1951 to 1959 he studied philosophy, psychology, and theology at the Catholic University of Louvain (Belgium), the University of Lyon (France), and the Gregorian University (Rome). He received the master's degree in philosophy and psychology in 1955 from Louvain with a thesis called "The Notion of Psychic Conflict in Freud" and the master's degree in theology in 1959 from the Theological Faculty of Lyon. He only applied for and received the doctorate in theology from Lyon in 1985, based on his entire theological corpus and in recognition of the permanent mark he had by then left on twentieth-century Christian thought.

After ordination to the priesthood in 1959, Gutiérrez began to teach theology to undergraduate lay students at the Pontifical Catholic University of Peru and to serve as advisor to the National Union of Catholic Students. In theology courses and during retreats for students of both the humanities and social sciences, he encouraged his listeners to examine the meaning of human existence and the place of God in the world in which they lived. This led him to set the questions and claims of faith in critical dialogue with modern thinkers such as

Albert Camus, Jean-Paul Sartre, and Karl Marx; film directors such as Luis Buñuel and Ingmar Bergman; and writers such as Peruvians José María Arguedas and César Vallejo.

As world Catholicism watched the extraordinary event of the Second Vatican Council unfold from 1962 to 1965, Gutiérrez followed developments closely, even attending the fourth session as a theological assistant to Bishop Manuel Larraín of Chile. Yet he paid equal attention to the flux of events, both ecclesial and sociopolitical, in his own country and across Latin America. To what he saw happening in both spheres he later applied the designation "irruption of the poor." Indeed, it is this irruption, a complex phenomenon known by Latin American social scientists as the *movimiento popular*, which constitutes the social context in which the theology of liberation was born and grew.[4] To neglect the sociopolitical matrix of the theology of liberation is to close one's eyes to the new praxis, new consciousness, and new relationship between God and humankind at the heart of the popular movement. In sum, he finds a new kind of society (characterized by justice), a new kind of human being (characterized by other-directedness), and a new kind of Christian disciple (for whom justice is a requirement of faith) all coming into being in those whose faith in God leads them to fight for freedom and justice, that is, for a *human* life. Absent historical grounding, such lofty claims may of course appear preposterous and even dangerous. Accordingly, Gutiérrez has devoted considerable attention to the methodological problem, that is, how to perceive and interpret the shift in human consciousness he believes he detects in the present historical juncture. The solution he has proposed (to be considered below) is threefold, incorporating social-scientific analysis, the utopian imagination, and Christian faith.

The years 1960 to 1965, then, saw what Gutiérrez came to consider significant breaks in the history of the church and the history of Latin America (and thus the world), namely, a new willingness by the church to embrace the world and the growing resolve of Latin Americans, and most notably Christian believers, to challenge the injustice of the societies in which they lived. It would not be inaccurate to say that this conjunction of events provided the stimulus for the genesis of the "theology of liberation."

In many respects the theology of liberation formed part of the trajectory of developments leading to the Second General Conference of the Latin American Episcopacy held in Medellín, Colombia, from August 26 to September 6, 1968. Among the few who can claim involvement at every step along the way to Medellín is Gutiérrez who felt mixed emotions as he listened to Pope Paul's closing words to the Vatican Council on December 7, 1965. Though he shared the joy of many at the church's new openness to the world, he also felt a sadness at the gap between the optimistic language of the Council and the reality of Latin America. As preparations began for the first post-conciliar meeting of the Latin American Episcopal Council (known by its Spanish acronym CELAM) in 1968, Gutiérrez was a member of the theological team at preliminary discussions on missions and on social reality. At the Medellín conference itself Gutiérrez played an indispensable role as official theological advisor to CELAM. In that capacity and as a member of two working subcommittees, he made outstanding contributions to the theological sections of the documents on "Peace" "Justice," and "Poverty of the Church." Yet his influence was even wider: besides contributing substantially to the theological underpinnings of the document on "Education," he also drafted the two major speeches of his bishop, Cardinal Juan Landázuri Ricketts of Lima, a co-president of the conference, to the plenary sessions of the assembly. Even a cursory reading of the final documents of Medellín reveals central axes of what was becoming Gutiérrez's theology of liberation, in particular the church's decision to make a pastoral option for the poor.

The influence of Gutiérrez in the final statements of Medellín is irrefutable; just as undeniable is the overwhelming approval of the final documents by the assembled representatives of the church of Latin America. While the Peruvian's role should not be minimized, neither can Medellín fairly be seen as an unwitting mistake by naïve bishops. The results of the Third General Conference of the Latin American Episcopate at Puebla, Mexico, a decade later with its clear delineation of the "preferential option for the poor" reaffirm the wisdom and commitment of Medellín.

What can be said more specifically about Gutiérrez's own contribution to the complex process which led to the creation of a theology of liberation? Chronologically, we might point to three key steps in his rethinking of the core of Christian teaching and practice. The first took place at Petrópolis, Brazil, in 1964 at a gathering of theologians concerned about how to relate Christian faith to the new historical movement through which Latin America was passing. In his presentation to the group, Gutiérrez raised the question of theological method by beginning with what he took to be the central pastoral problem of the day, namely, how to establish a salvific dialogue between God and concrete human beings in Latin America. His ideas were later set forth in the short treatise *La pastoral en la Iglesia en América Latina* (1968) in which he contrasted the prevailing pastoral approaches of the Latin American church with his conviction that the church is fundamentally convoked to speak and act prophetically in history.

A second step in the genesis of his thinking occurred three years later during a course Gutiérrez gave in 1967 at the University of Montréal on "The Church and Poverty." Here he dealt not only with theological method but more explicitly with content—specifically the three theological meanings of poverty.[5] It is instructive to compare his thoughts in Montréal with the final text of Medellín on the subject of poverty and the church. "A poor church condemns the unjust lack of this world's goods and the sin which begets it; preaches and lives out spiritual poverty as an attitude of spiritual childhood and of openness to the Lord; commits itself to material poverty. The poverty of the church is, in fact, a constant in the history of salvation" (Medellín, "Poverty of the Church," 4).

The third and decisive step in his own development took place, appropriately, in his own country of Peru. In July, 1968, a month before the Medellín conference, Gutiérrez presented a proposal for a "theology of liberation" at a gathering of priests of the National Office of Social Research (ONIS) in Chimbote, Peru. This marks the first time the term "theology of liberation" was used, in Latin America or anywhere else, as far as we can know.[6] Yet more important than the term is the theological content of "liberation" suggested by Gutiérrez. Already at Chimbote he linked salvation and liberation understood as the work of constructing a more humane temporal city, affirmed the uniqueness of Christian faith's contribution to the revolutionary process—namely, its simultaneous radicalization and relativization of human efforts at self-liberation—and warned of the danger of Christianity's irrelevance or worse if the significance of the kingdom of God for human history is not grasped by Christians. His thoughts circulated widely in Latin America via mimeograph and were published in 1969 in Montevideo as an essay called "Hacia una Teología de la Liberación" ("Toward a Theology of Liberation"). An invitation later that year to address a conference of the ecumenical Commission on Society, Development, and Peace (SODE-PAX), sponsored jointly by the Pontifical Commission on Justice and Peace and the World Council of Churches in Cartigny, Switzerland, on the "theology of development" allowed him to refine his thinking further. A résumé of that presentation was published in 1970 in the U.S. journal *Theological Studies* with the title "Toward a Theology of Liberation." With the publication in late 1971 in Lima of *Teología de la liberación: perspectivas,* Gutiérrez presented in detail the fruits of his intellectual labor and set his agenda for theological work for the future. The scope and depth of the book's challenge to current Christian thinking almost instantly gained for Gutiérrez the attention of the worldwide theological community. Formulations employed in key passages became classic, and a quarter of a century after the first Spanish edition Gutiérrez's masterpiece had been translated into at least ten other languages.

Gutiérrez himself has often pointed out that the notional threads which he was weaving together from 1964 to 1968 into the "theology of liberation" were part of the very fabric of intellectual life in Latin America during these years and that perhaps it was only a matter of time before something like the theology of liberation would appear. While there may be some truth in this, we now know that Gutiérrez's role was indispensable and his contribution unique. Fairness to an individual and a regard for historical facts are not all that is at stake here; as Gutiérrez himself has pointed out, the very *meaning* of liberation theology, much debated for nearly three decades now, depends to some degree on a grasp of the facts of its appearance in history.[7] Like all theologies, liberation theology is the product of a particular historical moment; unlike some theologies, liberation theology is fully aware of this fact.

THE CAREFUL LISTENER

The range and complexity of sources upon which Gutiérrez draws to understand what he takes to be the essentially prophetic character of the Judeo-Christian tradition give his thought its widely recognized depth, solidity, and fruitfulness. Yet nuance and intricacy also expose his writings to misunderstanding, unwarranted simplification, or ideological reduction. With any work of Gutiérrez, even if it appears straightforward, the reader is confronted with the distillation of a complex "conversation" between Gutiérrez and a host of interlocutors: the authors of the Judeo-Christian Scriptures; later commentators on the Bible (including those who presently speak as the official teaching authority of the Catholic church); theological colleagues from around the globe; social scientists from the past and present (including analysts such as Peruvian socialist José Carlos Mariátegui who are largely unknown outside Latin America); Peruvian literary giants such as the poet Vallejo and the novelist Arguedas); the scorned and crushed of history (which includes the vast majority of his own people) whose voices are not easy to discern; and finally, and most importantly, the God in whom he confides. Frankly, it is hard to imagine a better read person than Gustavo Gutiérrez, and not just among contemporary theologians.[8] Let us briefly examine this extraordinary range of influences on his thinking.

SCRIPTURE: SPIRITUAL ANCESTORS

Serious attention to the Bible and contemporary biblical scholarship permeates Gutiérrez's treatment of the Word of God and the doctrine of revelation and reflects his years of study at Lyon, a center of biblical studies in the 1950s.[9] Yet few outside Peru know that he preaches carefully crafted homilies nearly every Sunday as pastor of a parish in a poor neighborhood of Lima or that for seven years he provided biweekly commentaries on readings from the Catholic lectionary as a service to other preachers and to ordinary Catholics across the country.[10] His role as founder in 1971 and guiding spirit of Lima's "*Jornadas de reflexión teológica*" (popularly known as the "summer course" in theology) is widely recognized, though the extent to which Scripture figures in course lectures and discussion groups is perhaps less well known.[11] He has, of course, also produced a major biblical commentary (*On Job*, Spanish 1986) as well as a comprehensive biblical theology (*The God of Life*, Spanish 1989). It is easy to see why some critics, Christian and non-Christian alike, find Gutiérrez overly "traditional." Yet there is no way to understand his thought (or his life) apart from his appropriation of the Word of God.

Because "the Word [of God is] contained in Scripture and transmitted by the living tradition of the church,"[12] Gutiérrez takes his cue in interpreting that word from the actual experience of the ecclesial community itself. What he has noticed, and repeatedly pointed out in his writings, is that Christians not only find answers to their questions in the Bible but also frequently discover that the Word of God puts new questions to *them*. Thus, while *we* read the Bible, it is also true to say that *the Bible* "reads" us. Through Scripture God questions believers about the adequacy of their discipleship.[13] It is this second "reading" which has especially concerned Gutiérrez and which led him to set forth the hermeneutical principles he follows in attempting to understand God's questions to the ecclesial community.

Several principles of biblical interpretation arise from the Bible itself. The ineffable mysteriousness of the God of the Bible means that understanding begins, for Gutiérrez, with *faith* in the mystery. Furthermore, he leaves no doubt about the christocentric, or "christo-finalized," nature of his faith and therefore his scriptural exegesis.[14] Jesus Christ is "the primordial, and in a certain sense unique, source of revealed truth" and is himself the good news.[15] "Because he is the "fulfillment of the promise of the Father," he is "the only way to grasp the profound unity of the Old and New Testaments."[16] Thus, Gutiérrez sees biblical interpretation as a dialogue between believers of the past and people of faith today. He specifies even further that, "because the Bible is to a great extent the expression of the faith and hope of the poor and above all because it reveals to us a God who loves preferentially those the world passes over,"[17] we must listen with special regard to those who both believe *and* are poor.

Second, in the Bible "God's saving action manifests itself in historical events" which constitute the "language" of Scripture. But believers bring their own personal and collective histories to their reading of the Bible. For Gutiérrez this means, above all, his people's complex history of unjust suffering, struggles to protect its right to life, and hope in God. As a dialogue of histories—the history of past and present believers—biblical interpretation can "shed light on our present history, both collective and personal, and help us to see in it the intervention of the God who liberates."[18]

Third, Gutiérrez takes seriously the common experience of believers who can identify with the Word of God despite their distance in time and culture from the biblical authors. Yet a sense of the word's "nearness" does not excuse believers today from making the effort to understand the social, cultural, and religious contexts in which the biblical texts were written. Contemporary biblical scholarship, then, can help to overcome the distance we also feel from the scriptural texts. An adequate approach must overlook neither the Bible's nearness to us nor its distance from us.

Finally, believers today are not the first to ask questions of the Bible and in turn be questioned by Scripture. The church is in fact the historical community of those who question and are "questioned" by Scripture. Gutiérrez accordingly strives to take seriously the biblical "readings" of previous generations of believers.

ECCLESIAL COLLEAGUES:
TRADITION AND THE CHURCH'S MAGISTERIUM

From the beginning, Gutiérrez's work demonstrated his conviction that "a privileged *locus theologicus* for understanding the faith will be the life, preaching, and historical commitment of the church."[19] Church teaching is present (and often explicitly noted) on nearly every page of Gutiérrez's writings. Indeed, his views have been profoundly shaped by the believing community's theological tradition and its authoritative interpretation.

In his analyses Gutiérrez frequently discovers unsuspected riches, theoretical as well as practical, in the church's living theological tradition. At the same time he does not shy away from pointing out inadequacies in Christian thought and practice. His work in the 1960s, including the preparation of *A Theology of Liberation*, was largely devoted to rethinking the pastoral practice of the church in Latin America whose failings raised fundamental ecclesiological questions as well. The warning he issued in his 1978 essay on the eve of the Latin American bishops' conference in Puebla ("The Preparatory Document for Puebla: A Retreat from Commitment") doubtless contributed to the clarification of, and eventual consensus about, the notion of the "preferential option for the poor."[20] The notion that the God of the Bible sides with the poor and oppressed of history (a notion whose recovery owes much to the Peruvian theologian) today finds broad support from the Catholic church's magisterium.[21] The subtitle of Gutiérrez's 1986 work *The Truth Shall Make You Free: Confrontations* suggests the context of conflict in which the church's theological discussion has at times proceeded since the Second Vatican Council. The key to understanding Gutiérrez's part in the sometimes difficult conversation between liberation theologians and other sectors of the church, including its magisterium, is be found in the aforementioned fidelity he seeks to maintain to God and to the poor and the love and respect for the church which mark every sentence he writes.[22]

Gutiérrez has not to date produced a full-blown treatment of the problem of doctrinal development in the history of the church. But his own de facto view may be glimpsed in his analysis of theological breakthroughs in other times. His compelling and exhaustive study of the sixteenth-century debate in Spain, in which the Dominican friar and bishop Bartolomé de Las Casas took a leading role, over the *theological* meaning of the Conquest, the human and Christian status of the native inhabitants, and the correct method of evangelization to be employed by the church reveals Gutiérrez's conviction that theological development and renewal are often the fruit of a shift in historical context and, correspondingly, of a shift (conscious or not) in the vantage point from which theologians consider the mysteries of faith. When such a shift is consciously undertaken, it is possible only through profound personal conversion and, dialectically related to this, a shift in pastoral practice.[23] Thus, the history of theology demonstrates more than the simple application of Christian teaching to new historical contexts; what Gutiérrez finds is the Christian community's growing understanding of its own faith. When the church embraces and exercises the freedom offered as gift by the Spirit, it has often discovered that seemingly "secular" historical events may shed light on the meaning of its own tradition.

The foregoing means that Gutiérrez finds in the life of the church a genuine *locus theologicus;* while historical praxis serves as the indispensable medium through which the Christian community comes to understand God's revealed truth, about which "a great deal still remains to be learned"[24]:

> The ultimate criteria come from revealed truth, which we accept in faith, and not from praxis itself. It is meaningless—it would, among other things, be a tautology—to say that praxis is to be criticized "in the light of praxis."[25]

We must note, at the same time, that Gutiérrez speaks of "criteria" in the plural and that the modifier "ultimate" implies a legitimate role for less-than-ultimate criteria as well. Indeed, in Gutiérrez's view the practice of faith—discipleship—is one such criterion for the correct statement of Christian truth. But Christian praxis itself must always be linked to eschatology, the Christian affirmation of a world beyond the present life.[26] Thus, to say that "Jesus Christ is the hermeneutical principle for all understanding of the faith" implies "the fundamental hermeneutical circle: from humanity to God and from God to humanity, from history to faith and from faith to history. . . ."[27] The practice of faith in a concrete historical context, then, is the "indispensable condition" for a correct reflection on faith.[28] In Gutiérrez's view, the inescapable context in which Christian faith must be practiced today is the massive social, economic, and political marginalization of the majority of the earth's people.[29] This alarming and painful *fact* confronts Christian thinking and action; that is, it demands a response which is at one and the same time theoretical and practical.

CONTEMPORARY THEOLOGICAL COLLEAGUES

Though it is no show of false modesty when Gutiérrez claims to be a "part-time theologian," he has entered into some of the most significant theological conversations of the day with seriousness and gusto. Nor can anyone doubt that he has been heard, if not always well understood or welcomed by all, in that conversation.[30] His principal theological interlocutors may be divided into four groups: (1) European thinkers, Protestant and Catholic alike, who laid the foundations for the theology of the Second Vatican Council (among them Karl Barth, Dietrich Bonhoeffer, Rudolf Bultmann, M.-D. Chenu, Yves Congar, Jacques Maritain, Karl Rahner, Edward Schillebeeckx, Pierre Teilhard de Chardin, and Paul Tillich) and their heirs (among them Johann-Baptist Metz and Jürgen Moltmann); (2) the teaching of the Catholic magisterium (especially as formulated by Popes John XXIII, Paul VI, and John Paul II; the Vatican's Sacred Congregation for the Doctrine of the Faith; and the Latin American episcopate at its meetings in Medellín, Puebla, and Santo Domingo); (3) North American theologians, critics as well as supporters, and in a special way those who have developed feminist, Afro-American, and Hispanic theologies of liberation; and, finally, (4) colleagues from Latin America, Africa, and Asia.[31] Besides his writings, Gutiérrez's active participation in theological and pastoral conferences beyond counting testifies to his conviction that theological work must today be collaborative. (No one has yet figured out how Gutiérrez manages to do all the things he does in the time he has at his disposal.)

Let me suggest some of the ways these diverse theological conversation partners have influenced Gutiérrez's thought, in particular the Christian doctrine of salvation and its correlate, God's special love for the least of humanity. Though the size of Gutiérrez's theological corpus appears modest when compared to other major Christian thinkers of this century, the range of interlocutors as well as his own creativity give Gutiérrez's theology its widely acknowledged breadth *and* depth, its nuance, and its solidity—in short, its power to clarify, challenge, and convert.[32]

The earliest writings of Gutiérrez (from the years 1966–1971), including *A Theology of Liberation,* demonstrate his regard for the works of distinguished European theologians from World War I through the Second Vatican Council. Widespread postconciliar euphoria did not hide from his view the appalling situation of poverty in the world or the courageous if costly efforts underway to end oppression. Nor did he fail to note the challenge posed by these realities to the Christian doctrine of salvation. Soteriology, indeed, has been the central concern of all Gutiérrez's works from the 1960s to the present. At the heart of his formulation of a theology of liberation is the dialectical relationship he posits between God's free gift of salvation on the one hand and human efforts at liberation in history on the other. In a widely accepted (and frequently quoted) schema, he proposes that liberation be understood as a three-fold process which embraces (1) the creation of a just and humane socioeconomic and political order, (2) the emancipation of human consciousness from self-concern (in the case of those who abuse others for their own self-aggrandizement) or from the lack of a sense of self (in the case of those crushed in history by the selfishness of others) to solidarity with others, and (3) redemption by God from sin for a communion of love. Liberation, emancipation, and redemption: each term enriches the others in Gutiérrez's restatement of the theory of salvation. While the strength of Gutiérrez's soteriological model, indeed its whole point, lies in the unity he claims for the threefold process of liberation, he is careful to distinguish the three levels as well. Though he rejects both a causal and a chronological relationship among them, he also seeks to avoid a false identification and an equally false juxtaposition. A direct (immediate) relationship would open the door to politico-religious messianism; the denial of any meaningful relationship would allow for an idealistic, privatized faith ready to accommodate itself opportunistically to the unjust status quo in the world.

Gutiérrez's proposed reinterpretation of the doctrine of salvation and its relation to political praxis cannot be adequately understood apart from the mediating term—"utopia"—he has retrieved and added to the usual bipolar framework of faith and politics. In Gutiérrez's view, God's saving activity (third level) alone *unifies* the threefold but single liberation process, and thus grounds authentically Christian political praxis (first level). But it is the second level—utopia—which correctly and fruitfully *mediates* the relationship of political praxis and redemption from sin. Gutiérrez argues that a grasp of the utopian level not only expands our understanding of liberation processes in history; it also allows us to see how politically liberative praxis deepens our understanding of the Christian faith itself. Gutiérrez in no way disputes the soteriological priority of God's saving activity; he does assert the epistemological import of utopia.

For Gutiérrez, utopia refers to "a personal transformation by which we live with profound inner freedom in the face of every kind of servitude."[33] The transformation he has in mind is the movement from fear to trust, from resignation to initiative, and from isolation to solidarity. The achievement of this transformation alone makes possible "a real encounter among persons in the midst of a society without social inequalities."[34] While such a shift is only possible thanks to God's grace, it is also brought about by persons themselves, i.e., it is "human self-creation."[35] Those who think they find Pelagian tints here, or simply an irrational illusion, would be directed by Gutiérrez to examine the lives of Peru's poor who, though formerly "absent from history," are now becoming "active agents of their own history," a fact widely attested in the social-scientific literature of Latin America.[36] Despite old and new forms of oppression, such "new persons" have haltingly but surely initiated a "different history"[37] and begun to create a qualitatively different kind of society based on solidarity rather than the radical individualism characteristic of the modern West.[38] In the ongoing struggle of the poor to achieve their own liberation and the liberation of those who oppress them, Gutiérrez finds empirical support for Karl Rahner's restatement of a classic principle of Thomist theology, namely, the direct, not inverse, proportion between radical reliance on God and genuine human autonomy.[39] Gutiérrez knows that this principle is only truly understood by those who both experience themselves as free subjects responsible before God and who accept this responsibility. And he sees its concrete verification in the struggle of the marginalized to eliminate the margin itself: "the gratuitous gift of the kingdom is accepted *in their efforts* to free themselves from exploitation."[40]

The theory of salvation proposed by Gutiérrez reveals his debt to European colleagues; indeed, he notes the links between the political theology of Metz, for example, and his own liberation theology. But from the beginning he has also pointed out the differences, and even opposition, between the theology of liberation and modern European theology.[41] Far from being simply a more radical version of progressive European thought, the theology of liberation poses a direct challenge to the former because of the historical relationship between

Latin America and Europe. Written from the "underside" of the history of Western development (and not simply from an earlier stage of it), theology in Latin America must, in Gutiérrez's view, challenge any understanding of God which accepts the worldwide status quo and fails to get to the roots of the inhuman suffering Western "development" and "progress" have caused and continue to cause. While he acknowledges the urgency for Europeans of dialogue with secularized, nonbelieving "modern" persons, he is not willing to excuse his North Atlantic colleagues from addressing an even more pressing reality, but one more difficult for them to see: the shadow side of their own civilization.[42] Some would say that, despite a century of unparalleled crimes against humanity in Europe, the most incisive and original minds on that continent have not achieved the comprehensive critique of Western civilization and Western Christianity mounted by Latin American liberation theologians, led by Gutiérrez.[43] Thus, the question which his own Latin American context poses to him and which always serves as his theological point of departure—namely, how to tell those who suffer unjustly that God loves them—is in fact not simply a "Latin American" question. Gutiérrez's principal theological interlocutor—namely, the "non-person" of today (meaning those *treated* as non-persons by the world)—is the creation of the world of modernity itself. As such, "non-persons" pose universal, and not simply "local," questions to society and to the church.

Without a doubt Gutiérrez must be counted among those who have shaped the universal church's reception of the Second Vatican Council's teachings. The story of his role in the birth of a distinctively Latin American theology and the transformation of church's self-understanding largely remains to be told.[44] At the heart of both stands the principle of God's "preferential option for the poor,"[45] in Gutiérrez's view the outstanding contribution of Latin America to the world church. Though its implications remain the subject of discussion, the principle today permeates all levels of official Catholic church teaching.[46] Careful exegetical and theological scholarship and (equally importantly) pastoral experience have clarified the notion which was implicit at Medellín in 1968, ratified at Puebla in 1979, and reiterated at Santo Domingo in 1992. Indeed, some today see the promotion of justice (whose theological foundation is the preferential option), as having achieved a *status confessionis*—that is, it is now seen to be an element so fundamental to biblical revelation and church teaching that personal decisions made in regard to it become decisions for or against the faith itself.[47]

The contemporary church's grasp of the biblical God's predilection for the poor and the pastoral consequences of this preference owes no one a greater debt than Gustavo Gutiérrez. His recovery of this ancient and classic insight (see 1 Cor. 1:26–31) began with his recognition that the "inhuman misery" (Medellín, "Poverty of the Church," 1), "antievangelical poverty" (Puebla 1159), and "intolerable extremes of misery" (Santo Domingo 179) which characterize Latin

America constitute "institutionalized violence" (Medellín, "Peace," 16) and thus a violation of God's plan for the construction of a kingdom of life. The divine will to life, then, reveals itself most radically in God's choice as objects of special concern those whose lives, whose very existence stands at greatest risk. In the dialectic between the universality of God's love and the particularity of God's decision to stand with the poor, Gutiérrez finds mutual implication, not opposition. This represents one of the earliest affirmations of the theology of liberation.[48] Indeed, each pole demands the other; elimination of either results in a reductionism—either to an abstractionism literally fatal to the poor, or to a narrow sectarianism incompatible with the church's mandate to make the reign of God's love universally manifest. The church of the poor *is* the church of all.[49]

The terms "preferential" and "option," a literal translation of the Spanish *opción preferencial*, present English-speaking people with certain difficulties which require clarification. First, as used by Gutiérrez and the church's magisterium, the notion of God's *preference* for the poor signifies the priority the "nobodies" of history receive within the scope of God's care for *all* of creation. As Gutiérrez has put it,

> preference implies the universality of God's love, which excludes no one. It is only within the framework of this universality that we can understand the preference, that is, "what comes first."[50]

"Preferential," then, means "having priority."

Second, it must be noted that God's *option* for the poor, and thus the *church's*, is not something "optional" which Christians may take or leave and continue to be followers of Christ. "To opt for the poor" (*optar por los pobres* in Spanish) means to make a free decision to side with the oppressed and powerless in their fight for justice and to stand against all persons and structures that oppose their liberation. Perhaps, then, English-speaking Christians might best think of the "option" as "a decision to make a commitment." Taking sides with the poor transforms the world into a place of justice; in the process, of course, it transforms the lives of the poor *and* the lives of those (poor and non-poor) who make this choice.

It is also worth observing that the decision (option) Christians make vis-à-vis the poor is shaped by the angle from which reality is viewed. In Gutiérrez's opinion, the priority given by God to the poor carries epistemological consequences for both social and theological analysis. Assigning "epistemological priority"[51] to the struggle of the poor for life and dignity means adopting the standpoint or vantage point of the poor (that is, their *viewpoint* but not necessarily their *views*) in order to come to an accurate understanding of the *human* (or inhuman) character of any given context and an adequate *Christian* interpretation of that context.[52] To sum up: to make a preferential option for the poor means to choose to give the poor practical priority and to shape one's practice by looking at the world through the eyes of the outcasts.

A final word about the genesis of the notion of the preferential option for poor: though the formula itself is correctly associated with the Puebla conference (1979), the fundamental idea, which synthesizes three distinct elements, was already present in germ at Medellín (1968) and, indeed, in Gutiérrez's own thinking as early as 1967. This can be seen by examining the three meanings of the term "poverty" proposed by Gutiérrez at Montréal and adopted by the Latin American episcopate at both Medellín and Puebla. The correspondence between the three meanings of poverty and the three elements of the term "preferential option for the poor" is no coincidence since Gutiérrez himself developed both from the experience of his own people. As he explains, poverty refers to (1) the lack of what is necessary for a human life (privation); (2) openness to God's will rooted in a profound interior freedom ("spiritual childhood"); and (3) the vulnerability, material and otherwise, which comes from choosing to live in solidarity with those who suffer destitution through no choice of their own (analogous to the "voluntary poverty" championed by Dorothy Day). It is not hard to see that privation corresponds to "the poor," poverty of spirit makes a choice ("preference") possible, and solidarity represents the concretization of the choice made ("option"). With the expression "preferential option for the poor," Gutiérrez attempted to synthesize the three meanings of poverty in a single phrase.

A word should be said about the meaning of salvation and God's preferential option for the poor in relation to two classes of people whose struggles for liberation have provided the context for noteworthy North American contributions to the theological enterprise—namely, the struggles of African-Americans and of women. Gutiérrez has on many occasions acknowledged his debt to those who have developed other theologies of liberation, including a black theology of liberation and a feminist theology of liberation.[53] In recent years he has pointed out in no uncertain terms that Latin America is at one with other parts of the world in perpetuating racist and sexist societies.[54] Attention to racial and ethnic oppression should come as no surprise in his work: as a Peruvian of indigenous ancestry, Gutiérrez has long been among the keenest students of that country's racial-ethnic divides. Indeed, he dedicated his *Theology of Liberation* to "two dear friends: José María Arguedas, a Peruvian writer on Indian culture, and Henrique Pereira Neto, a black priest in Brazil."[55]

Nor should the significance of his reference to women in the opening sentence of his 1971 classic be underestimated. In language considered redundant at the time, he states the book's purpose: "This book is an attempt at reflection, based on the gospel and the experiences of men and women committed to the process of liberation in the oppressed and exploited land of Latin America."[56] Men *and* (especially) women were examples to him of the "new kind of human being" and protagonists of the "new history" he saw in the making. Men *and* (especially) women are building a qualitatively new kind of society. Gutiérrez's "novel" language thus reflected the *novum* he perceived bursting forth in human history. Perhaps the most representative response by Gutiérrez to the struggle of women for full liberation as human beings is to be found not in his writings, though he offers us groundbreaking insights in this regard,[57] but in his pastoral work, including his teaching. Beginning in the early 1960s in his capacity as national advisor to the National Union of Catholic Students (UNEC) of Peru, he organized seminars for women on such topics as "A Biblical Theology of Women"[58] and has long been a champion of theological education for women, especially poor and indigenous women in his own country and throughout Latin America.[59] None of this means, of course, that he does not recognize a debt of gratitude to those who in the ensuing years have helped him "to see with new eyes our [Latin American] racial and cultural world, and the discrimination against women."[60]

POETICAL TRUTH AND THEOLOGICAL TRUTH

Frequently overlooked among the sources of Gutiérrez's thought and discourse is the brilliant literature of his native Peru. At home Gutiérrez has long been recognized as an expert in this legacy as well as a master stylist of the Spanish language in his own right.[61] Yet his commentaries on the works of Peru's greatest writers, especially those of poet César Vallejo (1892–1935) and novelist José María Arguedas (1913–1969), reveal the profound effect they have had on his thinking. References to these two writers are seldom lacking in Gutiérrez's own writings, even the most rigorously theological.[62] It is Vallejo, writes Gutiérrez, "whose witness has helped me to understand the Book of Job and relate it more fully to my own experience."[63] No book of the Bible has received more attention from Gutiérrez as he has wrestled with the agonizing problem of how to affirm the gratuitous love of God at the origin of all things, the central theme of biblical revelation, in the face of the suffering of the innocent.[64] The author of the Book of Job puts the heart of his message into the mouth of God by "tapping his deepest poetical vein." Perhaps only a "poet-theologian"—such as Gutiérrez himself—can both embrace and give expression to the mystery at the heart of creation.[65]

Vallejo's significance notwithstanding, the most prominent literary figure in the thought-world of Gutiérrez is doubtless the novelist Arguedas, with whom he enjoyed a brief but profound friendship. No one should overlook the lengthy epigraph in *A Theology of Liberation* taken from Arguedas' novel *Todas las sangres*. This extended passage, omitted from the first English edition of Gutiérrez's *magnum opus* and included in the revised edition only in Spanish because of the difficulty of translating it, sums up the central theme of Gutiérrez's own book and, indeed, his theology. In Arguedas' creation of a dialogue between a poor, mixed-race sacristan and a visiting Spanish priest in a forgotten Andean town, the sacristan explains that oppressed Indians find God in their suffering and know that "the God of the masters is not the same. He makes people suffer with no consolation." Gutiérrez restates Arguedas's insight: "[The God of the masters] is not the God of the poor, not the God of the Bible. The biblical God is the one who proclaims the good news to the poor."[66] In the face of innocent suffering Arguedas asserts what Gutiérrez takes as a profound theological truth: "What we know is far less than the great hope we feel."[67]

With Arguedas, Vallejo, and earlier Peruvians, such as the sixteenth-century Peruvian *mestizo* writers Guamán Poma and Garcilaso de la Vega, Gutiérrez himself lives between two worlds, the world of the oppressor and the world of the victim. With them he embraces the whole of his nation—the powerful and the powerless—by beginning with the powerless. Gutiérrez's theology reflects the same interior conflict experienced by Arguedas's *mestizo,* who voluntarily joins the "fraternity of the miserable."[68] While Arguedas saw one era of Peru's history coming to an end and a new era beginning, Gutiérrez believes that we stand at the divide between two eras of salvation history, and thus universal history. If the old era belonged to the "God of the whip," who was the enemy of the poor and of all true revolutionaries, the new era begins with the proclamation of the God of life, who is the friend and ally of the poor—and who *is* poor. Only the epistemological rupture discussed above makes such a perception possible. By befriending those who were the old God's victims and enemies, Gutiérrez discovers who the God of the Bible really is, namely, the God who is Life, Hope, Freedom—Friend. The God of the poor draws close to, and can most clearly be "seen" by, those who find a way to draw near the poor. If *God* is our *friend,* we have the *theological* basis for overturning all structures of injustice. If in the poor and persecuted figure of Jesus Christ God is one of us, we are confronted not with the evaporation of God's transcendence, as some fear, but with the transcendence of our captivity. Liberated humanity does not overcome God; rather, in partnership with God human beings overcome their own enslavement.

As even the most strictly theological of his writings attest, Gutiérrez has, with Arguedas and Vallejo, lived in his heart and flesh the crisis and agony of his cherished Peru. He learned from them that the suffering of Peru derives from the encounter—or failed encounter—of cultures and worlds two and a half millennia in the making. Though such a meeting could never have been simple, it remains painfully incomplete 450 years after it began. With Arguedas and Vallejo Gutiérrez came to distinguish a true from a false future for Peru. He is convinced that a truly human (and thus a truly Christian) future for Peru cannot be achieved simply by following in the footsteps of the nations of the modern West. Yet he also knows that the precise shape of the new future cannot now be clearly perceived or known; it is, instead, a reality "felt" and hoped for. And while the previous era is not entirely finished, the new one has already begun. Furthermore, the clash between opposing worlds, cultures, and historical eras that Gutiérrez sees (and suffers) in Peru affords, he believes, a glimpse into the meaning of universal human history.

What are the signs of the new future that Gutiérrez perceives, however indistinctly? At present the false hope of personal self-realization achieved apart from others—the ideal of Western individualism—stands opposed to a project of constructing an "authentic fraternity in the bosom of a people." In the long run individualism would destroy humanity, and, as more than four centuries have shown, the "modernization" of Peru along Western lines would mean the expansion of privilege for the rich, not the incorporation of all into the nation's life.[69] By contrast, the nascent solidarity among the poor—dramatically seen in Peru, for example, when ethnic identity gradually gives way to a consciousness of social class—is the source of a genuine hope against the ubiquitous forces of death.

Yet the conflict between past and future, between individualism and fraternity, cannot give way to redemption if those who embody the former are simply obliterated. A source of hope for Gutiérrez, as for his Peruvian mentors, rests in the capacity of those who have been despoiled, whose humanity has been deformed, whose very soul violated, to safeguard their humanity even as they live through the nightmare of oppression. Though ravaged for centuries, the poor of Peru, and in particular the descendants of the indigenous inhabitants so despised by the conquerors, have never completely lost their human dignity. Rather it is the very ones thought for centuries to be barely human (and treated accordingly by those who have considered themselves superior) who alone "are capable of combating the dehumanization in the oppressors and in themselves."[70] The power of the poor, the disdained, and the persecuted lies not in their capacity to destroy those whose hearts of stone permit them to oppress, but to convert them and give them hearts of flesh.[71] For Arguedas the greatest punishment for the "city of oppressors" (symbolized by Lima) will be its transformation into a happy city where no one hates[72]; for Gutiérrez the present hell of injustice will be transformed into the heavenly Jerusalem where every tear will be wiped away (see Isa. 25:8; Rev. 21:4).

Signs of the new era and the new world emerging from within the old abound for those with eyes to see. *Compassion* is necessary in any truly revolutionary project because cruelty only destroys. *Love* alone makes communion possible in a multicultural society like Peru. Love is not an anti-revolutionary flight from history but the power that gives meaning and vitality to political commitment. *Memory* of the past with its joys and sufferings is not simple nostalgia but the source of renewal and subversion. *Repentance* (by those who wrong others) and *forgiveness* (by those who are wronged) together open the way to renewed relationship and life. In their innocence *music and beauty* nourish and express joy. Simple *kindness* saves through its power to refresh those who are tired. Finally, *suffering* accepted in order to end suffering is redemptive.[73] Compassion, love, memory, repentance and forgiveness, music and beauty, gentle kindness, and redemptive suffering: these are the means by which a new era in human history comes to be and the signs of its coming. In theological language they are the sacraments of God's reign.

It would not be too much to say that Gustavo Gutiérrez has a living relationship with certain non-theologian Peruvian predecessors whose sensitivity has shaped his life and thought—which means his life with God, his understanding of God, and thus his language about God. In writing about God he gives voice to *their* deepest concerns, sorrows, passions, and insights. And in writing about them Gutiérrez cannot, of course, avoid writing about himself.

> [Arguedas's] life, with all its achievements and limitations, was not truncated; turned toward the poor and scorned of the country, he showed us the way to keep on "sucking the juice from the earth in order to nourish those who live in our homeland."

"Arguedas is . . . the one who foretells the time that is coming," writes Gutiérrez.[74] The first task of the church is precisely this: to proclaim a new epoch. As a member of the church, he has vigorously taken up that task which, he believes, today requires recourse to avenues of knowledge formerly ignored or even scorned by the theological tradition, in particular the social sciences.

SOCIAL-SCIENTIFIC ANALYSIS AND THEOLOGICAL TRUTH

Gutiérrez insists on commitment to the poor and on the epistemological privilege of their vantage point on *theological* grounds, namely, the special care of the God of the Bible for the poor and God's choice of the oppressed as the favored instrument for the accomplishment of the divine will in history. All agree that Gutiérrez's incorporation of social-scientific thought into the work of theological reflection constitutes a significant methodological innovation in contemporary theology. Nevertheless, some have questioned the legitimacy of his proposition. For this reason it is important to delineate the nature of the relationship Gutiérrez asserts between theological inquiry and the disciplines of history, sociology, economics, anthropology, and psychology. There is no question here of "subjecting" divine revelation or theological truth to social-scientific judgment or verification; it is rather a matter of using the best tools available to achieve a sound understanding of the real world in which the church must carry out its mission of evangelization.

In Gutiérrez's view two central features of the contemporary world, and of Latin America in particular, require careful analysis: the fact of massive (and still increasing) poverty and the complex efforts of the poor to liberate themselves from poverty and its consequences. In his own effort to grasp this multifaceted situation, Gutiérrez takes a critical approach to social science. For example, he not only insists that the social sciences can be of inestimable value in penetrating reality; he also recognizes their incipient and nonabsolute character and notes the openness of science by its very nature to constant critical reexamination. He asserts that Christians must interpret the facts of poverty and struggles against it in the light of faith. He maintains a critical stance toward liberation movements, which, because they are immensely complex human processes, never escape a certain degree of ambiguity. He denies that any political program or system, however "scientifically" and carefully worked out, guarantees the quest for liberation. And he has frankly pointed out history's destruction of illusions about systems which claim to eliminate all evils.[75]

The principal touchpoints of controversy in Gutiérrez's use of social science have been his supposed uncritical acceptance of Marxist sociology and its influence in his theological opinions.[76] Because of the conceptual intricacies of the disciplines of theology and sociology and the necessarily complex nature of the dialogue between them which Gutiérrez has proposed, even professional theologians and sociologists may find themselves in deep water when they enter into truly interdisciplinary conversation. For this reason Gutiérrez has attempted to set forth his positions as clearly as possible, notably in his 1984 essay "Theology and the Social Sciences."[77]

While his primary interest centers on the dialogue between theology and the social sciences generally—and not the narrower conversation with Marxism—Gutiérrez sets forth guidelines for what he believes constitutes a legitimate theological use of Marxist analysis. First, he distinguishes between "Marxist analysis" and "Marxism" understood as a "total conception of life and therefore excluding Christian faith and its demands."[78] He also rules out "any totalitarian version of history which negates the freedom of the human person."[79] He points out that the question of the relationship between Marxist ideology and Marxist social analysis remains unresolved even among those who lay claim to Karl Marx's legacy. In this debate some have followed the lead of Friedrich Engels (and later Soviet Marxism) and take Marxism as an indivisible whole; others, such as Antonio Gramsci and the Peruvian Mariátegui, distinguished between Marxist analysis as a scientific method and "metaphysical materialism." For his part, Gutiérrez differentiates the ideological and philosophical aspects of Marxism from Marxist analysis as a science. He further warns against exaggerating the contribution of Marxist analyses (in the plural)—a tendency of both defenders and opponents—and insists that all such analyses be judged on social-scientific grounds alone.[80] Finally, to the surprise of some, especially in the English-speaking world, the Catholic church's highest teaching authority has on a number of occasions in the past century affirmed the *facts* of worldwide social conflict, class struggle rooted in the conflict between labor and capital, and the oppression of the working class.[81] The church's magisterium has also set forth guidelines for an authentically Christian method of analyzing these facts, which Gutiérrez affirms.[82]

Gutiérrez's treatment of the question of whether and how the social sciences may be legitimately used by the theologian helps to clarify his view of the principal tasks of theology and of those which lie beyond its competence. Like all theologies, liberation theology seeks an adequate language for speaking about God.[83] Today, given the profoundly inhuman conditions in which vast numbers of human beings live, such language both requires an understanding of poverty and its causes and seeks to make the Word of God efficacious in history by inspiring those who struggle for liberation from unjust poverty.[84] More precisely, while it does not fall to theologians "to offer strategic solutions or specifically political alternatives" to social problems, their work does become concrete (though not politically partisan) when they play a part in the proclamation of the Word, when they remind us that the transformation of human beings reaches deeper levels than that of sociopolitical structures (that is, on the aforementioned level of utopia), and when they call attention to the dialogue between God and human beings taking place at the heart of sociopolitical processes.[85] Leaving no doubt about his position on the matter, Gutiérrez asserts that constructing a social morality, not a political platform or program, is theology's proper task.[86] This means that he will refrain from "giv[ing] directives in fields that are the proper objects of human efforts," such as social liberation, but he will seek to show the relationship between these areas of endeavor and the reign of God and its ethical demands.[87]

How does one accomplish these properly theological tasks? For Gutiérrez, the conversion of theologians themselves constitutes a *sine qua non* for producing anything other than superficial theology. Perhaps it is this methodological requirement which, more than geography or culture, separates Gutiérrez from many of his critics. What has become ever more transparent in his writings is the *content* of such conversion: authentic conversion demands nothing less than a change of direction in life, "abandoning our own way . . . and entering the way of others—namely, our neighbors and, in particular, the poor."[88] This demand—a requirement, let us remember, for being able to think through the mysteries of God, Christ, or church adequately—is based on the claim that God's self-revelation in history is accomplished through the divine predilection for the weak.[89] Such a view, now solidly established by critical biblical scholarship[90] and incorporated into church teaching,[91] means that those who would question Gutiérrez—theologians or social scientists—must themselves speak from within an effective solidarity with the vast and complex movement of marginalized peoples for liberation underway today. Yet in Gutiérrez's view, such solidarity is only possible in the final analysis through God's gift of faith and the disciple's courageous acceptance of the gift.

FAITH AND THEOLOGY

With other theological giants of the twentieth century, such as Karl Rahner and Paul Tillich, Gutiérrez understands faith as trust in God which results in the "courage to be." While Tillich and Rahner focus on the struggles of individuals to accept themselves and the limitations of their own lives and see such acceptance as the proof of one's faith, Gutiérrez takes up two aspects he finds insufficiently attended to by his predecessors: the concrete and the social character of faith. As he points out, there is only one way to entrust one's life to God—namely by placing it in the hands of others. Furthermore, the gospel of Christ specifies who those "others" are—the "condemned of the earth." "God became flesh and is present in history, but because God is identified with the poor of the world, God's face and action are hidden in them." It is "there, in the poor, [that] the 'hidden God' questions and challenges us. . . ."[92] God's choice of the "despised and unimportant" of the world means that the Christian way to God must pass through those God attends to first, the poor.[93] But the social nature of faith derives not only from the fact that a whole category of persons mediates God's presence in history in a special way; it also means that disciples entrust their lives to God (through commitment to the poor) *together*. As Gutiérrez points out, Jesus' question about his true identity is directed to the disciples as a group. "Who do you [plural] say that I am?" The answer *I* give to the question cannot be separated from the answer *we* give.[94] To the modern Western mind such a statement is difficult to fathom; in the context of communitarian cultures (such as the Andean world), the divide between the self and the community to which one belongs cannot be so rigidly drawn. Certainly there can be no outright opposition between the terms "me" and "my community." Only coherence between the two allows me to speak of "my" community and "my" people.

Entrusting one's life to God constitutes a precondition for all adequate theological reflection. As I said above, fear, more than unbelief, is the enemy of faith and, consequently, of theology:

> Faith is not compatible with an attitude of apprehensiveness, it can indeed live through periods of darkness and it can, according to classic teaching, live in a kind of half-light, but it cannot live in fear. John reminds Christians who suffer persecution and insults that "there is no fear in love . . . and so one who fears is not yet perfect in love" (1 John 4:18). Cowardice in the face of what is new is contrary to faith. This explains the exhortation of the psalmist: "Sing to the Lord a new song" (33:3).[95]

Fear destroys self-confidence and trust of others, including trust in God. Fear also restrains hope, causing the fearful to abandon their dreams in favor of an empty "realism." In the process the fearful also deny, albeit unwillingly, God's promise to "create new heavens and a new earth" (Isa. 65:17; cf. Rev. 21:1). Most importantly, the fearful lose heart for the long, often painful, journey to freedom. Ultimately, of course, fear impedes love (grace) and keeps the fearful at a "safe" distance from others, especially from their suffering. But such a distance proves *un*safe. Begetting isolation for both parties and spawning indifference in the fearful, fear inexorably destroys the possibility of communion. Fear, then, with its offspring despair and indifference, undermines the ecclesial community called to set its course in faith, to go forward in hope, and to accomplish its task through love. Jesus' deeds of love frequently have a verbal preface: "Do not be afraid."

The complete record of a person's courageous acts on behalf of others (that is, acts of faith) is known to God alone, of course. Gustavo Gutiérrez's intellectual courage, however, is acknowledged with gratitude by many. With the believing poor, and in their name, he has challenged Christians paralyzed by fear of the cross, isolated in "upper rooms" far from the "scum of society,"[96] and cut off from the joy of a resurrection banquet of the "uninvited"[97] to stand with "those robbed of life and well-being."[98] And thus he invites the fearful among us to venture forth with Jesus' first disciples, to find courage and new life for ourselves by giving life to the "nobodies" of history, and thereby to allow God to reign on earth as in heaven.

One

TOWARD A NEW METHOD: THEOLOGY AND LIBERATION

Gustavo Gutiérrez has often noted the decisive role a reconsideration of theological method played in the birth of the theology of liberation and agrees with many others that a new method—rooted in a preferential option for the poor—constitutes a significant contribution of Latin America to theological reflection in the universal church. Chapter One of the present volume traces the development of the method he first proposed in the 1960s and continued to refine for the next three decades. These texts highlight the dialogue between theology and other literatures, particularly the social sciences, which he has pioneered.

1. TOWARD A THEOLOGY OF LIBERATION

In July 1968, Gutiérrez made a presentation in Chimbote, Peru, at a meeting of the National Office for Social Research, a Peruvian organization of priests committed to the liberating evangelization of the poor. His remarks were published a year later under the title "Hacia una teología de la liberación" ("Toward a Theology of Liberation") by the Servicio de Documentación MIEC–JECI, Montevideo (Uruguay). This first formulation of a "theology of liberation," later recognized as a turning point in the history of Christian thought, preceded the Medellín conference by one month. In remarkable fashion Gutiérrez sketched many of the main lines of the theological vision he would develop in succeeding decades. Among these were (1) the consequences for theological reflection of a serious commitment to liberative praxis and (2) the soteriological meaning of such praxis—that is, its significance for Christian discipleship. The English translation of Gutiérrez's talk is by Alfred T. Hennelly, S.J., and is found in the volume he edited called Liberation Theology: A Documentary History *(Maryknoll, N.Y.: Orbis, 1990), 62–77.*

As Christians come in contact with the acute problems that exist in Latin America, they experience an urgent need to take part in solutions to them. They run the risk, however, of doing this without a reexamination of their own basic doctrinal principles, a situation that can lead to dead ends and to action that is ultimately sterile.

In this talk I will distance myself from concrete issues in order to analyze these basic doctrinal principles. Actually, the distancing is only apparent, since the following reflections can only be understood within a broader and richer approach that includes pastoral action and even political action.

INTRODUCTION

First of all, let us examine what we mean by *theology*. Etymologically speaking, theology is a treatise or discourse about God—which really does not tell us very much. The classic meaning of theology is an intellectual understanding of the faith—that is, the effort of human intelligence to comprehend revelation and the vision of faith. But faith means not only truths to be affirmed, but also an existential stance, an attitude, a commitment to God and to human beings. Thus faith understands the whole of life theologically as faith, hope, and charity.

If, then, we say that faith is a commitment to God and human beings, we affirm that theology is the intellectual understanding of this commitment. It is an understanding of this existential stance, which includes the affirmation of truths, but within a broader perspective.

Faith is not limited to affirming the existence of God. No, faith tells us that God loves us and demands a loving response. This response is given through love for human beings, and that is what we mean by a commitment to God and to our neighbor.

Consequently, when we speak about theology, we are not talking about an abstract and timeless truth, but rather about an existential stance, which tries to understand and to see this commitment in the light of revelation.

But precisely because faith is above all an existential stance, it admits a differentiation according to circumstances and the different approaches to the commitment to God and human beings. To say that faith is a commitment is true for all ages, but the commitment is something much more precise: I commit myself here and now. The commitment to God and to human beings is not what it was three centuries ago. Today I commit myself in a distinctive manner.

When we speak of theology, we mean a theology that takes into account its variation according to time and circumstances. From this we can deduce three characteristics:

1. Theology is a progressive and continuous understanding, which is variable to a certain extent. If it were merely the understanding of abstract truth, this would not be true. If theology is the understanding of an existential stance, it is progressive, it is the understanding of a commitment in history concerning the Christian's location in the development of humanity and the living out of faith.

2. Theology is a reflection—that is, it is a second act, a turning back, a reflecting, that comes after action. Theology is not first; the commitment is first. Theology is the understanding of the commitment, and the commitment is action. The central element is charity, which involves commitment, while theology arrives later on.

This is what ancient authors said with regard to philosophy: *"Primum vivere, deinde philosophare*—first you must live, and then philosophize." We have interpreted this as first *la dolce vita,* and then some reflection if I have time. No, the principle is much more profound: philosophy, like theology, is a second act.

The pastoral consequences of this are immense. It is not the role of theology to tell us what to do or to provide solutions for pastoral action. Rather, theology follows in a distinctive manner the pastoral action of the church and is a reflection upon it.

3. If it is the intellectual understanding of a commitment, theology is an endeavor that must continuously accompany that commitment. The pastoral action of the church will be a commitment to God and the neighbor, while theology will accompany that activity to provide continual orientation and animate it. Every action of ours must be accompanied by a reflection to orient it, to order it, to make it coherent, so that it does not lapse into a sterile and superficial activism.

Theology, therefore, will accompany the pastoral activity of the church—that is, the present of the church in the world. It will accompany that activity continuously, to help it to be faithful to the Word of God, which is the light for theology.

But, I insist, the first and fundamental objective is the commitment of Christians. One should not ask of theology more than it can give. Theology is a science, and like any discipline, has a modest role in the life of human beings. The first step is action. As Pascal expressed it: "All the things in this world are not worth one human thought, and all the efforts of human thought are not worth one act of charity."

Theology is on the level of thought and reflection, and there is no theology that is the equivalent of an act of charity. The central issue is charity, commitment, action in the world. All this is what we understand by theology.

There is talk today of a theology of human liberation. Using this or other expressions, the theme has become a major preoccupation of the magisterium of the church in recent years.

If faith is a commitment to God and human beings, it is not possible to live in today's world without a commitment to the process of liberation. That is what constitutes a commitment today. If participation in the process of human liberation is the way of being present in the world, it will be necessary for Christians to have an understanding of this commitment, of this process of liberation.

This process constitutes what has been called since the Council a "sign of the times." A sign of the times is not primarily a speculative problem—that is, a problem to be studied or interpreted. For the reasons noted above, a sign of the times is first of all a call to action and secondly a call to interpretation. A sign of the times calls Christians to action.

The process of liberation is a sign of the times. It is a call to action at the same time that it is a new theme for reflection, new because it is a global term for the problems contained within it. Thus there is a certain deficiency in [certain] attempts that are being made with regard to a theology of liberation, . . . which leave me dissatisfied.

We will have to be much more concrete, but we will also be dependent on the progress of the science of economics for a more precise knowledge regarding the national and Latin American reality. A genuine theology of liberation can only be a team effort, a task which has not yet been attempted.

I will limit myself therefore to a sketch, to recalling a few paths of inquiry, as is suggested by my title, "Toward a Theology of Liberation." It really is *toward*. I believe we will have to go much further, but we can only achieve that through collaboration as a number of concepts become more precise.

We understand theology, then, as an intellectual understanding of the faith. But faith is above all a commitment to God and the neighbor. Although it implies the affirmation of truths, Christian truth nevertheless has the particular character of being a truth that is thought but that first of all is done. "To do the truth," the gospel text requires, and that is proper to Christian truth.

In this sketch we will consider three areas along the following lines:

1. The statement of the question
2. Human liberation and salvation
3. The encounter with God in history

1. THE STATEMENT OF THE QUESTION

The gospel is primarily a message of salvation. The construction of the world is a task for human beings on this earth. To state the question of a theology of liberation means, therefore, to ask about the meaning of this work on earth, the work that human beings perform in this world vis-à-vis the faith. In other words, what relationship is there between the construction of this world and salvation?

A theology of liberation, then, will have to reply first of all to this question: Is there any connection between constructing the world and saving it? . . .

Thus our own question is posed. The theology of liberation means establishing the relationship that exists between human emancipation—in the social, political, and economic orders—and the kingdom of God.

2. HUMAN LIBERATION AND SALVATION

Pope Paul VI said that what the church can appropriately contribute is a global vision of the human being and of humanity, a vision that situates the process of development within the human vocation. This had been affirmed by *Gaudium et spes*, and a reading of the texts will show us the theological progress that was accomplished by [the pope's encyclical] *Populorum progressio.* . . .

If we understand salvation as something with merely "religious" or "spiritual" value for my soul, then it would not have much to contribute to concrete human life. But if salvation is understood as passing from less human conditions to more human conditions, it means that messianism brings about the freedom of captives and the oppressed, and liberates human beings from the slavery that Paul VI referred to (*PP* 47).

The sign of the coming of the messiah is the suppression of oppression: the messiah arrives when injustice is overcome. When we struggle for a just world in which there is not servitude, oppression, or slavery, we are signifying the coming of the messiah. Therefore the messianic promises bind tightly together the kingdom of God and better living conditions for human beings or, as Paul VI said, more humane living conditions. An intimate relationship exists between the kingdom and the elimination of poverty and misery. The kingdom comes to suppress injustice.

These are two biblical themes, then, creation/salvation and the messianic promises, which demonstrate the extent to which the encyclical of Paul VI is anchored in revelation and the Word of God. Consequently, the pope can say that human development "constitutes a summary of all our duties." If then we can understand integral development as passing from less human conditions to more human conditions, and if within the most human elements we include grace, faith, and divine filiation, then we comprehend profoundly why it can be said that working for development is the summary of all our duties.

3. THE ENCOUNTER WITH GOD IN HISTORY

Gaudium et spes (45) tells us the following: "The Lord is the goal of human history, the focal point of the longings of history and of civilization, the center of the human race, the joy of every heart, and the answer to all its yearnings."

If there is a finality inscribed in history, then the essence of Christian faith is to believe in Christ, that is to believe that God is irreversibly committed to human history. To believe in Christ, then, is to believe that God has made a commitment to the historical development of the human race.

To have faith in Christ is to see the history in which we are living as the progressive revelation of the human face of God. "Whoever sees me sees the Father." This holds to a certain extent for every human being according to the important text of Matthew 25, which reminds us that an action on behalf of a human being is an action on behalf of God. If you gave food and drink, you gave it to me; if you denied it, you denied it to me. . . .

CONCLUSION

In closing, let us consider two well-known texts in the light of what we have been discussing. The first is from Karl Marx:

> The social principles of Christianity preach the need of a dominating class and an oppressed class. And to the latter class they offer only the benevolence of the ruling class. The social principles of Christianity point to heaven as the compensation for all the crimes that are committed on earth. The social principles of Christianity explain all the viciousness of oppressors as a just punishment either for original sin or other sins, or as trials that the Lord, in infi-

nite wisdom, inflicts on those the Lord has redeemed. The social principles of Christianity preach cowardice, self-hatred, servility, submission, humility—in a word, all the characteristics of a scoundrel.

How could he have presented such an image of Christianity? The other is a text from Isaiah:

For behold I create new heavens and a new earth; and the former things shall not be remembered and come into mind. [We will have changed reality in such a way that no one will remember the past. The result is a global change of structures.] But be glad and rejoice forever in that which I create; for behold, I create Jerusalem rejoicing, and her people a joy. I will rejoice in Jerusalem, and be glad in my people; no more shall be heard in it the sound of weeping and the cry of distress or an old man who does not fill out his days. . . . They shall build houses and inhabit them; they shall plant vineyards and eat their fruit. They shall not build and another inhabit; they shall not plant and another eat; for like the days of a tree shall the days of my people be, and my chosen shall long enjoy the work of their hands [65:17–22].

This very concrete reality is the kingdom of God. In it children will not die in a few days. The people will not work for others but for themselves, the city will be called a "rejoicing" and her people a "joy."

How could this have transformed into what was described in the text of Marx? Unfortunately, both images are true, from different perspectives. Although the messianic promises refer to concrete material things, Marx's vision of over a century ago continues to be repeated by human beings today.

The issue, then, is whether we are capable of realizing the prophecy of Isaiah and of understanding the kingdom of God in its integral reality, or whether we are going to give the counter-testimony that is reflected in the statements of Marx. This is precisely what is at stake in our epoch.

2. THEOLOGY AND LIBERATION

The Introduction to the original edition of A Theology of Liberation, *published for the first time in December 1971 by the Centro de Estudios y Publicaciones in Lima, makes clear the origin, intended audience, purpose, and procedure of what came to be recognized as the classic articulation of liberation theology. In this Introduction every word counts. Gutiérrez recognizes the novelty of the questions he poses and the inconclusiveness of his answers. His aim is to strengthen the commitment of Christian believers to the multifaceted liberation process underway in Latin America in the late 1960s. This passage is from* Theology of Liberation, xiii–xv.

This book is an attempt at reflection, based on the gospel and the experiences of men and women committed to the process of liberation in the oppressed and exploited land of Latin America. It is a theological reflection born of the experience of shared efforts to abolish the current unjust situation and to build a different society, freer and more human. Many in Latin America have started along the path of a commitment to liberation, and among them is a growing number of Christians; whatever the validity of these pages, it is due to their experiences and reflections. My greatest desire is not to betray their experiences and efforts to elucidate the meaning of their solidarity with the oppressed.

My purpose is not to elaborate an ideology to justify postures already taken, or to undertake a feverish search for security in the face of the radical challenges that confront the faith, or to fashion a theology from which political action is "deduced." It is rather to let ourselves be judged by the Word of the Lord, to think through our faith, to strengthen our love, and to give reason for our hope from within a commitment that seeks to become more radical, total, and efficacious. It is to reconsider the great themes of the Christian life within this radically changed perspective and with regard to the new questions posed by this commitment. This is the goal of the so-called *theology of liberation*.

Many significant efforts along these lines are being made in Latin America. Insofar as I know about them, they have been kept in mind and have contributed to this study. I wish to avoid, however, the kind of reflection that—legitimately concerned with preventing the mechanical transfer of an approach foreign to our historical and social coordinates—neglects the contribution of the universal Christian community. It seems better, moreover, to acknowledge explicitly this contribution than to introduce surreptitiously and uncritically certain ideas elaborated in another context—ideas that can be fruitful among us only if they undergo a healthy and frank scrutiny.

A reflection on the theological meaning of the process of human liberation throughout history demands methodologically that I define my terms. The first part of this book is devoted to that purpose. This will enable me to indicate why I pay special attention in this work to the critical function of theology with respect to the presence and activity of humankind in history. The most important instance of this presence in our times, especially in underdeveloped and oppressed countries, is the struggle to construct a just and fraternal society, where persons can live with dignity and be the agents of their own destiny. It is my opinion that the term *development* does not well express these profound aspirations. *Liberation*, on the other hand, seems to express them better. Moreover, in another way the notion of liberation is more exact and all-embracing: it emphasizes that human beings transform themselves by conquering their liberty throughout their existence and their history. The Bible presents liberation—salvation—in Christ as the total gift, which, by taking on the levels I indicate, gives the whole process of liberation its deepest meaning and its complete and unforeseeable fulfillment. Liberation can thus be approached as a single salvific process. This viewpoint, therefore, permits us to consider *the unity, without confusion*, of the various human dimensions, that is, one's relationships with other humans and with the Lord, which theology has been attempting to establish for some time; this approach will provide the framework for our reflection.

It is fitting, secondly, to show that the problem that the theology of liberation poses is simultaneously traditional and new. This twofold characteristic will be more evident if I analyze the different ways in which theology has historically responded to this problem. This will lead me to conclude that because the traditional approaches have been exhausted, new areas of theological reflection are being sought. My examination should help me remove the obstacles from my path and move ahead more quickly. The second part of the work deals with this matter.

The preceding analysis leads me to reconsider the "practice" of the church in today's world. The situation in Latin America, the only continent among the exploited and oppressed peoples where Christians are in the majority, is especially significant. An attempt to describe and interpret the forms under which the Latin American church is present in the process of liberation—especially among the most committed Christian groups—will allow me to establish the questions for an authentic theological reflection. These will be the first efforts along these lines. The third part of this treatise is devoted to this attempt.

The previous remarks make it clear that the question regarding the theological meaning of liberation is, in truth, a question *about the very meaning of Christianity and about the mission of the church.* There was a time when the church responded to any problem by calmly appealing to its doctrinal and vital resources. Today the seriousness and scope of the process that we call liberation is such that Christian faith and the church are being radically challenged. They are being asked to show what significance they have for a human task that has reached adulthood. The greater part of my study is concerned with this aspect. I approach the subject within the framework of the unity and, at the same time, the complexity of the process of liberation centered in the salvific work of Christ. I am aware, however, that I can only sketch these considerations, or more precisely, outline the new questions—without claiming to give conclusive answers.

The novelty and shifting quality of the problems posed by the commitment to liberation make the use of adequate language and sufficiently precise concepts rather difficult. Nevertheless, I present this study in the hope that it will be useful, and especially because I am confident that the confrontation necessarily implied in publishing will allow me to improve and deepen these reflections.

3. THEOLOGY: A CRITICAL REFLECTION

Theology understood as critical reflection on praxis is among Gutiérrez's best-known contributions to the discipline. In remarks to a gathering of Latin American theologians in 1964 in Petrópolis, Brazil, Gutiérrez argued for the "theological critique of certain pastoral options already made in Latin America"—including his own—as an appropriate task of the theologian. He thus gave expression for the first time to the perspective later to be known as "liberation theology." At Chimbote (1968) he spoke of "critical reflection on the presence and action of the church in the world in the light of faith" as one of three tasks of theology (the others are the pursuit of spiritual wisdom and rational knowledge). Three years later he was even more precise, describing this function as "critical reflection on historical praxis in the light of the Word "(Theology of Liberation, *11, emphasis added). In 1973 he claimed that in the Latin American context "theology will be a critical reflection from within and upon historical praxis in confrontation with the Word of the Lord lived out and accepted in faith" (in his essay "Liberation Praxis and Christian Faith," found in* Power of the Poor, *60). In 1988, after two decades of intense discussions of this question at many levels of the church, he depicted theology as "critical reflection [which] has for its purpose to read the complex praxis [of Christian existence] in the light of God's word" and whose "ultimate norms of judgment come from revealed truth that we accept by faith and not from praxis itself" (in "Expanding the View," the essay which serves as the introduction to the second edition of* Theology of Liberation, *xxiv). The following passages are from* Theology of Liberation, *3, 9–12.*

Theological reflection—that is, the understanding of the faith—arises spontaneously and inevitably in the believer, in all those who have accepted the gift of the Word of God. Theology is intrinsic to a life of faith seeking to be authentic and complete and therefore to the common consideration of this faith in the ecclesial community. There is present in *all believers*—more so in every Christian community—a rough outline of a theology. There is present an effort to understand the faith, something like a pre-understanding of that faith which is incarnated in life, action, and concrete attitude. It is on this foundation, and only because of it, that the edifice of theology—in the precise and technical sense of the term—can be erected. This foundation is not merely a jumping-off point, but the soil into which theological reflection stubbornly and permanently sinks its roots and from which it derives its strength.

But the focus of theological work, in the strict sense of the term, has undergone many transformations throughout the history of the church. "Bound to the task of the church, theology is dependent upon its historical development," writes Christian Duquoc. Moreover, as Congar observed recently, this evolution has accelerated to a certain extent in recent years: "The theological situation, including the very concept of theological work, has changed in the past twenty-five years.". . .

Theology must think critically about itself, about its own foundations. Only this approach can prevent theology from being a naïve discourse and make it aware of itself, in full possession of its conceptual elements. But we are not referring exclusively to this epistemological aspect when we talk about theology as critical reflection. We also refer to a clear and critical attitude toward economic and sociocultural factors which condition the life and reflection of the Christian community. To disregard these is to deceive both oneself and others. But above all, we take this expression as the theory of a particular practice. Theological reflection would then necessarily be a critique of both society and the church insofar as they are convoked and addressed by the Word of God; it would be a critical theory, worked out in the light of the Word accepted in faith and inspired by a practical purpose and therefore indissolubly linked to historical praxis.

31

By preaching the gospel message, by its sacraments, and by the charity of its members, the church proclaims and welcomes the gift of the kingdom of God at the heart of human history. The Christian community professes a "faith which works through charity." It is—at least ought to be—efficacious love, action, and commitment to the service of others. Theology is reflection, a critical attitude. The commitment of love, of service, comes first. Theology *follows;* it is the second step. What Hegel said about philosophy can be said of theology: it rises only at sundown. The pastoral activity of the church does not flow as a conclusion from theological premises. Theology does not generate a pastoral approach; rather it reflects upon it. Theology must be able to find in pastoral activity the presence of the Spirit inspiring the action of the Christian community. The life, preaching, and historical commitment of the church will be a privileged *locus theologicus* for understanding the faith.

To reflect upon the presence and action of the Christian in the world means, moreover, to go beyond the visible boundaries of the church. This is of prime importance. It implies openness to the world, gathering the questions it poses, being attentive to its historical transformations. In the words of Yves Congar, "If the church wishes to deal with the real questions of the modern world and to attempt to respond to them, . . . it must open as it were a new chapter of theologico-pastoral epistemology. Instead of using only revelation and tradition as starting points, as classical theology has generally done, it must start with facts and questions derived from the world and from history." It is precisely this opening to the totality of human history that allows theology to fulfill its critical function vis-à-vis ecclesial praxis without narrowness.

This critical task is indispensable. Reflection in the light of faith must constantly accompany the pastoral action of the church. By keeping historical achievements in their proper perspective, theology helps safeguard society and the church from regarding as permanent what is only temporary. Critical reflection thus always plays the inverse role of an ideology which rationalizes and justifies a given social and ecclesial order. On the other hand, by recalling the sources of revelation, theology helps to orient pastoral activity; it puts it in a wider context and so helps it avoid activism and immediatism. Theology as critical reflection thus plays a part in liberating humankind and the Christian community, preserving them from fetishism and idolatry, as well as from a pernicious and belittling narcissism. Understood in this way, theology has a necessary and permanent role in liberation from every form of religious alienation—often fostered by the ecclesiastical institution itself which impedes an authentic approach to the Word of the Lord.

As critical reflection on society and the church, theology is an understanding which both grows and, in a certain sense, changes. If the commitment of the Christian community in fact takes different forms throughout history, the understanding which accompanies the vicissitudes of this commitment will be constantly renewed and will take untrodden paths. A theology which has as its points of reference only "truths" which have been established once and for all—and not the Truth which is also a Way—can be only static and, in the long run, sterile. In this sense the often-quoted and misinterpreted words of Henri Bouillard take on new validity: "A theology which is not up-to-date is a false theology."

Finally, theology thus understood, that is to say as linked to praxis, plays a prophetic role insofar as it interprets historical events with the intention of unveiling and proclaiming their profound meaning. According to Oscar Cullmann, this is the meaning of the prophetic role: "The prophet does not limit himself as does the fortune-teller to isolated revelations, but his prophecy becomes preaching, message. He explains to the people the true meaning of events; he lets them know, at every moment, the plan and will of God." But if theology is based on this interpretation of historical events and contributes to the discovery of their meaning, it is with the purpose of making Christians' commitment within them more radical and clear. Only with the exercise of the prophetic function understood in this way, will the theologian be—to borrow an expression from Antonio Gramsci—a new kind of "organic intellectual." Theologians will be personally and vitally engaged in historical realities with specific dates and locations through which nations, social classes, and individuals struggle to free themselves from domination and oppression by other nations, classes, and individuals. Indeed, in the final analysis, the true interpretation of the meaning unveiled by theology is given in historical praxis. "The hermeneutics of the kingdom of God," observed Edward Schillebeeckx, "consists especially in making the world a better place. Only in this way will I be able to discover what these words mean: the kingdom of God." We have here a political hermeneutics of the gospel.

Theology as a critical reflection on historical praxis in the light of the Word does not replace the other functions of theology, such as wisdom and rational knowledge; rather it presupposes and needs them. But this is not all. It is not a matter of a mere juxtaposition. The critical function of theology necessarily leads to redefinition of these other two tasks. Henceforth, wisdom and rational knowledge will more explicitly have historical praxis as their point of departure and their context. It is necessarily in terms of this praxis that an understanding of spiritual growth based on Scripture should be developed, and it is in this same praxis that faith receives the questions posed by human reason. The relationship between faith and knowledge (science) will be situated in the context of the relationship between faith and society and thus in the context of liberating action. Given the theme of the present work, we will pay particular attention to this critical function of theology with the ramifications suggested above. This approach will lead us to be especially aware of the life of the church in the world and of commitments which Christians, impelled by the Spirit and in communion with others, undertake in history. We will give special consideration to participation in the process of liberation, an outstanding phenomenon of our times, which takes on special meaning in the so-called Third World countries.

This kind of theology, which begins by attending to a particular set of issues, will perhaps give us the solid and permanent, albeit modest, foundation for the *theology in a Latin American perspective* which is both desired and needed. Such an aim is not due to a frivolous desire for originality, but rather to a fundamental sense of historical efficacy and also—why hide it?—to the desire to contribute to the life and reflection of the universal Christian community. But in order to accomplish this, the desire for universality—as well as the contribution of the Christian community as a whole—must be present from the beginning. To concretize this desire would be to overcome a particularistic work—provincial and chauvinistic—and produce something *unique*, both our own and universal, and therefore fruitful.

"The only future that theology has is to become the theology of the future," Harvey Cox has said. But this theology of the future must necessarily be a critical reading of historical praxis, of the historical task in the sense we have attempted to sketch. Jürgen Moltmann says that theological concepts "do not limp after reality . . . but illuminate reality by showing its future." In our approach, to reflect critically on the praxis of liberation is not to "limp after" reality. In the praxis of liberation the present is, in its deepest dimension, pregnant with the future; hope forms an inherent part of our present commitment in history. Theology does not initiate this future which exists in the present. It does not create the vital attitude of hope out of nothing. Its role is more modest. It makes these explicit and interprets them as the true lifeblood of history. To reflect upon a forward-directed action is not to be fixed on the past. It does not mean being the caboose of the present. Rather it is to discern among present realities, in the movement of history, that which is driving us toward the future. To reflect by beginning with liberating historical praxis is to reflect in the light of the future which is believed in and hoped for. It is to reflect with a view to action which transforms the present. But it does not mean doing this from an armchair; rather it means sinking roots where the pulse of history is beating at this moment and illuminating it with the Word of the Lord of history, who irreversibly committed himself to the present moment of humanity's development in order to carry it to its complete fulfillment.

It is for all these reasons that the theology of liberation proposes for us not so much a new theme for reflection as a *new way* to do theology. Theology as critical reflection on historical praxis is a liberating theology, a theology of the liberating transformation of the history of humanity and also therefore that part of humanity—gathered into *ecclesia*—which openly confesses Christ. This is a theology which does not stop with thinking about the world, but rather tries to be a moment in the process through which the world is transformed. It is a theology which opens itself—in the protest against trampled human dignity, in the struggle against the plunder of the vast majority of humankind, in liberating love, and in the building of a new society of justice and fraternity—to the gift of the kingdom of God.

4. THE LIMITATIONS OF MODERN THEOLOGY: ON A LETTER OF DIETRICH BONHOEFFER

In many of his writings Gutiérrez assumes a critical yet nuanced stance toward complex historical developments. His view of modernity, for example, resists simple categorization. On the one hand, Gutiérrez acknowledges his own debt to progressive European theologians and recognizes the pertinence of their work in the context of their own secularized societies. Yet he also takes his distance from them, not only because the Latin American context is different from the European (i.e., it is neither secular nor "modern") but also because the two contexts are negatively linked. As social analysis makes plain, affluence and poverty, power and insignificance, are not unrelated. While some twentieth-century thinkers sensed the contradictions inherent in modern Western consciousness—the celebration of individual freedoms and the simultaneous enslavement of masses of people, for example—they have failed, in Gutiérrez's view, to see clearly enough that an adequate response to such inconsistencies can only come from beyond the modern bourgeois world, from the world of poverty and exploitation it has produced. Gutiérrez's reflections on Dietrich Bonhoeffer and others first appeared in 1979 as "Los límites de la teología moderna: un texto de Bonhoeffer" in Concilium. The passages below are taken from Power of the Poor in History, 222–24, 228–33.

Theological reflection is always carried on in a context of specific historical processes. It is accordingly bound up with these processes. The bourgeois revolutions and their intellectual consciousness, the Enlightenment, opened an age of important changes in the concrete life conditions of the Christian churches of the West. Simultaneously, therefore, they produced new challenges for systematic reflection upon the faith—challenges still charged with consequences in our own day.

The new threats were perceived, in their time, by two important thinkers in particular. One was that central figure of modern thought, who exerted such an influence, if rather a heterodox one, on theology, Georg Wilhelm Friedrich Hegel. The other was the "father of contemporary Protestant theology," Friedrich Schleiermacher. Until these two appeared on the scene, only Immanuel Kant, the theological sniper, was available for being "gone back to" ("Back to Kant!" the Protestant theologians loved to cry), all down the nineteenth century—and beyond. Another great questioner of Christianity took up these same challenges: Ludwig Feuerbach, whom Karl Barth was of course quite right to include in his *Protestant Theology in the Nineteenth Century*.

All these thinkers, especially Kant, Hegel, and Schleiermacher, were the heirs of a theological tradition altogether comfortable and at home in the modern "World come of age" of their eighteenth and nineteenth centuries. And now these same scholars would provide the fillip that Protestant theology, doubtless the broadest and most far-reaching theology of modern times, would need in order to take a new and important step forward. All this was taking place while the Catholic camp kept its distance from the world of ideas, tangling itself up in a mesh of endless, wearisome polemics with political liberalism over religious freedom and other modern liberties.

In the second half of the nineteenth century, liberal theology was even more outspoken in its acceptance of this modern, bourgeois world in which it had been born and bred. It continued the direction initiated by our three great thinkers, to be sure. But it left their criticisms and uneasiness behind. Now liberal theology would actually make the modern mentality the norm of faith, as well as of theology.

Much later, Dietrich Bonhoeffer would speak of the "easy terms of peace that the world dictated." The school of Albrecht Ritschl is a clear demonstration, in Barth's view, of this spontaneous, overtly bourgeois character of liberal theology. Theology is now more a culmination of the spirit of the Enlightenment than a challenge to it. By the end of the nineteenth century, liberal Protestant theology became the theology of a self-assured, middle-class Christianity.

Scholars recognize that it is only against this backdrop that the reaction of the three giants of twentieth-century Protestant theology—Karl Barth, Rudolf Bultmann, and Paul Tillich—can be understood. Serious, rigorous, and full of courage, these thinkers' stubborn questions challenged even the thought of the trio of giants who preceded them.

Bonhoeffer, who died in the Nazi extermination camp in Flossenburg in 1945, was a Christian theologian who sought to locate God at the very heart and center of human life. He refused to see God out on its periphery. As a result he is a theologian of great lucidity vis-à-vis the limitations of modern theology. In a number of pithy and penetrating observations—particularly in a passage in a letter of his dated June 8, 1944, which will serve us as our point of departure for certain reflections on bourgeois Christianity and the systematic reflection upon the faith that this Christianity produced—he provides the counterweight in favor of what is most progressive and advanced in that theology. He criticizes all three members of our mighty trio of twentieth-century theologians, confronting them anew with the very questions of the Enlightenment that provoked their theology.

Bonhoeffer's objection to the theology of Barth, Bultmann, and Tillich is that although they indeed questioned the Enlightenment and its theology, they failed to question it squarely and radically. Their critique was doubtless the best this type of theology had ever undertaken. Yet we feel in our bones the limitations of an effort to respond to the challenges of the modern world without criticizing it in its economic bases, as on its social and ideological levels. For, as we shall see, no one ever vanquished the modern, bourgeois mentality while remaining at its heart. This, it seems to me, is what Bonhoeffer's testimony communicates to us today. As we shall also see, it may even be that he surmised this himself.

Of course by taking up this passage from Bonhoeffer's letter as the vehicle of our reflections we shall be obliged to make an approach to reality in perhaps too narrow a purview—a purely theological purview, in which the historical moorings of our material, our vehicle, will appear only by way of occasional allusion. Indeed, in order not to wander afield in our theological considerations themselves, we shall have to renounce the opportunity for detailed discussion of certain observations and criticisms by our author in other quarters of theology itself. But I trust that by taking up the penetrating reflections of this great Christian and incisive theologian, who confronted the challenges of the modern world as perhaps no one before him, we may see both the grandeur and the historical limitations of his undertaking—and thereby discern, albeit vaguely at first, another path to take. . . .

As it had been for Barth, the proclamation of the gospel is Bonhoeffer's central concern. His theological reflection was always bound up with his pastoral ministry. Surely all great theologies are sprung from this same union. The intense degree of Bonhoeffer's political commitment during the last ten years of his life only served to sharpen his concern for the proclamation of the Christian message, lead him onto new terrain, and lay out before him a whole new problematic vis-à-vis his discourse on the faith. The question "How may one speak of God in a world come of age?" points up two themes he will concentrate on in his writings during his time in prison in Tegel: the world come of age we live in and the God we believe in. Ultimately what this question asks (and here Bonhoeffer broaches a third subject as well, one that spans the first two) is: "What is Christianity really?" That is, "Who actually is Christ for us today?" This is the question *theological* thinking asks—that is, nonreligious thinking.

For Bonhoeffer, Christian theology had become lost in misunderstandings, polemics, and apologetics with the modern world. There can be no doubt that he is thinking even of the great theological undertakings we have cited above—the work of our three twentieth-century giants. The basic reason, to Bonhoeffer's mind, for the failure of all these attempts is that humanity's adulthood had not been taken for what it was. Its real questions have not even been heard, let alone answered.

The expressions "world come of age" or "adulthood of the world," which Bonhoeffer began to use in his June 8 letter, are of course an allusion to the celebrated passage in which Immanuel Kant takes cognizance of the new situation obtaining in his own eighteenth century. Bonhoeffer proposes to take on the entire problem—to face squarely the fact of a humanity come of age, to accept this new world without reserve, to come to grips with its questions right in the middle of the field of battle, instead of heading rabbit-like for the bushes or the shadow of a massive old wall, to reason upon the faith without any nostalgia for what is no more—in short, to do everything that modern theology has not managed to do. This is the task to come, and Bonhoeffer feels he is in virgin territory now.

Nevertheless, at no time in the course of his attempt to come to grips with a grown-up world just as he finds it does Bonhoeffer point out that the historical agent of modern society and ideology is the bourgeois class—that is, a social class which has wrested economic and political power from the grasp of more traditional sectors and inaugurated a mode of production that is generating new forms of exploitation and new social classes. That humanity's adulthood would be built upon a world of poverty and plunder does not come into his field of vision. It is only the facts and events marking the mastery of nature and society by reason that figure in his account of the historical process leading to human autonomy. Concretely, these facts and events will be the great milestones in the ascent of the bourgeoisie.

The protest movements of the poor, from the late Middle Ages on, find no place in Bonhoeffer's historical focus, nor does the contemporaneous labor movement. It is remarkable that the phenomenon of Nazism, against which he struggled so courageously, did not lead Bonhoeffer to a deeper analysis of the "crisis in today's society." It was the Nazi phenomenon that seems to have provoked his judgment upon the ultimate values of modernity. Perhaps the explanation is that, taken up as he is with the fascist enemy and its attacks on liberal society from the rear, Bonhoeffer was less sensitive to the world of injustice upon which that society was built.

We must come to understand this new world, this world come of age. Of this Bonhoeffer is convinced. It is true that some of his expressions could lead one to believe that he postulated a mundane self-complacency instead. But no, he writes: "The world *must* be understood better than it understands itself, . . . [namely] on the basis of the gospel and in the light of Christ."

Eberhard Bethge is right when he says that it is the christological perspective that is basic for Bonhoeffer. He is right again that Bonhoeffer's reflections on humanity's adulthood are neither philosophy, nor phenomenology, but theology:

> The recognition of the world's coming of age is, with Bonhoeffer, neither philosophy nor phenomenology, but the knowledge of God, i.e., "theology," and that is a knowledge that seeks to follow God where he has already preceded us. That is why Bonhoeffer's statement about the world come of age is first and last a theological statement.

It is this attempt to "follow God where he has already preceded us" that requires us to reject the religious interpretation of Christianity—that we cease at last "to speak on the one hand metaphysically, and on the other hand individualistically." Both ways lead us out of the world—the former by locking God up in categories of "absolute" and "infinite," the latter by "the displacement of God from the world, and from the public part of human life," in order to relegate him to the "sphere of the 'personal,' the 'inner,' and the 'private.'" Here once more we have a criticism of theology's attempts to respond to the sudden attacks of the modern mentality by merely falling back instead of making a frontal assault.

For our author, when all is said and done, to seek to save the faith through religion is to fail to see that religion is always partial, whereas faith is global. It is an attempt to reduce the whole to one of its parts.

A comparison with Barth at this point is inescapable, and it will enable us to understand just what Bonhoeffer means by "religion." Bonhoeffer always recognized his debt to Barth, but there are clear differences between them as well. The first point of divergence is that, for Barth, religion is a necessary product of human striving. Of course, if this is what you begin with, holds Barth (and this is what his "friendly enemy," Schleiermacher, began with), you will never arrive at the God of the Bible. For Bonhoeffer, on the other hand, the religious interpretation of Christianity is something historically conditioned. It is a Western phenomenon, now fallen prey to the maturation of humanity. For Barth, religion is something inherent in human nature; for Bonhoeffer, it is a stage of history.

But there is a second, more important, difference. For Barth, religion is a way of gaining control of God. For Bonhoeffer, religion is a way of understanding God as dominator of the human person. Which of the two is it—the human being's power over God, or God's power over the human being? It is the latter notion that is Bonhoeffer's recognized adversary. Ultimately, he holds, the question facing us is not, "What is the modern spirit and what can it accept in the Christian faith?" The question now demanding our response is much more radical: "Who is God?"

The answer is, God is the God of Jesus Christ. That is, God is a God who saves us not through his domination but through his suffering. Here we have Bonhoeffer's famous thesis of *God's weakness*. It will make its mark in theology after he is gone. It is of this God, and only of this God, that the Bible tells us. And it is thus that the cross acquires its tremendous revelatory potential with respect to God's weakness as an expression of his love for a world come of age.

Here is a concept charged with force and power. "It is not the religious act that makes the Christian, but participation in the sufferings of God in the secular life." This is conversion. This is what it is to believe in the gospel. What makes a Christian a Christian is "being caught up into the messianic sufferings of God in Jesus Christ."

But here we strike bottom too. Here we are at the very heart of things. The cup of humanity's maturity must be drunk to the dregs. The correct response to modernity is not to place God beyond the limits of reason, or drag him into history from the outside, or domesticate him in "religious sentiment," or bottle him up in bourgeois mentality by making belief in him a human excellence. Nor again is it the answer to assert that to move away from him is the destruction of the root of all human culture. Nor, finally, is the answer to make of him the object of a free personal decision. God in Christ is a God suffering, and to share in his weakness is to believe in him. This is what it means to be a Christian.

But where is suffering today? Who are those who suffer? Thus Bonhoeffer finds himself driven to a question full of consequences. "What does this life look like, this participation in the powerlessness of God in the world?"

Bonhoeffer has walked, without fear and without reserve, down the road of the recognition of a world come of age—the world encountered by modern theology. And he walked it to the end, to full acceptance of that world. This is what enabled him to point to a new way of understanding God. But now of course he will need a new way of understanding God's presence in history. And here there is a fork in the road, and it is for us to make the choice. We may simply emphasize the world's adulthood, and keep on enthusiastically pulling out the consequences, without an analysis of the historical bases upon which this phenomenon has been erected—and then we shall have entered a blind alley, fruitless for any meaningful theology. Or we may understand this last theological effort of Bonhoeffer's as having led modern theology to a collision with its own dialectical demand for a change in perspective.

It will no longer do simply to continue to think in the modern mold, refusing to accept the theological datum that that mold, that mentality, has accompanied and justified the historical process that creates this new world of spoliation and injustice. Turning our backs, in our theological reflection, on the fact that the so-called modern spirit, which is the interlocutor of progressivist theology, is in large part the reflection of a capitalistic, bourgeois society will lead us merely to a few skirmishes with the rear guard of a world in decomposition. Or at most—and Bonhoeffer saw this himself—it will permit us to forge a discourse upon the faith for the "bourgeois, petty, and grand." Bonhoeffer's courage led him to a mountaintop, and from that mountaintop he could discern, through the mists, other roads to follow, even though he would be unable forthrightly to stride down them.

Indeed, the theme of God's suffering, to which Bonhoeffer was led by his analysis of the modern world, came to him another way as well. In an earlier text, composed before any of the letters of his prison experience, he speaks of an "apprenticeship" with which he had been favored in recent years:

> It is an experience of incomparable value to have learned to see the great events of the history of the world from beneath: from the viewpoint of the useless, the suspect, the abused, the powerless, the oppressed, the despised—in a word, from the viewpoint of those who suffer.

We may debate just to what extent this "apprenticeship" influenced Bonhoeffer's later theological reflection. But it is evident that it could not have influenced it at all, had it not first enabled him to look at the history of humanity in a new way.

It would be unwarranted to attempt to deduce from Bonhoeffer's use of terms such as "poor" and "oppressed" that we are in the presence of a critical analysis of modern society on grounds of that society's injustice and oppression. But there are weighty indications that Bonhoeffer had begun to move forward in the perspective of "those beneath"—those on the "underside of history." To cite just one example, Bonhoeffer wrote: "Jesus calls men, not to a new religion, but to life." This is a statement that calls for a frank acknowledgment of its total content. We dare not "water it down" with a spiritualistic interpretation explicitly rejected on several occasions by Bonhoeffer himself. Indeed, as he progressed in his reflections Bonhoeffer became more sensitized to the concrete, material things of human life: health, good fortune, and so on—the very things often missing from or denied to the fringes of modern society. For example, he was led to an examination of the notion of "blessing" in the Old Testament and its applicability today. He found that it includes the good things of earth, and that in it "the whole of the earthly life is claimed for God." One must appreciate the whole meaning of the passage in Luke that tells us that when Jesus' disciples were with him "they lacked nothing."

Thus Bonhoeffer's thesis that God suffers on the cross leads him to deplore the unjust suffering of the outcasts of society, and he proclaims the right to life in all its dimensions as an exigency of the Bible itself. Once more in the history of thought a profound sense of God has led someone to a new sensitivity to the plight of the poor. Their deprivations, and even the particular expressions of their faith in God, now become the object of Bonhoeffer's attention. True, he never really made this insight the center of his theological discourse. It remains focused first and foremost on the great challenges of modernity. But he did manage to engage these challenges directly, and this led him to sense the limitations of his own theological enterprise. His reflection is taking a tack whose origin is very deep in his personal experience, and this is why his testimony, and the paths he opens up, are charged with such potential for further advance.

Actually it was Barth who had broken the way for Bonhoeffer here. A great deal has been written recently about the influence of Barth's pastoral experience with the working classes on his theological positions, and it is a matter of record that this experience led him at one time to a clear socialist activism. Whatever may have been his precise political options, it is certain that his sensitivity to the new forms of spoliation and exploitation created by a capitalist society did play a role in his theological thinking: it made him attentive to the deterioration of God's word into a "bourgeois gospel" and alerted him to the need for a theology accommodated to the underclasses. It led him to a notion of God as taking sides with the poor against the powerful. It even led him to envision a role for the church in the struggle for social justice in the world of the oppressed.

Barth's thinking offers an example of the irruption of the perspective of the poor into the modern problematic—where, despite all, Barth's theology remains. But something very important is stirring at the theological limits reached by Bonhoeffer, and especially by Barth. Each of them discerns the glimmer of a dialectic in the history of the Christian faith. The modern, bourgeois mentality is not overcome in ideological dialogue, but in a dialectical opposition to the social contradictions this mentality represents in the real world of history. Only from beyond the frontiers of this modern bourgeois world will it be possible to respond to the challenges of that world. That is, only from within the world of poverty and exploitation that the bourgeois world produces can that same world be overcome.

It may be that the absence of social analysis prevented Bonhoeffer from carrying his intuition to its mature theological implications. But he had made a beginning. He had moved toward a perspective "from beneath"—not in the sense of proceeding from the human being to God (as in the expression, "Christology from beneath," or "low Christology," for example), but from a point of departure in the universe of oppression, and of aspirations for deliverance, in which the poor are languishing. He had moved toward a theological outlook whose point of departure is in a faith lived by exploited classes, condemned ethnic groups, and marginalized cultures. The heretofore "absent from history" are making the free gift of the Father's love their own today, creating new social relationships of a communion of brothers and sisters. This is the point of departure for what we call "theology from the underside of history."

5. THEOLOGY AND THE SOCIAL SCIENCES

If "the underside of history"—that is, the history of the abused—provides the most adequate standpoint for comprehending the Judeo-Christian message as Gutiérrez has argued (cf. section 4 above), the responsible theologian must seek a sound grasp of that "underside." This task is not, strictly speaking, theological, yet it must not be omitted from theological reflection. The enormous impact of Theology of Liberation *owed as much to the method Gutiérrez employed as to the theological conclusions he reached. In the decade following that landmark work, his use of social-scientific literature in particular provoked intense discussion within the church of the proper relationship between theology and the social sciences. In 1984 Gutiérrez spelled out his position in a widely-published article, "Teología y ciencias sociales," paying special attention to the much-debated question of Marxist analysis. The following passages from "Theology and the Social Sciences" are found in* The Truth Shall Make You Free, *53–55, 58–66.*

Reflection on the Word of God is intertwined with the way in which this word is lived and proclaimed in the Christian community. When a theology boldly, and in depth, makes its own the situation that the church is experiencing at a given moment of its history, then the context (even when past) in which the theology continues to be important. The substantial permanence of such a theology is the result of its ability to sink its roots both in the real problems of its age and in the faith experience of a particular community of the followers of Jesus. This is undoubtedly the reason why the thought of an Augustine of Hippo and a Thomas Aquinas (to mention but two great names) challenges us even today.

In recent centuries, the theology developed at the great classic centers of thought was forced to deal with a state of affairs produced by what we know as the "modern mentality." This mentality reached its mature form in a lengthy process and received a decisive stimulus from the industrial and social revolutions of the eighteenth century, as well as from the intellectual consciousness expressed in the events we know as the Enlightenment. At that time, the church found itself living in a social and intellectual setting in which the faith and the Christian way of life were being subjected to demanding criticism. That period has not yet come to a close. Time has smoothed down some rough edges and polished others, but theological reflection is still dealing with the situation in an effort to give new validity to the proclamation of the Lord's word in the modern world.

At the same time, however, a new situation, one brought about by the modern age itself, has begun to surface. I am referring to the increasingly more forceful and widespread historical presence of the poor and oppressed of this world. In many instances, this has occurred suddenly and in unforeseen ways; the result has been a new set of conditions in which the Christian community must live. For this reason, there is talk of a real "irruption of the poor" into contemporary society and the contemporary church. But if we try to get inside the process, it becomes easy to see that the suddenness is more apparent than real. For the movement has, in fact, deep historical roots that ensure the permanence of the historical phenomenon and show that we are not dealing with a passing curiosity.

The theological projects that have been undertaken in the setting of the so-called Third World countries, among the racial and cultural minorities of the affluent countries, and from the perspective of women, are expressions of the new presence of those who have hitherto been "absent" from history. These new projects have thus far been emerging in areas that have, theologically speaking, been barren but in which the Christian faith has ancient and deep roots. This fact explains the present fruitfulness of these areas.

One expression, among others, of these theological experiments is the discourse on the faith that has developed in the Latin American setting and is known as liberation theology. The faith of the poor of that continent plays an important part in liberation theology, which is therefore concerned, as Medellín and Puebla were, to understand the situation of poverty, its causes, and the efforts of those suffering under it to escape from it. It is at this stage that recourse to the social sciences becomes relevant, for these sciences are a means for gaining a more accurate knowledge of society as it really is and so to articulate with greater precision the challenges it poses for the proclamation of the gospel and thus for theological reflection as well. In the pages that follow, I shall limit myself to discussing the relationship between theology and the social sciences or, more accurately, to some aspects of this relationship.

RELATION TO THE SOCIAL SCIENCES

Talk of the poverty now existing in Latin America inevitably calls for descriptions and interpretations of this massive reality. This concern was present from the first theological essays we prepared. The episcopal conferences of Medellín and Puebla also undertook such descriptions and interpretations, as have many other ecclesial documents. In both cases (allowance being made for the nuances proper to magisterial texts and theological efforts) the goal—which ought to be made clear at the outset—is to examine social reality so as to then understand better—thanks to the light which comes from faith—the challenges and possibilities that this reality presents to the church in its work of evangelization. In other words, recourse is had to social analysis in order to understand a situation—not in order to use this analysis in the study of matters more strictly theological.

A CRITICAL APPROACH TO SOCIAL ANALYSIS

As I have pointed out a number of times in my books, the use of the social sciences is undeniably in its early stages and still marked by uncertainties. Nonetheless, these sciences do help us understand better the social realities of our present situation. We need discernment, then, in dealing with the social sciences, not only because of their inchoative character, which I just mentioned, but also because to say that these disciplines are scientific does not mean that their findings are apodictic and beyond discussion. In fact, the contrary is true. What is really "scientific" does not seek to evade critical examination but rather submits to it. Science advances by means of hypotheses that give various explanations of one and the same reality. Consequently, to say that something is scientific is to say that it is subject to ongoing discussion and criticism. This statement holds in a special way for the ever-new and changing field of social realities.

The same critical approach (which expresses an authentic rationality and personal freedom) must be taken to liberation movements. Like every human process, these are ambivalent. We must therefore be clear-sighted regarding them, not out of any aversion to history but, on the contrary, out of loyalty to the values they carry and solidarity with the individuals committed to them.

The longing for liberation is undoubtedly one of the "signs of the times" in our age. [As I have said,] "For many persons (going beyond this or that nuance or difference among them)—in Vietnam or Brazil, New York or Prague—this aspiration has become a norm for their behavior and a sufficient reason to dedicate their lives to others." In all these places, people will have to be faithful to a quest for freedom that no political system guarantees. This, even though the quest may cost them their lives—in capitalist societies, but also in the world of what today is called "real socialism." It was for this reason that I rejected, thirteen years ago, the attitude of "those who sought refuge in easy solutions or in the excommunication of those who did not accept their pat answers, schematizations, and uncritical attitudes toward the historical expressions of socialism."

Recent historical events have validated that rejection and have dispelled illusions regarding concrete historical systems that claim to eliminate all evils. As a result, we have launched out upon new and more realistic quests; quests, too, that are more respectful of all dimensions of the human.

SOCIAL SCIENCES AND MARXISM

Elements of analysis which come from Marxism play a part in the contemporary social sciences that serve as a tool for studying social reality. This is true of the social sciences generally, even when scholars differ from or are opposed to Marx (as in the case, for example, of Max Weber). But the presence of these elements does not at all justify an identification of the social sciences with Marxist analysis, especially if one takes into account what Father Arrupe, in a well-known letter on the subject, called "the exclusive character" of Marxist analysis.

The Theory of Dependency. The very fact that liberation theology has regarded the theory of dependence as important for an analysis of the Latin American social situation prevents the kind of identification just mentioned. For this theory had its origin in a development of the social sciences proper to Latin America, and is held by prominent theoreticians who do not regard themselves as Marxists. Nor may we overlook the fact that representatives of Marxism have severely criticized the theory. We are dealing here with a very important point of theory. Marx said: "The industrially more developed countries only present the less developed with an image of their own future." The theory of dependency, however, rejects this view. The Latin American social scientist A. Cueva writes that "to begin with, this theory challenged the supposedly 'linear' pattern of the evolution of human society and branded as 'eurocentric' Marx's own observations on the subject." Elsewhere, speaking of the views of Fernando Henrique Cardoso, the most important representative of the theory of dependency, the same writer says: Cardoso maintains a "theoretical posture that is worlds removed from that of Marx."

The nature of this article does not permit me to dwell on this point or to offer further evidence or go into the matter in greater depth. My intention in harking back to the theory of dependency—which was very much to the fore in early writings on liberation theology—is simply to make the point that neither the social sciences generally nor the Latin American contribution to them can be reduced to the Marxist version. I am not denying the contributions Marxism has made to our understanding of economic and social matters; I do, however, want the necessary distinctions to be clearly grasped.

Furthermore, the use (a critical use, as we have seen) of the theory of dependency does not mean a permanent commitment to it. In the context of theological work, this theory is simply a means of better understanding social reality.

Ideological Aspects and Marxist Analysis. In the contemporary intellectual world, including the world of theology, references are often made to Marx and certain Marxists, and their contributions in the field of social and economic analysis are often taken into account. But these facts do not, by themselves, mean an acceptance of Marxism, especially insofar as Marxism embodies an all-embracing view of life and thus excludes the Christian faith and its requirements. The matter is a complex one and would require a close study of texts, a presentation of divergent interpretations in this area, and the resultant distinctions and critical observations. Without getting into details, let us clarify some issues.

Let me begin by clarifying a first point. There is *no question at all* of a possible acceptance of an atheistic ideology. Were we to accept this possibility, we would already be separated from the Christian faith and no longer dealing with a properly theological issue. Nor is there any question of agreement with a totalitarian version of history that denies the freedom of the human person. These two aspects—an atheistic ideology and a totalitarian vision—are to be categorically discarded and rejected, not only by our faith but by any truly humanistic outlook and even by a sound social analysis.

The question of the link between the ideological aspects of Marxism and social analysis is a very controversial matter in the social sciences. The same is true even within Marxism itself: for some Marxists (in a line represented by Engels—Soviet Marxism, for example) Marxism is an indivisible whole; for others (Gramsci, J. C. Mariategui, and many more) Marxist analysis or the scientific aspects of Marxism are not inseparably linked to "metaphysical materialism."

I must make it clear, however, that in the context of my own theological writings, this question is derivative. In fact given the situation in which Latin America was living, it seemed to me more urgently necessary to turn to more clearly theological questions (in this I differed from European writings on similar subjects). That is why I wrote, in a note in *A Theology of Liberation:*

> We hope to present soon a study of certain questions concerning the ambiguities in the use of the term materialism and the various conceptions of Marxism as a total conception of life or a science of history. We hope therefore to situate the vision of human nature and atheistic ideology in Marxism.

In the promised study (the promise has only partially been fulfilled in courses and conferences), my intention was to deal in greater detail with the ideological and philosophical aspects of Marxism, as well as with the connection between these aspects and the more scientific levels of analysis. But my concern was equally to show that the contributions of Marxist analysis needed to be situated and criticized within the framework of the social sciences. Otherwise, the importance of these contributions is likely to be exaggerated both by their defenders and by their opponents.

Others have made a similar study and drawn similar boundaries. I wish to take part in the effort, and I hope for the opportunity to go into the matter more fully. But I must call attention to the fact that in a Christian perspective, importance does not attach exclusively to the theoretical side of the question. There are also pastoral concerns that are urgently important for all and especially for the church's magisterium. The latter has therefore recently issued several pronouncements on the subject and taken account therein of the new problematic and the set of theoretical and practical questions it raises. The encyclical *Pacem in terris* of John XXIII made some fruitful distinctions. The letter *Octogesima adveniens* of Paul VI touched on the subject in an open and authoritative way, pointing out the values and dangers of Marxism in this area (see esp. no. 34); it also pointed out the connections between analysis and ideology in Marxism and described the conditions required of a work that would go more deeply into the subject. The Puebla Conference returned to the question (see no. 92 and esp. nos. 543–45), noting the way in which these problems arise in the Latin American context.

The letter of Father Arrupe to which I referred earlier drew its inspiration from these documents of the magisterium. In that letter we find distinctions, appraisals, warnings, and rejections with which I am in full agreement and which must be taken into account both in pastoral practice and in any theoretical discussion of the subject.

THEOLOGY AND SOCIAL ANALYSIS

a. The purpose of my theology was stated in the opening of *A Theology of Liberation*: "This book is an attempt at reflection *based on the gospel and the experiences* of men and women committed to the process of liberation in the exploited and oppressed land of Latin America"—in the light, therefore, of the gospel, and in a world of poverty and hope.

At no time, either explicitly or implicitly, have I suggested a dialogue with Marxism with a view to a possible "synthesis" or to accepting one aspect while leaving others aside. Such undertakings were indeed frequent during those years in Europe . . . and were beginning to be frequent in some Latin American circles. Such was not my own intention, for my pastoral practice imposed pressing needs of a quite different kind.

As I have reminded the reader, once the situation of poverty and marginalization comes to play a part in theological reflections, an analysis of that situation from the sociological viewpoint becomes important, and requires recourse to the relevant disciplines. This means that if there is a meeting, it is between *theology and the social sciences,* and not between theology and Marxist analysis, except to the extent that elements of the latter are found in the contemporary social sciences, especially as these are practiced in the Latin American world.

b. Use of the social disciplines for a better understanding of the social situation implies great respect for the proper sphere of these human disciplines, and for the legitimate autonomy of the political realm. The description that these sciences give of a situation, their analysis of its causes, the trends and searches for solutions that they propose—all these are important to us in theology to the extent that they involve human problems and challenges to evangelization. It is not possible, however, to deduce political programs or actions from the gospel or from reflection on the gospel. It is not possible, nor should we attempt it; it is a matter of a different realm. . . .

c. In this area a permanent demand is made, motivated by the desire to do something concrete and active, but it can also distort the perspective and limits of theological reflection . . . . [As I have said before,] "liberation theology must be required to supply a concrete language. But we must not ask of theology what it cannot and ought not give."

It is not the function of liberation theology "to offer strategic solutions or its own political alternatives . . . . In my opinion, the 'theology of revolution' set out on that path, but it seems to me that it was not a theologically sound course to follow; in addition, it ended up 'baptizing' revolution—that is, it did not acknowledge the autonomy proper to the political sphere." It is, however, right "to ask theology to play a role in the proclamation of the word," for this is in keeping with the nature of a reflection that "positions itself in the light of faith and not in the light of sociology (I understand the temptations of sociologists; theologians, however, operate in the light of the faith as lived in the Christian community)."

Theology may also be asked to help us avoid losing a comprehensive vision of a given historical process and reducing it instead to its political dimension:

> Theology must be aware that the problem is not solved solely by changing economic, social, and political structures. Theologians must, on the contrary, be aware of deeper changes that can take place in the human person, of the search for a different kind of human being, of liberation in its multiple dimensions and not just in the economic and political dimension, although, of course, all these aspects are closely connected.

Most importantly:

> Theology must be asked to show the presence of relationship to God and the rupture of the relationship with God at the very core of the historical, political, and economic situation; this is something that no social analysis can ever bring to light. A sociologist will never come to see that sin—the breaking of the relationship with God and therefore with others as well—is at the very heart of any unjust situation. If a theology does not tell us this when it takes a social situation into account, then, in my opinion, theology is not reading the situation in the light of faith. Faith will not provide strategies, but it will indeed tell us, as Medellín says, that sin is at the heart of every breaking of brotherhood and sisterhood among human beings; it will therefore be a demand for a kind of behavior and a choice.

In my view, the requirements and tasks I have outlined here are fundamental for theology. They are part of its proper sphere; what is unacceptable is to turn theological reflection into a binding premise in the service of a specific political choice. This statement does not suggest a lack of interest in the serious questions raised by the struggle for social justice; it signifies only that we must be clear regarding the scope and limits of every contribution to a vast and complex subject.

d. The presence of the social sciences in theology at the point when it is important to have a deeper understanding of the concrete world of human beings does not imply an undue submission of theological reflection to something outside it. Theology must take into account the contribution of the social sciences, but in its work it must always appeal to its own sources. This point is fundamental indeed, for whatever the context in which theological reflection takes place, "theology must now take a new route, appealing also and *necessarily to its own sources.*"

Furthermore, the indispensable use of some form of rational discourse in theological work does not mean an uncritical acceptance of that form or an identification with it. [As I said in 1973]:

> theology is not be identified with a method of analyzing society or with a philosophical reflection on the person. . . . It never makes use of a rational tool without in some way modifying it. This is in the very nature of theology, and the entire history of theology is there to prove it.

It is a matter, then, of a classical question in which theology's own personality and the freedom which comes to theology from faith (its starting point) are at stake.

6. REVELATION AND THEOLOGICAL METHOD

The theological method Gutiérrez first developed in the mid-1960s, which regards theology as the "second step" after the experience of "contemplation and commitment" (note that these together constitute the "first step" for Gutiérrez), undergirds all contemporary liberation theologies. It also challenges all other theologies—"premodern," "modern," and "postmodern"—to acknowledge the necessarily historical character of the theological enterprise. A succinct statement of Gutiérrez's mature views on method is found in the Introduction to his 1985 commentary on the Book of Job, from which the following passage is taken (On Job, xi–xiv).

Theology is talk about God. According to the Bible, however, God is a mystery, and at the beginning of his *Summa Theologiae* Thomas Aquinas states as a basic principle governing all theological reflection that "we cannot know what God is but only what God is not." Must we not think, then, that theology sets itself an impossible task?

No, the task is not impossible. But it is important to keep in mind from the very outset that theological thought is *thought about a mystery.* I mention this here because it influences an attitude to be adopted in the effort to talk about

God. I mean an attitude of respect that is incompatible with the kind of God-talk that is sure, at times arrogantly sure, that it knows everything there is to know about God. José María Arguedas poses the question: "Is not what we know far less than the great hope we feel?" This question will bring an unhesitating, humble yes from those who believe in the God of Jesus Christ.

Let me make it clear, however, that when we talk of "mystery" with the Bible in mind, we do not mean something that is hidden and must remain hidden. The "mystery" in this case must rather be spoken, not silenced; communicated, not kept for oneself. E. Jüngel puts it well: in the Christian perspective, "the fact of having to be revealed belongs to the essence of mystery." According to Paul, revelation in this case is "the revelation of the mystery which was kept secret for long ages but is now disclosed and through the prophetic writings is made known to all nations, according to the command of the eternal God, to bring about the obedience of faith" (Rom. 16:25–26). The revelation of the mystery of God leads to its proclamation to every human being: this is the special characteristic of the biblical message regarding mystery. Reflection on the mystery of God must therefore begin with God's resolve of self-communication to "all nations" (Matt. 28:19). The framework and requirements of the proclamation are fundamental for theological work.

The point I have just made leads me to discuss two connections as I begin these pages on talk about God.

1. The first is the relationship between *revelation and gratuitousness.* Christ reveals that the Father who sent him on a universal mission is a God of love. This revelation assigns a privileged place to the simple and the despised: "At that time Jesus said, 'I thank thee, Father, Lord of heaven and earth, because you have hidden these things from the wise and the intelligent and revealed them to infants; yes, Father, for such was your gracious will'" (Matt. 11:25–26).

The words "wise and intelligent" refer to a social and religious minority in Israel: the teachers, or doctors, of the law, the high priests, and the scribes. These were the men who sat "on the chair of Moses" (Matt. 23:2) and had taken possession of "the key of knowledge" (Luke 11:52). They were the ones who attributed the works of Jesus to the power of Beelzebul (see Matt. 12:24). They were important and religious persons. When Jesus said that the revelation given by the Father was hidden from the teachers, he was directly opposing the accepted and usual view of his day. He was challenging the religious and social authority of the experts in the law and saying that, because of the Father's predilection for them, the ignorant have a capacity for understanding revelation. This statement is one more sign of the originality of Jesus' teaching. He was here attacking the very foundation of the religious world of his time—namely, the identification of the primary addressees of God's word.

Over against the wise and understanding are the "simple people." The Greek word Matthew uses here (*nepioi*—literally, "very young children") carries a clear connotation of ignorance. This is the point of the contrast with the "wise and intelligent." Scholars agree that *nepioi* here does not refer to moral or spiritual dispositions; rather the word has a certain pejorative overtone. The *nepioi* in this context are the simple, the ignorant, those who must be led along the right path because they do not know how to guide themselves.

The "simple people" are related to the poor, the hungry, and the afflicted (Luke 6:20–23); to sinners and the sick (who are despised on this account) (Matt. 9:12–13); to sheep who have no shepherd (Matt. 9:36); to the children (Matt. 10:42; 18:1–4); to those not invited to the banquet (Luke 14:16–24). All these categories form a bloc, a sector of the people; they are "the poor of the land!"

The ignorance in question is not in itself a virtue or a merit that explains the divine preference. What we see here is simply a situation of need. By the same token, wisdom is not a demerit or something that provokes divine rejection. The "wise" are not necessarily proud in the moral sense; they may be, and indeed that is a danger for them. So too the ignorant may be humble, but they are not always such; humility is simply a possibility for them. It follows that the condition of being privileged addressees of revelation is the result not primarily of moral or spiritual dispositions but of a human situation in which God undertakes self-revelation by acting and overturning values and criteria. The scorned of this world are those whom the God who is love prefers. This is a very simple matter, but for a mind that judges everything by merits and demerits, worthiness and unworthiness, it is difficult to grasp.

It must be said, however, that the reason for Jesus' gratitude is not primarily, as might appear, the fact that revelation has been hidden from some and granted to others. The structure of the sentence might suggest this interpretation, but the interpretation is wrong, as can be shown by a comparison with other passages that, like this one, use contrast in a distinctively Semitic way to emphasize a point. The fact that God hides "these things" from the wise and reveals them to the simple is the concrete occasion for grasping what is behind this behavior and gives it its meaning—namely, *the free and unmerited love of God* for every human being and especially for the poor and forgotten. This interpretation of Jesus' words is supported by the undeniable fact that the gospels treat this point as central to the message of Jesus.

The real reason, then, for Jesus' gratitude is his contemplation (in the full sense of the term as a form of prayer) of the Father's goodness and love that make the simple and the unimportant into the preferred. This predilection, which does not imply exclusivity, is underscored by the hiding of revelation from the wise and important. An entire social and religious order is hereby turned upside down.

The dominant element in the text as a whole is the gratuitous character of God's love. Puebla puts the matter very clearly:

The poor merit preferential attention, whatever may be the moral or spiritual situation in which they find themselves. Made in the image and likeness of God to be his children, this image is dimmed and even defiled. That is why God takes on their defense and loves them [§1421].

The ultimate basis of God's preference for the poor is to be found in God's own goodness and not in any analysis of society or in human compassion, however pertinent these reasons may be.

2. The second connection has to do with *the way or method of speaking about God*. The text I cited from St. Thomas above tells us of the limits or, if you prefer, the proper place of theological reflection. This brings us to a theme that is classical and central to liberation theology and its view of the theological task.

The point can be stated thus: God is first contemplated when we do God's will and allow God to reign; only after that do we think about God. To use familiar categories: contemplation and practice together make up what we call a *first act;* theologizing is a *second act*. We must first establish ourselves on the terrain of mysticism and practice; only subsequently is it possible to formulate discourse on God in an authentic and respectful way. Theologizing done without the mediation of contemplation and practice does not meet the requirements of the God of the Bible. The mystery of God comes to life in contemplation and in the practice of God's plan for human history; only in a second moment can this life inspire appropriate reasoning and relevant speech. (Given the two meanings of the Greek word *logos*—"reason" and "word"—theology is a reasoned word or reason put into words.) In view of all this we can say that the first moment is *silence*, the second stage is *speech*.

Contemplation and practice feed each other; the two together make up the moment of silence before God. In prayer we remain speechless, we simply place ourselves before the Lord. In a sense, we remain silent in our practice as well, for in our involvements, in our daily work, we do not talk about God all the time; we do indeed live in God, but not by discoursing on God. As Ecclesiastes says, "there is a time to keep silence, and a time to speak" (3:7b). Silence, the time of quiet, is first act and the necessary mediation for the time of speaking about the Lord or doing theo-*logy*, which is second act.

The moment of silence is the place of loving encounter with God and of prayer and commitment; it is a time of "staying with him" (John 1:39). As the experience of human love shows us, in this kind of encounter we enter depths and regions that are ineffable. When words do not suffice, when they are incapable of communicating what is experienced at the affective level, then we are fully engaged in loving. And when words are incapable of showing forth our experience, we fall back on symbols, which are another way of remaining silent. To offer a symbol, is to "not speak" but rather to let an object or gesture speak for us. This is precisely how we proceed in the liturgy; symbolic language is the language of a love that transcends words.

This is why images of human love are so often used in the Bible in speaking of the relations between God and the people of God. When two lovers fall silent and simply remain in each other's presence, they know that they are experiencing love of each other at a deeper level. Silence, contemplation, and practice are all necessary mediations in thinking about God and doing theology. Theology will then be speech that has been enriched by silence. This reflective discourse will in turn feed the silence of contemplation and practice, and give it new dimensions.

Gratuitousness and revelation, silence and speech: these are two presuppositions of the work of understanding our faith . . . . [In this work] we ask a question about God that comes from our experience in Latin America—that is, the experience of sharing life and faith of the poor of our continent.

7. TRUTH AND THEOLOGY

Gutiérrez's early formulations of a sound theological epistemology, and specifically of the link between the praxis of liberation and knowledge of religious truth, prompted a broad and deep discussion inside the church (as well as sometimes shallow extraecclesial debates). Gutiérrez himself has returned to the theme in lectures and in print on many occasions. In the climate of theological "confrontation" prevailing in the 1980s, he offered a careful statement of his thinking on the relationship between faith and culture, theory and practice, orthodoxy and orthopraxis. As presented in both the Hebrew and Christian Scriptures, truth is something to be "done" and not simply "known" (cf. John 3:19–21). Thus, for Gutiérrez, Christian truth is discovered—and believed—only in a life of discipleship. Only in doing the truth do we know the truth. The following selection is taken from Truth, 88–89, 94–98, 98–101, 101–105. This work's full title and subtitle (Spanish: La verdad los hará libres: confrontaciones*) together underscore the seriousness of the questions under discussion.*

The primordial, and in a certain sense unique, source of revealed truth is Jesus the Christ. The Christian message must be proclaimed to persons living in a particular historical and cultural situation, but it takes on its full meaning only when connected with Jesus, born of Mary and a member of human history, in whom we recognize the Son who invites us to a lasting, saving incarnation. The good news is Jesus Christ himself. Any reflection on the truths of Christianity and on the language needed for communicating them must start from him who is the truth. Believing in the truth and putting it into practice are two necessary and mutually implicative aspects of the following of Jesus, which is the obligatory setting of all theological reflection.

Theology is talk about God. Therefore, it derives its meaning from, and has its proper setting in, service of the church's proclamation of the gospel. Every sound theology is inspired by a desire to evangelize. This does not lessen its intellectual and critical demands, but it does give these their context and prevents theology from getting lost in digressions that keep it from saying, as the gospel puts it, "yes" for "yes" and "no" for "no" (see Matt. 5:37). . . .

In some Christian circles the word "truth" readily evokes the meaning given to it in traditional philosophy of Greek origin. According to that philosophy, truth resides in the essences of things, and we reach it via the connection that exists between any given thing and the idea we construct of it; if there is conformity between reality and idea, we possess the truth. This is a legitimate, intellectual approach that many regard as typical of the Greek world. It has left its impress on the history of Western philosophy.

The Semitic mentality, which is that of the Bible, has a very different conception of truth. The Hebrew word translated as "truth" (namely, 'emet and related words, from which comes our "amen") implies solidity, fidelity, trustworthiness, loyalty. The perspective here is concrete and historical; it reflects the world of the interpersonal, where what happens is as important as, or even more important than, what is.

More specifically: truth in the scriptures is a relation not between things and concepts but between promise and fulfillment. This relation is so basic that some have thought to see in it the central theme around which it would be possible to construct a theology of the Old Testament and even of the entire Bible. Be that as it may, it is certain that the dialectic of promise and fulfillment indicates a prior reference to God. It situates us in the context of a relation between persons and not between things and concepts. It points to the revelation of God in history through the fulfillment of God's promise of love and redemption. Promise and fulfillment serve as the broad arch within which are located the Old Testament idea of the covenant and the establishment of the new covenant by Jesus.

From the Christian viewpoint, this relation gives human history its deeper meaning, constantly carrying it beyond itself. For the fulfillment of the promise is not completed in the historical process: "The promise is gradually revealed in all its universality and concreteness: it is *already* fulfilled in historical realities, but *not yet* completely; it incessantly projects itself into the future, creating a permanent historical mobility."

In the Bible, God is called true because God does what God proposes, because God is faithful to God's promise and people. Psalm 89 says as much: "I will sing of thy steadfast love, O Lord, forever; with my mouth I will proclaim thy faithfulness to all generations. For thy steadfast love was established forever, thy faithfulness is firm as the heavens" (vv. 1-2). God's word is not retracted: "Yahweh swore to David a truth from which he will not turn back: 'The fruit of your bosom I will set on your throne'" (Ps. 132:11). This unshakable loyalty of God is what rouses and creates faith or *pistis*, that is, confidence in and surrender to God. God's fidelity to God's promises, encourages, and passes judgment on, our own fidelity.

The biblical idea of truth reaches its full meaning and all of its resonance in this relation between promise and fulfillment. For this reason, the element of time, of completion in the historical process, plays an important role in the idea of truth. Kasper writes: "The Hebrew idea of truth has a specifically historical character. . . . Truth must be verified in time, in the sequence of events."

The Father's promise of love is fulfilled in a sovereign and unparalleled way in Jesus the Christ. When Jesus says "I am the truth" (John 14:6), he is saying: in me the Father's promise is fulfilled. John also tells us in his gospel: "God so loved the world that he gave his only Son" (3:16). In this sending, in the Word made human flesh, a promise is fulfilled. God is revealed as true through the mission of Jesus: "He who sent me is true" (John. 8:26)—that is, faithful and worthy of faith, of self-surrender.

In all this, we are speaking, of course, of the way we approach God and understand God's fidelity to us. In Scholastic terms, our viewpoint is *quoad nos*. But the Bible also vigorously emphasizes God's transcendence and speaks of God independently of God's action in history; it adopts what we may call the *quoad se* viewpoint. For we may never forget, [as I wrote in *Power of the Poor*] that "the God revealed in history is a *God irreducible* to our manner of understanding, to our theology, even to our faith itself. It is impossible to appropriate to oneself this God who becomes present in events, this God who becomes history. . . . God is the utterly Other, the Holy One."

As Gerhard von Rad remarks, "It is in history that God reveals the secret of his person." Both aspects have to be preserved: our access to God through God's saving action in history, and the transcendent mystery of God's presence:

> It is certain that we know the Lord through the Lord's works, but these very works reveal to us that God liberates because God is a liberator, that God enters into agreements because God is faithful, that God does justice because God is just, and not the other way around, as we tend to think. God sanctifies because God is holy; God gives life because he is Life, because God is who God is. This is certainly the sense of Yahweh's self-description to Moses: "I am who I am."

Because God is who God is, God gives life, saves, and so on; because God is truth, God is revealed as true. The approach to the mystery of God is always a complex process and one that is, to a large extent, full of surprises.

The God who is "Wholly Other" (to use Karl Barth's expression) comes to meet us through the incarnation of the Son. If we accept the historical testimony of the actions and words of Jesus, we can attain to the Father: "He who has seen me has seen the Father" (John 14:9). Jesus is the way, apart from which there is no access to the Father and to the life that comes from him. God sent the Son "that whoever believes in him should not perish but have eternal life" (John 3:16). In Jesus Christ, who is the full and unexpected fulfillment of the Father's promise, history and eschatology are tied together, the present and the ultimate meaning of time. This is what is expressed in the words, "I am the truth." Jesus Christ is the first and last word, the alpha and the omega, the beginning and the end (Rev. 22:13).

The starting point of Christian life and therefore of theology is the encounter with Christ, in whom we recognize God to be love and Father, and other human beings to be our brothers and sisters. The truth that liberates is Christ himself and every action and word which come from him.

Christian life is, above all else, a *sequela Christi*, a following of Christ. The proper doing of theology (the method, the way) has its place within this movement (itself a way) toward the Father.

Jesus calls himself the truth, but he also describes himself as the way and the life (see John 14:6). His actions and words, his practice, show us the course to follow. The Lord proclaims a truth that must be put into practice; that is why works are regarded as so important throughout the New Testament. Passages to this effect abound, and there is no point in giving a list of them.

The Gospel of John, which is so concerned with the connection between truth and freedom, contains a passage that is especially interesting: "This is the judgment, that the light has come into the world, and people loved darkness rather than light, because their deeds were evil. For everyone who does evil hates the light, and does not come to the light, lest his deeds should be exposed. But he who does what is true comes to the light, that it may be clearly seen that his deeds have been wrought by God" (John 3:19-21). The passage pulls together some central themes of this gospel. The judgment passed on some is based on their rejection of the light "because their deeds were evil." "Doing the truth," on the other hand, means accepting the light—that is, Christ and his word, and thus doing deeds that are in accord with God. . . .

Does this perhaps mean that faith is reduced to works? Not at all. The contemplative dimension is an essential element of Christian life. Faith, however, must be translated into deeds; otherwise it is a dead faith (James 2:17). At the same time, as St. Paul vigorously reminds us, deeds do not save by themselves. Salvation is a gift, an expression of the unmerited and freely given love of God. But the two themes converge and require one another without being confused with one another: if we must "do the truth," the reason is that truth here is a saving truth, a truth that acts in history and gives life.

What has been said makes it possible to situate properly the concept of praxis, to which contemporary theology frequently appeals and which plays an important role in liberation theology. Praxis implies a transformative activity that is influenced and illumined by Christian love. *A Theology of Liberation* has a section entitled "Historical Praxis," which lists the various factors that have led to emphasis on this aspect in our time. They are as follows: "Charity has been rediscovered as the center of the Christian life" (and more specifically: it is "the *foundation of the praxis of Christians*, of their active presence in history"); the evolution of Christian spirituality; sensitivity "to the anthropological aspects of revelation"; "the very life of the church" seen as a *locus theologicus;* Blondel's view of "human action as the starting point for all reflection"; "the influence of Marxist thought," which has stimulated "theological thought, appealing to its own sources, to turn to reflecting on the meaning of the transformation of this world"; and finally the rediscovery of the eschatological dimension. These eight factors have led us to perceive "the importance of concrete behavior, of deeds, of action, of praxis in the Christian life." Six of the factors are theological in nature, and two (Blondel and Marx) are philosophical.

A lengthy passage which I wrote a few years ago clarified this point still further, taking into account a synthetic view of the idea of praxis. I think it worth citing here:

> What is really at stake . . . is not simply a greater rationality in economic activity, or a better social organization, but, over and above all this, a question of justice and love. These terms are classical and perhaps seldom employed in strictly political discourse. But they remind us of all the human density involved in the matter.
>
> These terms recall to our minds that we are speaking of real human persons, whole peoples, suffering misery and exploitation, deprived of the most elemental human rights, scarcely aware that they are human beings at all. *Liberating praxis*, therefore, to the degree that it starts out from an authentic solidarity with the poor and the oppressed, is, in short, a *praxis of love*. Real love—efficacious, historical, for concrete human beings. It is a praxis of love of neighbor, and of love for Christ in the neighbor, for Christ identifies himself with the least of our human brothers and sisters. Any attempt to separate love for God and love for neighbor gives rise to attitudes which impoverish in one way or anther.
>
> It is easy to oppose a "heavenly praxis" to an "earthly praxis" and vice versa—easy, but not faithful to the gospel of the Word who became a human being. It therefore would seem more authentic and profound to speak of a *praxis of love which sinks its roots in the gratuitous and free love of the Father*, and which turns into history in solidarity with the poor and dispossessed, and, through them, *in solidarity with all human beings*.

Liberating praxis, which is, in the, final analysis, a praxis of love, is thus based, without reductionism of any kind, on the gratuitousness of God's love. It brings us, through solidarity with the poor and oppressed, into solidarity with every human being. . . .

In relation to this praxis theology exercises a critical function "in the light of faith." This reference to the classical *lumen fidei* means that the critical reflection is not philosophical or sociological but theological. As Karl Lehmann remarks, faith "cannot be unqualifiedly identified with any type of praxis." Discernment is needed, and therefore recourse to the sources of revelation, for it is from the latter that the applicable criteria must be derived. . . .

The ultimate criteria come from revealed truth, which we accept in faith, and not from praxis itself. It is meaningless—it would, among other things, be a tautology—to say that praxis is to be critiqued "in the light of praxis." Moreover, this would in any case mean moving outside properly theological work. I think it important to assert this very clearly in order to clear up any ambiguities that the emphasis on the value of practice might produce in some minds. . . .

For this very reason, and also in order to avoid being too abstract, we must keep in mind that the criterion used in discernment comes from a faith that is lived and shared in the communion of the church. By this I mean, as I noted above, a faith that necessarily leads to concrete acts of love for neighbor, or, to put it differently, a faith that necessarily inspires a practice. Thus understood, it also helps us perceive aspects of the Christian message that would otherwise be hidden from us. The 1984 "Instruction on Certain Aspects of the 'Theology of Liberation'" can therefore say:

> Likewise the experience of those who work directly for evangelization and for the advancement of the poor and the oppressed is necessary for the doctrinal and pastoral reflection of the church. In this sense it is necessary to affirm that one becomes more aware of certain aspects of truth by starting with *praxis*, if by that one means a pastoral practice and a social practice of evangelical inspiration [*LN,* XI, 13].

The "deposit of faith" is not a set of cold, stored up truths but, on the contrary, lives on in the church, where it stimulates types of behavior that are faithful to the Lord's will, calls for its proclamation to all, and provides criteria for discernment in relation to the world in which the church finds itself.

A great deal still remains to be learned about revealed truth; we have not exhausted its wealth of meaning. The 1986 "Instruction on Christian Freedom and Liberation" says, therefore, that "a theological reflection developed from a particular experience can constitute a very positive contribution, inasmuch as it makes possible a highlighting of aspects of the word of God whose complete richness had not yet been fully perceived" (*LC,* no. 70). Revealed truth is life; hence the importance of ecclesial experience, as the same Instruction carefully states in a passage heavy with fruitful implications:

> But in order that this reflection may be truly a reading of the scripture and not a projection onto the word of God of a meaning it does not contain, theologians will be careful to interpret the experience from which they begin *in the light of the experience of the church itself.* This experience of the church shines with a singular brightness and in all its purity in the lives of the saints. It pertains to the pastors of the church, in communion with the successor of Peter, to discern its authenticity [ibid.; italics added].

It is significant that this passage speaks of "the light of the experience of the church." A kind of intellectualism has caused many to distrust giving Christian experience a role in theological work, perhaps because they improperly oppose experience and the affirmation of truth. In fact, Christian truths need to be lived if they are to be stated correctly and in a more than superficial way. The experience of the church includes the Christian message—that is, the deposit of faith; Christian truths are found in the people of God which is moving toward the

Father. The reference to the saints, the very persons who have lived the teachings of Jesus and put them into practice in a higher way, is especially stimulating for theological work.

Critical reflection "in the light of the word" is only one function of theology (the others are theology as wisdom and theology as rational knowledge), but it makes it possible properly to situate the relation between orthodoxy and orthopraxis, which has been so debated and is so open to misunderstandings and erroneous interpretations.

The emphasis on correct behavior or orthopraxis has polemical overtones when set over against an attitude that gives an almost exclusively privileged place to the doctrinal aspect (or what an intellectualist approach sometimes takes to be the doctrinal aspect) of the Christian message. This attitude undeniably exists, and both the magisterium and contemporary theology have referred to it, even before Vatican II but especially since, given the council's stress on concrete Christian life. The critique of that attitude was occasioned by the imbalance it introduced into the living out of the gospel. There is no doubt, of course, that the earlier mentioned emphasis of the contemporary mind on the practical aspects of human knowledge has played a part in creating the new sensitivity to orthopraxis. At the same time, however, this new sensitivity represents a revival of perspectives that have always had a place in the Christian community.

It is important also to observe that in liberation theology the subject of orthopraxis is studied in the context of the role played by eschatology in contemporary theology. The context is important, because this perspective opens us to the gift that gives ultimate meaning to history: the full and definitive encounter with the Lord and with other humans. The emphasis on historical practice is therefore directly connected with the Christian affirmation of a world beyond the present life.

The purpose in thus stressing the importance of orthopraxis is to throw into relief the role in Christian life of concrete commitment along the lines of that "doing of the truth" that we saw a few pages back. It should be clear that this is not at all to deny the meaning of orthodoxy, understood as a proclamation of and reflection on statements considered to be true. Right thinking is essential for a believer who has received the faith within the church.

The challenge is to be able to preserve the circular relationship between orthodoxy and orthopraxis and the nourishment of each by the other. Light is cast on this matter by Mark 8:27–35, a key passage, where the confession of faith in the messiah and the practical following of him imply one another. As Paul Tillich says, "Christian theology is rooted in a concept of truth in which there can be no separation between theory and practice, because this truth is saving truth."

Especially meaningful in regard to Christian freedom is the context of the statement that Christ is the truth that sets us free (John 8:32). To be free is to be a disciple (v. 31), to know the truth (v. 32), not to be self-sufficient (v. 33), not to practice sin (v. 35), to be a child of God (v. 35), and to welcome the word (v. 36).

The praxis of the Christian acquires its meaning in the following of Jesus, from the practice of the Lord himself. Encounter with Christ is the point of departure for our faith in ecclesial communion and for our understanding of it. Jesus Christ is the hermeneutical principle for all understanding of the faith. [As I wrote in *The Power of the Poor in History*]:

> In Jesus we encounter God. In the human word we read the word of the Lord. In the events of history we recognize fulfillment and promise. And all this because Jesus is the Christ of God, the one sent by the Father: the Son. "Yes, God loved the world so much that he gave his only Son" (John 3:16). For Jesus is the irruption into history of the one by whom everything was made and everything was saved. This, then, is the *fundamental hemeneutical circle:* from the human being to God and from God to the human being, from history to faith and from faith to history, from the human word to the word of the Lord and from the word of the Lord to the human word, from the love of one's brothers and sisters to the love of the Father and from the love of the Father to love of one's brothers and sisters, from human justice to God's holiness and from God's holiness to human justice. Theology—understanding faith—is *animated by the desire to help others live according to the Spirit.*

The truth that the understanding of faith aims to enter into more deeply and to know with all its demands upon believers is Jesus Christ himself. He is the supreme norm of theological discourse to the same extent that he is the supreme norm of our entire life. The indispensable condition for a correct reflection on faith, which is God's gift, is that we make his practice our own, make his way in history ours, and love as he loved us.

8. UNDERSTANDING THE GOD OF LIFE

The original version of the following text was given in February 1981 as the opening lecture of the eleventh annual "summer course" in theology in Lima. Gutiérrez's unceasing interest in the question of theological method reflects his conviction about its pastoral relevance, his abiding commitment to clarification of his thought, and his attention to ongoing scholarly debates on the matter. In its final (for now) edited form, Gutiérrez's thoughts on method presented below are taken from the Introduction to his 1989 work of biblical theology, El Dios de la vida (English: The God of Life, xiii–xvii), a shorter version of which was first published in 1982.

In a well–known passage Blaise Pascal contrasts the "God of Abraham, Isaac, and Jacob," the "God of Jesus Christ," with the "God of the philosophers." The words occur in the "Memorial," which Pascal always carried on his person and which gives expression to a profound mystical experience. In other words, the

God of the Bible is not the God of philosophy. This is an authentically Christian insight that has legitimately inspired many lived experiences and reflections. It is impossible not to agree with it.

As a matter of fact, philosophy—or at least a certain type of philosophy—has a great deal of trouble conceiving the God of biblical revelation. To give an example: for thinking that is based on Aristotle, it is difficult to say that God is love. Within the categories of Greek thought, love is a *pathos*, a passion; it implies a need and therefore a dependence on something or someone. For this reason, love cannot be attributed to the perfect being. Now, all this is not a matter simply of conceptual stumbling blocks; at issue is the way in which human beings approach God.

For the Bible, God is a mystery; that is to say, God is love that envelops everything. God is someone who is revealed within history and, at the same time, is present in the heart of each individual. This mystery must be communicated and not kept for oneself; it is not the possession of any individual or group. In Christ, says St. Paul, there has been revealed "the mystery kept secret for long ages but now . . . disclosed, and through the prophetic writings . . . made known to all the Gentiles, according to the command of the eternal God, to bring about the obedience of faith" (Rom. 16:25–26).

To believe is a vital and communal experience. The mystery of God must be accepted in prayer and commitment; this is the moment of silence and practice. Within this moment there arise the categories and language needed for communicating it to others; this is the moment for speaking. This communication must be made with profound respect; we must know how to situate ourselves before God. In a passage that is steeped in the Old Testament faith, Paul again shows us the way: "Oh the depth of the riches and wisdom and knowledge of God! How unfathomable are his designs and how inscrutable his ways! 'For who has known the mind of the Lord or who has been his counselor?' 'Or who has given him anything that he may be repaid?' For from him and through him and for him are all things" (Rom. 11:33–35; see Isa. 40:13).

The profound insight of Pascal does not, however, do away with the necessity of conceiving the God of biblical revelation; rather it warns us not to follow the wrong way of doing it. My intention in these pages is to reflect on the God of Abraham, Isaac, Jacob, and Jesus Christ. Jesus has shown us the way: "Whoever has seen me has seen the Father" (John 14:9). Augustine of Hippo tells us that Christ is the key to the Scriptures. He makes known to us who God is, because "no one knows the Father except the Son" (Matt. 11:27). It is well known that in the Bible "knowledge" is a very rich concept that is not limited to the intellectual realm but also connotes taste, friendliness, and love. Knowledge here is immediate and profound and embraces all dimensions of the person who is known and loved.

Consequently, it is in the Son, with him, and through him that we love the

Father. This love puts its stamp on our knowledge of God. Because we are God's friends and because God loves us, the Lord makes known to us "everything I have heard from my Father" (John 15:15). It is as friends of Jesus that we wish to reflect on our common Father. This revelation is the area in which I shall be making this present effort at understanding the biblical faith. In the community of the followers of Christ—in the church—we read the Word.

Biblical revelation receives its unity in Christ: according to Vatican II, which cites St. Augustine, God so ordered the two testaments "that the New should be hidden in the Old, and that the Old should be made manifest in the New" (*Dei verbum* 16). For this reason, my reflection seeks to include the entire Bible. The profound continuity of the Bible does not mean forgetting the novelty to be found in "the words and works . . . [the] death and glorious resurrection" of Jesus Christ (*DV* 4). The break entailed in this witness and proclamation . . . explains why under one and the same section heading I deal separately with the texts of each testament.

The Lord tells us, moreover: "Do not think that I have come to abolish the law or the prophets. I have come not to abolish but to fulfill" (Matt. 5:17). The demands that this "fulfillment" makes on the understanding of Scripture provide the basic criterion of my presentation of the theme of God in the Bible. "The most intimate truth which this [divine] revelation gives us about God and the salvation of humanity shines forth in Christ, who is himself both the mediator and the sum total of Revelation" (*DV* 2). . . .

Human beings believe in God in the context of a particular historical situation; after all, believers are part of a cultural and social fabric. For a long time, for example, the consciousness of their own limitations and their realization of their dependence on the external world, both natural and social, led human beings to emphasize God's power and omnipotence. The consciousness of their finiteness sensitized them to the infinity of the supreme being. In our age, the assertion of the human person as subject of its own history, as well as our increasing ability to transform nature, have gradually led to a different approach to God. In the context of the phenomenon we call "secularization" (there is no need here of introducing nuances and distinctions) there is a growing sensitiveness to a God who is revealed in humility and suffering. Confronted with human beings who are conscious of their strength, theology speaks of a God who is "weak."

From the experience of death of the poor, a God who liberates and gives life is nevertheless affirmed. The lived experiences of God and the reflection on God that originate in the impoverished and marginalized sectors of the human race emphasize this perspective. "I feel God differently," says a character in a book of J. M. Arguedas in the light of her experience as a woman, a human being who is neglected and looked upon as inferior. The same claim can be made by the unimportant people of this world, those who suffer abuse in body and dignity from the mighty. The experience of death leads to the affirmation of the God of life.

The mystery of God cannot be reduced to any one of the approaches I have schematically described. Each of them carries certain values and reveals to us aspects of a reality that is ineffable; the framework they supply enables us to perceive the complexity of the mystery we are approaching. But precisely because the Bible is to a great extent the expression of the faith and hope of the poor, and above all because it reveals to us a God who loves preferentially those whom the world passes over, the last approach just described has a broad and fruitful biblical foundation. I am interested in making this explicit while taking into account the challenges posed to us by our Latin American situation and by the lived experience of Christian communities here. These communities also "feel" the Bible differently and enter into a fruitful and complex dialogue with it. The avenues followed in this exchange have left their mark on [my reflections on the God of the Bible].

I approach the Scriptures in an attitude of faith. The intention of the books of the Bible is to speak to us of God and to communicate the faith of their authors and of persons, groups, and an entire people. This is said in various ways in these works. A passage from the Gospel of John sums up the approach: "Now Jesus did many other signs in the presence of his disciples that are not written in this book. But these are written so that you may [come to] believe that Jesus is the Messiah, the Son of God, and that through this belief you may have life in his name" (John 20:30–31). The intention, then, is to rouse faith in the Lord, to call the reader to life. Not everything that happened is recounted; the author proposes only to offer a selection of events (see the final verse of the same Gospel, 21:25). To read the Bible is to begin a dialogue *between faith and faith*, between the believers of the past and those of today: a dialogue that is taking place today within the ecclesial community, a pilgrim in history.

The books of the Bible tell us stories, sometimes about an entire people, sometimes about a community; or they tell of personal journeys. These books in turn have their own history; they took form through a process of reading and rereading. The stories, whether they be based on real situations or are literary fictions, give voice to an authentic faith experience. The stories told are not inspired by any urge for scientific accuracy; they do not constitute a history written according to contemporary canons. They are testimonies. Their aim is to show the saving action of God. This is what matters. God's saving action manifests itself in historical events which are its reference point and its language. I approach the Scriptures in terms of my own history, in terms of the situation of a people that suffers abuse and injustice but is organizing to defend its right to life and is keeping its hope in God strong. There is thus a dialogue *between history and history*. The biblical stories shed light on our present history, both collective and personal, and help us to see in it the intervention of the God who liberates.

The Christian people of Latin America whose knowledge of, and facility with, the Bible has grown and deepened so much in recent years, perceive the Word of God as very close to them. They hear it speaking directly to their everyday lives. When a passage is read, it is not unusual for someone to say, for example: "That is what just happened to me." Among the people there is a quick and extensive identification with the biblical texts. This experience of nearness is undoubtedly very valuable. The Bible is not a book like any other; it is the Word of the Lord who, according to Deuteronomy, always speaks to us "today." At the same time, however, we cannot forget that we are dealing with writings that took shape thousands of years ago, in languages and cultural settings that are not our own. We must therefore make the effort to distance ourselves from them and to acquire knowledge of the social, cultural, and religious context of the texts. Numerous and serious historical, social, and literary studies now allow us to know this background. These studies are a basic tool to be used in drawing near to writings that we must at the same time admit are distant from us. The dialogue with the Scriptures will be more fruitful if we are aware that our relationship to the biblical texts is one of both *nearness and distance.* On the one hand, we will then avoid a facile approach and even a possible manipulation of the Bible, but at the same time we will be prevented from succumbing to a literalism that pays no heed to human and social circumstances and turns every word into an absolute.

To have contact with the Bible means reading it. It is a text. We go to it with the questions, worries, and hopes that derive from the reality we are living. Such has been the church's practice throughout its history. This is what is called the pre-text with which we approach the Bible and continually read and reread it. John Paul II spoke of this in Brazil: "The church has meditated on these texts and messages from its own beginnings, but it is aware that it has still not penetrated their meaning as it would like (will it perhaps be able to do so some day?). In different concrete situations it *rereads these texts* and studies this message with the desire of finding a *new application* of it" (emphasis added). But when believers read Scripture, they also know that the Scriptures question them. The Bible is not a kind of depository of answers to our concerns; rather it reformulates our questions and launches us on unexpected paths. We can truly say that we read the Bible. But it in turn reads us, "penetrating even between soul and spirit, joints and marrow, and able to discern reflections and thoughts of the heart" (Heb. 4:12). The dialogue must therefore also be a relationship between *one reading and another reading.* When the reading of the Bible is done as a community, as a church, it is always an unexpected experience.

In summary, our starting point is our faith: we *believe* in the God of life. We aim to *think through* this faith by going ever deeper into the content of biblical revelation. And we do this while taking into account the way in which the poor *feel* God. Faith and reflection on God feed each other.

9. THEOLOGICAL LANGUAGE: FULLNESS OF SILENCE

On October 26, 1995, Gutiérrez was formally inducted into the Academia Peruana de la Lengua Española (Peruvian Academy of the Spanish Language) in Lima, only the third priest to be a member of the prestigious society. In his acceptance address Gutiérrez explored the present state of the theological language which is being forged in Latin America. This is a language characterized by the attempt to "sink roots into the complex and dense human condition of our peoples, to begin with our social and cultural universe in its expression, and to take seriously the narrative dimension of the Christian faith." The three parts of the address were titled "The God Who Is Both Patient and Nurse," "Between Babel and Pentecost," and "The Narrator Narrated." The excerpt below, published here for the first time in English, contains the second and third parts of the address. The original may be found in Páginas *137 (1996), 66–87. The translation is by the present editor.*

Theology is a language. It attempts to speak a word about the mysterious reality that believers call God. It is a *logos* about *theos*.

I have said "mysterious reality" and I would like to make it clear that I am taking the word "mystery" in its biblical sense. The French philosopher Gabriel Marcel helped us to understand the matter by drawing a distinction between "problem," "enigma," and "mystery." God is not a problem before which we stand impersonally and that we treat as an object. Nor is God an enigma, something utterly unknown and incomprehensible. In the Bible God is a mystery to the extent that God is an all-enveloping love. In Marcel's terminology, God is the mystery of the Thou that we can only acknowledge and invoke.

Hence—and always speaking from a biblical standpoint—mystery is not ineffable in the literal meaning of the word. It must—with all the proper qualifications—be spoken and communicated. To conceal it, to keep it withdrawn to a private sphere, or to limit it to a few initiates is to ignore its very essence. The mystery of God's love must be proclaimed. Doing so presupposes a language, a means of communication—a language located more in the disturbing certainty of hope than the serenity brought about by an innocuous knowledge.

Believing is an experience that is both interior and shared in community. Faith is a relationship between persons; that is why we said it is a gift. The mystery of God must be accepted in prayer and in human solidarity; it is the moment of silence and of practice. Within that moment—and only from within it—will there arise the language and the categories necessary for transmitting it to others, for entering into communication, in the strong sense of the term: in communion with those others; that is the moment of speaking.

In a beautiful passage, the Book of Ecclesiastes tells us that throughout human life everything has its moment and season: "a time to be silent and a time to speak" (3:7). These moments are not simply set side by side, but rather one depends on the other, and they nourish one another. Without silence there is no true speaking. In listening and meditation, what is to be spoken begins to be sketched faintly and hesitatingly. Likewise, expressing our inner world will lead us to gain new and fruitful areas of personal silence and encounter. That is what happens in theology.

Keeping in mind these preliminary considerations, I would like to offer some observations on the present situation of theological language, [in particular] on the connection between theological language and the human condition. Such observations may perhaps help us to appreciate the magnitude of a major development: for some decades now in Latin America and beyond it, a way of speaking of God is stammeringly coming to birth, a way of speaking marked by the cultural diversity of humankind and the conditions created by poverty and marginalization. . . .

BETWEEN BABEL AND PENTECOST

Genuine theological language requires sinking roots into what André Malraux called "the human condition." To do so, such speech must keep in mind the cultural diversity of humankind. A reflection on a biblical paradigm that is now part of the common heritage of humankind can offer us some insight.

Mythical accounts arise in order to account for fundamental but disputed matters. The passage in Genesis known as the tower of Babel seeks to explain something that is lost in the obscurity of time, namely the variety of tongues spoken by the human race. This narrative, generally read as a punishment by God for what is assumed to be a Promethean effort, has struck the imagination of the Western world over the centuries. The punishment meted out to those who wanted to "make a name for themselves" (Gen. 11:4) by building a tower that could reach up to the sky is said to have done away with an original single language (Gen. 11:1); those who were involved in the pretentious (Gen. 11: 8–9) building project were struck with bewilderment and could no longer understand each other.

Such is the most common interpretation, the one prevailing in the popular imagination of the West. Nevertheless, the matter is worth reconsidering in relation to the topic that interests us, namely, the task of theology.

DANTE AND THE VERNACULAR LANGUAGES

At different points in his work, Dante Alighieri alludes to the question of the vernacular languages which in his time were beginning to break away from Latin. He finally takes up the topic in a curious, unfinished treatise written in Latin, *De Vulgari Eloquentia (Vernacular Eloquence)*.

As a medieval man, Dante accepts the historicity of the tower of Babel story. He regrets the loss of humankind's proto-language and regards the diversity of languages as the result of a divine punishment. To this point we find nothing especially remarkable; Dante seems to accept at face value the prevailing interpretation of the Genesis text in his time. The fact is, however, that ultimately he introduces substantial changes in it.

He does not hide his intention. The opening lines in his book speak of the vacuum that he is seeking to fill. "No one before us," he says, "had treated the doctrine of the vernacular tongue." That is the point. The vernacular language is the one "we learn" he says, "without any rule, imitating our wet nurse." He regards it as the one best fitted for expressing feelings of joy and love. The vernacular language is hence the poetic tongue par excellence. For Dante the vernacular can be given no higher praise.

Dante says that the Babel episode is "worth recalling." What does he mean? Reading his treatise, one has the impression that he says this not so much because it reminds us of an exemplary chastisement to human audacity but because it opens the way to the vernacular languages. Babel thus becomes something of a *felix culpa*, a "happy fault" to which we owe the existence and the wealth of different languages, enabling us to express ourselves poetically. Punishment becomes reward, curse becomes blessing.

All of this does not mean that there is no yearning for a universal language in Dante. For him, however, that does not mean returning to the past; such yearning is toward the future and is aimed at overcoming the linguistic conditions arising at Babel. The *Divine Comedy*, for example, testifies to that yearning and search.

CURSE OR BLESSING?

Dante's questioning interpretation of the Genesis text was not the only assault on the ordinary understanding of this passage, but it is certainly one of the most significant. His contribution was to raise doubts about the idea that diversity of language was purely and simply a punishment from God.

Contemporary archaeological and historic research on the region of Mesopotamia has proved that in antiquity there were many cities built around very high towers. This has led some researchers to say that the first reference to the actual history of humankind that we find in the Book of Genesis is precisely the tower of Babel account.

Such facts surely served as ingredients for the author or authors of the account. Moreover, the history of the Jewish people and a careful reading of other texts in the Bible sharpen the picture of the motivations for this story. On a number of occasions, for example, the Jews saw their territory occupied by the great empires of the region, and they were put into forced labor by the political leaders of the enemy country.

Hence, many modern exegetes say that the text must be read as the fruit of the painful historical experience of a subjugated people. All these elements enter into a literary composition that thereby becomes a paradigm of the life of humankind and takes its place beyond its location at a particular place and time.

Unquestionably, we have here a rejection of the haughtiness of those building the city and the tower. But more than a Promethean enterprise of rivalry with God, it is a political attempt, totalitarian in nature, to dominate people. To the extent that it is such, it is indeed an offense against God. Hence, the single language is not—in the story we are examining—the expression of an idyllic unity of humankind, nor must it be an ideal yearned for; instead, it must be seen as the imposition of an empire. Such a language facilitates centralized power and the political yoke. As the experience of history demonstrates, the matter arises spontaneously in those who hold power in their hands or are close to it. This is the topic, as we all recall, of the letter that Nebrija sends to Queen Isabel to offer her his new and classic *Gramática Castellana (Spanish Grammar)*. The terms are well known.

Observation of history has convinced him that "language has always gone hand in hand with empire." They grow and flourish together and together they fall. The scholar Nebrija argues on behalf of his work by rooting it in the situation in 1492. He regards his book as especially timely at the moment when the queen has "under her yoke many barbarian peoples and nations of far off tongues"—peoples that he says must receive "the laws that the victor imposes on the vanquished." Nothing better for that purpose than to learn "our language" suggests Nebrija, something that those nations can do better and more rapidly now, thanks to the grammar that he is placing in his sovereign's hands.

Elsewhere, at another moment that is equally decisive, politically speaking, this view of language makes a reappearance. Within the tumult of the social movements and debates of the French Revolution, an effort is made to forge a single nation with a firm central power. The paradigm of the confusion of Babel is again recalled. The utopian thinkers of the sixteenth century had also invoked it, but at this point we are witnessing the actual erection of a modern state. The famous Abbé Gregory denounces what to his eyes appears to be a great contradiction: "with thirty dialects, we are like Babel with respect to language, whereas we stand at the forefront of the nations with regard to freedom."

The variety of languages is thus evidence of a very serious backwardness; that variety must be done away with if progress toward modernity is to be made. The fateful legacy of Babel must be eradicated. Regional languages must disappear; establishing a single language for all would seal national unity. The single language becomes an important political tool in a modern world then taking its first steps. It will contribute to the development of the totalitarian thrust of what Jürgen Habermas calls "instrumental reason."

Nebrija and Gregory (as well as many others we could easily mention) thus stand on the side of power. Matters look different to those who suffer the consequences of an imperial and even totalitarian will. Just as it is denounced in Dostoyevsky's always terrifying legend of the Grand Inquisitor which makes people believe that they enjoy freedom. That would be the message of the Genesis text and the reason for rejecting the fiction of a human community expressed in a single language so as no to impede the flow of orders coming from the central authority.

Against this background, the diversity of languages for oppressed peoples, far from being a punishment, helps protect their freedom. It prevents a totalitarian power from imposing itself with no resistance. If there is punishment, it is directed at the effort of some to impose, and not the different nations speaking their own languages. Well-known contemporary exegetes and theologians have pointed out that this biblical passage does not speak of punishment.

Those same scholars have also observed that in the Book of Genesis as a whole the diversity of peoples and languages is presented as a great treasure for humankind and as desired by God.

We are clearly dealing with a polysemic text. For our purposes it suffices to say that an interpretation being put forth today is not only one that can claim ancient intuitions and can be traced through the history of the reading of this account over the centuries, but that is also based on a rigorous contemporary approach to the text and its context. Moreover, the current appreciation of ethnic and cultural pluralism opens new possibilities for understanding this foundational myth about the diversity of languages.

ALL IN THEIR OWN LANGUAGE

We are thus led to be reminded of one of the most significant developments for contemporary Christianity: Christian faith has not only begun to arise in the hearts of non-Western peoples and cultures, but it has grown and matured there.

In an influential article seeking to assess Vatican Council II, Karl Rahner said that from a theological standpoint, three great periods could be discerned in the history of the church: first, the short time between Jesus and Paul of Tarsus, linked to the Jewish world; then, the period between Paul and the eve of Vatican II in the twentieth century, linked to the Western world. The third moment, which began with Vatican II, faces the major challenge of dealing with universality in diversity. Historians might dispute Rahner's periodization, but it is undeniably stimulating and even provocative.

Recognition of the (culturally and ethnically) other is a major demand of our time. Over untraveled paths and unforeseen shortcuts the experience of neglected and abused peoples is becoming fruitful for the two great dimensions of Christian life: mysticism and human solidarity. It is there that a discourse on God is sinking its roots, a discourse that is not merely a reflection of what is occurring in places where Christianity has existed for many centuries.

Forced to become acclimated in a different environment and to take nourishment from the sap that comes from other lands, theological language gives hardy fruits whose flavor is somewhat different from the one to which many were accustomed, but they are not thereby less tasty and nutritious. The demands of what is now called inculturation—a new term for something quite old—which was emphasized by John Paul II and the bishops meeting several years ago in Santo Domingo (1992), go further than adaptation. They call for a renewal of mental categories.

This effort encompasses many current efforts to speak of God. What Dante said of the vernacular languages is true for theological language rooted in a particular social and cultural world. As they express in a unique way the initial feelings of joy and love (that is why they are the proper language of poetry), likewise the paths taken today by the word about God based on particular experiences are best fitted for powerfully and authentically giving voice to delight and pain, and to hope and love. Discourse on God is not real and challenging except in the diversity with which it is formulated.

In this apology for particularity, however, what space remains for universality? The first point to be made is that theological languages are converging approaches toward the mystery recognized and invoked in faith, the root of every word about God. However, although fundamental, it is not the only basis for unity and universality; such words also depend on the human density that theological language bears within itself.

"A provincial of this world," [Peruvian novelist] José María Arguedas calls himself at one point. The human universality toward which Arguedas moves, starting with the Peruvian Indian and *mestizo*, bears the mark of the suffering and hope, the anguish and gentleness of those who are sometimes regarded as human refuse. Far from limiting his perspective, this stamp gives it breadth and effective power. "In the sound of the *charango* and the *quena*, I shall hear *everything*," he says as he finishes his *Ultimo Diario?* His is the concrete universality which, as Hegel said, is expressed in the singular.

To the extent that language about God takes on the human condition with its doubts and certainties, generosity and self-seeking, insecurity and constancy, laughter and tears, it passes through the density of the social, of gender, of the ethnic, and of the cultural so as to reach the deepest dimensions of the human. "If language thus loaded with strange essences," said Arguedas perceptively, "enables us to see the deep human heart, if it communicates to us the story of its movement over the earth, universality may perhaps be a long time in coming; it will nevertheless come, however, for we know very well that humans owe their preeminence and their dominion to the fact that they are one and unique." That is why he used to say mischievously, "I am a provincial of this world."

We will not have a lively language about God without a lucid and fruitful relationship with the culture of a time and a place. At the same time, the various particular theologies must establish close communication with one another, because they are striving for a word about singular situations situated in an ever more interdependent world.

The episode of Pentecost, sometimes regarded as the paradigm of a universal language, illustrates this necessary communication out of diversity. It is not about speaking a single language, but about being able to understand one another. The story tells of persons who have come from different places and have heard the disciples of Jesus and understood them— three times, it says—in their own language (Acts 2:6, 8, 11). All are speaking their own language but they understand one another. Hence Pentecost, far from being a paradigm of anti-

Babel, signifies instead that each of the various ethnic groups present in Jerusalem is prized. There is only one reservation: the legitimate linguistic differences between them must not only not hinder mutual understanding but favor it.

Language about God takes its inspiration from the Christian message but also—and inseparably—in the manner in which it made up of life. This depends on very specific historic circumstances. No theology is without its own accent in speaking of God. A flavor, a special taste, which is what the word "accent" also means. The differences in such speaking must be respected. It is not imposed uniformity that is required, but understanding in diversity.

THE NARRATOR NARRATED

With its starting point in the density of human life, a language about God anchored in a particular cultural world must be capable of narrating the experience of Jesus and of those who have accepted his witness.

The Bible is composed of a wide variety of narrations—it is more stories than a single story or history. These accounts speak of the great issues of human concern: the origin of time, the reason for all that exists, the life and death of human beings, and the relationship with nature. Through the accounts, God—or more specifically God's humanity, Jesus—becomes present to those who accept God in their lives. The word about God must therefore bear this narrative imprint. The famous line by Blaise Pascal contrasting "the God of Abraham, Isaac, Jacob, and Jesus Christ" with the "God of the philosophers" is precisely the opposition between the God of narration and the God of concept and abstraction.

To tell of Christian practice, inspired by trust in love and in faith, means exchanging experiences. Such interchange, as the ever-acute Walter Benjamin put it, is "the surest reality among things that are sure." That is what Jesus did.

A FLAVORFUL KNOWLEDGE

In the early days of Christianity, theology was simply a meditation on the Bible aimed at enriching the believer's everyday life or Christian practice. Theological language took the form of wisdom, again in the biblical meaning of the word: a knowing that has not lost its connection with savor, a delicious knowledge. [Throughout this passage there is a wordplay between *saber* ("to know," "knowledge") and *sabor* ("flavor," "taste")—Ed.] A speaking that also meant enjoying [*distrutar*—word play on "fruit"—Ed].

Contact with the Greco-Roman world, and especially with philosophy, launched theology along the path of discourse and argumentation where the background was metaphysical. This encounter with Greek reason, and today with contemporary critical reason, led, and leads, to theological reflection of significance. It also shows its limits and its gaps, however.

For that reason it is obvious in our own time that, without discounting the contribution that we have just noted, it is important to highlight the narrative dimension mentioned earlier. For a long time, the philosophical perspective led to an interpretation of the well-known line of John's Gospel "in the beginning was the word" (1:1) in the sense of the Greek *logos*, that is, concept and human reason. The complexity of the term with its Hebrew substrate was accordingly pushed to one side. Beneath the word *logos* used by John is the Hebrew *dabar* which means simultaneously word and event. It is the *dabar*, thus understood with its double meaning, that stands at the beginning. It is the word made human flesh.

An event must be told, spoken. The story heard gives rise to other tellings. "What we have heard—that we tell," says a psalm. The result is a chain of narrative, composed of both the memory of past events and the imprint of other new ones. A believing community is always a narrating community.

Let us take, by way of example, a text familiar to us, the parable that we customarily call "The Good Samaritan". Prompted by the question, "Who is my neighbor?" Jesus tells the story of two somewhat prominent individuals within the Jewish people (both connected to religious worship) who remain unmoved by the suffering of someone they did not know, perhaps for reasons of ritual purity. The third individual is a Samaritan, who therefore belongs to a people and a religion that were then held in contempt. The Samaritan approaches the injured man and becomes his neighbor. The passage concludes with a short and unequivocal statement from Jesus to the individual to whom he has told the story: "Go and do likewise" (Cf. Luke 10:29–39).

The text does not offer us a definition of the category "neighbor" nor a speech on charity or human solidarity. We stand before a simple but compelling comparison that calls us to have the capacity to be moved in the presence of a person who is abused and suffering and to effectively act to help that person.

Let us look at another gospel text. This time it is not a parable, but the story of something Jesus does. I have in mind what we hastily call "The Multiplication of the Loaves." The story speaks to us of sensitivity to people's hunger, of sharing, and of knowing how to do so with the little that is at hand. At the end of the passage, the twelve baskets set in the middle of the grass are a call to keep sharing. Indeed, from now on sharing what one has must be the sign of those who accept the story. Hence, it is likewise the criterion making it possible to be discerning about human behavior.

There is no argument here based on definitions and doctrinal boundary setting, but rather a deed of love expressed in the sharing of bread. Here also we find a challenge to continue to do so throughout history. The great biblical accounts as well as the one that tells us the story of the life and death of Jesus have a value—today we would call it performative—for those who come into contact with them.

Jesus was a story teller. His stories give rise to others that one way or another speak of him and of his witness. Jesus is the narrator narrated. From that standpoint, Christianity is simply a saga of stories. Story-telling is the proper way of speaking about God; this is not simply a literary form, much less a pedagogical device, as we are inclined to say of the gospel parables; it is the proper language for speaking about God. Parables belong to the very nature of the gospel.

Narration incorporates the hearer within it. It tells an experience and makes it an experience of those who hear it. The characteristic feature of the story is invitation, not obligation; its terrain is freedom, not command. A theology that takes its stand in story, that knows how to narrate faith, will be a theology that is humble and backed up by personal commitment, a theology that offers and does not seek to impose, one that listens before speaking. Truth emerges from silence, said Simone Weil shortly before her death. This is also true of speaking about God.

A HERMENEUTIC OF HOPE

Theology, says Paul Ricoeur, emerges at the intersection between "a space of experience" and "a horizon of hope." In that space there occurs a personal contact with the witness of Jesus, a Galilean itinerant preacher, whom we know through the biblical story. That hope is expressed not in the repetition of that narration, but in its recreation in the life of those who feel called by the experience of Jesus and his friends. Theology is truly a hermeneutic of hope, a hermeneutic that must be done and redone continually. In scripture it is called "giving an account of hope" (1 Peter 3:15).

The witness of Jesus is ever challenging and disturbing. He tells us that human life reaches its full meaning only in total and daily surrender. The fact that he is the reference point is not a fixation on the past, but rather a way of bringing him into the present, so much so that memory of him has been regarded as dangerous for a history that is dominated by selfishness and injustice.

To recall, for example, the life and death of a man of our own time like Archbishop Oscar Romero is to tell faithfully and creatively the life and death of Jesus in the present of Latin America. With the Master, he could say, "No one takes my life from me; I lay it down on my own" (John 10:18). We can find this supreme act of freedom in other stories, many of them simple and everyday, and thus having less public impact. They all challenge those who live isolated from the suffering of others, but they are likewise invitations to a change of attitude. Such proposals leave it up to our freedom and inventiveness to find the ways and also—why not?—the motivations that each one of us would like to have, leading to the practice of human solidarity.

The point is not that there is no room for logical argument and systematic thought in theology, but rather that they must always draw nourishment from a faith that reveals its full meaning only in a living and life-giving story. Although the telling is itself already a way of interpreting, there is undoubtedly a moment for narrating and a time for presenting arguments.

Theology must protect the categories of story and memory if it wants to remain faithful to its sources and to play a role in liberating human beings from whatever hinders them from having their dignity respected and developing all their potentialities.

10. UPSTREAM TO THE SOURCE

In 1992, the quincentenary of the Spanish conquest of the Americas, Gutiérrez published a massive study (nearly 650 pages of text and 150 pages of notes) of the thought of Dominican Bishop Bartolomé de Las Casas, best known as the sixteenth-century "defender of the Indians" (En busca de los pobres de Jesucristo: El pensamiento de Bartolomé de Las Casas; English translation: Las Casas: In Search of the Poor of Jesus Christ, 1993). Though not, strictly speaking, a work of theology but rather of the history of theology, the tour de force nevertheless constitutes a challenge to those who undertake theological reflection today. For the discerning reader, Gutiérrez's treatment of Las Casas also offers notable insights into Gutiérrez himself.

In the volume's introduction, "Upstream to the Source," Gutiérrez explains how Las Casas's attempt to discover the source of the suffering of indigenous peoples in the Americas not only led him to seek a remedy for that suffering, but also guided him to a rediscovery of the very source of Christian life, namely, the love of Christ. The following passage is taken from Las Casas, *1–4.*

In the prologue of his *History of the Indies,* citing an ancient author, Bartolomé de Las Casas reminds us that history is the "teacher of life" and the "life of our memories." This is especially the case with the testimony of Bartolomé himself. With Bartolomé, deeds and commitments are inseparable. Each sheds light on, and sustains, the other. To study them is to infuse with life the memory of his reflections. He was a witness of his time—of the fact that, in this "Indian world, I have seen suffering," as he said. He speaks to us from an era whose pace had accelerated at the sight of a widening of the then-known world.

His long life prevented him from simply remaining under the impact of the first events of the Indies. He was able to get beyond this stage and conceive, as far as possible, a complete, integral notion of his era. "I am perhaps the oldest and, of those alive today, the most experienced" in these matters, he declares, not without a touch of pride, "with the possible exception of one of two others in all of these West Indies." In this ample period of time, he always learned from reality; he conceived a thousand projects, was on the mark with some of them and missed it with others, fought with impressive tenacity, knew how to analyze situations with great lucidity, survived numerous attacks, achieved many of his objectives, evolved in his thinking.

But above all Bartolomé was moved by "the charity of Jesus Christ, which knows neither measure nor rest as long as it is a pilgrim on this earth." Indeed, neither did Las Casas rest. He was always moved by "the sight of the faith of Jesus Christ being so vituperated, affronted, and brought low in this New World," its inhabitants being the victims of such rapacity. Therefore—he says at the close of his life—he has walked "in dedication to the task of acquiring a remedy for the native folk of what we call the Indies," in order that "the havoc and massacre committed there, counter to all reason and injustice," might cease.

This is the living context of his reflections. He never ceased revising and deepening those reflections with a view to a better understanding of what was occurring in his time in the Indies and in Europe. Conscious of the sixty-one years that had elapsed since he had seen "these tyrannies begin," and the forty-eight he had labored "to inquire and study and bring the truth out into the open," Las Casas says, in a delicate moment of his life, writing to the Dominican friars of Chiapa and Guatemala: "I believe, if I am not deceived, that I have plumbed the depths of these things and managed to reach the headwaters." Upstream to the source: Las Casas always sought the waters that would write *finis* to the sterility and suffering of the Indies he knew. These deep waters are the material of the present book. Like him, we too shall have to travel upstream, to the headwaters, for we seek the source of his own writings and testimony. In traveling up this stream, we shall attempt to make his historical journey of the past a challenge and "teacher of life" for us today.

FACING THE TRUTH

We are currently celebrating the fifth centenary of an occurrence of capital importance in the history of humanity. The event to which we refer changed the life of Bartolomé de Las Casas as well. We mean the encounter (or collision), unexpected on both sides, not only between the peoples of the territory today called America and those who lived in Europe, but including Africa, as well—a third continent promptly and violently incorporated into the process of which we speak. This event is regarded as a *discovery* by those who see history from the old continent (as they themselves call it). A *covering,* others call it—referring to a history written in blatant disregard of the viewpoint of the inhabitants of the so-called New World. The *"Conquista"* it was dubbed in the old history books; "invasion" some prefer to call it today.

One thing is certain: the matter is a complex one, and one that we have not yet adequately interpreted. Individuals of a number of different spiritual families devote attention to it. As might be expected, diverse, even opposed, focuses come into confrontation, for we are dealing with the historical course of a reality whose wounds are old and still open. The fifth centenary has endowed with renewed vitality polemics that have basically never ceased to smolder. A further contributing factor, doubtless, is the better understanding we have today, thanks to a great deal of research, of the manner in which the Indian peoples themselves have always read this same history.

The controversy kindles mighty passions and produces towering indignation. And with good reason. Let us take just one fact: whatever calculation we accept of the original population of America, the decline in population over the seventy or eighty years following the arrival of Columbus can be regarded only as an authentic demographic collapse. Add to this the disappearance of cultures that for one reason or another were unable to offer resistance to the invaders, along with so many other, similar factors.

The very mention of these matters is deeply distasteful to many in certain European nations: Spain and Portugal, present at the beginning and constituting the principal European presence ever since; France, England, and Holland, which later arrived on the scene; Germany, with its episodic financial investments and presence in the Indies; and Italy, through the presence and influence of certain personages. All of these countries are proud of what they have accomplished in the Indies, and actually regard it as civilizing and evangelizing. It is important, however, to remember that Spain alone had the courage to hold a comprehensive debate on the ethics and morality of the European presence in the Indies. In the other countries of the old world, the right to occupy these lands was regarded as too obvious to be questioned.

True, the discussion could be overwhelmed today by a flood of data and documents. We could be trapped in a fog of emotions, or hand down judgments that would be anachronistic in the face of history's advance and the presence of irreversible situations. A consideration of what happened from the sixteenth century onward must not be transformed into an invitation to turn back the clock of history. History cannot be remade. This is simple realism. But this must not prevent us—on the contrary, it should stimulate us—to see the meaning for us today of an honest interpretation of the events that have occurred since that time. That time, to quote Las Casas, was "altogether new, and unlike any other." Now is a crucial moment, therefore, for a realistic understanding of our present, and of the promise that present holds for the future.

The question becomes more urgent—and more difficult—when we take account of the fact that, in this controversial encounter, the gospel of Jesus, too, came to these lands. What are we to think of the enormous human cost to which the evangelization of the Indies has de facto been linked? How are we to understand the role of the church in these events? In what way do these occurrences mark the current situation of the Christian community on this continent? What can we learn today from Christians' first reactions to the demands on, contempt for, and death of the Indian populations? To what extent ought the protests, reflections, and engagements of so many missionaries of the sixteenth century in the face of the Indians' suffering be guidelines for our own days?

With the most profound respect for the historical coordinates of the past, we necessarily address that past out of our present concerns and anxieties. The effort will require courage and honesty. Only by looking historical truth full in the face shall we be able to embark upon the times to come with responsibility and efficacy.

We do not seek solely an understanding of history and of the society in which we live. Also at stake is the *intellectus fidei*—the "intelligence" or understanding of Christian faith. After all, it is impossible to divorce the experience of faith and reflection on that experience from the history of peoples. A hope for and welcome of the reign of life must necessarily call in question, and radically, a political reality of oppression and injustice. Las Casas said that the Indians were being "stripped of their lives before their time" and thus despoiled of "space for their conversion."

Unfortunately, something of the same must be said of the poor of today in Latin America, who continue to suffer a premature, unjust death. From the outset, the so-called controversy of the Indies had an important theological dimension. It could not have been otherwise in an age and a country like that of Spain of that time, where the Christian element weighed so heavily in the balance. At a distance of several centuries, something of the sort is occurring today. Today once more, in these same lands of the Indies, the process of a reflection upon faith has been leading rapidly to an effective commitment in an awareness of the situation of poverty and injustice in which the majority of the population of Latin America live and under the inspiration that should animate the quest for a liberation that takes account of the complexity of the human person. It is for these reasons that we find the testimony of Bartolomé de Las Casas so meaningful today. Here was someone driven to proclaim the reign of God in a fitting manner, through a defense of the life and freedom of persons in whom his faith enabled him to perceive Christ himself.

Two

HERMENEUTICAL PRINCIPLE: PREFERENTIAL OPTION FOR THE POOR

Most theologies, past and present, have claimed universality and objectivity based on an alleged freedom from sociohistorical conditioning in the reception of divine revelation. By contrast, the theologies of liberation assert that all theology is contextual and particular, and consequently none can be impartial in a world of conflicting social interests. Because the theologian's social location itself prevents theology from being disinterested, Gutiérrez urges a careful determination and forthright acknowledgment of one's fundamental allegiance among conflicting sociopolitical forces.

But recognizing distinct vantage points does not imply assigning equal value for theology to all of them. Among the theological norms advanced by Gutiérrez, Jesus Christ stands preeminent as "the hermeneutical principle of faith, and hence the foundation of all theological reasoning" (Power of the Poor, 61). In the years since Vatican II—thanks in large part to Gutiérrez—the church has deepened its understanding of Jesus Christ through the notion of God's "preferential option for the poor." It may not be easy to perceive the theological import of a genuine identification with the cause of the marginalized of the world; but if, as Gutiérrez claims, God loves preferentially the poor and oppressed whose situation of premature and unjust death contradicts the divine will in history, God's choice tells us more about who God is than who the poor are. For this reason the preferential option is a theological norm. Furthermore, if Scripture itself is the product of God's choice of the poor, and if the revelation of God is mediated by the poor, an authentic solidarity with the poor of today becomes an indispensable precondition for a firm grasp of the biblical message. The process by which the church has come to perceive and appropriate the "epistemological privilege" of the poor has at times been arduous. Nevertheless, the pastoral, theological, and ecumenical fruits of this growing awareness are undeniable. Gutiérrez himself believes that a grasp of the preferential option for the poor will be the enduring legacy of liberation theology to the church. The texts of Chapter Two illustrate the evolution of Gutiérrez's thinking about the preferential option for the poor and, when placed beside official papal, episcopal, and curial teaching, suggest the debt owed Gutiérrez by the universal church in this regard.

11. HISTORY IS ONE

The strength of Gutiérrez's theological positions often resides in the balance, or better, tensive unity, he achieves between two or more apparently conflicting poles. One of his first theological concerns—the nature of history—arose from what he believed to be the inadequacy of the church's understanding of its relationship to, and thus its role in, the world. With others, Gutiérrez sought to avoid the dualism of "two histories, one profane and one sacred," and at the same time to safeguard the gratuitous character of God's offer of salvation. He accomplished this by asserting that all human history is "christo-finalized." Yet Gutiérrez was not satisfied with mere abstract assertion; the important question is how history can be both God's and ours. In other words, how can we link the ideas that the outcome of personal histories and collective human history is genuinely in our hands and, at the same time, fully in God's custody?

Gutiérrez answers this question in two steps. First, he demonstrates that the historical experience of (political) liberation called the Exodus allows us to see that human self-creation is not incompatible with divine redemption. Indeed, as the Hebrews learned, all creative acts are redeeming and all redemptive acts are creative. And second, he holds that for the Bible the eschatological promises of God are not only made in history but are in the process of being fulfilled in history. Thus the "complete encounter with the Lord will take place in history" (Theology of Liberation, 97), *not after or beyond history. Yet the promise of fulfillment itself relativizes every partial actualization of the promise in history. Hence, the proper Christian stance before history is one of total commitment and, simultaneously, permanent detachment. Only by maintaining such a practical and conceptual tension can we give adequate expression to a theological truth. The following text about the meaning of history, taken from* Theology of Liberation *(86–97), lays one of the foundation stones for the notion of the preferential option for the poor (to be taken up in succeeding selections in this chapter).*

There are not two histories, one profane and one sacred, "juxtaposed" or "closely linked." Rather there is only one human destiny, irreversibly assumed by Christ, the Lord of history. His redemptive work embraces all the dimensions of existence and brings them to their fullness. The history of salvation is the very heart of human history. Christian consciousness arrived at this unified view after an evolution parallel to that experienced regarding the notion of salvation. The conclusions converge. From an abstract, essentialist approach we moved to an existential, historical, and concrete view which holds that the only human being we know has been efficaciously called to a gratuitous communion with God. All reflection, any distinctions which one wishes to treat, must be based on this fact: the salvific action of God underlies all human existence. The historical destiny of humanity must be placed definitively in the salvific horizon. Only thus will its true dimensions emerge and its deepest meaning be apparent. It seems, however, that contemporary theology has not yet fashioned the categories which would allow us to think through and express adequately this unified approach to history. We work, on the one hand, under the fear of falling back again into the old dualities, and, on the other, under the permanent suspicion of not sufficiently safeguarding divine gratuitousness or the unique dimension of Christianity. Although there may be different approaches to understanding it, the fundamental affirmation is clear: there is only one history—a "christo-finalized" history.

The study of two great biblical themes will allow us to illustrate this point of view and to understand better its scope. The themes are the relationship between creation and salvation and the eschatological promises.

CREATION AND SALVATION

The Bible establishes a close link between creation and salvation. But the link is based on the historical and liberating experience of the Exodus. To forget this perspective is to run the risk of merely juxtaposing these two ideas and therefore losing the rich meaning which this relationship has for understanding the recapitulating work of Christ.

CREATION: THE FIRST SALVIFIC ACT

The Bible does not deal with creation in order to satisfy philosophic concerns regarding the origin of the world. Its point of view is quite different.

Biblical faith is, above all, faith in a God who gives self-revelation through historical events, a God who saves in history. Creation is presented in the Bible, not as a stage previous to salvation, but as a part of the salvific process: "Praise be to God the Father of our Lord Jesus Christ. . . . In Christ he chose us before the world was founded, to be dedicated, to be without blemish in his sight, to be full of love; and he destined us—such was his will and pleasure—to be accepted as his sons through Jesus Christ" (Eph. 1:3–5). God did not create only in the beginning; he also had an end in mind. God creates all to be his children. Moreover, creation appears as the first salvific act: "Creation," writes von Rad, "is regarded as a work of Yahweh in history, a work within time. This means that there is a real and true opening up of historical prospect. No doubt, creation as the first of Yahweh's works stands at the very remotest beginnings—only it does not stand alone, other works are to follow." The creation of the world initiates history, the human struggle, and the salvific adventure of Yahweh. Faith in creation does away with its mythical and supernatural character. It is the work of a God who saves and acts in history; since humankind is the center of creation, it is integrated into the history which is being built by human efforts.

Second Isaiah—[in A. Jacob's view] "the best theologian among the Old Testament writers"—is an excellent witness in this respect. His texts are frequently cited as one of the richest and clearest expressions of the faith of Israel in creation. The stress, however, is on the saving action of Yahweh; the work of creation is regarded and understood only in this context: "But now this is the Word of the Lord, the word of your creator, O Jacob, of him who fashioned you, Israel:

Have no fear; for I have paid your ransom; I have called you by name and you are my own" (43: 1; cf. 42:5–6). The assertion is centered on the redemption (or the Covenant). Yahweh is at one and the same time Creator and Redeemer: "For your husband *is* your maker, whose name is the Lord of Hosts; your ransomer is the Holy One of Israel who is called God of all the earth" (54:5). Numerous psalms sing praise to Yahweh simultaneously as Creator and Savior (cf. Pss. 74, 89, 93, 95, 135, 136). But this is because creation itself is a saving action: "Thus says the Lord, your ransomer, who fashioned you from birth: I am the Lord who made all things, by myself I stretched out the skies, alone I hammered out the floor of the earth" (Isa. 44:24; cf. also Amos 4:12ff.; 5:8ff.; Jer. 33:25ff.; 10:16; 27:5; 32:17; Mal. 2:10). Creation is the work of the Redeemer. Rolf Rendtorff says: "A more complete fusion between faith in creation and salvific faith is unimaginable."

POLITICAL LIBERATION: SELF-CREATION OF THE HUMAN BEING

The liberation from Egypt—both a historical fact and at the same time a fertile biblical theme—enriches this vision and is moreover its true source. The creative act is linked, almost identified with, the act which freed Israel from slavery in Egypt. Second Isaiah, who writes in exile, is likewise the best witness to this idea: "Awake, awake, put on your strength, O arm of the Lord, awake as you did long ago, in days gone by. Was it not you who hacked the sea monster Rahab in pieces and ran the dragon through? Was it not you who dried up the sea, the waters of the great abyss, and made the ocean depths a path for the ransomed?" (51:9–10). The words and images refer simultaneously to two events: creation and liberation from Egypt. Rahab, which for Isaiah symbolizes Egypt (cf. 30:7; cf. also Ps. 87:4), likewise symbolizes the chaos Yahweh had to overcome to create the world (cf. Pss. 74:14; 89:11). The "waters of the great abyss" are those which enveloped the world and from which creation arose, but they are also the Red Sea which the Jews crossed to begin the Exodus. Creation and liberation from Egypt are but one salvific act. It is significant, furthermore, that the technical term *bara,* designating the original creation, was used for the first time by Second Isaiah (43:1, 15; cf. Deut. 32:6) to refer to the creation of Israel. Yahweh's historical actions on behalf of the people are considered creative (41:20; 43:7; 45:8; 48:7). The God who frees Israel is the Creator of the world.

The liberation of Israel is a political action. It is the breaking away from a situation of despoliation and misery and the beginning of the construction of a just and comradely society. It is the suppression of disorder and the creation of a new order. The initial chapters of Exodus describe the oppression in which the Jewish people lived in Egypt, in that "land of slavery" (13:3; 20:2; Deut. 5:6): repression (Exod. 1:10–11), alienated work (5:6–14), humiliations (1:13–14), enforced birth control policy (1:15–22). Yahweh then awakens the vocation of a liberator: Moses. "I have indeed seen the misery of my people in Egypt. I have heard their outcry against their slave-masters. I have taken heed of their sufferings, and have come down to rescue them from the power of Egypt. . . . I have seen the brutality of the Egyptians toward them. Come now; I will send you to Pharaoh and you shall bring my people Israel out of Egypt" (3:7–10).

Sent by Yahweh, Moses began a long, hard struggle for the liberation of the people. The alienation of the children of Israel was such that at first "they did not listen to him; they had become impatient because of their cruel slavery" (6:9). And even after they had left Egypt, when they were threatened by Pharaoh's armies, they complained to Moses: "Were there no graves in Egypt, that you should have brought us here to die in the wilderness? See what you have done to us by bringing us out of Egypt! Is not this just what we meant when we said in Egypt, 'Leave us alone; let us be slaves to the Egyptians'? We would rather be slaves to the Egyptians than die here in the wilderness" (14:11–12). And in the midst of the desert, faced with the first difficulties, they told him that they preferred the security of slavery—whose cruelty they were beginning to forget—to the uncertainties of a liberation in process: "If only we had died at the Lord's hand in Egypt, where we sat round the fleshpots and had plenty of bread to eat" (16:3). A gradual pedagogy of successes and failures would be necessary for the Jewish people to become aware of the roots of their oppression, to struggle against it, and to perceive the profound sense of the liberation to which they were called. The Creator of the world is the Creator and Liberator of Israel, to whom is entrusted the mission of establishing justice: "Thus speaks the Lord who is God, he who created the skies, . . . who fashioned the earth. . . . I, the Lord, have called you with righteous purpose and taken you by the hand; I have formed you, and appointed you . . . to open eyes that are blind, to bring captives out of prison, out of the dungeons where they lie in darkness" (Isa. 42:5–7).

Creation, as we have mentioned above, is regarded in terms of the Exodus, a historical-salvific fact which structures the faith of Israel. And this fact is a political liberation through which Yahweh expresses love for the people and the gift of total liberation is received.

SALVATION: RE-CREATION AND COMPLETE FULFILLMENT

Yahweh summons Israel not only to leave Egypt but also and above all to "bring them up out of that country into a fine, broad land; it is a land flowing with milk and honey" (3:8). The Exodus is the long march toward the promised land in which Israel can establish a society free from misery and alienation. Throughout the whole process, the religious event is not set apart. It is placed in the context of the entire narrative, or more precisely, it is its deepest meaning. It is the root of the situation. In the last instance, it is in this event that the dislocation introduced by sin is resolved and justice and injustice, oppression and liberation, are determined. Yahweh liberates the Jewish people politically in order to make them a holy nation: "You have seen with your own eyes what I did to Egypt. . . . If only you will now listen to me and keep my covenant, then out of all peoples you shall become my special possession; for the whole earth is mine. You shall be my kingdom of priests, my holy nation" (19:4–6). The God of Exodus is the God of history and of political liberation more than the God of nature. Yahweh is the Liberator, the *goel* of Israel (Isa. 43:14; 47:4; Jer. 50:34). The Covenant gives full meaning to the liberation from Egypt; one makes no sense without the other. . . . The Covenant and the liberation from Egypt were different aspects of the same movement, a movement which led to encounter with God. The eschatological horizon is present in the heart of the Exodus. Casalis rightly notes that "the heart of the Old Testament is the Exodus from the servitude of Egypt and the journey toward the promised land. . . . The hope of the people of God is not to return to the mythological primitive garden, to regain paradise lost, but to march forward toward a new city, a human and comradely city whose heart is Christ."

Yahweh will be remembered throughout the history of Israel by this act which inaugurates its history, a history which is a re-creation. The God who makes the cosmos from chaos is the same God who leads Israel from alienation to liberation. This is what is celebrated in the Jewish passover. . . . The memory of the Exodus pervades the pages of the Bible and inspires one to reread often the Old as well as the New Testament.

The work of Christ forms a part of this movement and brings it to complete fulfillment. The redemptive action of Christ, the foundation of all that exists, is also conceived as a re-creation and presented in a context of creation (cf. Col. 1: 15–20; 1 Cor. 8:6; Heb. 1:2; Eph. 1:1–22). This idea is particularly clear in the prologue to the Gospel of St. John. According to some exegetes it constitutes the foundation of this whole Gospel.

The work of Christ is a new creation. In this sense, Paul speaks of a "new creation" in Christ (Gal. 6:15; 2 Cor. 5:17). Moreover, it is through this "new creation," that is to say, through the salvation which Christ affords, that creation acquires its full meaning (cf. Rom. 8). But the work of Christ is presented simultaneously as a liberation from sin and from all its consequences: despoliation, injustice, hatred. This liberation fulfills in an unexpected way the promises of the prophets and creates a new chosen people, which this time includes all humanity. Creation and salvation therefore have, in the first place, a christological sense: all things have been created in Christ, all things have been saved in him (cf. Col. 1:15–20).

Humankind is the crown and center of the work of creation and is called to continue it through its labor (cf. Gen. 1:28)—and not only through its labor. The liberation from Egypt, linked to and even coinciding with creation, adds an element of capital importance: the need and the place for human active participation in the building of society. If faith "desacralizes" creation, making it the area proper for human work, the Exodus from Egypt, the home of a sacred monarchy, reinforces this idea: it is the "desacralization" of social praxis, which from that time on will be the work of humankind. By working, transforming the world, breaking out of servitude, building a just society, and assuming its destiny in history, humankind forges itself. In Egypt, work is alienated and, far from building a just society, contributes rather to increasing injustice and to widening the gap between exploiters and exploited.

To dominate the earth as Genesis prescribed, to continue creation, is worth nothing if it is not done for the good of humanity, if it does not contribute to human liberation, in solidarity with all, in history. The liberating initiative of Yahweh responds to this need by stirring up Moses' vocation. Only the *mediation of this self-creation*—first revealed by the liberation from Egypt—allows us to rise above poetic expressions and general categories and to understand in a profound and synthesizing way the relationship between creation and salvation so vigorously proclaimed by the Bible.

The Exodus experience is paradigmatic. It remains vital and contemporary due to similar historical experiences which the People of God undergo. As Neher writes, it is characterized "by the twofold sign of the overriding will of God and the free and conscious consent of humans." And it structures our faith in the gift of the Father's love. In Christ and through the Spirit, persons are becoming one in the very heart of history, as they confront and struggle against all that divides and opposes them. But the true agents of this quest for unity are those who today are oppressed (economically, politically, culturally) and struggle to become free. Salvation—totally and freely given by God, the communion of human beings with God and among themselves—is the inner force and the fullness of this movement of human self-generation initiated by the work of creation.

Consequently, when we assert that humanity fulfills itself by continuing the work of creation by means of its labor, we are saying that it places itself, by this very fact, within an all-embracing salvific process. To work, to transform this world, is to become a human and to build the human community; it is also to save. Likewise, to struggle against misery and exploitation and to build a just society is already to be part of the saving action, which is moving toward its complete fulfillment. All this means that building the temporal city is not simply a stage of "humanization" or "pre-evangelization" as was held in theology until a few years ago. Rather it is to become part of a saving process which embraces the whole of humanity and all human history. Any theological reflection on human work and social praxis ought to be rooted in this fundamental affirmation.

ESCHATOLOGICAL PROMISES

A second important biblical theme leads to converging conclusions. We refer to the eschatological promises. It is not an isolated theme, but rather, as the former one, it appears throughout the Bible. It is vitally present in the history of Israel and consequently claims its place among the People of God today.

HEIRS ACCORDING TO THE PROMISE

The Bible is the book of the Promise, the Promise made by God to human beings, the efficacious revelation of God's love and self-communication; simultaneously it reveals humankind to itself. The Greek word which the New Testament uses to designate the Promise is *epangelia,* which also means "word pledged," "announcement," and "notification"; it is related to *evangelion.* This Promise, which is at the same time revelation and Good News, is the heart of the Bible. Albert Gelin says that "this Promise lies behind the whole Bible, and it makes it the book of hope, the slight hope stronger than experience, as Péguy said, which persists through all trials and is reborn to greater strength after every setback." The Promise is revealed, appeals to humankind, and is fulfilled throughout history. The Promise orients all history toward the future and thus puts revelation in an eschatological perspective. Human history is in truth nothing but the history of the slow, uncertain, and surprising fulfillment of the Promise.

The Promise is a gift accepted in faith. This makes Abraham the father of believers. The Promise was first made to him (cf. Gen. 12:1–3; 15:1–16) that he and his posterity would be, as St. Paul says in a vigorous and fertile expression, "the heirs of the world" (Rom. 4:13). For this reason Jesus, John the Baptist (Luke 3:8; 13:16; 16:22; 19:9), and Paul (Gal. 3:16–29; Rom. 4; Heb. 11) place Abraham at the beginning of the work of salvation. This Promise is "given to those who have such faith" in Jesus Christ (Gal. 3:22). The Promise is fulfilled in Christ, the Lord of history and of the cosmos. In him we are "the 'issue' of Abraham, and so heirs by promise" (Gal. 3:29). This is the mystery which remained hidden until "the fullness of time."

But the *Promise* unfolds—becoming richer and more definite—in the *promises* made by God throughout history. [As Gelin writes,] "The first expression and realization of the Promise was the Covenant." The kingdom of Israel was another concrete manifestation. And when the infidelities of the Jewish people rendered the Old Covenant invalid, the Promise was incarnated both in the proclamation of a New Covenant, which was awaited and sustained by the "remnant," as well as in the promises which prepared and accompanied its advent. The Promise enters upon "the last days" with the proclamation in the New Testament of the gift of the kingdom of God.

The Promise is not exhausted by these promises nor by their fulfillment; it goes beyond them, explains them, and gives them their ultimate meaning. But at the same time, the Promise is announced and is partially and progressively fulfilled in them. There exists a dialectical relationship between the Promise and its partial fulfillments. The resurrection itself is the fulfillment of something promised and likewise the anticipation of a future (cf. Acts 13:23); with it the work of Christ is [as Gelin says] "not yet completed, not yet concluded"; the resurrected Christ "is still future to himself." The Promise is gradually revealed in all its universality and concrete expression: it is *already* fulfilled in historical events, but *not yet* completely; it incessantly projects itself into the future, creating a permanent historical mobility. The Promise is inexhaustible and dominates history, because it is the self-communication of God. With the Incarnation of the Son and the sending of the Spirit of Promise this self-communication has entered into a decisive stage (Gal. 3:14; Eph. 1:13; Acts 2:38–39; Luke

24:29). But by the same token, the Promise illuminates and fructifies the future of humanity and leads it through incipient realizations toward its fullness. Both the present and future aspects are indispensable for tracing the relationships between Promise and history.

ESCHATOLOGY: THE FUTURE AND THE HISTORICAL PRESENT

In recent years the eschatological dimension of revelation—and consequently of Christian existence—has been rediscovered.

In traditional dogmatic theology, the treatise on the "last things" (death, judgment, heaven, hell, the end of the world, the resurrection of the dead) was a kind of appendix not too closely related to the central themes. This treatise began to be referred to as eschatology. Its etymology suggested its appropriateness: *escatos*, "last," and *logos*, "treatise."

Toward the end of the nineteenth century, the eschatological theme appeared in liberal Protestant theological studies (Johannes Weiss, Albert Schweitzer) on the message of Jesus and the faith of the primitive Christian community. Jürgen Moltmann points out the impact of the rise of this line of thinking, but recalls also the pointlessness of these first efforts. "Dialectical theology" came onto this scene from another vantage point and made eschatology the center of its thinking. The "first" Barth is its best representative. Under the influence of Kant, Barthian eschatology is what Urs von Balthasar calls "transcendental eschatology": eternity is the form of true being; time is nothing but appearance and shadow; the ultimate realities are the first principle of everything and therefore the limit of all time. It was this viewpoint, according to Moltmann, "which prevented the break-through of eschatological dimensions in dogmatics."

But the eschatological theme has continued to gain in importance. The term is controversial, the notion much debated. One idea, however, has emerged: the Bible presents eschatology as the driving force of salvific history radically oriented toward the future. Eschatology is thus not just one more element of Christianity, but the very key to understanding the Christian faith.

Basing his study on a rigorous exegesis of the Old Testament, Gerhard von Rad has completed an important attempt at clarification in this area. He believes it is inaccurate to think of the eschatological sphere as a "consistent body of ideas, made up of complex cosmic and mythological expectations about the future, from which the prophets drew what they wanted." To reserve the term *eschatological* to designate the end of time, the fulfillment of history, that is to say, extrahistorical events, he thinks is not enough. For von Rad, the prophets have "eschatologized" Israel's conceptions of time and history. However, what is characteristic of the prophets is, on the one hand, their orientation toward the *future* and, on the other, their concern with the *present*.

It is due to their posture toward the *future* that the prophets are the typical representatives of the Yahwist religion. What is characteristic of the prophets' message is that the situation they announce "cannot be understood as the continuation of what went before." Their starting point is an awareness of a break with the past; the sins of Israel have rendered it unacceptable; the guarantees given by Yahweh are no longer in force. Salvation can come only from a new historical action of Yahweh which will renew in unknown ways the earlier interventions in favor of the people; the signs announcing this action come to be dimly seen by the prophets' rereading those earlier events. The Exodus is a favorite theme of the prophets; what they retain of it is fundamentally the break with the past and the projection toward the future. This causes von Rad to conclude that "the message of the prophets has to be termed eschatological whenever it regards the old historical bases of salvation as null and void," and he notes that "we ought then to go on and limit the term. It should not be applied to cases where Israel gave a general expression of her faith in the future, or . . . in the future of one of her sacred institutions." Von Rad ends by saying that "the prophetic teaching is only eschatological when the prophets expelled Israel from the safety of the old saving actions and suddenly shifted the basis of salvation to a future action of God." The core of eschatological thought is in this tension toward that which is to come, toward a new action of God. Hope in new acts of God is based on Yahweh's "fidelity," on the strength of his love for his people which was manifested in the past initiatives on their behalf. These new actions lead to and are nourished by an act to take place at the end of history.

But there is another facet of the prophetic message which we have already considered and which will help us—despite its apparent opposition to the orientation toward the future which we have just mentioned—to pinpoint the notion of eschatology. We refer to the prophets' concern for the present, for the historical vicissitudes which they witness. Because of this concern the object of their hope is very proximate. But, this "closeness" does not exclude an action of Yahweh at the end of history. Indeed, the prophetic message proclaims and is realized in a proximate historical event; at the same time, it is projected beyond this event. This has been perceptively and clearly explained by Steinmann with respect to messianism in his comments on Isaiah's oracle of the "soul." The author distinguishes two meanings in this prophecy: the first, the only one comprehensible to his contemporaries, points to something "immediately offered by Yahweh to remedy the tragic situation created in Jerusalem by the onslaught of the Syro-Ephraimitic League"; this is the birth of a new heir to the crown. The second sense is but dimly perceived by the prophet: "It is through the gift of a child that Yahweh will save the world." The eschatological prophecy refers, therefore, to a concrete event, and *in* it to another fuller and more comprehensive one to which history must be open. What is especially important for an accurate understanding of eschatology is the relationship between these events. The relationship is found in the projection toward the future included in the present event. From a similar point of view, von Rad interprets Deuteronomy, the book which contains the theology of the Covenant:

It is certain, literally, that Deuteronomy comes from the time after the conquest, for it speaks of the people on Mt. Horeb; thus it functions as fiction; because they had been living on the land for a long time. But here we see a clearly eschatological feature which permeates the whole. All the salvific benefits which it mentions, including a life of "rest," are proposed to the community again, now that it is called to decide for Yahweh. We are faced with one of the most interesting problems of Old Testament theology: the promises which have already been realized historically are not invalidated, but continue to be true in a new context and somewhat different form. The promise of the land was preached again without interruption as a future good, even after it had been achieved.

This interpretation allows him to speak of the eschatological scope of Deuteronomy, an opening to the future which is not only not suppressed by the implementations in the present, but is rather affirmed and dynamized by them.

The historical implementations of promises in the *present* are—insofar as they are ordered toward what is to come—as characteristic of eschatology as the opening to the *future*. More precisely, this tension toward the future lends meaning to and is expressed in the present, while simultaneously being nourished by it. It is thus that the attraction of "what is to come" is the driving force of history. The action of Yahweh in history and at the end of history are inseparable. It has been said often in recent years that the expression used in Exod. 3:14 *(Ehyeh asher 'ehyeh)* is correctly translated not as "I am who am," which can be interpreted within our categories in the sense of a vigorous but static assertion of God's transcendence, but rather as "I will be who will be." A new kind of transcendence is emphasized: God is revealed as a force in our future and not as an ahistorical being. Grammatically both translations are valid. It would be better perhaps to use an expression which emphasizes the characteristic of permanence: "I am he who is being." But the use of similar expressions (thirty–one times throughout the Bible) and the context of the Covenant in which the above passage is found, lead us rather to stress the active sense of the terminology employed. "To be" in Hebrew means "to become," "to be present," "to occupy a place." "I am" would mean "I am with you," "I am here ready to act" ("When I put forth my power against the Egyptians and bring the Israelites out from them, then Egypt will know that I am the Lord" [Exod. 7:51]). "I am the Lord, I will release you. . . . I will rescue you. . . . I will adopt you as my people. . . . I will lead you to the land. . . . I will give it to you for your possession" (Exod. 6:6–9; cf. also 3:10, 17; 8:18).

The full significance of God's action in history is understood only when it is put in its eschatological perspective; similarly, the revelation of the final meaning of history gives value to the present. The self-communication of God points toward the future, and at the same time this Promise and Good News reveal humanity to itself and widen the perspective of its historical commitment here and now.

ESCHATOLOGICAL PROMISES: HISTORICAL PROMISES

What has been said will help us to frame better a classic question regarding the interpretation of Old Testament texts. We refer to the so-called spiritualizing influence which the New Testament has on them.

According to this hypothesis, what the Old Testament announces and promises on the "temporal" and "earthly" level has to be translated to a "spiritual" level. A "carnal" viewpoint kept the Jewish people from seeing the hidden, figurative sense of these announcements and promises, which is revealed clearly only in the New Testament. This hermeneutical principle is strongly held in Christian circles. And it is not new. A famous text of Pascal's echoes this ancient tradition: "The prophecies have a hidden and spiritual meaning to which this people were hostile, under the carnal meaning which they loved. If the spiritual meaning had been revealed, they would not have loved it."

Let us take as a recent and representative example of this line of interpretation the opinion of a well-known exegete. Regarding the prophetic promises, Grelot asserts with his usual precision that there is a fundamental misunderstanding of the object of these promises. "On the one hand," he writes, "they seem to refer to the *temporal redemption* of Israel, freed from secular oppression and reestablished in its past status in such a way that all nations participate in its privileges and enjoy with it the earthly goods promised at the time of the first Covenant. But on the other hand, they also seem to refer to the *spiritual* redemption of all, as can be inferred from some of the brightest pages, not the longest but the purest." In order to clarify this ambiguity, it is necessary to argue from the principle that the true object of the promises is veiled by the figurative language used by the prophets. The problem at hand, therefore, is to discover "what has to be taken literally and what is to be understood figuratively." The answer is clear: the object of these promises is the "permanent *spiritual* drama of humanity which touches directly on the mystery of sin, suffering, and salvation, which constitutes the substance of its destiny"; the texts which transmit these promises to us, however, have only an "accidental relationship with *political* history. The true sense is therefore the "spiritual" one. The New Testament will make this sense perfectly clear.

But is this really a true dilemma: either spiritual redemption or temporal redemption? Is there not in all this an "excessive spiritualization" which Yves Congar advises us to distrust? All indications seem to point in this direction. But there is, perhaps, something deeper and more difficult to overcome. The impression does indeed exist that in this statement of the problem there is an assumption which should be brought to the surface, namely a certain idea of the spiritual characterized by a kind of Western dualistic thought (matter-spirit), foreign to the biblical mentality. And it is becoming more foreign also to the contemporary mentality. This is a disincarnate "spiritual," scornfully superior to all earthly realities. The proper way to pose the question does not seem to us to be in terms of "temporal promise or spiritual promise." Rather, as we have mentioned above, it is a matter of partial fulfillments through liberating historical events, which are in turn new promises marking the road toward total fulfillment. Christ does not "spiritualize" the eschatological promises; he gives them meaning and fulfillment today (cf. Luke 4:21); but at the same time he opens new perspectives by catapulting history forward, forward toward total reconciliation. The hidden sense is not the "spiritual" one, which devalues and even eliminates temporal and earthly realities as obstacles; rather it is the sense of a fullness which takes on and transforms historical reality. Moreover, it is only in the temporal, earthly, historical event that we can open up to the future of complete fulfillment.

It is not sufficient, therefore, to acknowledge that eschatology is valid in the future as well as in the present. Indeed, this can be asserted even on the level of "spiritual" realities, present and future. We can say that eschatology does not lessen the value of the present life and yet expresses this in words which might be misleading. If by "present life" one understands only "present *spiritual* life," one does not have an accurate understanding of eschatology. Its presence is an intrahistorical reality. The grace-sin conflict, the coming of the kingdom, and the expectation of the parousia are also necessarily and inevitably historical, temporal, earthly, social, and material realities.

The prophets announce a kingdom of peace. But peace presupposes the establishment of justice: "Righteousness shall yield peace and its fruit [shall] be quietness and confidence forever" (Isa. 32:17; cf. also Ps. 85). It presupposes the defense of the rights of the poor, punishment of the oppressors, a life free from the fear of being enslaved by others, the liberation of the oppressed. Peace, justice, love, and freedom are not private realities; they are not only internal attitudes. They are social realities, implying a historical liberation. A poorly understood spiritualization has often made us forget the human consequences of the eschatological promises and the power to transform unjust social structures which they imply. The elimination of misery and exploitation is a sign of the coming of the kingdom. It will become a reality, according to the Book of Isaiah, when there is happiness and rejoicing among the people because "they shall build houses and live to inhabit them, plant vineyards and eat their fruit; they shall not build for others to inhabit nor plant for others to eat. . . . My chosen shall enjoy the fruit of their labor" (65:21–22) because the fruit of their labor will not be taken from them. The struggle for a just world in which there is no oppression, servitude, or alienated work will signify the coming of the kingdom. The kingdom and social injustice are incompatible (cf. Isa. 29:18–19 and Matt. 11:5; Lev. 25:10ff. and Luke 4:16–21). "The struggle for justice," rightly asserts Dom Antonio Fragoso, "is also the struggle for the kingdom of God."

The eschatological promises are being fulfilled throughout history, but this does not mean that they can be identified clearly and completely with one or another social reality; their liberating effect goes far beyond the foreseeable and opens up new and unsuspected possibilities. The complete encounter with the Lord will mark an end to history, but it will take place in history. Thus we must acknowledge historical events in all their concreteness and significance, but we are also led to a permanent detachment. The encounter is present even now, dynamizing humanity's process of becoming and projecting it beyond its hopes (1 Cor. 2:6–9); it will not be planned or predesigned. This "ignorance" accounts for the active and committed hope for the gift: Christ is "the Yes pronounced upon God's promises, every one of them" (2 Cor. 1:20).

12. ENCOUNTERING GOD IN HISTORY

With most biblical scholars, contemporary theological opinion, and the Second Vatican Council itself, Gutiérrez asserts that "human history is the space of our encounter with God, in Christ" and that humanity is the "temple of God." In the first part of the following selection, Gutiérrez emphasizes the universality of God's presence—in the very heart of every human being—and then turns to a central ramification of that presence, namely, that "love for God is unavoidably expressed" through love of one's neighbor." In the following selection from A Theology of Liberation, *106–10, Gutiérrez laid the foundation for the principle of God's choice of the poor, which he would later develop in greater detail.*

The purpose of those who participate in the process of liberation is to "create a new humanity." We have attempted to answer our first question, namely, what is the meaning of this struggle, this creation, in the light of the Word accepted in faith? We can now ask ourselves what this option means for the *human being.*

In their political commitments, people today are particularly sensitive to the fact that the vast majority of humankind is not able to satisfy its most elementary needs; often they seek to make the service of those who suffer from oppression or injustice the guiding principle of their lives. Moreover, even Christians evaluate "religious" things in terms of their human meaning. This approach is not without ambiguities, but many prefer, in the words of José María González Ruiz, "to err on the side of the human."

We mentioned earlier that theology is tending more and more to reflect on the anthropological aspects of revelation. But the Word is not only a Word about God and *about* human nature: the Word is *made* human. If all that is human is illuminated by the Word, it is precisely because the Word reaches us through human history; Gerhard von Rad comments that "it is in history that God reveals the secret of his person." Human history, then, is the location of our encounter with God, in Christ. Recalling the evolution of the revelation regarding the presence of God in the midst of the people will aid us in clarifying the form this encounter in history takes. Both God's presence and our encounter with God lead humanity forward, but we celebrate them in the present in eschatological joy.

HUMANITY: TEMPLE OF GOD

The biblical God is a God who is near, a God of communion with and commitment to the human person. The active presence of God in the midst of his people is a part of the oldest and most enduring biblical promises. In connection with the first Covenant, God said: "I shall dwell in the midst of the Israelites, I shall become their God, and by my dwelling among them they will know that I am the Lord their God who brought them out of Egypt. I am the Lord their God" (Exod. 29:45–46; cf. 26:11–12). And in the proclamation of the new Covenant, God said: "They shall live under the shelter of my dwelling; I will become their God, and they shall become my people. The nations shall know that I the Lord am keeping Israel sacred to myself, because my sanctuary is in the midst of them forever" (Ezek. 37:27–28). This presence, often with the connotation of a dwelling, that is to say, a presence in a particular place (*shekinah*) characterizes the type of relationship established between God and human beings. Thus, Congar can write: "The story of God's relations with his creation and especially with man is none other than the story of his ever more generous, ever deeper Presence among his creatures."

The promise of that presence was fulfilled in different ways throughout history until it reached its fullness in a manner which surpassed all expectations: God became human. Henceforth God's presence became both more universal and more complete.

At the outset of the history of the chosen people, God's self-revelation took place especially on the *mountain*. Sinai was a privileged place for meeting God and for God's manifestations (Exod. 19). Yahweh ordered Moses, "Come up to me on the mountain" (Exod. 24:12; Deut. 10:1), because on the mountain rested the glory of the Lord (Exod. 24:16–17). The God of Israel was known for a long time as "a god of the hills and not a god of the valleys" (1 Kings 20:28). The presence of Yahweh came closer when it was linked to the *tent* which accompanied the Israelites in their pilgrimage through the desert. This was a place of encounter with Yahweh which Moses placed outside the camp and here spoke with Yahweh whenever Israel needed detailed instructions (Exod. 33:7–11; Num. 11:16, 24–26; Deut. 31:14). The same was true of the *Ark of the Covenant*, which also in a sense implied a dwelling place of Yahweh; in it Moses spoke with Yahweh (Num. 1:1). The idea of a dwelling was stressed to the point that there was even a curious identification between Yahweh and the Ark: "Whenever the Ark began to move, Moses said, 'Up, Lord, and may thy enemies be scattered and those that hate thee flee before thee.' When it halted, he said, 'Rest, Lord of the countless thousands of Israel'" (Num. 10:35–36; cf. also Josh. 4:5, 13; 1 Sam. 4:17).

The tent, the Ark (and even the mountain) underscore the mobility of the presence of the Lord, who shared the historical vicissitudes of the people (2 Sam. 7:6–7). In a certain way, they precluded any precise, physical location. The situation changed with the temple. The land of Canaan was initially designated as Yahweh's dwelling place. It was the land promised by Yahweh, who was not to be found outside it. David feared exile because he did not wish to be far from Yahweh (1 Sam. 26:19–20). After the prophet Elisha cured his leprosy, Naaman took a handful of the soil of Canaan to be able to offer sacrifices beyond its borders (2 Kings 5:15–19).

Certain places in the land of Canaan were privileged: these were the sanctuaries, generally located in high places. But very soon, especially after the Deuteronomic reform, there was but one official sanctuary in Jerusalem: Solomon's temple. The different traditions converged there: the obscurity of the Holy of Holies recalled the darkness through which Moses climbed Mt. Sinai; the Ark was placed in the temple; the temple is the heart of Jerusalem, and Jerusalem is the center of the land of Canaan—hence the importance of the temple in the life of the Israelites. The connotation of house, dwelling, was greater than in the previous cases (2 Sam. 7:5; 1 Kings 3:1–3; Amos 1:2; and Isa. 2:2, 37:14; Ps. 27:4).

But at the same time—and to keep the balance—it was proclaimed that no temple could contain Yahweh. This idea was expressed forcefully in the famous prophecy of Nathan, motivated by David's desire to erect a temple for Yahweh (2 Sam. 7). Moreover, at the very moment that the temple was consecrated, Solomon admitted that heaven is Yahweh's dwelling place: "Hear the supplication of thy servant and of thy people Israel when they pray toward this place. Hear thou in heaven thy dwelling and, when thou hearest, forgive" (1 Kings 8:30). The theme of the dwelling place of God in the heavens was old (cf. Gen. 11:5; 18:21; 28:12; Exod. 19:11; Deut. 4:36; Ps. 2:4), but it emerged clearly—and with the full strength of its transcendence and universality— at the very moment when the Israelites erected a dwelling, a fixed place, for the privileged encounter with Yahweh. The idea of a heavenly abode gathered strength gradually, especially after the exile. In the temple itself, the Holy of Holies was an empty space: God dwells everywhere.

While these notions of transcendence and universality were taking shape and becoming established, the prophets were harsh in their criticism of purely external worship. Their censure extended to places of worship; God's presence is not bound to a material structure, to a building of stone and gold. "Men shall speak no more of the Ark of the Covenant of the Lord," writes Jeremiah. "They shall not think of it nor remember it nor resort to it; it will be needed no more" (Jer. 3:16). And regarding the temple: "These are the words of the Lord: heaven is my throne and earth my footstool. Where will you build a house for me, where shall my resting place be? All these are of my own making and these are mine. . . . The one I will look to is downtrodden and humble and distressed, one who reveres my words" (Isa. 66:1–2). The last phrase indicates the essence of the criticism:

Yahweh's preference is for a profound, interior attitude. To this effect, in proclaiming the new Covenant, Yahweh says: "I will take the heart of stone from your body and give you a heart of flesh. I will put my spirit into you and make you conform to my statutes, keep my laws and live by them" (Ezek. 36:26–27; cf. Jer. 31:33). God will be present in the very heart of every human being.

This proclamation was completely fulfilled with the *incarnation* of the Son of God: "So the Word became flesh; he came to dwell [pitch his tent] among us" (John 1: 14). Nathan's prophecy was accomplished in a most unexpected way. Christ not only announces a prayer "in spirit and in truth" which will have no need for a material temple (John 4:21–23), but he presents himself as the temple of God: "Destroy this temple . . . and in three days I will raise it again." And John specifies: "The temple he was speaking of was his body" (2:19, 20). And Paul tells us: "It is in Christ that the complete being of the Godhead dwells embodied" (Col. 2:9; cf. Eph. 2:20–22; 1 Pet. 2:4–8). God is manifested visibly in the humanity of Christ, the God-Man, irreversibly committed to human history.

Christ is the temple of God. This explains Paul's insistence that the Christian community is a temple of living stones, and that each Christian, a member of this community, is a *temple of the Holy Spirit:* "Surely you know that you are God's temple, where the Spirit of God dwells. Anyone who destroys God's temple will himself be destroyed by God, because the temple of God is holy; and that temple you are" (1 Cor. 3:16–17). "Do you not know that your body is a shrine of the indwelling Holy Spirit, and the Spirit is God's gift to you?" (1 Cor. 6:19). The Spirit sent by the Father and the Son to carry the work of salvation to its fulfillment dwells in every human being—in persons who form part of a very specific fabric of human relationships, in men and women who find themselves in particular historical situations.

Furthermore, not only is the Christian a temple of God; every human being is. The episode with Cornelius shows that the Jews "were astonished that the gift of the Holy Spirit should have been poured out even on Gentiles." Peter draws the conclusion. "Is anyone prepared to withhold the water for baptism from these persons, who have received the Holy Spirit just as we did ourselves?" (Acts 10:45, 47; cf. 11:16–18 and 15:8). For this reason the words of Christ apply to everyone: "Anyone who loves me will heed what I say; then my Father will love him, and we will come to him and make our dwelling with him" (John 14:23). "Many constitute the temple, but invisibly," says Congar referring to the well-known expression of Augustine of Hippo: "Many seem to be within who are in reality without and others seem to be without who are in reality within." In the last instance, only the Lord "knows his own" (2 Tim. 2:19).

What we have here, therefore, is a twofold process. On the one hand, there is a universalization of the presence of God: from being localized and linked to a particular people, it gradually extends to all the peoples of the earth (Amos 9:7; Isa. 41:1–7; 45:20–25; 51:4; and the entire Book of Jonah). On the other hand, there is an internalization, or rather, an integration of this presence: from dwelling in places of worship, this presence is transferred to the heart of human history; it is a presence which embraces the whole person. Christ is the point of convergence of both processes. In him, in his personal uniqueness, the particular is transcended and the universal becomes concrete. In him, in his Incarnation, what is personal and internal becomes visible. Henceforth, this will be true, in one way or another, of every human being.

Finally, let us emphasize that here there is no "spiritualization" involved. The God made flesh, the God present in each and every person, is no more "spiritual" than the God present on the mountain and in the temple. God is even more material. God is no less involved in human history. On the contrary, God has a greater commitment to the implementation of peace and justice among humankind. God is not more "spiritual," but is closer and, at the same time, more universal; God is more visible and, simultaneously, more internal.

Since the Incarnation, humanity, every human being, history, is the living temple of God. The "pro-fane," that which is located outside the temple, no longer exists.

13. THE HISTORICAL POWER OF THE POOR

*The following passages are taken from the article "La fuerza histórica de los pobres,"
which served as the introduction to the 1978 collection of Latin American church documents,* Signos de lucha y esperanza: Testimonios de la Iglesia en América Latina. *Here Gutiérrez draws up a balance sheet of the "struggles and hopes" in the life of
the Latin American church during the ten years since Medellín. Seeking to overcome
"historical amnesia" and the oppression it abets, he takes as the framework of his evaluation the nearly five centuries of oppression, rebellion, and Christian faith in Latin
America and highlights acts of resistance and liberation that reveal "a people's will to
self-affirmation." Though the fight has been long, and is still far from over, he is convinced that the power of the poor to change the course of history will prove invincible.
This claim, of course, rests in the first instance not on the poor but on faith in the God
whose promise to establish a reign of justice takes flesh in a special love for the poor. In
an observation adopted by the bishops at Puebla (cf. no. 1142), Gutiérrez points out
that "God loves the poor just because they are poor, and not necessarily, or even primarily, because they are better believers . . . or morally firmer than others." When the
mission of the church is considered in relation to the newly won self-affirmation of the
poor and their renewed Christian faith, the convergence (not identity) of conscientization, or political consciousness-raising, and evangelization comes into view. While
the latter addresses the relationship between the human person and God and the former the relationship between the person and the world, both aim at liberating human
consciousness—that is, persons' views of themselves and their purpose in the world.
Though distinct, evangelization and conscientization can thus be mutually reinforc-
ing. The following passages are taken from* The Power of the Poor in History,
77–83, 87–88, 89–90, 94–99.

Bartolomé de Las Casas and a number of other remarkable figures of the sixteenth century in Latin America constitute an exception to the bloody beginnings of the path of murder and death that is the saga of colonial domination in Latin America. Their descriptions of the encounter of the poor person, the Amerindian, with the dominator, the conquistador, are anything but a portrait of the idyllic embrace that we are often pressured to accept today. Those noble persons were of the culture, nationality, and ethnic makeup of the oppressors; but their faith experience was different. Prophetically they denounced the brutal exploitation of the hapless Indian masses and their "death before their time."

From the very beginning, then, this "premature death" which cut short the right to life, was present as an essential component of the social order then being established. Even today it has not ceased to assault what Pedro de Cordoba, another witness of those times, called "the life and temporal increase" of the poor. Yet at the same time, through a nearly incredible and difficult conversion to Christ present in the Indians, there were also those who from the very beginning cried "no" to the murder of the poor and affirmed their elemental right to life. This oppression is ancient but wears new guises today and persecutes those who rise up against it.

AVOIDING HISTORICAL AMNESIA

This story of captivity and deliverance—which must be retold, now, from the viewpoint of the oppressed—is the constant undercurrent of our contemporary praxis in Latin America. These years have given us many occasions to speak of the rise of a new political consciousness among Latin American peoples. But this new awareness is nothing other than our new perception of the concrete situation in which we live—the world of death created by the conquistadors. Of course, we gained our perception all the more rapidly as the prevailing system became the more oppressive and repressive—until this new popular awareness could burst forth as a social force in the popular liberation struggles of the 1960s. Latin American social situations differ from land to land, however, and the people's struggle reflects their variety. The dominant sectors take the occasion of this variety to allege that liberation struggles are the work of minority factions—little groups of radicals, students, and a few priests out of touch with the people—thus altogether ignoring the historical significance of these struggles. They are abetted in certain ecclesiastical circles by individuals and groups who repeat the rightist "party line."

But reality is complex. This simplification is either contrived or extremely naïve. The dominators are clearly seeking to invalidate what has happened in these years or perhaps to protect what is left of their charge that efforts at change were the work of radicals. But what is certain is that the distortion of the facts blinds them to what is occurring in the deep undercurrents of history's flowing waters. They are thus unable to identify the precise points of breach and continuity that shape that history. And the upshot is that they fail to grasp what is really at stake here today after all the failures and false hopes but also the advances and a realism which disturbs the privileged of the present social order.

Another expression of our Latin American people's new political awareness is their better grasp of the socioeconomic realities of the continent. What is called the "theory of dependency"—to the degree that it was able to place relationships of domination within a context of confrontation between social classes—contributed fruitfully to this knowledge of reality. Despite all its limitations, this attempt to rethink our distinctive historical process in categories peculiar to that process was stimulated by the liberation movements of the 1960s and contributed to the strength of those movements. It helped the popular class to reject the politics of compromise and conformism during that decade. However, the present situation of the popular movement and the level attained by the internationalization of capital are creating new practices and new theoretical requirements. . . .

The birth of a popular movement with greater backbone and organization, with new instruments of analysis, and with an anticapitalist project which is clear in some cases or searching for a more precise shape in others, was savagely repressed in both its radical and moderate expressions alike. This is what happened in Brazil, Guatemala, Colombia, Peru, Bolivia, and, at the beginning of the 1970s with unheard-of refinement and violence, in Chile (where a socialist program was being implemented), Uruguay, and Argentina.

With the armed forces, all political resources, and the public media firmly in their grasp, dominators have sought to dismantle all organized protest against the economic exploitation that lies at the base of the system from which they reap their profit of lordship. They have tried to "take the wind out of the sails" of any and all movements daring to represent the interests of the oppressed. And they have tried to isolate these efforts, together with the groups of persons engaged in them, from contact with the masses of the poor, among whom these movements had been begun with such enormous difficulty. But they had been begun, and the masses were awakening to a new political awareness. As far as the dominant groups were concerned, this development had to be crushed, nipped in the bud. Of course at the same time they were very much concerned to demonstrate that "nothing had happened" in Latin America; that these occurrences were the deed of some lunatic fringe, unaccountably at odds with "our Western Christian civilization."

Those who today uncritically accept and repeat on cue—particularly in ecclesiastical circles—the interpretation given out by the dominant classes might do well simply to ask themselves whether the huge military, political, and ideological apparatus mounted in those years to eliminate what they considered "tiny groups" was not after all somewhat out of proportion to the alleged threat. Why so many bounces if the playing field was level?

Of course, there was nothing level about the playing field at all. We had begun to perceive the "social disparity" (would the experts allow us to speak of "disparity of life"?), and never again would the poor hesitate to defend their rights. Nor would blows and repression any longer deter them from their quest for a socialist way and a genuine democracy.

All these experiences in the life of the popular masses, in the 1960s as today, have been the hotbed of intense life, in Christian communities of a popular makeup and involvement. The attempt to reflect on these experiences in the light of faith is what we call the theology of liberation. For it is life experience that both affords this theology its strength and assigns it its limits. The theology of liberation is rooted in this historical, popular process. It has its roots in the faith as lived in this social experience—the experience of following Jesus in the defense of the rights of the poor, in the proclamation of the gospel in the midst of the struggle for liberation. This is this theology's turf and terrain, and so of course it will attend much more to what is transpiring on this terrain than to the analyses and critiques of the world of academic theology, however worthy these analyses and critiques may be in themselves.

The adversaries of a theology that so doggedly stresses the outlook of the poor, and the liberation of the poor, will naturally be most concerned to draw attention away from that which nurtures the substratum that gives life to this theology. Its adversaries, falsifying reality, say that its seedbed is a desert. They deny that it draws its sustenance from the radicalism of a faith lived deep in the effort of the masses to extricate themselves from the throes of a system that so marginalizes and despoils them. Our adversaries think that by thus ignoring the spring and source of this theology in a living faith—a faith rooted in popular experience—they can disqualify it as theology. They cannot admit that what the poor of Latin America have begun to do can be theology. Then too, of course, the dominant ideology feels less threatened by theological alternatives that do *not* have their roots sunk in the challenges of social conflict.

The defenders of the existing social system seek to disqualify our effort of reflection by claiming that its protagonists are not a people awakening to a new awareness, but a little group of partisans isolated from that people. This is what they are saying, really, when they attempt to deny a connection between the struggles of today and yesterday—when they try to cut off a people's memories, as they have succeeded in doing in some countries, and so keep them from perceiving what the battles they are waging owe to the battles of a few years back.

Defenders of the present social order are even enjoying a certain success in some Christian circles—circles that for one reason or another have not kept terribly close to the popular struggles of more than a decade now, and who only today are rediscovering the role of the poor and lowly of Latin America in their self-liberation. Surely this rediscovery is under way, and it is daring and creative. But it runs the risk of falling into the trap of the dominator and contributing in some way to the "historical amnesia" with which the latter seeks to infest the people. For this memory of past battles is not a matter of reassuring nostalgia and pleasant reveries. It is a subversive memory, and it lends force and sustenance to our positions, refuses to compromise or equivocate, learns from failures, and knows (by experience) that it has the capability of overcoming every obstacle, even repression itself.

THE OPTIMISM OF ACTION

The myth of a euphoria that is supposed to have held sway in Latin America in the years around 1968 is but another facet of this same effort to disqualify everything new that came to light at that time. It is normal for hopes, and even illusions, to rise when something new happens. And the new breadth, and radical depth, of the popular struggles of the late 1960s were certainly a new happening. But to assert that anyone entertained the illusion that revolution and the new society were just around the corner is to make a travesty of historical reality.

What was happening during those years—in Brazil, Bolivia, Peru, Argentina, Mexico, and even Chile, along with the continuing tragedy of Paraguay, Nicaragua, and many other countries—did not permit any light-minded illusions, but a fertile and disturbing hope, yes. It is not difficult to see why certain political events of the early 1970s, and of course, the direction undertaken by the Latin American bishops themselves at Medellín, provoked a certain optimism in Latin America; this was legitimate. But I want to make it clear that this attitude was not present before. Let us be clear: what conservative elements are attempting to do here, by insisting that euphoria existed in 1968, is to pull the rug out from under what was born then. They are trying to undermine the significance of the involvement of Christians in the liberation process which, at the level of thought, sought verbalization in the theology of liberation, and was later expressed with the power and prophetic tone of Medellín which we remember and long for.

Some, today, owing to a faulty grasp of what was at stake in those years, or understandably shaken by the new, refined forms of repression with which we live in Latin America today, uncritically repeat, and without wanting to, lend legitimacy to what certain groups say, groups intent on falsifying a reality which disturbs them.

Romantic illusions? No, rather a clear awareness that something new was afoot, something no repression could ever again crush: a people's will to self-affirmation and to life. José Carlos Mariátegui, assailing the "idealistic optimism" of José Vasconcelos, said: "Pessimism comes from reality, optimism from action." For indeed what is so sorely needed here is not a condemnation of reality, but a conviction that that reality can and must be transformed by the action of the popular classes. This is the affirmation of a utopia on the way to becoming a historical reality—through difficulties and hard struggles, to be sure, and with an open-eyed awareness of the present situation. Only with a determination to transform the present situation shall we ever be able to acquire an authentically realistic view of that situation. This is a "utopianism" opposed to the "realism" of the capitalist oppressor who is incapable of appreciating the rationality that springs from the power of the poor. In the final analysis, there is nothing more revolutionary, nothing more pregnant with liberative utopia, than the ancient and profound oppression of the poor of Latin America.

Curiously—or perhaps significantly—the same persons who characterized the mood of ten years ago as illusion-filled and euphoric are the ones giving us a pessimistic and whining description of the Latin American situation today. According to them, repression, national security, and fascism, have battered the popular movement and taken the whole continent captive. We are told that we are faced with an entirely and radically new situation. But our interlocutors and their "realism" are doubly in error. Actually, there was neither such optimism before, nor are things now so bad as they think. And both views converge in a single result: to create confusion and impede the development of revolutionary energy among the popular classes and liberating faith in the popular Christian communities. It is for this reason—because such development matters to us and not out of a detached interest in historical accuracy—that it is incumbent upon us to expose what stands behind these pseudo-realistic interpretations.

Contrary to what one so often hears, especially outside Latin America, the popular movement is currently enjoying a period of strength, not of weakness. Silent strength, if you will. But real strength. Yes, this is a moment of great difficulty and hardship. But it is a moment of unprecedented vitality and vigor, as well; a period of repression, but also of creativity, for the masses; a period of self-criticism regarding indiscretions committed but above all, a moment of unreserved criticism of the system that exploits, marginalizes, and assassinates the poor.

The masses of the people have suffered cruel blows, but they have also learned important lessons. The popular movement is aware of its steps backward, of the ambiguity of some of the paths it has taken, and of the vagueness of some of its social proposals. This is proper to every historical process. But the popular movement also knows about determination, hope, when to be silent, and political realism. The exploited masses have demonstrated their capacity for resistance, and that capacity is most disconcerting to dominators. It even surprises revolutionary groups, which until recently were carrying forward certain liberation projects and today are undergoing such brutal repression.

Recent social and political events (doubtless still ambivalent) in countries with Indian and *mestizo* majorities who live in dire poverty and age-old captivity, and where no facile illusions are possible, have demonstrated that, beneath a surface of repression and ambiguity, the popular movement has continued to press forward. Nicaragua, Peru, Bolivia, and Ecuador are the most obvious examples.

Those who had begun to convince themselves that popular protest against age-old repression had been extinguished are beginning to grow uneasy. This will be just one episode in a long struggle. There will be other setbacks, but there will also be new, more decisive advances in a process which is, at bottom, irreversible. As Antonio Gramsci insisted, historical processes can be analyzed calmly and with realism only if we study sufficiently long segments of time. Otherwise, we overestimate the importance of passing phenomena and we lose sight of the deeper movement. No, it's clear that the die has not yet been cast, but in history's shakers the dice can already be heard.

It is in this complex but stimulating setting that grassroots Christian communities are born and live. Here the Word of the Lord becomes rich, concrete, and creative, for here that word becomes history. And by this very fact, the word challenges every reality of the present, prevents it from becoming established, and fills it with the future—a future of the fullness of love expressed today in our love for our sister and brother in circumstances that are difficult and often ambiguous. In these circumstances it is not easy to make decisions and then move ahead with the choices we have made. But something deeply evangelical is in the making, something new, as the love of Christ is always new. . . .

THE RIGHTS OF THE POOR

All this makes for a complicated and explosive setting for the presence and voice of the church in Latin America. The coming of age of the popular masses' political awareness over the last decade, the growing involvement of Christian groups in the liberation process, and the fact that repression has begun to strike the official church to a degree hitherto unknown, coupled with the brutality shown by repressive regimes during these same years, have moved bishops' conferences and other church groups to undertake a vigorous defense of human rights. At times, the church's voice was the only one to be heard in the face of human rights abuses and helped to make them known to the world, and in this way the church helped to limit the scope of such abuses.

At the same time, a structural analysis better suited to Latin American reality has led certain Christians to speak of the "rights of the poor" and to interpret the defense of human rights within this framework. It is not just a matter of words. This alternative language represents a critique of the liberal approach which presupposes an equality in our society that in fact does not exist. It tries not to forget what really hangs in the balance here, namely, the misery and spoliation of the poorest of the poor, the conflictive character of Latin American life and society, and the biblical roots of the defense of the poor.

One of the traps that may yet ensnare the church in Latin America will be a facile, naïve acceptance of so-called "restricted democracy" which allows certain liberties and individual rights to be formally restored but which leaves intact profound social and economic inequality. The condemnation of violations of human rights by an important and progressive part of the church would have little effect if we were to accept an opening of society to democracy for the middle class which would only enhance the flexibility with which the prevailing system exercises its domination over the popular masses.

Only from within the world of the poor of Latin American society (and whoever uses the term "poor" has taken a collective point of view and pointed out the conflictive nature of society) is it possible to grasp the true meaning of, and the biblical demand for, the defense of human rights. Only thus will it be clear that, for the church, this task is an expression of the proclamation of the gospel in Latin America today. The church may not, then, content itself with alleviating the most blatant forms of repression while the causes of what Medellín called "institutionalized violence" remain in place. In this way the church will also avoid a subtle form of asserting its own power even as it defends the poor or of presenting itself as a political alternative in Latin America.

PERSECUTED IN THE CAUSE OF JUSTICE

The hand of the dominator does not beat around the bush in punishing any protest on the part of the oppressed, any attempt at altering a social order that manufactures poor people. One of the significant facts of Latin American life in recent years is that repression has reached Christian circles with openness and brutality. I am referring to persons and groups explicitly calling themselves Christian, including many who exercise official responsibilities in the institutional church.

These realities, already in the making ten years ago, today are commonplace. They are a painful but unmistakable sign, full of consequences, that our Christian community is moving ever closer to the poor of Latin America, that we have actually begun to experience the lot of the poor. These Christians—farmhands, laborers, priests, bishops, university students, nuns—are not jailed, tortured, and murdered for their "religious ideas" but for their social and evangelizing practice. They are persecuted because, believing as they do in a God of liberation, they condemn the injustices done to the poor and commit themselves to the poor, to their lives and struggle, because they try to rethink their faith from the standpoint of solidarity with the liberation of the oppressed. Frequently they are persecuted by governments themselves claiming to be Christian and which, in defense of "Western Christian civilization," see themselves as champions of the faith and protectors (!) of the church. This monstrous lie has been condemned by many, but scandalously accepted by some, and even supported and justified by what has been called a "theology of massacre." Still others prefer to keep silent in the face of this taking of the name of the Lord in vain, be it out of cowardice, or out of a secret, unconfessed complicity.

I cite the persecution of Christian groups. But I am by no means suggesting that Christians constitute the most persecuted sector of the Latin American population. I only wish to underscore the fact that being a Christian, or even a priest or bishop, no longer (thank God!) automatically confers immunity from the assaults of the oppressor's might. On the contrary, being Christian has become subversive in the eyes of the powerful and dangerous for those who have committed their lives to the poor. The entire phenomenon also sets in relief the degree to which the dominant classes have become exasperated in defense of their interests. . . .

Its lists of martyrs is one of the great riches of the Latin American church today—and for a poor, exploited, and believing people. The dominators view it with no little surprise when someone actually lays down their life for a faith that, to them, means no more than serenity and religious justification for age-old social injustice. Hence their attempt to explain these deaths with reasons that have nothing to do with faith or hope in Christ the liberator which seem so foreign to their experience. They look on with surprise, as I said, but even more with alarm, for these martyrs are testifying that there are poor people in Latin America and that the poor are calling the status quo into question. This is a reality that the dominators would prefer to forget or to attribute to nonstructural causes—or, even worse, they seek to spiritualize the poor so that, instead of raising challenges with their disturbing material poverty, the poor offer us solutions through an inoffensive, badly misinterpreted (and hence unbiblical) "spiritual poverty." The martyrs of Latin America attest to the fact that the poor "die before their time," from hunger or the bullet. As someone said in a Christian commentary, their very corpses are subversive, and this is why the powerful refuse to surrender them, *or* to release data that would make public the true cause of death, as happened in the case of Bishop Enrique Angelelli, in Argentina, for example. The dominator fails to appreciate that passing through the experience and crisis of the empty tomb was for the friends of Jesus, and is for his followers today, what allows them to grasp the fullness of the life of the risen Christ who conquers all death.

The names of the bishops and priests, and perhaps the nuns and some of the lay persons, who have been kidnapped, imprisoned, tortured, or murdered, are fairly well known. Their number and positions in the church are proof of the polarization underway in Latin America. Less well known of course, but by no means less important, are the numerous campesinos, laborers, and students who have suffered the same fate. These are the anonymous ones of this history of repression and of hope, just as the poor from whom they spring and for whom they die are anonymous. The blood of those persecuted in the cause of justice quickly grants to those whom the Bible calls the "poor of the land" new rights to the land they claim in order to be able to work it and live as human beings. Their blood revives faith in the power of God the liberator who conquers fear and death.

Rarely have so many deaths given so much life to a people and a church. For truly, as the prophet Ezekiel reminded us, there are no dry bones or death except when there is no hope. But the living God is with his people. His Spirit is present in these dead, fills them with life, and raises up a whole people, "a great, an immense army" (Ezek. 37:10). Yahweh makes his people a promise: "I shall put my spirit in you, and you will live, and I shall resettle you on your own soil; and you will know that I, Yahweh, have said and done this—it is the Lord Yahweh who speaks."[Ezek. 37:14]. . . .

TAKING THE ROAD OF THE POOR

The interpretation of the faith which comes from the poor marks a break with
the dominant theology but stands in continuity with a history we do not know
well but which looks richer and more promising all the time. It is a true theology, an oppressed theology, one frequently rejected by political forces with the
complicity of important ecclesiastical elements.Our record of this interpretation
of the faith is generally fragmentary and oral, as manifested in customs, rites,
and the like. Only rarely in the past has it been possible to express it openly. An
example would be Bartolomé de Las Casas, or, in more fragmentary fashion,
certain other missioners of the same era, who genuinely took sides with the Indians. The poor themselves have had to follow an even more difficult road in order
to make themselves heard. And yet the memory of history, the memory of faith,
is there, awaiting reconstruction. The task will be complex, and it is urgent. The
memory of the poor is always subversive of a social order that robs and marginalizes them.

Subterranean Currents. This suppressed theology sprang forth from the life and
struggles of the poor who believed in the living God. Consequently it suffered
the same fate as those who tried to make themselves heard by means of this theology: destruction and oblivion. To follow the road of the poor through history
will be rather fruitful for the theology of liberation, for here that theology must
grapple with the crucial question of its own historical continuity.

The reflections of the poor upon their faith are not found in the histories of
theology which are limited to the academic version theology. But the perspective of the poor is not entirely absent from academic theology; certain "oases" in
the desert are sporadically watered by underground springs which manage to
break to the surface here and there. But the perspective of the poor never constitutes the central element of academic expressions of theology.

We usually find the theology of the poor emanating from spiritual movements of the poor, which are frequently social movements as well. Certain
streams of medieval piety would be a good example of this tendency. This is significant, for the life and reflection of the poor always have a contemplative and
mystical dimension—and at the same time a dimension of protest and social
transformation.

Perhaps the reason for all this will become clearer if we refer to the biblical
sources of the privileged position of the poor in the gospel message. Jesus called
the poor "fortunate." In spite of stubborn resistance recently, spiritualistic interpretations of this basic starting point for understanding the meaning of the
kingdom of God have been losing ground. The faith experience of the poor
themselves as well as serious exegetical studies, such as Jacques Dupont's work
on the Beatitudes, make the point clearly: the gospel of Jesus proclaims to us the
love of God for the poor for being just that—poor—and not necessarily, or even

primarily, for being more believing, kinder, or better, morally speaking, than others. God loves them simply because they are poor, because they are hungry, because they are persecuted. Only on this basis is it possible to appreciate subsequent efforts to enrich or define precisely the evangelical meaning of the poor person.

This may sound harsh to some. For example, it may seem to them that this view shows little interest in persons' spiritual attitudes. It might even seem to express something like an indifferent disdain toward the personal qualities of the poor. But this would be to get ahead of ourselves, to lose sight of what comes first, and thereby to create an interminable labyrinth of distinctions and apparent contradictions that in the end only yield ideas devoid of interest or historical impact. And this is to say nothing of being unfaithful to the gospel. The Beatitudes are in fact more a revelation about God than about the poor. They tell us who God is and which kingdom is God's. They speak to us of God as the defender of the poor, as their protector, their liberator. Only in this way is it possible to grasp the privileged role of the poor—concrete poor people, the dispossessed, and the oppressed—in God's kingdom.

And here we are confronted with a paradox. If we "spiritualize" this gospel message about the poor too soon, as it were, and maintain that the gospel refers first and primarily to the "spiritually" poor rather than to the "materially" poor, then we "humanize" God. We make God more accessible to human understanding. God would then love, by preference, those who are good because they deserve it—just as we do ourselves. But if, instead, we hold to the first and more direct meaning of God's love for the poor—precisely as poor people (materially speaking, if you want to use that language)—we then stand before the mystery of God's revelation and the gift of his kingdom of love and justice. We stand before something which challenges our categories, the mystery of a God who will not be reduced to our mode of thinking, and who judges us on the basis of our concrete, historical actions toward the poor (Matt. 25). Now we face a God who blocks the path of a false love which forgets sisters and brothers while claiming to direct itself spiritually toward God, more to domesticate God than to feel itself questioned by God's word (see 1 John 4:20). Thus, in order to know and to love God, one must know the concrete life situation of the poor today, and radically transform a society that produces them.

This is the meaning of the kingdom of God revealed to us in Jesus' practice— a messianic practice which inverts not only values, but historical realities and social roles as well (see 1 Sam. 2:4–8; Luke 1:51–53). Jesus' actions are directed toward testifying to the love of God for every human being through the historical, conflictive, and preferential love for the poor (Luke 4:16–20). This practice led him to a violent death, an expression of solidarity with the death which the oppressed of this world undergo. But we cannot say of Jesus what someone has written about another person in history (was it written with irony or ingenuously?), namely, that "at the end of his days, he died." The resurrection of Jesus marks the affirmation of life not in the face of a death "at the end of his days" but rather a death "ahead of time," an execution. The resurrection confirms Jesus as the Christ, the Messiah, and makes his message of justice and life definitive, a message which challenges a homicidal society.

To be a disciple of Jesus is to make our own his messianic practice, his message of life, his love for the poor, his condemnation of injustice, his sharing of bread, his hope in the resurrection. The Christian community, the *ecclesia*, is made up of those who take up that messianic practice of Jesus and use it to create fraternal social relationships—and thereby accept the gift of being children of the Father. Messianic practice is the proclamation of the kingdom of God in the transformation of the historical conditions of the poor. It is the word of life, backed up by the liberating deed.

An Exploited and Believing People. The term "poor," as we have said above, always has a collective connotation and implies social conflict. In the Bible the "poor person" is part of a social group, a whole people, "the poor of the land." They are a people poor and humiliated, robbed of the fruits of their labor, suffering the oppressor's injustice. It is this complex and fertile sense of "poor" that I have in mind when I say that in Latin America the poor who are at the same time Christian constitute a concrete starting point full of consequences for theological reflection and the life of the church. This is precisely the situation of the poor of our continent: they are both poor and believing. In them we have two dimensions but also two potentialities, both residing in the same people.

Their situation of oppression and exploitation is well known, but we must examine it in its present forms. It is a concrete situation which requires concrete analysis. Nothing exempts us from seeking a serious, scientific knowledge of the nature of the exploitation that the popular classes are suffering. It is equally urgent that we be able to differentiate between various strata and groups within the popular masses—that we come to recognize which are more advanced and which are more backward, fundamentally through their relationship to the productive process but also through their potential and their experience of mobilization.

The exploitation which the popular classes suffer and the presence among them of the dominant ideology naturally cultivate fear, social climbing, and a search for individual, selfish solutions to problems. But these are simple rough spots in a road that leads in a more important and decisive direction and which arises from the very situation of exploitation: the desire for radical change, the revolutionary potential. It is not enough, then, to call attention to the spoliation and oppression in which the popular classes live. One must also see that these classes create the objective conditions in which they may begin the struggle for their rights and for power in a society that has refused to recognize them as human beings at all. In the struggle, the people gain greater and greater consciousness of being a social class, the active subject of the revolution and of the construction of a different society. Their revolutionary potential is something to be developed and organized, with a view to concrete efficaciousness in history.

A second vector, closely linked to the previous one, is the fact that the people believe in God. This is evident not only in their explicitly religious expressions, but in some sense in their life as a whole. This is what Mariátegui called the "religious factor" in the existence and history of the people of Peru. What is known as popular piety is one of its expressions, but it is not the only one. The "religious factor," unfortunately, has frequently been, and still is today, an obstacle to the people's progress in the perception of their situation of oppression. Much in popular religion is still a manifestation of the dominant ideology. This is why any form of "religious populism" that ignores what I just pointed out must be avoided. We are faced with a complex reality here, and our approach must take the complexity into account.

The believing dimension of the people also implies, as their practice demonstrates, the presence of an immense potentiality of liberating faith. This faith has come to expression in different forms throughout history, accompanying and inspiring dogged resistance to oppression, and even open rebellion against it. Those who have this faith—who believe in the God of the Bible—are oppressed. But in a certain way their faith is also oppressed and imprisoned at the heart of a capitalistic, dehumanizing society. The liberating potential of faith must also be developed. Otherwise, the complex and rich life of the Latin American people will be maimed, and we will be deprived of the message God wishes to reveal to us through the understanding the poor and simple have of him.

At the service of this development, and out of the very dynamism of this faith, the popular Christian communities arise, and a church is being born from this people, a popular church under the impulse of the Spirit of truth and freedom. This liberating faith disturbs dominators who prefer not to believe it exists, prefer not to believe in its capacity to reveal God in our concrete history. But in denying this faith, dominators reveal themselves for what they really are—the "fool" of the Bible, the atheist who refuses to believe in the liberating God. It is necessary to emphasize that we cannot separate these two situations and two possibilities. The potential of a liberating faith is linked to the capacity for revolution, and vice versa, in the concrete life of this poor and oppressed people. Hence it is impossible to try to develop one of these possibilities without taking the other into account. This is what makes the growth of the people's political consciousness and Christian consciousness disturbing. The work of many of Latin America's basic Christian communities has developed within a perspective of unity shaped by taking the exploited and Christian people as the starting point. From this real-life grounding, then, it is possible to overcome (while avoiding oversimplifications) the dichotomy certain theologies impose but which is foreign to the people's practice and which their reflection has critiqued for some time now. But the unity of these two aspects in the heart of the people is a process; inevitably the political dimension and the faith dimension develop at different rates. At times one element will grow faster than the other. The need for unity is serious and stems from the biblical message and from the very situation of the people. Nevertheless, this unity must be achieved through reflection, elaboration, and systematization. This complex reality conditions our work, but it also points to a task.

Let us be clear about what it means to take this as our starting point and to accept the consequences of such a point of departure: it means rejecting completely all attempts at "reductionism" in the task of evangelization, both the reductionism of a disincarnate spiritualism masquerading as "religion," and the reductionism of a political-action approach that idealistically ignores the reality of the people's faith. Both reductions are one-sided and unreal and thereby betray an ignorance of the situation and the potential of the popular classes. We know the pitfalls of this.

I continue to be convinced—and the practice of the poor confirms me in this conviction—that a fertile, imaginative challenge lies in "contemplation in action," in action which transforms history. I am referring to finding God in the poor, in our solidarity with the struggle of the oppressed, and in a faith full of hope and gladness lived out in the very heart of a liberation process whose agents are the popular classes themselves.

To reject for this reason what I called "political reductionism" in no way means ignoring the role of revolutionary political action or, even less, its character as sign within a unitary approach to the work of evangelization. This final unity is one which calls attention to the dialectical character of the relationship between act (sign) and word. Reductionisms show no awareness of this dialectic, nor do they perceive the relationship between the desire for social transformation and liberating faith in the concrete life of the people.

Reductionisms, then, mutilate a rich historical reality and idealistically remain ignorant of it. Going against what a growing practice tells us, reductionisms refuse to go to the very heart of the matter, where political radicalism and gospel radicalism meet and strengthen each other.

14. IN A FOREIGN LAND

On many occasions Gutiérrez has invited a non-poor audience into the alien world of the poor, "alien" even to the poor themselves because of the humiliating poverty and premature death to which they are condemned. As Gutiérrez demonstrates, a compassionate identification with those who suffer unjustly (and with those non-poor people who take their side) ought to lead to a commitment to alleviate their suffering. But it also makes possible a sharper perception of the situation. Indeed, indifference may cloud the mind more than passion. The following passage from We Drink from Our Own Wells, *9–13, illustrates in addition how nontheological sources—in this case ancient Amerindian wisdom and modern social science—can enhance a believer's grasp of Christian faith. At issue in this text is the biblical notion of judgment.*

The situation created by the process of liberation—a process that in its varied embodiments is attacking the age-old wretchedness and exploitation that have characterized Latin America—is raising serious questions about a certain approach to Christian life. It is causing persons to break with that approach and launching them on new quests. Familiar reference points are being obscured; confusion, frustration, and defensive withdrawal are experienced on a wide scale. But a process of reevaluation is also in evidence and new paths are being opened. All this is a judgment being passed by history: a history in this case that the poor and the dispossessed—those who are the privileged ones in God's kingdom—have begun to create. The judgment is thus also one being passed by God. Let me point out some of the more salient aspects of this *krisis* or judgment.

AN ALIEN WORLD

Latin American reality is characterized by a poverty that the Final Puebla Document (PD) describes as "inhuman" (no. 29) and "anti-evangelical " (no. 1159). Such poverty represents a situation of "institutionalized violence," to use the well-known phrase of Medellín ("Peace," no. 16).

The real issue in this situation is becoming increasingly clear to us today: poverty means death. It means death due to hunger and sickness, or to the repressive methods used by those who see their privileged position being endangered by any effort to liberate the oppressed. It means physical death to which is added cultural death, inasmuch as those in power seek to do away with everything that gives unity and strength to the dispossessed of this world. In this way those in power hope to make the dispossessed an easier prey for the machinery of oppression.

Perception of the reality of death penetrating a rural area that has become alien is well expressed in a heart-rending letter that came from Haiti, the poorest country in Latin America. Faced with the threat of the eviction of rural populations because of a government project, a group of Christians writes:

> These fields are our entire life, our entire support. They give us food. Thanks to them we can send our children to school. . . . Farmhands can no longer find work, even as day laborers. How are we to live? . . . Where can we go? If we move to Port-au-Prince our situation will only be worse, because there is such misery there. If we go to the mountains, what kind of land can we expect to till? Must we, then, leave Haiti—get on a boat in order to discover the misery in other places? We do not deserve this torture.

The conclusion bespeaks a bitter realism: "Wherever we look, we see death."

It is this that is really meant when we talk of poverty and of the destruction of individuals and peoples, cultures and traditions. In particular, it is what is meant when we speak of the poverty of those most dispossessed: Amerindians and Latin American blacks, and the women of these doubly marginalized and oppressed sectors of the population. Consequently, despite what is sometimes thought, we are not dealing here simply with a "social situation," as though it were a state of affairs unrelated to the fundamental demands of the gospel message. Rather we are confronted with a reality contrary to the reign of life that the Lord proclaims.

In the Bible the land is one object of the promise of life. The children of God are promised a land of their own in which they will live as the proper inhabitants and not as outsiders or strangers. A foreign land, on the contrary, is a place of injustice and death (for the Jewish people the prototypes of such a land were, first, Egypt and, later on, Babylon, as in Psalm 137 from which I have taken the title of the present chapter). A "foreign" land is one that is hostile and has therefore lost its meaning as a gift from God.

Age-old oppression, intensified by the repressive measures with which the powerful seek to hinder all social change, creates a situation in which the vast Latin American majorities are dispossessed and therefore compelled to live as strangers in their own land. For this reason, the breakthrough of the poor into Latin American history and the Latin American church is based on a new and profound grasp of this experience of estrangement. The exploited and marginalized are today becoming increasingly conscious of living in a foreign land that is hostile to them, a land of death, a land that has no concern for their most legitimate interests and serves only as a tool for their oppressors, a land that is alien to their hopes and is owned by those who seek to terrorize them.

This experience has historical roots in the vision of the sixteenth-century Amerindians of Peru: their land had become a foreign territory, a world turned inside out by the European conquerors. The situation therefore called for a radical change, a cosmic cataclysm (*pachacuti* is the Quechuan term), that would put the universe back on its feet by establishing a just order.

Exiled, therefore, by unjust social structures from a land that in the final analysis belongs to God alone—"all the earth is mine" (Exod. 19:5; cf. Deut. 10:14)—but aware now that they have been despoiled of it, the poor are actively entering into Latin American history and are taking part in an exodus that will restore to them what is rightfully their own. This struggle for their rights is located within a quest for the kingdom of God and its justice—in other words, the struggle is part of a journey to a meeting with the God of the kingdom. It is a collective undertaking of liberation in which the classic spiritual combat is making more searching demands because it has taken on social and historical dimensions.

The result is that those who involve themselves in this struggle likewise become "strangers" to Latin American society and even to some sectors of the church. They are in fact alienated from the status quo and its beneficiaries, who regard themselves as the owners of lands, goods, and persons. In these circumstances, efforts to change the situation can come only from "outside." For (according to the privileged) the Latin American poor are content with their lot;

they cherish only the hope of receiving something when they extend their hands and beg, and they thank their generous benefactors for such kindness. And, paradoxically, at bottom the powerful of Latin America are right: the tenacious determination that things must change comes in fact from a land that the powerful have turned into a foreign land for the poverty-stricken masses.

Given these circumstances, it is no surprise that Latin America is today living in an age of suspicion. To those in control every action aiming at liberation and the recovery for the people of what belongs to it, all talk that openly starts with the realization of alienation, is subversive and calls for punishment by the political, military, or ideological authority in the hands of the ruling class. The present situation—which the exploited have now begun to challenge—has been so completely accepted by some and so completely taken to be the proper order of things that every expression of disagreement becomes unnatural and is grounds for suspicion; this holds true even in certain sectors of the church.

At the present time, then, men and women who try to side with the dispossessed and bear witness to God in Latin America must accept the bitter fact that they will inevitably be suspect. They may even be regarded not as followers of Jesus Christ but as intruders: they come from outside, make their way in, and create problems, simply because they think—and, be it said, live—differently. It is hard for them to accept suspicion for something that is so deeply a part of them as their personal honesty and, above all, their faith in the Lord. Such suspicion is an attack on what the old morality used to call a person's "honor," which is a basic right of every person. But honor of this kind can bring persecution, imprisonment, or death. Archbishop Oscar Romero was an example of someone suspected of not being a good Christian. Some of those who entertain such suspicions are simply fearful of the future to which the Lord is calling us. Suspicion within the Christian community itself is nowadays a component of the cross of Christians who seek to bear witness to the God of the poor . By that very fact, it is also a factor that serves to purify their commitment.

15. THE EVANGELIZING POTENTIAL OF THE POOR

The first passage below is taken from a lengthy reflection written shortly after the Puebla conference ("Pobres y liberación en Puebla," April 1979). In this text Gutiérrez considers a singular insight rooted in the pastoral experience of the Latin American church, proclaimed at Puebla, and now shared with the universal church: the realization by non-poor persons that they have been evangelized by the poor. Here again Gutiérrez had led the way in an earlier article ("The Historical Power of the Poor," 1978) when he had spoken of "two-way evangelization." This selection is from Power of the Poor, *148–52.*

When Puebla was in preparation, there was a great deal of searching to identify the primary and most urgent challenge to the task of evangelization in the church. After all, this would be the theme of the conference itself. But when the conference convened, there was no hesitation. Puebla stated its position at the very beginning. Hence we too may enter at once upon the point that interests us here—the relationship between gospel and liberation, from the perspective of the poor:

> The situation of injustice described in the previous section forces us to reflect on the great challenge our pastoral work faces in trying to help human beings to move from less human to more human conditions. The deep-rooted social differences, the extreme poverty, and the violation of human rights found in many areas pose challenges to evangelization. Our mission to bring God to human beings, and human beings to God, also entails the task of fashioning a more fraternal society here [§90].

Bringing God to human beings implies the building of a society of brothers and sisters. A dominant theme in Puebla will be this relationship between the proclamation of the gospel and the struggle for justice—the relationship between salvation and that "justice for the poor" that is the teaching of the Magnificat (§1144).

Puebla takes up a position from one of the richest gospel perspectives when it recalls: "The poor are the first ones to whom Jesus' mission is directed (Luke 4:18–21), and . . . the evangelization of the poor is the supreme sign and proof of his mission (Luke 7:21–23)" [§1142].

But given the concrete situation of the poor in Latin America, this evangelization will take on a liberating perspective. This is why, after pointing out that service rendered to the poor is the "privileged gauge" of the following of Christ, Puebla asserts: "The best service to our fellows is evangelization, which disposes them to fulfill themselves as children of God, liberates them from injustices, and fosters their integral advancement" [§1145].

The passage is brief but precise. It explains the meaning of a liberating evangelization by placing it within the context of the three planes of integral liberation, which we saw above and which we saw to be inseparable. This is the context in which the preferential option for the poor is situated:

> The objective of our preferential option for the poor is to proclaim Christ the Savior. This will enlighten them about their dignity, help them in their efforts to liberate themselves from all their wants, and lead them to communion with the Father and their fellow human beings through a life lived in evangelical poverty [§1153].

The option is demanded by the "scandalous reality of . . . Latin America," as we saw (§1154). It "should lead us to establish a dignified, fraternal way of life together as human beings and to construct a just and free society" (§1154). The proclamation of the gospel is a contribution to liberation from whatever oppresses the poor in the here and now of the social injustice in which they live.

It summons them to live as children of God and to enter into communion with the Father. The prerequisite for this proclamation of the gospel is "the lived experience of evangelical poverty" (§1157)—which we now know to be solidarity with the poor and rejection of the situation of spoliation in which the vast majority in Latin America live.

But Puebla goes a step further along these lines, echoing the rich experience of the Latin American church in recent years. In the document "The People of God Are in the Service of Communion," the conference asserts that the post-conciliar years have been marked in Latin America "by a rising awareness of the masses of the common people" (§233). This and other considerations lead the Puebla bishops to demand in another document that the Latin American poor "be taken into account as responsible people and subjects of history, who can freely participate in political options, labor-union choices, and the election of rulers" (§135).

Accordingly, conscious of the fact that "the common people . . . construct the pluralistic society through their own organizations, "the church must contribute to the construction of "a new society *for* and *with* the common people" (§1220; emphasis added). These observations and demands, concerning the people as agent of its own history, are also expressed in a most meaningful way in a context of evangelization. Puebla's document "A Preferential Option for the Poor" says:

> Commitment to the poor and oppressed and the rise of grassroots communities have helped the church to discover the evangelizing potential of the poor. For the poor challenge the church constantly, summoning it to conversion; and many of the poor incarnate in their lives the evangelical values of solidarity, service, simplicity, and openness to accepting the gift of God [§1147].

This notion had been expressed with great lucidity in the contribution of the Peruvian episcopate to Puebla's preparatory phase, in a section devoted to "the poor in Latin America as addressees and agents of evangelization" (§§435–41). The bishops speak of discovering the "evangelizing charism of the poor" and go on to explain that

> The church's commitment to the poor and oppressed, and the growth of the basic church communities among the common people, from Medellín on, have led it to discover, and recognize the value of, the evangelizing charism of which the poor and oppressed are the bearers. For they constantly question the church and call it to conversion, and many of them live a life of evangelical values themselves—solidarity, service, simplicity, and openness to receive the gift of God.

The similarity of the two texts speaks for itself. The Peruvian statement helps us better understand what Puebla means. What is being reflected here is a deep and fertile experience of the Latin American church, proceeding, as the text says, from a practice that intimately intertwines two elements: a commitment to the poor and oppressed, and the growth of the grassroots church communities. It had been in this solidarity, and in the rise of active and responsible Christian communities in the popular sectors, that the church had had the experience of the poor actually evangelizing—proclaiming the gospel themselves. To them, and not to the learned and prudent, is the love of the Father revealed (cf. Matt. 2:25). It is the poor who receive it, understand it, and announce it, in their own distinctive, demanding way. This is what Puebla means when it says that the ones the Bible calls the poor are not only the privileged recipients of the gospel; they are also, by that very fact, its messengers.

Puebla's conviction is the fruit of praxis. Here we have an expression of the life of the Latin American church that bureaucracy and fear did not succeed in suffocating.

In this same connection, some observations on the basic Christian communities, the grassroots Christian communities, will not be out of place. This was a bone of contention in Puebla. Persons unfamiliar with concrete pastoral work, and perhaps influenced by connotations that certain terms have in other parts of the world, looked on this phenomenon—one of the most fertile in the life of the church in recent years—with a certain diffidence at first. But here again, life is not easily ignored.

There is nothing more solid or blunt than reality itself, and every effort to make it vanish or to falsify it is eventually shattered by reality. It was the Brazilian bishops—without a doubt one of the most outstanding delegations at Puebla—along with other bishops and nonbishops (members of the Latin American Conference of Religious [CLAR], for example) who made people understand the meaning of these Christian groups born in, and committed to, the world of the common people. By whatever name they are called, they express a lived experience of the gospel, in communion with the church, of great wealth and promise for the presence of the church of Jesus Christ in Latin America. Hence Puebla notes with approval: "The poor, who have also been inspired by the church, have begun to organize in order to live out their faith in an integral way, and hence to reclaim their rights" (§1137).

What we have here is a rich vein which in fact the Latin American people have not neglected. Rather they have found a way to carry forward their fight against social injustice, their liberation projects, and their experience of the gospel, all with a sense of realism, ability, and courage. In an important text full of consequences, the Puebla bishops declare their approval and support for the common people. The passage comes from the document "Evangelization and the People's Religiosity":

> The gap between rich and poor, the menacing situation faced by the weakest, the injustices, and the humiliating disregard and subjection endured by them radically contradict the values of personal dignity and solidary fellowship. These are values which the people of Latin America carry in their hearts as imperatives received from the gospel. That is why the religiosity of the Latin American people often becomes a cry for true liberation. It is a demand which

is still not satisfied. Motivated by their religiosity, however, the people create or utilize within themselves space for the practice of brotherhood in the more intimate areas of their lives together: e.g., the neighborhood, the village, their labor unions, and their recreational activities. Rather than giving way to despair, they confidently and shrewdly wait for the right opportunities to move forward toward the liberation they so ardently desire [§452].

From the perspective of the evangelizing potential of the poor, a position which constitutes a definite advance over that of Medellín because it seeks creative continuity with its predecessor, it is possible to comprehend better the meaning of the liberating evangelization on which both Medellín and Puebla and above all the practice of the Latin American church have so much insisted in recent years.

16. CONFLICT IN HISTORY

While the fact of social conflict in human history is indisputable, some in the church have preferred to ignore it or "wish it away," while others have not seen it as a specifically Christian concern. As Gutiérrez points out, social conflict arising from the oppression of groups of persons on the basis of race, class, sex, or any other characteristic, presents the church with an obvious and serious pastoral problem. Hostile divisions among people, Christian or not, challenge a church whose mission is to be the sacrament of God's love for the world. But social conflict also poses a theoretical difficulty: how can divine love—necessarily universal—be reconciled with God's solidarity with those who suffer oppression?

The reality of sociopolitical conflict led Gutiérrez to examine the relationship between theory and practice and the tension between love and preference in a section of Theology of Liberation *entitled "Christian Fellowship and Class Struggle." Because of misunderstandings, he rewrote this section for the second edition of his classic work in 1988, calling it "Faith and Social Conflict." It should be noted that his fundamental position remains unchanged. Indeed, references to recent documents of the church's magisterium lend it greater force. His most detailed treatment is found in his 1986 essay on "Theology and the Social Sciences," from which the following passages are taken (found in* The Truth Shall Make You Free, *67–70, 70–80).*

[The subject of conflict in history] is a sensitive area, one in which it is difficult at times to see our way clearly; it stirs strong feelings. At the same time, however, it is a subject that cannot be avoided.

THE PASTORAL PROBLEM

Some persons say they are shocked that this aspect of reality should even be considered. Let me begin by saying that to a great extent I understand their reaction. No one agrees with a situation in which human beings come into conflict. And in fact the situation is not "acceptable," either humanly or in a Christian perspective. Conflict is undoubtedly one of the most painful phenomena in human life. We should like things to be different, and we ought to look for ways of getting rid of these oppositions, but on the other hand—and this is the point I want to make—we cannot avoid facing up to the situation as it actually is, nor can we disregard the causes that produce it. Neither can we give up on something urgently necessary: to see the situation in the light of faith and of the demands of the kingdom.

In this area, the most important biblical—and traditional—theme is that of the relationship between peace and justice. Peace is a gift brought by God's reign, but authentic peace presupposes the establishment of justice. Therefore, drawing their inspiration from Paul VI, the bishops at Medellín could say in quite specific terms: "If 'development is the new name for peace' (Paul VI), Latin American underdevelopment, with its own characteristics in the different countries, is an unjust situation that promotes tensions that conspire against peace"(*Peace,* no. 1).

Christians may not give up on the promotion of peace, but the peace they are promoting must be built on authentic, permanent, and just foundations. "Peace is, above all, a work of justice" (Medellín, *Peace,* no. 14). It is not possible, of course, to conceal the fact that this places us at times in boundary situations, where theological reflection advances only by trial and error, and where the result is often inadequate. Despite this, it is impossible that we should give up on trying, within our limits, to bring a faith-illumined clarity to these extreme situations.

The history of theological reflection on war, that deadly scourge of humanity, is an example of what I mean. European theologians have long and direct experience in this area, which we in other parts of the world do not always understand in all its details. Even so, their theological thinking on the subject has never been entirely satisfactory, because of the sensitivity and slipperiness of the subject itself. Theological reflection on war is always tentative and in process. The divergent and in some ways opposed positions recently taken by the North American and European episcopates on nuclear weapons are examples of what I am saying.

Living in Latin America and trying to get close to the "inhuman wretchedness" (Medellín, *Poverty,* no. 1), the boundless and "antievangelical . . . poverty" (Puebla, no. 1159) of its people, means living in the midst of conflict that we do not want and in which as human beings we cannot possibly take pleasure. But neither can we deny it. To deny it would be to deny our own selves as human beings who are bound in solidarity to our fellows and as Christians who must live out both the universality of God's love and God's preference for the poor. For this reason, I wrote in *A Theology of Liberation:*

> To become aware of the conflictual nature of the political sphere should not mean to become complacent. On the contrary, it should mean struggling— with courage and clarity, deceiving neither oneself nor others—for the establishment of peace and justice among all people.

It is perhaps not easy for those who lack direct experience of these situations to understand all the demands they make. For myself, the question I have always asked and have repeated at every step has been this: How are we to meet all the requirements of love of God in a situation of conflict in which individuals end up opposed to one another? To put it more concretely: a situation in which persons and social groups or nations, with various forms of power at their disposal, confront other persons, groups, and countries that have no power and no historical importance. Once again, I see the question as urgent because of my pastoral experience. Many Christians who were committed to the liberation process, and were fully aware of the conflictual aspects of the situation, were having problems with regard to the meaning of Christian love in such a situation. I therefore thought it absolutely necessary to discuss the problem, and to do so in the language of the time.

One conviction presided over my thinking in this area: there are no situations, however difficult, that amount to an exception or a parenthesis in the universal demands of Christian love. It is not enough, however, simply to assert this conviction; it is also necessary to apply it to concrete situations and seek adequate answers. This is what I tried to do in *A Theology of Liberation*, while allowing for all the difficulties and risks involved. There I focused on one manifestation—perhaps the most extreme and problematic, in the judgment of many Christians—of conflict within history—namely, the fact of class struggle. I thought it my pastoral duty not to shrink from this hard question, which many were asking at that time as they confronted various events and political situations in Latin America. In my discussion of the subject the conclusion I reached was clear: "it must be a real and effective combat, not hate. This is the challenge, as new as the gospel: to love our enemies." That requirement comes from the universality of God's love.

A QUESTION OF FACT

My purpose at that time was to pose the pastoral and theological problem of love of neighbor in light of the historical fact of conflict, including the struggle between classes. Let me specify several points in this regard.

To speak of conflict as a social fact is not to assert it apodictically as something beyond discussion, but only to locate it at the level of social analysis. I cannot, for pastoral or theological reasons, simply deny social facts; that would be to mock those Christians who must confront these facts every day. For this reason I made the following statement over ten years ago, during a discussion of the subject and at a bishop's request:

> The problem facing theology is not to determine whether or not social classes are in opposition. That is in principle a matter for the sciences, and theology must pay careful attention to them if it wishes to be *au courant* with the effort being made to understand the social dimensions of the human person. The question, therefore, that theology must answer is this: If there is a struggle (as one, but not the only form of historical conflict), how are we to respond

to it as Christians? A theological question is always one that is prompted by the content of faith—that is, by love. The specifically Christian question is both theological and pastoral: How are Christians to live their faith, their hope, and their love amid a conflict that takes the form of class struggle? Suppose that analysis were to tell us one day: "The class struggle is not as important as you used to think." We as theologians would continue to say that love is the important thing, even amid conflict as described for us by social analysis. If I want to be faithful to the gospel, I cannot disregard reality, however harsh and conflictual it may be. And the reality of Latin America is indeed harsh and conflictual.

The conditional sentence ("Suppose that analysis . . . ") in that paragraph is important for situating the problem, for it leaves the door open, in an undogmatic way, to other possibilities. . . .

When I speak of conflict in history I always mention different aspects of it. That is why I continually refer to races discriminated against, despised cultures, exploited classes, and the condition of women, especially in those sectors of society where women are "doubly oppressed and marginalized" (Puebla, no. 1134, note). In this way, I take into account the noneconomic factors present in situations of conflict between social groups. The point of these constant references is to prevent any reduction of historical conflict to the fact of class struggle. I said earlier that in *A Theology of Liberation* I was discussing the class struggle aspect of the general problem because it is the one that poses the most acute problems for the universality of Christian love. If it is possible to clear that obstacle, then we have an answer to the questions raised by other, perhaps less thorny, kinds of conflict. For it is evident that history is marked by other forms of conflict and, unfortunately, of confrontation between persons.

There are those who seem without further discussion to identify the idea of class struggle with Marxism. As we know, this is incorrect and indeed was rejected by Karl Marx himself. In his well-known letter to J. Weydemeyer, he says: "As for me, mine is not the merit to have discovered either the existence of classes in modern society or the struggle between them. Much before me bourgeois historians had described the historical development of this class struggle and the bourgeois economists had studied its economic anatomy."

Marx thought that his own contribution was to have established the connection between class struggle and economic factors (as well as the dictatorship of the proletariat). These economic factors are often presented as operating historically in a deterministic manner. I am not concerned here with the important debate on this point or with the varying interpretations that the debate has produced within Marxism itself. The point I want to make is simply that an economically based determinist view of class struggle is completely alien to liberation theology.

In this connection, experts on Marx have always pointed out the very limited space (a few paragraphs amid thousands of pages) given to class struggle in Marx's principal work, *Capital.* . . .

Nevertheless, there are in Marxism expressions which turn class struggle from a simple fact into "the driving force of history" and, in more philosophical versions, a "law of history." An analysis would have to be made to determine the meaning and importance of this transformation of fact into historical principle. My only concern here is to insist that this approach does not reflect my own thinking and that therefore I have never used such expressions. . . .

THE REQUIREMENTS OF CHRISTIAN LOVE

NEUTRALITY AND SOLIDARITY

I have been criticized for saying that when faced with a situation of this magnitude, neutrality is impossible and that it calls for our active participation. And yet the context of my statements made it clear that passivity or indifference is not permissible when the issue is justice and the defense of the weakest members of society. Passivity or indifference would be neither ethical nor Christian. This does not mean that the alternative is to promote conflict. As I wrote in *A Theology of Liberation*, "Those who speak of class struggle do not 'advocate' it— as some would say—in the sense of creating it out of nothing by an act of [bad] will. What they do is to recognize a fact and contribute to an awareness of that fact." They acknowledge, that is, the reality of social conflict and the necessity of becoming aware of it so as to get rid of it by attacking its causes.

In this area John Paul II has made an enlightening distinction. In no. 11 *Laborem exercens* he says:

> This conflict, interpreted by some as a socioeconomic class conflict, found expression in the ideological conflict between liberalism, understood as the ideology of capitalism, and Marxism, understood as the ideology of scientific socialism and communism, which professes to act as spokesman for the working class and the worldwide proletariat. Thus the real conflict between labor and capitalism was transformed into a *systematic class struggle* conducted not only by ideological means, but also and chiefly by political means.

The "real conflict" takes place in the factual world, and it is to this that the reflections in the same number of the encyclical apply. This real conflict can be transformed into a "systematic class struggle" as an all-embracing political strategy. The latter was not my position when I raised the question of the existence of conflict and the demands it makes of us. The real conflict and the systematic class conflict are two different things: that is precisely my own position. Confusions in this area are indeed possible, but for that very reason the pope's distinction between reality and strategy is especially enlightening.

The facts are hard to grasp and disputed, but this does not excuse us from having to make a choice. The real issue here, the real requirement, is solidarity. I realize, of course, that if we evade the issue with a few general phrases or if we simply recall the principles regarding social conflict, we will have fewer problems. But it is not possible to remain neutral in face of the situation of poverty and the justice of the claims made by the poor. . . .

All this is not simply past history. As Pope John Paul II has written, "There must be continued study of the subject of work and of the subject's living conditions. In order to achieve social justice in the various parts of the world, in the various countries and in the relationships between them, there is a need for ever new *movements of solidarity* of the workers and with workers." More than that, the pope says that "the church is firmly committed to this cause for she considers it her mission, her service, a proof of her fidelity to Christ, so that she can truly be the 'church of the poor.'"

No one is unaware of what this solidarity of the church with worker movements (a solidarity the pope looks upon as a "proof of her fidelity to Christ") means concretely. The church's task amid the social confrontations that this solidarity implies is to proclaim the gospel of love, peace, and justice. We know what consequences this solidarity has entailed for many Christians in Latin America, where confrontations are becoming more acute. The case of Archbishop Romero is a clear, painful, and yet happy example of this evangelical witness. But so are the accusations brought against and the harassments suffered by so many other members (laity, religious, priests, and bishops) of the church in Latin America.

There is obviously no question of identifying a preferential option for the poor with an ideology or a specific political program that would serve as framework for reinterpreting the gospel or the task of the church. Nor is there any question of limiting oneself to one sector of the human race. I regard these reductive positions as utterly alien. But I have dealt with this matter on various occasions and need not insist on the point once again.

I do, however, wish to discuss a question I regard as important. I said earlier that the universality of Christian love is incompatible with any exclusion of persons but not with a preference for some. I think it worth citing here a passage from Karl Lehmann, a theologian and presently archbishop of Mainz:

> There can undoubtedly be situations in which *the Christian message allows only one course of action.* In these cases the church is under the obligation of decisively taking sides (see, for example, the experience of Nazi dictatorship in Germany). *In these circumstances, an attitude of unconditional neutrality in political questions contradicts the command of the gospel* and can have deadly consequences.

There is no passage in my own writings that so incisively stresses specificity and points to one course of action as the only possible course. But, faced with so strong a statement, I cannot but ask: Does not what held for the experience of Nazism in Europe hold also for the Latin American experience of wretchedness and oppression? In both cases, we are faced with boundary situations, but that is precisely what I said at the beginning of this section, and it is to this kind of situation that Archbishop Lehmann is referring.

The important point is that according to the German theologian *there are cases* in which "the Christian message allows only one course of action." Would anyone dare brand this claim unchristian and reductivist? In this case, proximity to the horror of Nazism showed that the claim is theologically acceptable in an extreme situation. In such situations, the judgment one makes depends not simply on social analysis but on the ethical reaction (see John Paul II's notion), which we experience in face of a situation that we analyze and, above all, live through. Perhaps it is this very last point—living in the situation—that makes the difference in outlooks. For there is no doubt that behind Archbishop Lehmann's words lies the complex and painful experience of the German people and German Christians. But there are other experiences no less painful and scandalous.

THE UNIVERSALITY OF CHRISTIAN LOVE

All that has preceded brings me to a final, but fundamental, point. When we speak of taking social conflict (including the fact of class struggle) into account and of the need of overcoming the situation by getting at the causes that give rise to it, we are asserting a permanent demand of Christian love. We are thus recalling a basic injunction of the gospel: love of our enemies. In other words, a painful situation that may cause us to regard others as our adversaries does not dispense us from loving them; quite the contrary. When, therefore, I speak of social conflict, I am referring to social groups, classes, races, or cultures, but not to persons.

There are indeed times in the struggle for justice when conflict may seem to be with individuals. Speaking of unions, John Paul II says:

> They are indeed a mouthpiece for the struggle for social justice, for the just rights of working persons in accordance with their individual professions. However, this "struggle" should be seen as a normal endeavor "for" the just good: in the present case, for the good that corresponds to the needs and merits of working persons associated by profession; but it is not a struggle "against" others [*Laborem exercens,* no. 20].

He goes on to say, more specifically: "Even if in controversial questions the struggle takes on *a character of opposition* toward others, this is because it aims at the good of social justice, not for the sake of 'struggle' or in order to eliminate an opponent" (ibid., emphasis added). In these difficult questions there is indeed a de facto opposition between persons, but even amid this opposition the Christian ethos does not allow hatred.

In *Quadragesimo anno* Pius XI acknowledged the existence of class struggle and even accepted it in some situations as something that can gradually change "into an honest discussion of differences founded on a desire for justice" and that "can and ought to be the point of departure *from which to move forward* to the mutual cooperation of industries and professions" (no. 114). But he also pointed out a basic condition required for that kind of change and progress: "if class struggle abstains from enmities and *mutual* hatred." This is indeed an absolutely fundamental Christian requirement.

The same call for a universal Christian love is to be found in the other passages I have cited regarding what John Paul II calls "the real conflict" between social classes. Bishop Lehmann also reminds us of the same obligation in words that continue the already cited passage regarding situations in which neutrality on the part of the church "contradicts the command of the gospel and can have deadly consequences." He goes on to say, and rightly: "But when seen from the viewpoint of the gospel, *a decisive commitment to specific groups* must never be allowed to overshadow a fundamental part of the Christian message—namely, that the church has an obligation to communicate God's love to all human beings without exception." Even the extreme case, "in which the Christian message allows only one course of action," does not do away with the requirement of universal love. This is all the more true, then, when there is question of respecting both the universality of love and the *preferential* option of which I have spoken. This point has always been clearly made in my writings, and I have always regarded it as fundamental.

17. THE SUFFERING OF OTHERS

While some have mistakenly believed that a preferential option for the poor concerns only the non-poor, Gutiérrez has steadfastly argued that the option is incumbent upon all Christians, including the poor themselves, because conversion and solidarity are the vocation of every disciple. In fidelity to the God of life, the poor must make a decision to enter into solidarity with persons of their own race, class, or culture—that is, with people condemned to the same situation of marginalization. In his masterful reading of the Book of Job, Gutiérrez argues that a turning point in Job's relationship with God occurs when the afflicted man comes to see that, unfortunately, he is far from alone in suffering unfairly. Indeed, the awareness of others' suffering (and its injustice) leads Job to free himself from a theology of reward and punishment and to begin to embrace the mystery of gratuitous love and the tasks to which it gives rise. Gutiérrez treats this shift in Job's consciousness in chapter 5 of On Job *(Spanish original 1986), from which the following excerpts are taken (31–38).*

The dialogue of Job and his friends advances at an uneven pace, but it does advance. The friends repeat themselves and become increasingly aggressive, but Job sees more deeply into his own experience and refines his thinking. An important point is reached in this progress when he realizes that he is not the only one to experience the pain of unjust suffering. The poor of this world are in the same boat as he: instead of living, they die by the roadside, deprived of the land that was meant to support them. Job discovers to his grief that he has many counterparts in adversity.

The question he asks of God ceases to be a purely personal one and takes concrete form in the suffering of the poor of this world. The answer he seeks will not come except through commitment to them and by following the road— which God alone knows—that leads to wisdom. Job begins to free himself from an ethic centered on personal rewards and to pass to another focused on the needs of one's neighbor. The change represents a considerable shift.

THE LOT OF THE POOR

As his friends continue to insist on the doctrine of temporal retribution, Job ceases to look only at his individual case and asks why it is that the wicked prosper [see Job 21:6–9]. This first enlargement of the field of personal experience will supply him with a further argument in the debate with his friends. From the new vantage point he will be able to see the weakness of the arguments brought against him. . . .

"At the very thought" [that the wicked still live on]: Job recalls a fact of daily life, which anyone can verify. The wicked prosper—that is, the very persons who neither serve God nor pray to God [Job 21:13–15, 17–18]. . . .

These cases show that the arguments of Job's friends in support of the theory of temporal retribution are in fact worthless; they also show the inadequacy of his friends' references to experience. Job therefore says to them: "So what sense is there in your empty consolation? Your answers are a deception" (21:34). The answers do not reflect reality. Job's own experience gives them the lie; furthermore, Job now sees that the question being debated does not concern him alone. This realization gives new vigor to the protest of supposedly "patient" Job, who asks in challenge and complaint: "So God is storing up punishment for his children?" (21:19). . . .

Job will reflect more fully on this phenomenon and thus be able to broaden his personal experience still further. As a result, he will distance himself even more quickly and fully from the ethico-religious language of his friends. Moreover, his line of argument will now change radically, as a result precisely of his realization that poverty and abandonment are not his lot alone. For he sees now that this poverty and abandonment are not something fated but are caused by the wicked, who nonetheless live serene and satisfied lives. These are the same ones who tell the Lord, "Go away!" The wicked are both rejecters of God and enemies of the poor—two sides of the same coin. All this leads the author of the book to put into the mouth of Job the most radical and cruel description of the wretchedness of the poor that is to be found in the Bible, and also to have Job utter a harsh indictment of the powerful who rob and oppress the poor [Job 24:2–14]. . . .

The description is full of detail and shows careful attention to the concrete situation of the poor. The poverty described is not the result of destiny or inexplicable causes; those responsible for it are named without pity. Job is describing a state of affairs caused by the wickedness of those who exploit and rob the poor. In many instances, therefore, the suffering of the innocent points clearly to guilty parties. The daily life of the poor is a death, says the Bible. The oppressors of the poor are therefore called murderers. The Book of Ecclesiasticus says it bluntly: "The bread of the needy is the life of the poor; whoever deprives them of it is a murderer. To take away a neighbor's living is to murder him; to deprive an employee of his wages is to shed blood" (34:21–22; see Jer. 22:13–17; Amos 5:11–12; Mic. 2:9–10).

The injustice is even more scandalous because the poor who lack everything and suffer hunger and thirst are the very ones who work to produce for others the food they cannot have for themselves. There is no respect for their basic right to life, though this is the foundation of all justice. With this situation in mind the prophet promises, in words that recall this contrasting passage in Job, that on the day when Yahweh creates new heavens and a new earth "no more shall there be . . . infants who live but a few days, or adults who do not fill out their days. . . . They shall build houses and inhabit them; they shall plant vineyards and eat their fruit. They shall not build and another inhabit; they shall not plant and another eat" (Isa. 65:20–22). This is the promise of the God of *life*, and it should even now begin to transform the situation of *death* in which the poor live.

The oppressors who kill the poor (the orphan, the widow, the unpaid worker) do their deeds at night, hoping perhaps that the darkness will hide their crimes [Job 24:14]. But the cause of the poor is God's cause. And Job realizes that his own cause is linked to that of the poor. Where, then, is God in the midst of it all? Will God be deaf to the prayer of the poor? This time, Job's cry is not simply for himself, for he knows that he is part of the world of the poor. It is in that setting that he asks his question, and it carries with it the questions of all those whom he has just recognized as his fellows in misfortune.

THE WAY OF THE WICKED

When Zophar, who thinks as always within the framework of the theology of temporal retribution, describes the lot of the wicked, he lists among their faults their behavior toward the poor [20:15–19]. . . .

Job's theologian friends, who know the biblical tradition, are well aware that it is a serious sin to amass wealth through exploitation of the poor. Such behavior contradicts the very meaning of the people's life in the Promised Land, which was meant to be the opposite of life in Egypt, the land of oppression and injustice. Mistreatment of the helpless is an offense against God; for that reason (Zophar goes on to say) the gladness of the wicked is transitory [20:20–2]. . . .

The prophetic view of the poor thus makes a fleeting appearance in the speeches of Job's friends, but is immediately shackled, as it were, by the doctrine of temporal retribution.

Eliphaz repeats the doctrine at greater length in his final speech, thus spending his last ammunition. It must be acknowledged that his aim has improved.

He has taken note of the attacks on an abstract theology. Job, in ending his series of answers to his friends, has once again called them to task: "What sense is there in your empty consolation? Your answers are a deception" (21:34). Eliphaz responds by making his arguments more pointed. He had earlier spoken of the sinfulness of all human beings (chap. 4) and of sin generally as deserving punishment (chap. 15); now he directly accuses Job of serious sins:

> Do you think he is punishing you for your piety and bringing you to justice for that? No, for your great wickedness, more likely, for your unlimited sins! You have exacted unearned pledges from your brothers, stripped people naked of their clothes, failed to give water to the thirsty and refused bread to the hungry; handed the land over to a strong man, for some favored person to move in, sent widows away empty-handed and crushed the arms of orphans [22:4–9].

The details of the list are very significant. The emphasis is not on public worship: Was or was not Job a religious man? Eliphaz takes a clearly prophetic stance and finds fault with Job's behavior vis-à-vis the poor. The position that authentic worship presupposes the practice of love and justice is characteristic of the prophetic tradition. Eliphaz adopts it here as he points out that because Job has not practiced the works of mercy, he has failed both justice and God. That is why he finds himself in his present situation [22:10-11]. . . .

Eliphaz's final speech is thus an assertion of the rights of the poor. A key element in his argument is the assumption—for no evidence is adduced—that Job has been guilty of these sins. In fact, Job vehemently denies it, as we shall see in a moment. . . .

In Eliphaz's view, then, Job behaves like all the other wicked who do not believe that God sees their deeds. This is a typical reproach leveled at evildoers. Eliphaz seems to argue that if Job denies temporal retribution, it can only be because he thinks God is unaware of what goes on among human beings. In fact, then, the prophetic standpoint that this theologian has to some extent adopted in this speech has not led him to abandon the doctrine of retribution, which he and his two friends have been so fervently defending. His reasoning, as we have already seen, is this: Job is suffering, therefore he *must* have committed these sins. Job will appeal to facts and reject this argument that is based solely on doctrinal principles and undeterred by any concern to check it against reality.

On the basis of what he has said, Eliphaz urges Job to conversion [Job 22:21–30]. . . . The conversion Eliphaz has in mind supposes that Job acknowledges his sin and separates himself from it: "Drive wickedness from your tent." Job is being urged to depart from the "ancient trail" of the wicked (22:15) in order that "light" may shine "on your path" (22:28). Thus the darkness that keeps him from seeing his way will be dispersed (see 3:23). The way (Hebrew, *derek*) of the just is here contrasted with the way of the wicked and refers to the conduct of those who advance toward God by doing God's will. Eliphaz ends with the promise of deliverance: "He rescues anyone who is innocent; have your hands clean [that is, practice justice], and you will be saved" [22:30].

It must be recognized that within the limits imposed by his theology, Eliphaz has made a great effort to be reconciled with Job. Meanwhile, Job's outlook has been broadened by his realization of the suffering and injustice that are the lot of the poor. Consequently, even when denying the misdeeds of which Eliphaz accuses him, he sees more clearly that to be just means paying heed to the poor and setting them free.

His friend's argument will help Job to launch a significant process in which his individual situation becomes less and less the focus of the debate. He will broaden his perspective to include the sufferings and injustices to which the poor fall victim, as we saw above. This broadening of outlook will in turn enable him to sketch a new language about God.

Job's other two friends, Bildad and Zophar, also deliver their final speeches. These amount to repetitive indictments incapable of carrying further the bold attempt made by Eliphaz, who undoubtedly has the sharpest mind of the three. For this reason, they succeed only in angering Job [27:2–7]. . . .

The three friends have said what they had to say; their store of arguments is exhausted. They will not speak again. Disagreeing with them, Job has asserted his integrity and uprightness. His conviction of his innocence has become a solid rock within him. He now solemnly assures them that he will maintain this position to the end of his life. Nothing will persuade him to the contrary. This is a matter of conscience, but of a conscience that has a lofty sense of truth. Were he to agree with his friends, he would be lying; neither his faith in God nor his state of mind will allow him to do it. He will not fall back on deception in order to ease his situation and achieve a degree of repose. His truthfulness leaves him isolated and almost defenseless. Who is the adversary he has in mind [when he says, "Let my enemy meet the fate of the wicked, my adversary, the lot of the evil-doer!" (27:2–7)]? His friends? God? Someone else? Scholars are in disagreement.

From the legal standpoint that Job several times adopts, the possible guilt of anyone challenging him will be proof of his own innocence. In the verse to which I have just referred, Job is not really accusing anyone; he has his own interests in mind. His words, especially if they refer to God, are harsh; yet, much to his regret, the whole form that the theological debate with his friends has taken down to this point forces him to utter them. He is exhausted, and so is the debate. The road they have been traveling has led into a blind alley; Job has had the courage to follow the road to the end in order to prove that this is where it must lead. Fresh air is needed, and a radical change of perspective.

The author's poetic genius will see to it that our legitimate longing for an answer to the questions formulated does not itself remain rudimentary and unmediated. It must mature, penetrate each of us more deeply, and take historical form. The question we face here is not one that can be handled by what Blaise Pascal calls the *esprit géométrique*, or mathematical mind, which reasons in an orderly way from definitions and principles. What is needed is rather the *esprit de finesse*, or intuitive mind, which is implies a penetrating, comprehensive vision of a reality present to all. The poet helps us sharpen this vision by giving us now a beautiful poem on wisdom (chap. 28) and placing us (as if in a temporary rest between the preceding debate and the last and more important speeches of the book) before the greatness of God and the mystery of knowing God's intentions for the human race.

Gently, and in verses of great beauty, the author reminds us that this requires a prudence (discernment) that wisdom alone gives. To possess this wisdom is to respect the Lord. The poem tells us that human beings know where to find silver, iron, and a great many other things, but that where wisdom is concerned, "God alone understands her path and knows where she is to be found" (28:23). At the same time, he also shows in a subtle way that something new is needed if we are to enter into the knowledge of God. Chapter 28 thus serves as a poetic hinge, so to speak, in the development of the book.

18. THE GOD WHO COMES

According to Gutiérrez, for the Christian the preferential option for the poor is based neither on social analysis nor on "Christian compassion" for those who suffer. In the final analysis it is a theocentric option, that is, a choice made by believers, individually and collectively, founded on their understanding of who God is. Gutiérrez's most complete study of the God portrayed in the Bible is The God of Life *(1989). Chapter 5 of that work, "The God Who Comes," considers the question of where God can be found in the world. Yet in answering that question Gutiérrez inevitably speaks of who God is. As he demonstrates, the God of the Bible cannot be found by those who practice injustice or hypocritical religious ritual (that is, in the "empty temple"). On the contrary, God makes a home in history among the victims of injustice and scorn (that is, in a "foul-smelling stable"). However, God is also present in the cosmos ("clothed in beauty"). Gutiérrez finds the dialectics of transcendence/historical presence and of revelation/hiddenness at the heart of the Bible's portrait of God. These same two pairs must ground the church's option for the poor. The following passages are taken from* The God of Life, *69–91.*

The God of the Bible is the God who comes to the people. Yahweh says: "I have come down to rescue them from the hands of the Egyptians" (Exod. 3:8; see 18:20), and "I will come to you" (Exod. 20:24). John the Evangelist says of the Word: "He came to his own house" (John 1:11, literal) and he "made his dwelling among us" (v. 14). The Apocalypse begins (Rev. 1:4, 8) and ends (Rev. 22:20) with the promise of the definitive coming of the Lord. God is present where God's life-giving plan takes flesh. This prompts me to reflect on a dialectic often found in the Bible: the tension between God's visibility and invisibility, between God's obviousness and hiddenness. This tension is renewed—in continuity and discontinuity—by the incarnation of the Son of God. The tension provides us with new forms of God's presence and absence in history.

1. GOD HAS DEPARTED

Whenever and wherever God's reign and demand that we "do what is right and just" are denied, God is not present. There is a philosophically inspired theology that has difficulty in handling the biblical assertion of God's absence. As children we learned that God is everywhere, and knows and sees everything. From a metaphysical viewpoint that is correct. But the Bible also and quite frequently speaks to us of God's absences, of spaces deprived of God's presence. If we restrict ourselves to the categories of traditional philosophy, we will see these biblical statements as absurdities: What kind of a God is it who is *not* in a particular place? If we take that approach, we will be guilty of confusing a particular philosophy with reflection on the God of the Bible.

The Scriptures offer us three important examples of God's absence that will help us think about the God of biblical revelation.

THE EMPTY TEMPLE

The temple is clearly a place where God must necessarily dwell. Yet the Bible says that God is not there, if those trying to find God do not put into practice the commandment of life and justice [see Jer. 1:1–7]. . . .

The prophet is calling for a radical conversion in those who wish to find God. He makes it fully clear that until there is a commitment to the rights of the poor, God will not dwell with them in the temple; God will be absent. Observe that Jeremiah is speaking here of a holy place—that is, a space that has classically been God's dwelling place. Even so, God orders the prophet to proclaim that God will not be found there if those who claim to be approaching God are exploiting the poor and shedding the blood of the innocent. Here God is absent from the temple because the people do not practice justice, especially toward the weakest among them.

The prophet therefore criticizes those who claim to be seeking help in the temple but who in fact profane it by their behavior: "And yet [they] come to stand before me in this house which bears my name, and say: 'We are safe; we can commit all these abominations again.' Has this house which bears my name become in your eyes a den of thieves? I too see what is being done, says the Lord" (Jer. 7:10–11).

Jesus likewise forcefully rejects the hypocrisy that such an attitude represents. Using various passages from the Old Testament (Isa. 56:7; Zech. 14:21; Ps . 69:10), the Synoptic evangelists tell us of the expulsion of the traders from the temple. It is significant that while the Synoptics place this incident toward the end of Jesus' ministry, John places it at the beginning. One of the passages to which Jesus alludes is the one just cited from Jeremiah, which helps us understand the meaning of the passage in the Gospels:

They came to Jerusalem, and on entering the temple area he began to drive out those selling and buying there. He overturned the tables of the money changers and the seats of those who were selling doves. He did not permit anyone to carry anything through the temple area. Then he taught them, saying, "Is it not written: ' My house shall be called a house of prayer for all peoples?'" But you have made it a den of thieves. [Mark 11:15–17]

Here we have Jesus confronting the leaders of the Jewish people (the first of his confrontations with them according to the parallel passage in John). The Lord is in Jerusalem (John says he is there to celebrate Passover, the feast of liberation) and, when he enters the temple, he finds an especially scandalous kind of oppression of the people. Money has become a mediator between God and the faithful, with the result that the latter are faced by an oppressive tyrant and not by the Father who liberates them from slavery. The house of the God who loves the people and sets them free has been turned into a marketplace that exploits and degrades. The business transacted in the temple enriches the high priests; it is they who are behind the trade. The sellers of animals and the money changers who accept Roman money (which is pagan and cannot be offered in a holy place) and give in exchange money minted by the temple itself, are simply intermediaries.

The expulsion by Jesus is therefore an attack on powerful interests, the interests of those who, without denying God with their lips, have replaced God with greed, which Paul regards as idolatry. The substitution is adroit and disguised, and paradoxically, often justified by religious arguments. No one is free to engage in such a perversion of the faith. The special harshness with which Jesus treats the sellers of doves is worth noting (John also emphasizes it). The fact is that the dove, being the smallest and cheapest of animals, is for that reason used by the poorest in sacrifices of purification. The people engaged in selling doves are therefore using worship to exploit the poor. This is why such business is especially scandalous, and it is why Jesus is so resolute in his expulsion of the dove sellers. We may hide our desire for power and money behind arguments and even religious motives; but the Lord, who knows what is in human nature (as John says at the end of his account of the expulsion: 2:25), will not allow "his name to be taken in vain" (see Exod. 20:7).

The service of money ends in oppression of the poor. Whether God dwells or does not dwell in a particular place depends on whether true worship is offered there, the worship that the Gospel of John describes as "worship in Spirit and truth" (John 4:24). If such worship is being offered, then God is there for all and especially for the scorned and unimportant. Citing a universalist text from Second Isaiah (56:7), Jesus says that the temple shall be called a house of prayer "for all peoples" (Mark 11:17). In the passage parallel to the one on which I am commenting, Matthew notes that "the blind and the lame approached him in the temple area, and he cured them" (Matt. 21:14). The healing is a prophetic gesture that underscores his rejection of what was going on in the temple; his giving of life is the opposite of the exploitation of the poor and the substitution of money for God. It is not surprising, therefore, that the people affected by the attitude of Jesus react aggressively. Immediately after the incident, Mark tells us, "The chief priests and the scribes came to hear of it and were seeking a way to put him to death, yet they feared him because the whole people was spellbound at his teaching. When evening came, they went out of the city" (Mark 11:18–19).

THE WORLD OF BRIBERY

Those in authority over the people are obligated to respect the law and to establish right and justice. They do not always do so in practice. [The prophet Micah indicts] . . . the mighty of the nation [who] are betraying their responsibility and causing the death of the innocent [Mic. 3:9–12]. All of this is an assault on the will of the God of life.

When the prophet attacks those who "build up Zion with bloodshed" [Mic. 3:10], he is attacking greed, the idolatry of mammon—that is, the bribery, the pay, and the money that turn judicial and religious activities into a commodity. Yet "they rely on the Lord" [Mic. 3:11]! The prophet is infuriated; these idolaters even claim their actions are devout; they claim that God is with them and that God guarantees their security. Since the argument from God's presence is manipulated to justify unjust behavior, God himself maintains that he will abandon Zion and punish it for the sins of its leaders—that is, the very men whose responsibility it is to teach the people and lead them to faith in Yahweh. God is absent from these men because they are idolaters; in fact . . . St. Paul [says] that the greedy, those who worship money, are idolaters [cf. Eph. 5:5; Col. 3:5].

In one of his harshest attacks on the religious leaders of his people, Jesus rebukes them to their faces: "Woe to you, blind guides, who say, 'If one swears by the temple, it means nothing, but if one swears by the gold of the temple, one is obligated.' Blind fools, which is greater, the gold, or the temple that made the gold sacred?" (Matt. 23:16–17).

As the reader will know, a great deal of money was stored in the temple as a result of the offerings made by devout Jews. If this money had any meaning, it derived it from the place in which it was stored. But, to the scandal of having money thus accumulate, there was added the scandal created by the priorities that the beneficiaries of this treasure had introduced into temple practice.

"Which is greater, the gold or the temple?" The question is a cutting indictment. Jesus is bringing to light a profound deviation in those who claim to represent the law of God, although in fact they "love places of honor at banquets, seats of honor in synagogues, greetings in marketplaces, and the salutation 'Rabbi'" (Matt. 23:6). Honors and money give these religious leaders a power that makes them unable to put up with Jesus.

Theirs is an intolerance that does not fear even committing murder when they see their privileges questioned and the dishonesty of their religion exposed. God is not with religious leaders who betray their task nor does God give them backing. The blood of Jesus can seal the new covenant, which he inaugurates because he dies as a just man at the hands of those who refuse to accept the God of life whom he preaches. But the covenant of love will abide; it will carry the indelible mark of the lamb of God, of the Lord's sacrifice, but also of his resurrection.

EVIL DEEDS

We are familiar with the many passages in which the prophets denounce acts of worship that they regard as empty of content, because those performing them: do not practice justice [e.g., Amos 5:21–24]. . . . As I said earlier, offerings to Yahweh, the God of the covenant, must be linked to the establishment of what is right and just. Otherwise they are not acceptable to God; they are hollow actions [and not] "a fast, a day acceptable to the Lord" [Isa. 58:5–7].

Sharing our bread with the poor, making of them our companions, that is, our "bread-sharers" (this is the etymology of "companion"): that is the fast God wants. Only under these conditions will God be present [cf. Isa. 58:9]. . . .

A passage of the New Testament repeats these reasons for the absence of God from allegedly religious activities:

> Not everyone who says to me, "Lord, Lord" will enter the kingdom of heaven, but only the one who does the will of my Father in heaven. Many will say to me on that day, "Lord, Lord, did we not prophesy in your name? Did we not drive out demons in your name? Did we not do mighty deeds in your name?" Then I will declare to them solemnly, "I never knew you. Depart from me, you evildoers." [Matt. 7:21–23]

"I never knew you; depart from me" is a classical formula of the Bible for a complete and unconditional rejection. "On that day" those rejected will be termed "evil-doers," because they did not feed the hungry or give drink to the thirsty (see Matt. 25:31–45). The actions that such people claim as religious (prophesying, expelling demons, working miracles) were simply ritual gestures empty of concrete love for brothers and sisters, for the poor; therefore God was not in these actions. Moreover, the exercise of these charisms becomes the practice of evil (in Greek: *anomia*, lawlessness); that is, the very opposite of love (Greek: *agape*), which is God's law as explained in the Sermon on the Mount, of which this passage is a part. "Evil-doers" is a bold and harsh term that allows no loopholes. When one tries to justify the failure to love the poor and the oppressed by claiming that one is occupied in worshiping, one is in fact doing evil. God is not bound to accept our religious works; if they are not inspired by the desire for life and justice, God is not present in them.

All these passages recall different ways in which God is absent: from the temple, from the leaders of the people, and from religious activities. But all these absences have a single theological meaning: God is not there because the reign of God is not accepted; because God's will is not carried out. As the elderly sacristan says in [José María Arguedas's novel] *Todas las sangres*: "God is here in Lahuaymarca. He has left San Pedro, and, I think, forever." God departs from places and persons that have subjected the Indian to so many humiliations and injustices. The philosophical argument offered by the priest—"God is everywhere, everywhere"—is irrelevant. The old sacristan ponders: "Was God in the hearts of those who broke the body of innocent Master Bellido?" In the hearts of those who rob and kill? No, God has left them. Arguedas's poetic intuition matches the biblical outlook. When the grace of God's reign is not accepted, when God's demands are not met, the God of the kingdom is absent.

2. DWELLING OF GOD

The presence of God is one of the major themes of the Bible. There is an exact term that expresses God's dwelling within history: the *shekinah* of Yahweh. The people of Israel are profoundly convinced of God's nearness, and this nearness motivates a permanent thanksgiving. "What great nation is there that has gods so close to it as the Lord, our God, is to us whenever we call upon him?" (Deut. 4:7). God is present in the midst of the people, but not only there, for God is also present in the cosmos—that is, in everything that is the result of God's creative action. The coming of Christ hastens and deepens this presence in history and in the least of history's participants.

THE COSMOS SPEAKS OF GOD

The poetry found in many books of the Bible has for one of its favorite themes the traces of God in the natural world [in which] God is clothed in beauty [see, e.g., Ps. 104]. . . .

God's presence is signaled by these beautiful garments; God is found in the "tent" from which his message reaches us. The natural world speaks of God: "The heavens declare the glory of God, and the firmament proclaims his handiwork " (Ps. 19:2). . . .

In part, perhaps, because it springs from a rural world, the Bible likes to sing of this presence of God and to do so along with the rest of creation. A fine example of this approach is the beautiful hymn of the three young men, Hananiah, Azariah, and Mishael, in the Book of Daniel [Dan. 3:62–66]. . . .

It is important, however, to observe that the main reason for these exclamations of wondering praise is not the fact that heaven, earth, and the phenomena of nature raise questions that human beings have difficulty in answering, so that they fall back on mystery and try to find God in what is hidden and in interstellar space. The Bible does indeed refer to this experience, but its emphasis on the theme is due much more to the fact that it sees God revealed in the grandeur and harmony of the cosmos, in the majestic beauty of the natural world. Like Dante at the end of his *Divine Comedy*, the Bible speaks to us of "the love that moves the sun and the stars." . . .

This vision of things is extremely important, and we need to recover it through contemplation and the celebration of the liturgy. It represents the phase of silence [which precedes attempts to speak about God]. If we lose the dimension of beauty, we deny ourselves access to the God who loves us, as well as to an understanding of liturgical language. All the symbols used in such language are realities of the natural world: fire, water, light, fruits. The presence of God undoubtedly spurs us to stress the ethical perspective, but no less certainly the finding of God in contemplation has an aesthetic dimension. Do we not see this in the experience of the great mystics, such as St. John of the Cross ("Seeking my loves, I will go o'er yonder mountains and banks") in his relationship with nature? The sensitivity of the Bible to this aspect of reality causes it to assert the presence of God in the beauty of the universe. In the addresses of God in the Book of Job (chapters 38–41), for example, the beautiful description of the natural world serves as a revelation of the gratuitousness of God's love.

On the other hand, approaching the mystery of God moves along avenues that are apparently opposed among themselves. This is because we are engaged in a dialectical approach to the ineffable. God is revealed through events that cannot fail to be seen and even produce fear: the storm, for example, and devouring fire [see, e.g., Exod. 19:16–18]. . . . But God is also present in situations that rise into consciousness only if we are attentive to them, as, for example, the light breeze [see 1 Kings 19:11–13]. . . . God is manifested on the mountain and in the storm, and in fire amid thunder and lightning. But God is also manifested in the "tiny whispering sound" of a breeze, in the light caress that restores calm after the terrifying storm. In these different ways that are based on events of nature the Bible seeks to approach the immeasurable fullness of God's presence.

Let us note, however, that in all cases it is the same God who is revealed and makes identical claims. Thus the manifestation of God in the form of a light breeze does not relieve Elijah of the necessity of covering his face when Yahweh is near, nor does it soften the terms of the mission he receives. On the other hand, the theophany in the storm on the mountain does not keep Moses from speaking frankly to Yahweh and experiencing Yahweh's intimate presence.

I SHALL DWELL IN YOUR MIDST

God is present in the cosmos, but God is also present in the midst of history. The living God is present and active in the historical movement of human society. God has decided that it should be so. God's being with us is a central and profound idea, and one that is not reducible to simplistic visions of reality. The prophets supply two correctives against errors of interpretation that can occur in the effort to understand this presence more fully and define it more closely.

The first is to remind their hearers that no space and no time can contain God fully. God dwells in the cosmos and in concrete human history, but these cannot enclose God or set limits to God's presence. The holy mountain cannot, nor can the ark or the temple or any reality or dimension of society; neither can any experience or any historical event set limits to the divine action. This is one of the reasons why the Old Testament is so opposed to the making of images: God cannot be represented; God transcends any likeness.

For this reason, when the Jewish people, remembering the presence of God on Mount Sinai and their experience of God's company in the wilderness, build a temple for God—that is, a particular spot in which God's dwelling is fixed—the prophets immediately broaden the horizon and caution that the true dwelling place of God is in the heavens. Thus, in the presence of the imposing temple built of cedar of Lebanon to be a house for Yahweh, Solomon exclaims before the entire assembly: "Can it indeed be that God dwells on earth? If the heavens and the highest heavens cannot contain you, how much less this temple which I have built!" (1 Kings 8:27).

Implicit in the conviction that no place and no historical event is capable of containing God is the great biblical idea that God cannot be manipulated. God is beyond the reach of every effort to limit the scope of God's freely adopted plans. Human beings must not delude themselves: Yahweh agrees to the building of a temple, but this is not the sole place in which God dwells, nor is God's dwelling there guaranteed. For the same reason temporal limits cannot be imposed on God; that is, God cannot be enclosed in time. When the rulers of the city of Betulia decide that they will hand the city over to the enemy if Yahweh does not come to its aid within five days, Judith responds in the purest prophetic tradition: "God is not like a human being, to be threatened, or like a mere mortal, to be won over by pleading ultimatum" [Jth. 8:16].

This fine passage clearly asserts the transcendence of God and the utter freedom with which God loves. Those who demand guarantees of God do not understand God: you cannot give God ultimatums. God is beyond all space and all time. God will act, utterly freely, if it pleases God to do so.

The prophets constantly recall the majesty of Yahweh and thus counteract the tendency, often found in believers, to seek to domesticate faith in God. For this reason they frequently met with resistance and hostility among their own people. In our own day, even to speak of God and the poor is to go counter to a world that creates a religion for its own private use, one that sees no problems and raises no questions.

The second corrective of the prophets relates to a point to which I have already referred. Isaiah puts it this way: "Truly with you God is hidden, the God of Israel, the savior!" (Isa. 45:15). The Lord certainly dwells within history, but, as the prophet makes clear, God's presence is often hidden; God is present in what is insignificant and anonymous. On many occasions God brings a work of justice or salvation to completion in a hidden manner. God's dwelling in history is not simple and obvious, so that it may be found quickly, directly, and unmistakably. God is present in human history with its tensions, successes, and conflicts, but finding God requires a search.

Searching, as I said earlier, is a profound spiritual theme in every discussion of the way to reach God, in every reflection on the always unprecedented ways of coming to this hidden God, who most often accomplishes the work of salvation in ways that are not ours, as Isaiah says (Isa. 55:8). Consequently, if we are to find God acting in history, we must have an attitude of faith that is open to novelty and mystery. The Lord cannot be manipulated, nor can we invent a God who will meet our expectations. On the contrary, we must agree to be constantly challenged by God.

3. EVERYTHING BEGINS WITH AN ENCOUNTER

God's dwelling in history reaches its fullness in the incarnation in Jesus the Galilean, the poor man of Nazareth. A verse in the Prologue of John's Gospel puts it in a warm-blooded, concrete way: "And the Word became flesh and made his dwelling among us" (John 1:14). The *Biblia Española* version reads: "And the Word became a man and camped among us." These are different ways of expressing the same certainty: the dwelling of God in history. This central theme of the Bible finds its fullest realization in the incarnation. Matthew stresses this point by applying the prophecy of Isaiah: Jesus is Emmanuel, a name which, as the evangelist specifically points out, means "God with us" (Matt. 1:23; see Isa. 7:14).

IN THE WORD WAS LIFE

The Gospel of John is determined to bring home to us the importance of this encounter. His Prologue touches on all the major themes of his work; it resembles a symphonic overture announcing the material that will be developed later. In these eighteen opening verses of the Gospel we find in fact the dialectic of death-life, light-darkness, truth-lie, grace-sin, the theme of witnessing, and the relationship of freedom and slavery; all this in addition to the historical perspective, which is more important in John's Gospel than is commonly thought. The essence of the passage consists in the repeated assertion of various ways in which the word became flesh and pitched his tent in our midst. All this has its source in the primordial experience of John, the beloved disciple and author (though not necessarily the redactor) of this Gospel—that is, in his personal encounter with Jesus (see John 1:35–42). The central ideas in the Prologue cross at this point.

The first thing that calls for our attention and is of major importance for understanding John's theological purpose is the opening words: "In the beginning was the Word" (1:1). The Bible as a whole opens with the words "in the beginning" (Gen. 1:1), as it speaks of God the Creator, whose Spirit "swept over the waters" (Gen. 1:2). John uses the same words for the opening of his Gospel: "In the beginning was the Word, and the Word was with God" (John 1:1). The Greek words *en pros*, which are translated "was with," signify a direction and movement: "was directed toward." For this reason, some have given the translation: "was face to face with God." The words are a way of expressing the divinity of the word.

Verse 2 repeats, in a kind of summary, the idea of the divine origin of the word: "He was in the beginning with God."

Verse 3 again forcefully brings out the divinity: "All things came to be through him, and without him nothing came to be." The word is not created but creative.

The next verse adds an important idea to that of creation: "In him was life" (REB). The God who is revealed in the Bible is fundamentally life. This is the main characteristic of God in the Bible and a fertile theme of the fourth Gospel. A little further on, Jesus will say to us: "Just as the living Father sent me and I have life because of the Father, so also the one who feeds on me will have life because of me" (John 6:57). Jesus transmits the Father's life to us; possession of this life is the purpose of God's creative work and salvific action. "And this life was the light of the human race" (v. 4). The word is life and it is light. The perspective of life sheds light on the message. This was John's own experience: his meeting with Jesus was a source of illumination for him. The option for life becomes the definitive criterion for being and acting as Christians. Everything that involves giving life in various ways is characteristic of the followers of the Lord. By contrast, everything that entails rejection, poverty, exploitation, and contempt for life means a covenant with death and a denial of the God of Jesus.

When I speak of life, I mean all life. At the new beginning of creation that follows the flood, God says to Noah and his family that the covenant is "with you and your descendants after you . . . and with all the animals that were with you, . . . with all living beings, with everything that lives on earth" (Gen. 9:9–10, 17). The covenant is with the various forms of life, which all come from God. The important and pressing concern for ecology in our day finds in the Bible a solid and fertile basis, provided we set aside an exclusively anthropocentric interpretation of ecology. From the standpoint of the poor of this world we ought to pay increasing attention to this subject.

The Book of Job teaches us a major lesson in this regard when it reminds us that not everything was created for the service of human beings; there are many things in the natural world that human beings may consider "useless" but in which God finds delight. Human beings, made as they are in the "image and likeness of God," occupy a privileged place among living things and are called to the grace of full communion with God. But Paul reminds us that the whole of creation waits for its liberation through the children of God (Rom. 8:21–22). The activity of Jesus is directed toward communicating this fullness of life: "I came so that they might have life and have it more abundantly" (John 10:10).

Life is light, and darkness is what hinders it. The contrast between light and darkness is a theme that runs throughout the Gospel of John. Thick darkness is to light what death is to life. This idea has various roots. In Genesis, darkness precedes light; it "covered the abyss" (Gen. 1:2) and is a component of chaos;

but there is an important nuance here, as compared with John: the darkness is not actively opposed to the light. In John, on the other hand, the image of darkness is laden with hostility: the darkness is expressly opposed to the acceptance of the word. The reign of death is opposed to the reign of life. Darkness in John is connected with the world of falsehood, which, as we know, is another major theme of his Gospel. The world of falsehood is the work of human beings or, more accurately, the result of the refusal to accept the Lord, who is truth (see John 14:6). Darkness stands for sin, opposition, hostility. Light, on the other hand, is the milieu of love. There is antagonism between the darkness and the light, but John tells us that "the light shines in the darkness, and the darkness has not overcome it" (v. 5). The Lord is the light of the world: "Whoever follows me will not walk in darkness, but will have the light of life" (John 8:12). To follow Jesus means to set free and to give life.

In this setting of creation, life, and light a prophet makes his appearance: John the Baptist, "a man . . . sent by God" (v. 6); in him we begin to touch the history of a people. The precursor came to bear witness to the light; but only they who have experienced it can be witnesses. This is a thought that John repeats in the prologue of his first Letter: "What we have seen and heard we proclaim now to you" (1 John 1:3). Here, at the beginning of John's Gospel, another John, the Baptist, is presented to us as a witness. His light is a reflected light; he is a man who has received the light he needs in order to help others and illumine the way that leads to the Lord. John the Evangelist knew the Baptist and had been his disciple; that is why he knew that the Baptist "was not the light, but came to testify to the light" (v. 8).

The word alone is "the true light, which enlightens everyone" (v. 9), but makes himself known through messengers. All are called to believe; as soon as they enter this world, the light is present to them, because it is God's intention that human beings should reach the fullness of life. By a free act, which no one else can do by proxy, every person must choose light or darkness. And this freedom itself is the result of life received.

It is in the world of history that we accept or reject the word. The decision we make is heavy with consequences. The world was made by the Word; if the world does not know him—that is, does not accept and love him—it denies its very self. Its refusal amounts to rejecting the life that gave it its beginning, and therefore to fall back into darkness and chaos, this time definitively.

Beginning in verse 11 the author introduces the central theme of the Prologue: the dwelling and reception of the Word in history: "He came to what was his own [or: to his own home], but his own people did not accept him." In his own journey of faith, how often had John the Evangelist himself failed to "accept" the Lord? Behind the seemingly abstract language of the Prologue stands living experience.

Those who accept the word receive the gift of becoming children of God; this is an expression of the life that was in the word. The gift here given signifies a power or force: God makes us sons and daughters. We respond actively to this gift by ourselves in turn accepting the daughters and sons of the Father whom we meet on our journey to him.

HE MADE HIS DWELLING AMONG US

"He came to what was his own" (v. 11); he "became flesh" (v. 14): these are expressions showing the word's entrance into history. In the Bible "flesh" means the human being, sometimes with the connotation of weakness. In this short phrase John sums up the theme of emptying to which Paul will give sublime development in the second chapter of Philippians. The word entered history and accepted the human condition, including what makes it most fragile: "For your sake he became poor although he was rich" (2 Cor. 8:9).

"He made his dwelling among us" (v. 14): this fine image is taken from the Old Testament. We are told in Exodus that "the tent, which was called the meeting tent, Moses used to pitch at some distance away, outside the camp" (Exod. 33:7). The tent played a very important role for the Israelites during their crossing of the wilderness toward the promised land. The shadow of this tent of repose, which gave meaning and energy for the long journey, provided an anticipated taste of the goal reached after forty years of journeying. The presence of the tent transforms an experience of desolation into an incipient and comforting encounter with God, just as, according to Saint-Exupéry, the existence of a well in the middle of a desert transforms it into a life-giving space that gives us courage and spurs us on our quest.

According to John, the flesh that the Word assumes is the tent of a new encounter. We are called to become one in it; to be a disciple of Jesus means to live, believe, and hope under this tent. Paul expresses the same idea when he says that Christians are members of the body of Christ. The Word "camped" among us and then, laden with humanity, rose once more to the Father: "And we saw his glory, the glory as of the Father's only Son" (v. 14). John traces a thought-provoking pattern: the Word was with God in the beginning; he enters history to bring life; and he returns to the Father. Christ becomes one of us and then raises us up to contemplation of the glory he has received from the Father. That is why the evangelist says in verse 16: "From his fullness we have all received, grace upon grace." The incarnate Word gives us his own life; he communicates his own fullness by making us daughters and sons of the Father: "grace and truth came through Jesus Christ" (v. 17).

The Prologue ends with a restatement of the transcendence of God: "No one has ever seen God" (v. 18). The incarnation does not strip God of holiness, radical otherness. God is completely different; God does not belong to this world. That is what is implied in invisibility. But the Son sees God and therefore can reveal God: "the only Son who is close to the Father's heart, has revealed him" (v. 18). John is here reverting to his claim that if one is to give testimony, to reveal, one must have seen and experienced. The Son, who is face to face with the Father, is the only one who can reveal him.

4. AN IRRUPTION SMELLING OF THE STABLE

Despite appearances, the Gospel of John, including the Prologue, is steeped in concrete history and personal experience. But the more narrative language of the other Gospels undoubtedly provides us with a different and complementary approach to the presence of the Lord.

AN HISTORICAL FAITH

The Gospel of St. Luke tells us that "in those days a decree went out from Caesar Augustus that the whole world should be enrolled. This was the first enrollment, "when Quirinius was governor of Syria" (2:1–2). The Gospel of Matthew adds that Jesus was born "in Bethlehem of Judea, in the days of King Herod" (2:1).

These simple texts convey a profound message: Jesus was born in a particular place at a particular time. He was born under Emperor Octavius, who had himself named Augustus when he reached the pinnacle of power; when Quirinius was governor of Syria; during the reign of Herod, who was traitor to his people and had sold out to the occupying power. It was during this time that Jesus was born, a man of no importance in the eyes of the cynical and arrogant authorities as well as in the eyes of those who disguised cowardice as peace and political realism.

He was born in Bethlehem, "one of the little clans of Judah" (Mic. 5:1 NRSV), surrounded by shepherds and their flocks. His parents had come to a stable after vainly knocking at numerous doors in the town, as the Gospels tell us; we are reminded of the popular Mexican custom of *las posadas*. There, on the fringe of society, [as Manuel Días Mateos puts it,] "the Word became history, contingency, solidarity, and weakness; but we can say, too, that by this becoming, history itself, our history, became Word."

It is often said at Christmastime that Jesus is born into every family and every heart. But these "births" must not make us forget the primordial, massive fact that Jesus was born of Mary among a people that at the time were dominated by the greatest empire of the age. If we forget that fact, the birth of Jesus becomes an abstraction, a symbol, a cipher. Apart from its historical coordinates the event loses its meaning. To the eyes of Christians the incarnation is the irruption of God into human history: an incarnation of littleness and service in the midst of the power and arrogance of the mighty of this world; an irruption that smells of the stable.

Christian faith is a historical faith. God is revealed in Jesus Christ and, through him, in human history and, within it, in the least important and poorest sector. Only with this as a starting point is it possible to believe in God. Believers cannot go aside into a kind of dead-end corner of history and watch it go by. It is in the concrete setting and circumstances of our lives that we must learn to believe: under oppression and repression but also amid the struggles and hopes that are alive in present-day Latin America; under dictatorships that sow death among the poor, and under the "democracies" that often trade on their needs and dreams.

The Lord is not intimidated by the darkness or by the rejection of his own. His light is stronger than all the shadows. Entering into our own history—here and now—and nourishing our hope with the desire for life that belongs to the poor of our continent are the unavoidable conditions for dwelling in the tent the Son has pitched in our midst. If we do so, we shall experience in our flesh the encounter with the word who proclaims the kingdom of life.

This proclamation calls believers together as a "church," as a community whose vocation it is to continue the mission of the Word. At the end of the first chapter of his Gospel, John tells us of the meeting of two disciples of John the Baptist with the Word made flesh, and how these two straightaway went and told others what they had seen and heard. Andrew says to his brother Simon: "'We have found the Messiah' (which means Anointed). Then he brought him to Jesus" (John 1:41–42). Thus the passing on of the good news gave birth to the community of Jesus' disciples, destined to bear witness to the God of history.

In an earlier section I reminded the reader that according to the Bible nothing can contain God. The same cannot be said without qualification of Jesus, the only Son. Yet, while bearing in mind this new situation, the corrective offered by the prophets can open up meaningful ways of understanding God's relation to history. Indeed, the New Testament speaks of the fullness of time in connection with Christ, but at the same time it tells us that Christians who are incorporated into the body of Christ by baptism have a historical journey to make.

This body, the head of which is Christ, is required for the fullness (*pleroma*) of Christ, of which the Apostle speaks. Given this perspective, it is possible to understand a certain ongoing validity to the prophetic concern mentioned above. In the present situation, this concern is focused rather on the body, of Christ, the *ekklesia*, which is a pilgrim in history and whose visible boundaries are nevertheless not those of God's presence in the world. This means that God is not contained within these boundaries. The *parousia* or return of the Lord will seal the completion of the fullness of time.

Hope of the *parousia* is an integral element in our life of faith. The Lord's second coming, to which we seldom give much thought, is not a marginal question nor can it be dealt with in passing. The *parousia* signifies the fullness of God's presence in history and the fullness of history in God. Before it happens, there is a journey to be made, a march toward the full implementation of the promise. With the incarnation we have entered into the fullness of time, though we still have a distance to go; the body of Christ is now present in history. The time of the church is that of the process whereby God dwells in history.

THE FACES OF THE LORD

The Son of God was born into a little people, a nation of little importance by comparison with the great powers of the time. Furthermore, he took flesh among the poor in a marginal area—namely, Galilee; he lived with the poor and emerged from among them to inaugurate a kingdom of love and justice. That is why many have trouble recognizing him. The God who became flesh in Jesus is the hidden God of whom the prophets speak to us. God is such precisely in the measure that he is present via those who are the absent, anonymous people of history those who are not the controllers of history—namely, the mighty, the socially acceptable, "the wise and the learned" (Matt. 11:25).

In the Old Testament God appears as defender of the poor. This fact leads to the assertion that mistreatment of the deprived is an attack on God. The Book of Proverbs, for example, says: "Those who oppress the poor insult their Maker, but those who are kind to the needy honor him" (Prov. 14:31; see also Prov. 17:5; Lev. 19:14; Sir. 34:20). But the identification Jesus posits between such people and the least members of society is unique and original (see Matt. 25:31–46).

Several other passages bring us close to the same idea. For example: "Whoever receives one child such as this in my name, receives me" (Mark 9:37). In this context, we should not forget that in the culture of that time children were among those to whom no heed was paid. But no passage of the Gospel has the power of the always startling text of Matthew on the final judgment. A good deal might be said of it, [but for] the moment, I am interested in calling attention to what it says about the presence of God among us.

This well-known passage, Matthew 25:31–46, sheds light on two important identifications. The one coming to judge is the Son of man who "will sit on his glorious throne" (v. 31). A great deal has been written on the expression "Son of man," which Jesus uses so often to designate his mission. Let us note that in Matthew's own Gospel it is found several times in various contexts: Jesus' suffering and surrender of his life (17:22; 26:2), his service (24:27), and the eschatological judgment (25:31). The present passage goes on to say that it is the king who will judge (v. 34). Son of man and king, then, signify the same person.

The Gospel of John makes the same identification in one of its densest and profoundly theological passages (18:28–19:22). Here John focuses on the royalty of Jesus (mentioned here twelve times, out of sixteen occurrences in the Gospel as a whole). Before Pilate, who represents the most powerful government of that age, the Lord acknowledges that he is a king, but that his kingdom is of a different kind. "So Pilate said to him, 'Then you are a king?' Jesus answered, 'You say I am a king'" (18:37). A moment before, Jesus had made the point that "my kingdom does not belong to this world" (18:36); that is, the power exercised in it is used not to dominate, as was the case with the Roman authorities, but to serve. Jesus is a king who identifies with the least members of society, those whom society scorns. That is why they make fun of his claim to kingship (see 19:2–3). This king is then led forth and presented as "the man" (or: the Son of man) (19:5).

A passage in Mark [10:35–45] explains power that is used for service . . . [and demonstrates how James and John], two of Jesus' closest followers show their lack of understanding by asking for places of honor. The Lord answers their petition with (once again!) a question: Are they able, like he, to pay the price in suffering and death that the proclamation of the kingdom of life demands? The announcement that Jesus himself must suffer and die has already elicited a first reaction of rejection from Peter (see Mark 8:31–32). Self-surrender to others and not personal glory is the lot Christ sets before his servants. The disciples are indignant at James and John, not because the latter are mistaken regarding the message of Jesus but because they have beaten the others in asking for what all of them want. In point of fact, it is not easy to understand what it means to receive the kingdom; one of the most serious misunderstandings disciples can have is to think that our status as Christians or our responsibilities in the church make us "absolute lords" over others. That is, that these give us a right to personal glory as understood according to the categories prevailing among the great of our society.

Jesus, the Messiah, turns the reigning order upside down. In his effort to help his disciples advance along the way they have entered upon, he tells them that the truly great one among them is the one who serves and that he who would be first must be "the slave of all." This is the "messianic inversion" that is a central element in the gospel message. The inversion begins with the Lord himself who, when he became one of us, intended not to be served but to serve. Service does not mean passively accepting the present state of affairs. Rather it implies initiative and creativity, the knowledge and hard work needed to build a human, just, and fraternal world. What the Gospel rejects is power viewed as domination, as the quest to have others acknowledge us as "bosses"; it does not reject power understood as service.

This distinction helps us to understand better the second identification. Ten of the sixteen verses in Matthew's story of the judgment speak of the Lord identifying himself with the least, with the unimportant. To give life (or refuse it) to the poor is to encounter (or reject) Christ himself. This is the point being made in the Greek word used here: *elachistos* ("least"). Matthew uses the same word to describe the littleness of Bethlehem (Matt. 2:6), which is nonetheless destined for greatness because "from it will come the Messiah." Every person who is poor and forgotten is, like Bethlehem, unimportant, but from this person the Lord comes to us. It is in commitment to the marginalized that we find the meaning of our lives as believers and as human beings. When we serve the poor we serve the Christ in whom we believe; when we are in solidarity with the neediest we recognize the lowly royalty of the Son of man. There is no other way of "inheriting the kingdom.". . . .

There, in the poor, the "hidden God" questions and challenges us, especially if, like Puebla, we put ourselves in the presence of today's concrete poor, without indulging in any fantasies about them. God became flesh and is present in history, but because God is identified with the poor of the world, God's face and action are hidden in them. The Lord hides his presence in history, and at the same time reveals it, in the life and suffering, the struggles, the death, and the hopes of the condemned of the earth. But we must also remember—standing right there—that this rejection of the kingdom of life is the reason for God's absence. The dialectic between God's transcendence and God's presence in history, as well as the dialectic between revelation and hiddenness, are set forth in the Bible in a complex and fruitful way that requires historical discernment and attention to what that unforgettable pope, John XXIII, called the signs of the times.

Vallejo with his poetic intuition spoke to us of this God who is hidden in the wretched:

> The lottery ticket seller who cries "A thousand-dollar winner!"
> contains I know not what depths of God. . . .
> And I wonder on this tepid Friday that
> struggles on beneath the sun:
> Why should the will of God be dressed as a seller of lottery tickets?
> [César Vallejo, "La de a mil," in his *Los Heraldos Negros*]

The lottery ticket seller passes by and offers us "a thousand-dollar winner." We will never know whether if we had bought the ticket we would have won the lottery. But this tattered fellow, who shows us "I know not what depths of God" and who despite his seeming inability to love, can, like God, "give us heart," is thereby able to revive our lost hopes and shatter our boredom. Fortune, which is fickle, uncontrollable, impossible to subdue, seems to elude even the farsightedness of the lottery ticket seller, "this bohemian god." We do not know whether in meeting this crier of lottery tickets we might run into fortune and encounter God. That is why the poet asks about the will of God, about this God who so mysteriously is linked to the marginalized of history and who conceals himself, hides himself, works and dresses as a seller of lottery tickets, a towncrier, and a street vender.

19. PREFERENTIAL OPTION FOR THE POOR

A year before his first attempt to sketch a "theology of liberation" in Chimbote, Peru (July 1968), Gutiérrez offered a course at the University of Montréal on "the church and the problem of poverty." Twenty-six years later, in accepting a doctorate honoris causa *from that university's Faculty of Theology, he summarized his thinking about the "preferential option for the poor." As always, Gutiérrez began by tracing the his-*

torical development of the notion from Pope John XXIII through the Second Vatican Council and the Latin American bishops' conferences at Medellín (1968), Puebla (1979), and Santo Domingo (1992). He then attempted to clarify each term of the phrase—poverty, preference, and option. He concluded his remarks by considering another notion under discussion in the church today, that of the "new evangelization." An English translation of his talk was published in Promotio justitiae 57 *(1994) 11–18. The following passage contains the clarification of terms in the second part (14–16). Since it is not a redacted text, the translation preserves its original oral character.*

Perhaps the best way to grasp the challenges contained in this expression is to take it word by word: poverty, preference, and option.

POVERTY

The poverty to which I refer encompasses economic, social, and political dimensions, but it is certainly more than all that. In the final analysis poverty means death: unjust death, the premature death of the poor, physical death. It is unfortunately not only in Latin America that people die of sicknesses which medical science has long since overcome in other places. There is no reason why people should die of cholera, yet it kills many victims in my own country Peru, just as it kills people in other parts of the world, in Asia and wherever there are poor people.

Poverty therefore leads to physical death, to say nothing of situations in which people are repressed. But we must also mention cultural death. When a people is not taken into account, when a people is despised in one way or another, then in a certain sense the persons who belong to that people are also being killed. In Latin America we have a great variety of races, cultures, and languages. If these social groups are despised, then the people who belong to them are being killed. Anthropologists often say that culture is life; well, if a culture is despised, then that life is despised. This also happens when women are not accorded their full human rights.

Poverty therefore means death. In saying this, I am not trying to discount the social, economic, or political dimensions; I only want to insist on this other meaning of poverty in order to tell you that what is ultimately at stake is life itself. This is why Christian communities in Latin America often speak of the God of Life and reject unjust physical and cultural death, as well as other manifestations of selfishness and sin.

So what then do we mean by "poor"? I do not think there is any good definition, but we come close to it by saying that the poor are non-persons, the *in-significant*, those who do not count in society and all too often in Christian churches as well. A poor person, for example, is someone who has to wait a week at the door of the hospital to see a doctor. A poor person is someone without social or economic weight, who is robbed by unjust laws; someone who has no way of speaking up or acting to change the situation. Someone who belongs to a despised race and feels culturally marginalized is *in-significant*. In sum, the poor are found in the statistics, but they do not appear there with their own names. We do not know the names of the poor; they are anonymous and remain so. They are insignificant in society but not before God.

People often say to me, "You are a Latin American and so you are poor." In fact I am not poor because I am not *in-significant* since I am a priest. This must be said straight out. I try to live with the poor, but as a priest and a theologian I would be lying if I said that I was someone insignificant in my country. It would be false modesty (and to tell the truth all forms of modesty are false). It is best to acknowledge things as they are and then try, with a certain humility, to live close to the poor.

A final remark on the topic of poverty: if you talk about the poor, people will probably regard you as sensitive and generous. But if you talk about the causes of poverty, they will say to themselves, "Is this a Christian speaking? Isn't such language really political?"

On the other hand, the life of the poor is not simply one of deprivation. The poor also have a great richness to contribute. In speaking about the option for the poor, we are not speaking only of people who have absolutely nothing because they are insignificant; they also possess a great human richness.

PREFERENCE

I have often met people who find it strange to use the term "preference." Would it not be better to say simply "option for the poor" since "preferential" sounds too gentle? I do not agree. Preference implies the universality of God's love, which excludes no one. It is only within the framework of this universality that we can understand the preference, that is, "what comes first." The Bible speaks of God's preference for the poor. In Genesis, why does God prefer Abel to Cain? Nowhere does it say that Abel is better or that Cain has something evil about him. But Abel was the younger brother, the last. God preferred the sacrifice of Abel to that of Cain. Cain's sin was his refusal to accept God's preference for Abel, and so he killed him. The rejection of the preference means failing to grasp that we must combine the universality of God's love with God's preference for the poorest. And this was the expression typical of Pope John XXIII, "The Church of all, and particularly the Church of the poor." As Christians we cannot say, "Only the poor count." Such an attitude is not Christian; neither is claiming to love everyone while in fact loving no one. Holding the two aspects together—universality and preference— is not easy. It is a great challenge.

But why this preference? An analysis which lets me understand poverty is not what brings us to prefer the poorest. Analysis is surely useful, but it is not enough. Or one might think that one should prefer the poor out of human compassion. Such compassion is very important, but it is not the ultimate reason. Or again, you might say, "You talk so insistently about the poor because you are Latin American." I always answer these people, "Please try not to jump to conclusions. If I talk about poverty, it is first of all because I am a Christian, and secondarily because I am Latin American." The geographical factor, however important, comes second.

All the poor are good, some say, in order to justify the preference for them. Someone who says that gives me the impression of never having seen a poor person up close. For the poor are human beings; they include very good people, but there are also some among them who are not good. We should prefer them not because they are good (if they are, fine!) but because first of all God is good and prefers the forgotten, the oppressed, the poor, the abandoned. The ultimate and final reason for the "preference" lies in the God of our faith. This affirmation places an obligation on us because you and I believe in the same God. What I have just said applies to everyone because no one can evade this preference for the poor. How to do it?—that is another question. But if we believe in the same God, then we should walk side by side in history. The preference stems from God's goodness and it stems from God's gratuitous love, a central idea of the gospel message. God first loved us. Our lives should respond to this gratuitous initiative of God. This is the meaning of "spiritual poverty."

The great mystics—St. John of the Cross, for example—teach us how the God who gratuitously loves us constitutes the heart of the spiritual life. This does not oppose social and political commitment. Without contemplation, without prayer, we cannot conceive of Christian life. But without solidarity with the poor there is no Christian life either. So here are two dimensions which we must strive to hold together.

OPTION

The curious remark is sometimes made that "the option for the poor is something which [only] the non-poor have to make." This is not quite true, for the poor also have to opt in favor of their sisters and brothers by race, social class, and culture. And so the option for the poor is a decision incumbent upon every Christian.

20. GOD'S MEMORY

In the Introduction to Part Three of Las Casas: In Search of the Poor of Jesus Christ *called "God's Memory" (193–95), Gutiérrez claims that Las Casas's commitment to the salvation of believers and unbelievers alike, to the proclamation of the gospel to both groups, and to the life and liberty of the Indians led him to question the prevailing theology of salvation. Gutiérrez's analysis of Las Casas provides a clue to his own view of how doctrine develops in the history of the church, namely through critical reflection on the practice of faith.*

In the Indies, Europeans encountered entire nations that had no knowledge of the gospel. This was an altogether new experience for them. Furthermore, these unbelievers, or infidels, were not enemies, nor were they usurpers of Christian lands. Nothing of the kind had ever been known to medieval Christendom, which, for that matter, was little concerned (apart from the remarkable case of Raymond Lull) with the evangelizing of the Jews or the Muslims. To this it must be added that the historical relationship of Jews or Muslims to Christian nations was very different from that of the dwellers of the Indies.

The novelty was so overwhelming that it gave rise to strange theses about the Indians—such as that they were descendants of the lost tribes of Israel or of peoples who had once received a proclamation of the gospel by the apostle Thomas. Bartolomé de Las Casas's concerns were different. He never entertained such bizarre notions. One of the reasons he held aloof from theories like these—and the point is worthy of mention—was that certain individuals appealed to them to justify the wars being waged on the Indians. After all, in the supposition of an earlier Christianization or evangelization, the natives of the Indies would have to be regarded as apostates from the faith, which they had once received, or at least as recalcitrant hearers of a gospel that had been proclaimed to them once upon a time. On this supposition, in the thinking of the age, acts of violence against the Indians—in defense of the true faith, which they had abandoned—became legitimate. There is no innocent theology!

The proclamation of the gospel, as we have seen, was the major concern of the great missionary Bartolomé de Las Casas. But precisely here, on this central point of the Christian message—the proclamation of the gospel—Bartolomé's experience of the New World stirs him to a rereading that will lead him to interesting theological intuition, and distance him from the Western, and ultimately comfortable, theology of salvation dominant in his time. The concrete problem with which Bartolomé de Las Casas begins, without knowing where it will lead, is how to proclaim salvation in the Indies, that is, under the conditions (and with the implications) dictated by the concrete reality. We speak of "intuitions," and of a "distancing" from a certain theology of salvation, because in fact we are dealing with something rich and promising but still incipient. It could scarcely have been otherwise.

God's salvific activity is the content of evangelization and "is the end, or final cause, for which these [Indies] have been granted by the church to the Sovereigns of Castile and León, who until now have had no stake in them." This "final cause" is the criterion which allows one to sift events of the Indies and by which the legitimacy or illegitimacy of the Spanish presence in the Indies must be judged. On this foundation, then, a norm of behavior arises. The required behavior will be "obligatory under pain of the eternal damnation" for those who have responsibility in these matters. The idea is plain and exacting: the eternal salvation of believers is rightly linked to that of unbelievers. . . .

Salvation of unbelievers and believers, proclamation of the gospel to both, and defense of the Indians' life and liberty: here are Las Casas's great concerns. They all have their foundation in his experience—and his notion—of God, whose solicitude for the abandoned of history Bartolomé expresses in a beautiful phrase of profoundly biblical inspiration: "God has a very fresh and living memory of the smallest and most forgotten.". . .

The questions presented to Las Casas by the deadly reality of the Indies with respect to the salvation of unbelievers [are further complicated by the] thorny matter of human sacrifices. This endows the problem with all the more urgency once freedom in religious matters is presumed to be required. How is this concrete reality to be appraised from a theological viewpoint? As he begins to address the subject, Bartolomé is forced into uncharted territory. The only map he has consists of the distinctions he finds in scholastic theology, which he makes use of but goes beyond as well, and on more than one occasion.

Bartolomé begins with the theology that has been bequeathed to him, but he endeavors to extract from it the greatest possible advantage for his combat in defense of the life and rights of the Indians. His notion of God and his concern for the eternal destiny of those who call themselves Christians will assist him in broadening his perspectives. Las Casas will not divorce salvation from justice. The achievement of the latter is a condition for gaining the former.

The theology of the age was very rigid concerning the salvation of non-Christians. But Las Casas, like certain others of his time, gradually comes to perceive that the new facts do not fit into the abstract mold of the dominant doctrine. This leads him to glimpse pathways little trodden in his day. Paradoxically, along these "new" routes he rediscovers positions maintained in the first centuries of the church (and thus more traditional than the theology of salvation of his time), which theology and the magisterium of the church have recovered in our own day. Once more his sense of the mystery of God and of the certainty of God's love for the last and least of history enables him to chart new routes.

Three

THEOLOGICAL AXIS:
THE GRATUITOUSNESS
AND EXIGENCE OF LOVE

The central axis of Gutiérrez's entire theology is the gratuitous yet demanding, universal yet preferential, love of God. The richness and complexity of these dialectical pairs are the source of the originality, profundity, and potency of Gutiérrez's understanding of God, humanity, salvation, Jesus Christ, and the church. Texts that deal with the second pair (the universality and preference of divine love) are found in Chapter Two of this volume. The selections in Chapter Three illustrate the evolution and the continuity of Gutiérrez's views on grace.

At bottom Gutiérrez believes that the free gift of God's love, made concrete above all in the gift of life, may awaken a sense of gratitude in the one who accepts it. Gratitude, however, does not stop at contemplating the gift; thankfulness gives rise to the desire to love in return. Here is the source of the "demand" to love, especially through life-giving acts. The exigency to which Gutiérrez refers, then, is interior to love; that is, it comes from love, and cannot be commanded from without, even by God. In this framework, to say that love makes demands on those who receive it as a free gift does not erase its gratuitous character. Gratuitousness and exigency together typify love; each implies the other.

21. CONVERSION TO THE NEIGHBOR

While joining many others in asserting the unity of love of God and love of neighbor, Gutiérrez also saw as few others did in the first years after the Council a further inescapable consequence of God's identification with humankind. Thanks in no small measure to his work, it has now become difficult to overlook the fact that the neighbor who most mediates the presence of God is "not the one whom I find in my path, but rather the one in whose path I place myself." As Gutiérrez's extended commentary on the parables of the last judgment (Matt. 25:31–46) and good Samaritan (Luke 10:29–37) makes clear, "neighbor" denotes in particular the wounded or needy. Taken from Theology of Liberation *(110–16), the following text is an expansion of a 1966 article called "Caridad y amor humano" ("Charity and Human Love") in which*

Gutiérrez joined European theologians in asserting the primacy of love in Christian life and therefore in theology. The text below sets the stage for the later development of the notion of the preferential option for the poor. Here we can already see how our option for the poor must be based on God's prior choice of the needy with its twofold purpose: their rescue and our conversion. The term "conversion" suggests the difficulty that privileged persons may have in genuinely "turning to" (that is, recognizing, identifying with, and standing alongside) their abused or neglected neighbors.

The modes of God's presence determine the forms of our encounter with God. If humanity, each person, is the living temple of God, we meet God in our encounter with others; we encounter God in the commitment to the historical becoming of humankind.

TO KNOW GOD IS TO DO JUSTICE

The Old Testament is clear regarding the close relationship between God and the neighbor. This relationship is a distinguishing characteristic of the God of the Bible. To despise one's neighbor (Prov. 14:21), to exploit the humble and poor worker, and to delay the payment of wages, is to offend God: "You shall not keep back the wages of a man who is poor and needy, whether a fellow-countryman or an alien living in your country in one of your settlements. Pay him his wages on the same day before sunset, for he is poor and his heart is set on them: he may appeal to the Lord against you, and you will be guilty of sin" (Deut. 24:14–15; cf. Exod. 22:21–23). This explains why "a man who sneers at the poor insults his maker" (Prov. 17:5).

Inversely, to know, that is to say, to love Yahweh is to do justice to the poor and oppressed. When Jeremiah proclaimed the New Covenant, after asserting that Yahweh would inscribe the law in the hearts of human beings, Jeremiah said: "No longer need they teach one another to know the Lord; all of them, high and low alike, shall know me" (31:34). But Jeremiah advises us exactly on what knowing God entails:

Shame on the man who builds his house by unjust means, and completes its roof-chambers by fraud, making his countrymen work without payment, giving them no wage for their labor! Shame on the man who says, "I will build a spacious house with airy roof-chambers, set windows in it, panel it with cedar, and paint it with vermilion"! If your cedar is more splendid, does that prove you are a king? Think of your father: he ate and drank, dealt justly and fairly; all went well with him. He dispensed justice to the cause of the lowly and poor; did this not show he knew me? says the Lord (22:13–16).

Where there is justice and righteousness, there is knowledge of Yahweh; when these are lacking, it is absent: "There is no good faith or mutual trust, no knowledge of God in the land, oaths are imposed and broken, they kill and rob;

there is nothing but adultery and license, one deed of blood after another" (Hos. 4:1–2; cf. Isa. 1). To know Yahweh, which in biblical language is equivalent to saying to love Yahweh, is to establish just relationships among persons, it is to recognize the rights of the poor. The God of biblical revelation is known through interhuman justice. When justice does not exist, God is not known; God is absent. Medellín asserts: "Where this social peace does not exist there will we find social, political, economic, and cultural inequalities, there will we find the rejection of the peace of the Lord, and a rejection of the Lord himself" (*Peace* §14).

On the other hand, if justice is done, if the alien, the orphan, and the widow are not oppressed, "[t]hen I will let you live in this place, in the land which I gave long ago to your forefathers for all time" (Jer. 7:7). This presence of Yahweh is active; Yahweh "deals out justice to the oppressed. The Lord feeds the hungry and sets the prisoner free. The Lord restores sight to the blind and straightens backs which are bent; the Lord loves the righteous and watches over the stranger; the Lord gives heart to the orphan and widow but turns the course of the wicked to their ruin." So "the Lord shall reign forever" (Ps. 146:7–10).

This encounter with God in concrete actions toward others, especially the poor, is so profound and enriching that by basing themselves on it the prophets can criticize—always validly—all purely external worship. This criticism is but another aspect of the concern for asserting the transcendence and universality of Yahweh. "Your countless sacrifices, what are they to me? says the Lord; I am sated with whole offerings of rams. . . . The offer of your gifts is useless, the reek of sacrifice is abhorrent to me. . . . Though you offer countless prayers, I will not listen. There is blood on your hands. . . . Cease to do evil and learn to do right, pursue justice and champion the oppressed; give the orphan his rights, plead the widow's cause" (Isa. 1:10–17). We love God by loving our neighbor: "Is not this what I require of you as a fast: to loose the fetters of injustice, to untie the knots of the yoke, to snap every yoke and set free those who have been crushed? Is it not sharing your food with the hungry, taking the homeless poor into your house, clothing the naked when you meet them and never evading a duty to your kinsfolk?" (Isa. 58:6–7). Only then will God be with us, only then will God hear our prayer and will we be pleasing to God (Isa. 58:9–11). God wants justice, not sacrifices. Emphasizing the bond between the knowledge of God and interhuman justice, Hosea tells us that Yahweh wishes knowledge and not holocausts: "O Ephraim, how shall I deal with you? How shall I deal with you, Judah? Your loyalty to me is like the morning mist, like dew that vanishes early. Therefore have I lashed you through the prophets and torn you to shreds with my words; loyalty is my desire, not sacrifice, not whole-offerings but the knowledge of God" (Hos. 6:4–6).

Although it is true that in the texts cited the neighbor is essentially a member of the Jewish community, the references to aliens, who together with widows and orphans form a classic trilogy, indicate an effort to transcend these limitations. Nevertheless, the bond between the neighbor and God is changed, deepened, and universalized by the Incarnation of the Word. The famous text so often quoted in recent years, Matt. 25:31–45, is a very good illustration of this twofold process.

CHRIST IN THE NEIGHBOR

The parable of the final judgment, which concludes Matthew's eschatological discourse, seems to many to summarize the essence of the gospel message. Exegetes are alarmed by the way that many theologians use this text and by the consequences which have been deduced for Christian life. Various recent studies have attempted to deal with these new questions; they have not, however, delved into the basic problems. There are many factors involved in the reevaluation of the text. It is fertile soil for research by exegetes and theologians.

Jean-Claude Ingelaere, author of the most extensive and detailed of the studies made along these lines, observes that this pericope poses two fundamental questions: who are the nations judged by the Son of God and who are "the least of the brethren" of the Son of man? In relation to these two questions, Ingelaere distinguishes three lines of interpretation of this text which have developed to date: some believe that this is a judgment of all persons—Christians and non-Christians—according to their love of neighbor, and particularly of the needy; others see in this a judgment of Christians with regard to their behavior toward the disadvantaged members of the Christian community itself (Origen, Luther); and finally, a minority believe it refers to the judgment of pagans based on their attitude toward Christians. The author obviously opts for the third interpretation. Although the work is thorough and well documented, it is less than convincing. The two restrictions involved in this third exegesis—although they do easily resolve various minor questions (for example, the failure to recognize Christ implied in the question, "When did we see you hungry?" etc.)—go against the obvious sense of the text and the context, which stress the universality of the judgment and the central and universal character of charity. This is actually an attempt to revive an old thesis of H. J. Holtzmann, hardly mentioned by Ingelaere, which M. J. Lagrange, based on Loisy, Weiss, and Wellhausen, characterized as "strangely illogical." The majority of the exegetes opt for what Ingelaere considers the first interpretation. The henotheistic expression "all nations" (v. 32) is considered to have a "clearly universal sense." According to Mühlen, it includes "not the pagans as distinguished from the Jews and the Christians, but in fact all persons: pagans, Jews, and Christians. On the other hand, there is also a general consensus regarding the universality of the content of the expression: "the least of my brethen" (v. 40). This term designates "all the needy, whoever they may be, and not only Christians."

This is the line of thinking we will follow. The passage is rich in teachings. Basing our study on it and in line with the subject which interests us, we wish to emphasize three points: the stress on communion and fellowship as the ultimate meaning of human life; the insistence on a love which is manifested in concrete actions, with "doing" being favored over simple "knowing"; and the revelation of the human mediation necessary to reach the Lord.

The human person is destined to total communion with God and to the fullest fellowship with all other persons. "Dear friends, let us love one another, because love is from God. Everyone who loves is a child of God and knows God, but the unloving know nothing of God. For God is love" (1 John 4:7–8). This was Christ's revelation. To be saved is to reach the fullness of love; it is to enter into the circle of charity which unites the three persons of the Trinity; it is to love as God loves. The way to this fullness of love can be no other than love itself, the way of participation in this charity, the way of accepting, explicitly or implicitly, to say with the Spirit: "Abba, Father" (Gal. 4:6). Acceptance is the foundation of all communion among human persons. To sin is to refuse to love, to reject communion and fellowship, to reject even now the very meaning of human existence. Matthew's text is demanding: "Anything you did not do for one of these, however humble, you did not do for me" (25:45). To abstain from serving is to refuse to love; to fail to act for another is as culpable as expressly refusing to do it. This same idea is found later in John: "The man who does not love is still in the realm of death" (1 John 3:14). The parable of the Good Samaritan ends with the famous inversion which Christ makes of the original question. They asked him, "Who is my neighbor?" and when everything seemed to point to the wounded man in the ditch on the side of the road, Christ asked, "Which of these three do you think was neighbor to the man who fell into the hands of the robbers?" (Luke 10:29, 36). The neighbor was the Samaritan who *approached* the wounded man and *made him his neighbor.* The neighbor, as has been said, is not the one whom I find in my path, but rather the one in whose path I place myself, the one whom I approach and actively seek. The other aspects of the Christian life become meaningful if they are animated by charity; otherwise, in Paul's words, they simply are empty actions (cf. 1 Cor. 13). This is why Matthew's text says we will be definitively judged by our love for others, by our capacity to create comradely conditions of life. From a prophetic viewpoint, the judgment ("crisis") will be based, according to Matthew, on the new ethic arising from this universal principle of love.

But this charity exists only in concrete actions (feeding the hungry, giving drink to the thirsty, etc.); it occurs of necessity in the fabric of relationships among persons. "Faith divorced from deeds is barren" (James 2:20). To know God is to do justice: "If you know that he is righteous, you must recognize that every man who does right is his child" (1 John 2:29). But charity does not exist alongside or above human loves; it is not "the most sublime" human achievement like a grace superimposed upon human love. Charity is God's love in us and does not exist outside our human capabilities to love and to build a just and friendly world, to "establish ties" as Saint-Exupéry says. "But if a man has enough to live on, and yet when he sees his brother in need shuts up his heart against him, how can it be said that the divine love dwells in him? My children, love must not be a matter of words or talk; it must be genuine and show itself in action" (1 John 3:17–18). Loving us as a human, Christ reveals to us the Father's love. Charity, the love of God for human beings, is found incarnated in human love—of parents, spouses, children, friends—and it leads to its fullness. The Samaritan approached the injured man on the side of the road not because of some cold religious obligation, but because "his heart was melting"(this is literally what the verb *splankhnizein* means in Luke 10:33; cf. Luke 1:7, 8; 7:13; 15:20), because his love for that man was made flesh in him. . . .

We turn to the third idea we wished to consider in connection with this text of Matthew: human mediation to reach God. It is not enough to say that love of God is inseparable from the love of one's neighbor. It must be added that love for God is unavoidably expressed *through* love of one's neighbor. Moreover, God is loved in the neighbor: "But if a man says, 'I love God,' while hating his brother, he is a liar. If he does not love the brother whom he has seen, it cannot be that he loves God whom he has not seen" (1 John 4:20). To love one's brother, to love all persons, is a necessary and indispensable mediation of the love of God; it is to love God: "You did it for me, . . . you did not do it for me." In his perceptive homily at the closing of the Council, Paul VI commented on Matthew's text saying that "a knowledge of humankind is a prerequisite for a knowledge of God"; and he summarized the objective of the Council as "a pressing and friendly invitation to humankind of today to rediscover in fraternal love the God [to use the words of St. Augustine] 'to turn away from Whom is to fall, to turn to Whom is to rise again, to remain in Whom is to be secure, to return to Whom is to be born again, in Whom to dwell is to live.'". . .

But really this conclusion is valid not only for Christians, but for all persons who, in one way or another, welcome the Word of the Lord into their heart. God's presence in humanity, in each person, which is expressed, for example, in the idea of the temple mentioned above, seems to us more fruitful and richer in ramifications. It is in the temple that we find God, but in a temple of living stones, of closely related persons, who together make history and fashion themselves. God is revealed in history, and it is likewise in history that persons encounter the Word made flesh. Christ is not a private individual; the bond which links him to all persons gives him a unique historical role. God's temple is human history; the "sacred" transcends the narrow limits of the places of worship. We find the Lord in our encounters with others, especially the poor, marginated, and exploited ones. An act of love toward them is an act of love toward God. This is why Yves Congar speaks of "the sacrament of our neighbor," who as a visible reality reveals to us and allows us to welcome the Lord: "But there is one thing that is privileged to be a paradoxical sign of God, in relation to which men are able to manifest their deepest commitment—our Neighbor. The sacrament of our Neighbor!"

Nevertheless, the neighbor is not an occasion, an instrument, for becoming closer to God. We are dealing with a real love of persons for their own sake and not "for the love of God," as the well-intended but ambiguous and ill-used cliché would have it—ambiguous and ill-used because many seem to interpret it in a sense which forgets that the love for God is expressed in a true love for persons themselves. This is the only way to have a true encounter with God. That my action toward another is at the same time an action toward God does not detract from its truth and concreteness, but rather gives it even greater meaning and import.

It is also necessary to avoid the pitfalls of an individualistic charity. As has been insisted in recent years, the neighbor is not only a person viewed individually. The term refers also to a person considered in the fabric of social relationships, to a person situated in economic, social, cultural, and racial coordinates. It likewise refers to the exploited social class, the dominated people, the marginated. The masses are also our neighbor as M.-D. Chenu asserts. This point of view leads us far beyond the individualistic language of the I-Thou relationship. Charity is today a "political charity," according to the phrase of Pius XII. Indeed, to offer food or drink in our day is a political action; it means the transformation of a society structured to benefit a few who appropriate to themselves the value of the work of others. This transformation ought to be directed toward a radical change in the foundation of society, that is, the private ownership of the means of production.

Our encounter with the Lord occurs in our encounter with others, especially in the encounter with those whose human features have been disfigured by oppression, despoliation, and alienation and who have "no beauty, no majesty" but are the things "from which men turn away their eyes" (Isa. 53:2–3). These are the marginal groups, who have fashioned a true culture for themselves and whose values one must understand if one wishes to reach them. The salvation of humanity passes through them; they are the bearers of the meaning of history and "inherit the kingdom" (James 2:5). Our attitude toward them, or rather our commitment to them, will indicate whether or not we are directing our existence in conformity with the will of the Father. This is what Christ reveals to us by identifying himself with the poor in the text of Matthew. A theology of the neighbor, which has yet to be worked out, would have to be structured on this basis.

22. FREEDOM AS A GIFT AND TASK AT PUEBLA

Freedom, like the love it makes possible, is understood by Gutiérrez as both a gift and a task. While the theology of Vatican II largely moved beyond an earlier view of Christian discipleship as a straightforward matter of obedience to divine authority, the Council favored the language of moral exhortation, which continues to understand authority in extrinsicist terms. In Gutiérrez's formulation of the theology of liberation, the human task arises out of profound gratitude for God's freely given gifts (freedom and love). In this framework human beings accept God's gift precisely in dedicating themselves to others, especially the most vulnerable. Thus, Gutiérrez insists on the purpose for which God frees us, namely to love (and not simply to be able to obey divine commands). In this paradigm, then, Christian life is understood as both gift and task, the unity of which originates in the very gratuitousness of God's love. Such a dialectic forms the central axis of nearly all of Gutiérrez's writings, including the following passage from his 1979 commentary on the results of the Puebla conference, "Pobres y liberación en Puebla." The English translation (revised here) is found in Power of the Poor, *145–48.*

Medellín had spoken of the muffled cry for liberation of millions of Latin Americans (*Poverty* §2). Puebla asserts that, ten years later, things have changed: "The cry might well have seemed muffled back then. Today it is loud and clear, increasing in volume and intensity, and at times full of menace" (§89).

Puebla recognizes that the yearning for liberation in Latin America has become even more urgent and demanding than before. In his addresses in Santo Domingo and Mexico [in 1979], the pope had already spoken in this vein more than once, and now Puebla takes up the theme—frequently employing the adjective "integral." Hence it is important to see what Puebla means by "integral." One text is especially worthy of note. It expatiates on the integral character of true liberation, and makes some important precisions. This passage, part of the contribution of the Commission on Human Dignity, is so long (§§321–29) that we can cite only a few extracts, paraphrasing and condensing the rest.

After asserting that freedom is a gift and a task, which "cannot be truly achieved without integral liberation (John 8:36)," and which "in a real sense . . . is the goal of human beings, according to our faith," Puebla cites a text from St. Paul that has played an important role in our thinking about liberation—Galatians 5:1. The apostle says, "When Christ freed us, he meant us to remain free" (§321). Puebla goes on to say that to turn the establishment of community and of active participation (rooted in freedom understood as the capacity to take charge of ourselves) into definitive realities is something which must be done "on three inseparable planes: our relationship to the world as its master, to other persons as brothers or sisters, and to God as God's children" (§322). There follows a detailed presentation of these three planes (§§323–25). Finally, their intimate links with one another are expounded, as based upon a profound unity:

Through the indissoluble unity of these three planes, the exigencies of communion and participation flowing from human dignity appear more clearly. If our freedom is fully realized on the transcendent plane by our faithful and filial acceptance of God, then we enter into loving communion with the divine mystery and share its very life (*Gaudium et spes,* 18). The opposite alternative is to break with filial love, to reject and despise the Father. These are the two extreme possibilities, which Christian revelation calls grace and sin respectively. But these two possibilities do not occur without simultaneously reaching the other two planes. This has enormous consequences for human dignity [§326].

The last two points are an effort to identify the relationship between the third plane—one's relationship with God—and the other two: the relationship among persons and the relationship between persons and the material world (§323). The link between the third and second planes will be "first and foremost a labor of justice":

> The love of God, which is the root of our dignity, necessarily becomes loving communion with other human beings and fraternal participation. For us today it must become first and foremost a labor of justice on behalf of the oppressed. The fact is that "one who has no love for the brother he has seen cannot love the God he has not seen" (1 John 4:20) [§327].

This "labor of justice," then, means the effort of liberation. The link with the first plane is expressed in a transformation of the material world with a view to the construction of a just lordship there—one that will consist in a true communion of sisters and brothers:

> Authentic communion and participation can exist in this life only if they are projected on to the very concrete plane of temporal realities, so that mastery, use, and transformation of the goods of this earth and those of culture, science, and technology find embodiment in humanity's just and fraternal lordship over the world—which would include respect for ecology [§327].

Next, the document reaffirms the inseparability of the planes, following the schema of grace and sin indicated above. First, grace: the document sets forth the concrete social and historical demands of the love of God, of friendship with God:

> Confronted with the realities that are part of our lives today, we must learn from the gospel that in Latin America we cannot truly love our fellow human beings, and hence God, unless we commit ourselves on the personal level, and in many cases on the structural level as well, to serving and promoting the most dispossessed and downtrodden human groups and social classes, with all the consequences that will entail on the plane of temporal realities [§327].

There is no love for God without love for one's brothers and sisters, particularly those who are most poor, and this means—the document could not be clearer—a commitment on the level of social structures, "with all the consequences that will entail on the plane of temporal realities."

Now the document looks at what happens in the other half of the schema: sin. Of course the picture just presented is only reinforced. The concrete, historical consequences of sin—breach of friendship with God—are inevitable:

> Sinfulness on the personal level, the break with God that debases the human being, is always mirrored on the level of interpersonal relations in a corresponding egotism, haughtiness, ambition, and envy. These traits produce injustice, domination, violence at every level, and conflicts between individuals, groups, social classes, and peoples. They also produce corruption, hedonism, aggravated sexuality, and superficiality in mutual relations (cf. Gal. 5:19–21) [§328].

All this is a description of the creation of a situation of sin, a notion that, as we have already mentioned, was central in Medellín and which Puebla here takes up again with greater force and insistence: "Thus they establish sinful situations which, at the worldwide level, enslave countless human beings and adversely affect the freedom of all" (§328).

Sin, the breach with God, is not something that occurs only within some intimate sanctuary of the heart. It "always" moves into interpersonal relationships, the document says, and hence is the ultimate root of all injustice and oppression—as well as of the social confrontations and conflicts of concrete history, whose existence among us the document makes no attempt to sidestep.

This is how far one must go if one wishes to grasp the meaning of Christ's liberation and all its implications. As Medellín says, in a now familiar passage:

> It is the same God who, in the fullness of time, sends his Son in the flesh, so that he might come to liberate all people from the slavery to which sin has subjected them: hunger, misery, oppression and ignorance, in a word, that injustice and hatred which have their origin in human selfishness [*Justice* §3].

Puebla takes up the same idea, in the conclusion of this long passage on manner of understanding the expression "integral liberation"—and reasserts from this viewpoint the inseparability of the three planes that have now been so carefully expounded:

> It is from this sin, sin as the destroyer of human dignity, that we all must be liberated. We are liberated by our participation in the new life brought to us by Jesus Christ, and by communion with him in the mystery of his death and resurrection. But this is true only on the condition that we live out this mystery on the three planes described above, without focusing exclusively on any one of them. Only in this way will we avoid reducing the mystery to the verticalism of a disembodied spiritual union with God, to the mere existential personalism of individual or small-group ties, or to one or another form of social, economic, or political horizontalism (John Paul II, Opening Address at Puebla, III, 6) [§329].

Puebla has the perspicacity to insist on the pope's integral focus—which condemns not only horizontal reductionism (the shibboleth of the polemicists) but the vertical as well, so frequently passed over in silence.

The passage is crystal clear. And the precision of its language recaptures the best of Latin American reflection on the point at issue. Puebla does not fall prey to the terrorist attitudes of those who undertake to ignore the complex, rich meaning of the term "liberation" as it has been used during recent years—years of increasing commitment, in the form of Christian practice and reflection, to the struggles of an exploited community of believers to build a humane and just society. Their communion with the death and resurrection of Jesus Christ, at the heart of this battle, is the magnificent witness of this people during these years.

To live the love of Christ to the point of giving one's life for one's sisters and brothers, affirming one's hope in the life of the resurrected Christ who vanquishes all death and injustice, is the central element of the power of the poor in history. This is why the aspirations and struggles of the poor for liberation are a threat to the great ones of this world, those who reap the benefits of a social order where they sow death—but fail to stifle hope.

This long passage, then, is the key to the correct understanding of the term "integral liberation," so frequently used in Puebla. It is in light of this notion of integral liberation that the whole series of Puebla documents on the subject should be read.

23. FREE TO LOVE

From the beginning Gutiérrez's work stressed the theological *link between freedom and love. His 1966 study of love in the Bible ("Caridad y amor humano") concluded that "the disciples are chosen for love; that is why they are sent and that will be their testimony." Employing a Pauline intuition, he notes in* Theology of Liberation *that, in the final analysis, liberation serves a purpose beyond freedom. "Free for what? Free to love" (24). Consequently, love must guide the process of liberation. The introduction to Part Three of* We Drink from Our Own Wells *(1984; 91–94) summarizes his thinking on the subject.*

Encounter with the Lord, a life according to the Spirit, a wayfaring that embraces all aspects of life and is done in community: these are dimensions of every journeying in search of God.

In this process the way is carved out as we go, because no previously traced route exists. Spirituality, as I have said repeatedly, is the area of the Spirit's action; it is therefore characterized by freedom. To quench the Spirit (1 Thess. 5:19) is to do away with the fruit of the Spirit: love and those actions in relation to God and neighbor in which love finds expression; with regard to these "there is no law" (Gal. 5:23). Law in this context is external coercion and, as such, is associated with the flesh and death.

St. James can therefore say: "So speak and so act as those who are to be judged under *the law of liberty*" (James 2:12). The law of freedom, the law of the Spirit, is the law by which will be judged the works without which faith is dead (James 2:14, 26). We know too that, according to the Letter of James, these works are above all those done for the "poor in the world" whom God has chosen as "heirs of the kingdom which he has promised to those who love him" (2:5).

Jesus gives us an example of freedom as a distinguishing trait of a life in the service of others. This service is expressed in and acquires its meaning from the way in which Jesus controls the surrender of his own life: "No one takes [my life] from me, but I lay it down of my own accord" (John 10: 18). This is the attitude of one who comes to decisions without being influenced by external pressures, and who makes these decisions out of love for others. Jesus freely decides to give his life in *solidarity* with those who are under the power of death. Freedom exercised within a communion of life: such is the meaning of Christian freedom, such is the context for its full development.

[Earlier] I analyzed certain passages of Paul (e.g., Gal. 5:1 and 13). It was these texts that gave rise to the familiar distinction, taken over by St. Thomas Aquinas among others, between freedom *from* and freedom *for*. "Freedom from" refers to freedom from sin, from selfishness, from injustice, from need; all these are conditions that call for a liberation. "Freedom for" states the purpose of the freedom acquired: freedom for love, for communion; the attainment of love and communion is the final stage in liberation. "Free to love": this phrase, inspired by Paul (another text in the same line is that of 1 Cor. 9:19: "though I am free from all men, I have made myself a slave to all [*edoulosa*]") expresses the full meaning of the process of liberation to which many Latin American Christians are committed. In the final analysis, to set free is to give life—communion with God and with others—or, to use the language of Puebla, liberation for communion and participation.

In this context of the struggle for liberation for the sake of love and justice, a distinctive way of following Jesus is coming into existence in Latin America. A new spirituality is in the germinal stage there; because it is germinal it cannot as yet be sketched out in detail for the purposes of labeling it and circumscribing it by characteristic traits. At present we are in the position of those trying to decide whom a newborn child resembles. Some will say the father, others the mother; some will even find that the child has this grandfather's nose or that aunt's eyes, whereas still others will even be of the opinion that the child does not remind them of any family features known to them. Better to photograph the child and decide later on whom it resembles.

I am aware of this difficulty. But lest I dwell too long on the point, I shall take the risk of singling out some characteristic features of the spirituality that is now developing in Latin America. What I shall really be attempting is to organize certain experiences and the reflections they provoke; we still lack the necessary perspective and distance to proceed in any other fashion. The traits I shall point out will therefore not be sharply defined and will call for a good deal of nuancing; some of them may have to be dropped, others added.

As in the case of other spiritual ways that I have previously called to the reader's attention, the major themes of collective Christian experience in Latin America are those proper to Christian existence in its entirety. Here, too, reorganization is being carried out in view of some central intuitions regarding the demands of the historical moment. Our experiences in the framework of commitment to the poor and oppressed of Latin America are sending us back to fundamental ideas in the gospels. It could not be otherwise. These experiences are suggesting new approaches and raising new questions. But at the same time the biblical message is challenging our experiences and shedding light on them.

I shall keep this circular relationship in mind when trying to suggest some features of the spirituality that is arising among us. The experience of solidarity calls for a conversion, which is the point of departure for any following of Jesus. A commitment within history calls for effective action within history, but the effort to achieve efficacy brings with it a deeper penetration into God's gratuitous love as the source of everything else and as a power that sweeps us along with it. The Latin American situation is characterized by profound suffering out of which comes a new, paschal experience of joy that flows from the gift of life. "Inhuman" and "anti-evangelical" poverty is a massive reality in our midst, but commitment to the poor and the oppressed leads to the rediscovery of a central gospel theme: spiritual childhood. Solidarity with the dispossessed has brought many Christians a painful experience of loneliness due to the isolation into which they are thrown, the suspicion that their actions arouse, or the imprisonment they suffer; this loneliness proves nonetheless to be a privileged means of grasping the deeper meaning of ecclesial community.

I think that the characteristic traits of the "walking according to the Lord" that is developing in Latin America are due to the relationships I have just described. It is important, however, not to isolate the various factors, because only when they are interconnected is it possible to grasp what is peculiar to each of the traits. When they are linked as I have linked them we shall perhaps better understand what it means to live in community or what the attitude of spiritual childhood really is. Joy in the gratuitous gift of God's love calls upon us to break with sin, injustice, and death in contemporary Latin America.

As I attempt to sketch a profile of the new way that is coming into existence among us, I shall illustrate what I am saying by stringing together texts that attempt to express the spiritual experiences that are at the heart of solidarity with the poor and dispossessed. I make no claim to completeness. The subject deserves a more comprehensive and detailed book that is presently beyond my abilities. The texts I shall cite are meant to be representative of many others, perhaps even others that are far richer. My purpose here is simply a first approach to the subject.

The fact is that daily contact with the experiences of some, a reading of the writings of many, and the testimony of still others have convinced me of the profound spiritual experiences that persons among us are having today. They are a gift from the Lord and therefore have a good deal of the ineffable about them. My hope is that what I say will not betray, even if it inevitably diminishes, the way in which the presence of the God of life is being experienced in these lands of premature and unjustly inflicted death.

24. THE CHURCH OF THE BEATITUDES

Among New Testament texts the parable of the Last Judgment (Matt. 25:31–46) and the Beatitudes of Matthew (5:1–12) and Luke (6:20–26) have occupied a central place in Gutiérrez's theology from the beginning. From the Hebrew Bible he draws most frequently on Second Isaiah and the Psalms. The story of the Exodus, while important, is not foundational for Gutiérrez. [See Jeffrey S. Siker, "Uses of the Bible in the Theology of Gustavo Gutiérrez: Liberating Scriptures of the Poor," Biblical Interpretation 4 (1996) 40–71.] In analyzing the Beatitudes, Gutiérrez is guided by the principle of the preferential option for the poor, which allows him to perceive a complementarity in the two versions based on the dialectic of gratuitousness and exigency. Refuting a commonly presumed Matthean "spiritualization" of Luke's more "material" concerns, Gutiérrez believes that Luke's version highlights the gratuitousness of God's love while Matthew emphasizes the ethical requirements inherent in God's free gift. The following passage forms the concluding section of "The Preferential Option for the Poor," a part of Gutiérrez's long essay "The Truth Shall Make You Free." It is found in The Truth Shall Make You Free *(1986; 160–64).*

According to *Libertatis conscientia,* [published in 1986 by the Vatican's Sacred Congregation for the Doctrine of the Faith] "the Beatitudes . . . enable us to situate the temporal order in relation to a transcendent order, which gives the temporal order its true measure, but without taking away its own nature" (no. 62). We must ask why they have this function.

As everyone knows, we have two versions of the Beatitudes: one in the Gospel of Luke, the other in the Gospel of Matthew. The divergence between them has given rise to many commentaries and observations. The first Beatitude sets the tone for both the similarities and the differences. Luke has: "Blessed are you poor"; Matthew adds a phrase: "Blessed are the poor in spirit"; according to both, "yours (theirs) is the kingdom of God (heaven)." Has Matthew "spiritualized" Luke's version?

Some commentators think so. On the other hand, no one can deny that the Gospel of Matthew is notably insistent on the need for concrete and "material" actions toward others and especially toward the poor (see Matt. 25:31–46). This emphasis does not seem to be compatible with a supposed Matthean "spiritualism." The seeming contradiction between the two approaches to the Beatitudes is perhaps the result of an application to the first gospel of categories that do not do justice to the originality of its outlook. Let us try to enter into the outlook.

In Luke, the first Beatitude refers to the real poor, those poor in material things. Of whom would Matthew have us think when he speaks of "the poor in spirit"?

In the biblical outlook (and the Semitic outlook generally), "spirit" indicates a relationship to something dynamic: breath, vital force. It is something which finds expression in knowledge, understanding, virtue, and decision-making. Spirit is the dynamic aspect of the human being.

The Old Testament often uses the expression "in spirit" as an addition that changes the basic meaning of certain words and gives them a figurative meaning. In Proverbs 16:18, for example, the words "lofty in spirit" are to be translated as "haughty"; in Isaiah 29:24 "erring in spirit" refers to one who has gone astray. "Poor in spirit" is a comparable expression and means something more than a lack of, or detachment from, material goods.

The verse in Matthew has at times been translated "blessed are they who choose to be poor." The intention is to avoid the spiritualist interpretation mentioned above, but, despite the good intention, the expression is somewhat defective and an ambiguity remains. On the positive side, the choice of poverty brings out the dynamic aspect of Christian life as seen in solidarity with the people at the bottom of the historical scale. On the negative side, I think that spiritual poverty refers to a situation that is more basic and more comprehensive than the choice of real poverty.

Spiritual poverty means spiritual childhood, which is a key idea in the gospel. It is a matter of complete availability to the Lord and the recognition that the Father's will is our food, as Jesus says in the Gospel of John. Spiritual childhood is the attitude of those who know themselves to be sons and daughters of God, and brothers and sisters of their fellow human beings.

"Poor in spirit" is a synonym for "disciple of Christ." The other seven Beatitudes of Matthew spell out various attitudes proper to those who are followers of the Lord. They display a peculiar characteristic of this Gospel: the emphasis on ethical requirements: to get along well with others (this is the meaning of "meek"), to practice justice, to be merciful, to be a peacemaker, and so on.

In the perspective just explained ("poor in spirit" equals "disciples"), it makes sense to say that Christians should choose a poor lifestyle. The reason is not that being poor is an ideal to be striven for but that to be a disciple *today* includes being in solidarity with the real poor, those who lack the necessities for living in the way that their dignity as human beings and children of God calls for. As Medellín reminds us, poverty according to the Bible is an evil, a situation not desired by the God of life.

It will be helpful here to look at the key role played by the theme of justice in the Matthean Beatitudes (see 5:6 and 5:10). As *Libertatis conscientia* says, "Read and interpreted in their full context, the Beatitudes express the spirit of the kingdom of God, which is to come. But, in the light of the definitive destiny of humankind thus manifested, there simultaneously appear with a more vivid clarity the foundations of justice in the temporal order" [no. 62]. It is not possible, in effect, to separate these two questions.

The establishment of justice and right is a central theme of the Old Testament, and we find it in countless passages of the Bible. The word "justice" has a twofold meaning: it is a gift of God, but it also implies a relationship between human beings. It is therefore the work of God, but it is likewise the work of the king, of the people, and of believers generally. It is both gift and task. The two aspects are closely connected. It is in the relationship between human beings that the gift of God's justice receives its historical embodiment.

Seen against this backdrop, the idea of justice proves to be extremely important and fruitful for the interpretation of the Beatitudes. In Matthew's Gospel we find seven mentions of justice, five of them in the Sermon on the Mount. In the Beatitudes themselves, justice occupies a key place.

If we look closely at the Beatitudes in Matthew, it is easy to see that they are divided into two distinct groups. The first group is inspired directly by Luke (or Luke's source) and ends with the fourth Beatitude: "Blessed are those who hunger and thirst for righteousness." The second group is Matthew's own contribution and does not have the element of contrast that the Beatitudes have in Luke. This second group also ends with a mention of justice (righteousness) in its relation to the gift of the kingdom: "Blessed are those who are persecuted for righteousness' sake, for theirs is the kingdom of heaven."

The practice of justice is required of the disciples of Christ. Therefore they are blessed if they desire ("hunger and thirst") to establish it, and they are blessed as well if they are persecuted because of it. The connection between the kingdom of God and the justice God requires is a close one throughout the Sermon on the Mount, where we find this important and indeed decisive verse: "Seek first his kingdom and his righteousness, and all these things shall be yours as well" (Matt. 6:33). As the preceding verse (32) shows, the kingdom and its justice are from the Father, and this explains their primacy in Christian life.

The practice of justice by the disciple finds expression in lifegiving actions on behalf of the neighbor and especially the most defenseless: the poor. Matthew is careful to point this out in a passage that is part of the unit in which the Beatitudes are found.

The passage on the Beatitudes ends with v. 12, but what follows is fully integrated with it. Disciples are persons called to bear witness by concrete actions. What they do must be seen by others in order that the latter may receive the message of the Beatitudes. "Good works" (5:16) is a technical expression in the Bible; it refers to "works of mercy," which are enumerated for us, in a now classic list, in Matthew 25:31–46. The visibility of these good works ("light," "lamp") is not for the sake of personal ostentation; they are to be done for the glory of God. This glorification is the ultimate purpose of the works done by the disciples of Jesus; through these works human beings are to be led to the Father. To glorify the Father means to acknowledge the primacy of his love, to adhere to his will, to be faithful to his plan for the human race.

The works done by disciples are their way of reaching the Father; in this manner they make their own the way taken by Christ. The passage on the Beatitudes really ends with v. 16 and shows us the role played by works in the attitudes proper to followers of Jesus. "Blessed are the poor in spirit" and the other Beatitudes mean: Blessed are the disciples, those who practice justice by works of love and life, and who thereby glorify the Father. This approach to the Beatitudes makes it possible to establish a fruitful relationship between the beginning of Matthew 5, where the preaching of Jesus starts, and Matthew 25, where that preaching ends. Blessed are the disciples, because they give food to the hungry and drink to the thirsty, and because they clothe the naked and visit the prisoner; in other words, because by means of concrete actions they give life and thus proclaim the kingdom.

The Beatitudes in Luke put the emphasis on the gratuitousness of the love of God, who has a predilection for the poor. The Beatitudes in Matthew fill out the picture by specifying the ethical requirements that flow from this loving initiative of God. The two approaches are complementary. Matthew does not "spiritualize" the Beatitudes; rather, if I may coin a word, he "disciple-izes" them. The Matthean approach is especially demanding: the followers of Jesus are those who translate the grace they have received into works for the neighbor and especially the poor; on this account they are called blessed and fit to enter the kingdom "prepared for you from the foundation of the world" (Matt. 25:34).

The life of disciples unfolds between gratuitousness and demand. In the passage on the Beatitudes Matthew stresses the need of specific behavior toward others. Such behavior is, a requirement flowing from the gift of the kingdom. There is nothing which demands greater solidarity with others than the gratuitousness of God's love. The church of the poor is the church of the Beatitudes, a church committed to the poor and oppressed of this world and, at the same time, completely dedicated to proclaiming the gratuitous love of God.

25. GRATUITOUSNESS AND THE FREEDOM OF GOD'S LOVE

Led to the study of the Book of Job by his own people's anguished cry for justice, Gutiérrez produced a penetrating analysis of the Hebrew masterpiece in his 1986 work Hablar de Dios desde el sufrimiento del inocente: Una reflexión sobre el libro de Job. *(English translation:* On Job: God-Talk and the Suffering of the Innocent*). A summary of this book became chapter 8 of* The God of Life, *"My Eyes Have Seen You," from which the following text is taken (1991; 154–63). Here again Gutiérrez asserts both the gratuitousness of God's love and the value of human works.*

However, as Job came to learn, it is not simply a matter of "balancing" the two; rather, the quest for justice must be situated within the framework of God's gratuitous love. There is no opposition or competition between grace (love) and justice because the gratuitousness of God's love—and this alone—makes it possible to perceive the divine predilection for the victims of injustice, a partiality which in turn impels believers to dedicate themselves to transforming the face of the earth.

The relationship between God and the poor that Job sketches and Elihu confirms [see Job 33:8–14; 34:19–30; 36:6] retrieves the ethical perspective, but in a different context and with a different meaning than it had in the doctrine of temporal retribution. As a result, a face of the Lord is now seen that has not appeared previously. Belief in God certainly brings with it the demand for certain kinds of behavior, in particular a solidarity with the poor and the oppressed. But there is now another dimension of language about God that had been hinted at in the beginning and receives increasingly strong emphasis as the Book of Job moves through its course.

BLESSED BE THE NAME OF YAHWEH

As the reader knows, the major part of the book on which I am commenting consists of a series of discourses by Job, his friends, and finally God. The theme of all the discourses is the meaning to be assigned to God's action in connection with what happens to the personage in question. But even before the discourses begin, Job himself has, in the prologue, given one interpretation of what has been happening to him. Having lost all his possessions, Job, now poor, accepts the situation, places himself in God's hands, and exclaims:

> Naked I came from my mother, naked I shall return again.
> Yahweh gave, Yahweh has taken back.
> Blessed be the name of Yahweh! [Job 1:21]

So too, in a second stage in which Job suffers from a cruel illness and is reduced to sitting on a garbage heap, he refuses to accept the impatient view of his wife who rebukes him: "Why persist in this integrity of yours? Curse God and die." He answers her: "That is how a fool of a woman talks. If we take happiness from God's hand, must we not take sorrow too?" The paragraph ends with the author of the book saying of Job: "And in all this misfortune Job uttered no sinful word" (2:8–10). That is to say, he did not speak ill of God despite his poverty, isolation, and sufferings. "He uttered no sinful word"; on the contrary, he voiced a deep sense of the gratuitous love of God. Everything comes from God and is God's gracious gift; no one, therefore, has a right to make claims on God.

Job's language is of a kind often heard among poor but believing people. On so many occasions I myself have heard unsophisticated people talking like Job: "God gave him (or her) to me, God has taken him (or her) away." The words do not express a mere resignation; there is something deeper here that an enlightened faith finds it difficult to put a finger on. The faith of the people displays a keen sense of the lordship of God; it has a spontaneous awareness of what Yahweh says in the Book of Leviticus: "Land will not be sold absolutely, for the land belongs to me, and you are only strangers and guests of mine" (Lev. 25:23). The faith of the people is marked by a profound conviction that everything belongs to the Lord and everything comes from the Lord. This conviction is finely expressed in a beautiful prayer of David: "Everything is from you, and we only give you what we have received from you. For we stand before you as aliens: we are only your guests, like all our fathers" (1 Chron. 29:15).

These initial reactions of Job contain, in inchoative form, the language of contemplation, which will take clearer shape as Job enters more deeply into his experience. It is certain, however, that if the language of the believing people remains at this inchoative level, it cannot successfully stand up to the onslaught of ideologized forms of talk about God. As a result, it is open to manipulation by theologies that are alien to the experience of ordinary folk. Furthermore, as in the case of Job, persistent poverty and suffering raise difficult questions; withdrawal and evasion in the face of these questions can end in an acceptance of evil and injustice, and even a resignation to it, which are in the final analysis contrary to faith in the God who liberates. It is necessary therefore to go more deeply into this intuition shown by the faith of the people and to strengthen it, but this process involves some ruptures.

These ruptures will come in Job's reaction to the efforts that his friends make to justify his sufferings.

CONFRONTATION WITH GOD

The three friends argue from certain principles and endeavor to apply these to the case of Job: "Hear, and know it for yourself" (5:27). These competent but mistaken theologians are sure of what they teach; Bildad will even say with a certain smugness: "Think, and then we'll talk" (18:2). In the view of these men, Job is a stubborn and rebellious man who has failed to think (the idea that Job is "patient" will not stand up to a careful reading of the book).

Job too feels certain, not about a doctrine that he is perhaps unable to refute, but about his own experience of life: *he is innocent.* The arguments of his friends seem weak to him when set over against this deep conviction. On the other hand, Job experiences moments of hopelessness. He says, for example:

If I prove myself upright, his mouth may condemn me, even if I am innocent, he may pronounce me perverse. I am innocent; life matters not to me, I despise my existence. It is all one, and hence I boldly say: he destroys innocent and guilty alike. When a sudden deadly scourge descends, he laughs at the plight of the innocent. When a country falls into the power of the wicked, he veils the face of its judges. Or if not he, who else? [9:20–24]

Bold words, these, that have their source in unbearable suffering. But his complaint is directed to a God in whom he believes; thus he is paradoxically asserting God's presence. A few verses later, Job states his wish that some "arbiter" might intervene as mediator in his dispute with God [9:32–33]. . . .

This mediator, as will become increasingly clear in the course of the book, is God. Biting protest and unsteady confidence characterize the first phase in Job's spiritual struggle. . . . While Job's friends mock him, suffering makes him "weep before God" [16:20] with increasing intensity. On this occasion, he calls for a witness, someone to defend him in his suit against God—whom, be it noted, he calls his "friend." The identity of the witness remains unclear as yet, but, knowing himself to be innocent, Job demands that there be someone to testify to his integrity. He hopes that this person will appear soon, for his own years are numbered and, once they are finished, it will be too late to see justice done.

Nevertheless, doubts and uncertainties beset and torture him [17:16]. . . . Despite these doubts Job continues to insist on the same point of departure; that is, he tries to understand God's action in the light of his own experience and not of abstract principles. Amid his confusion (and in reaction to the friends who accuse him of blaspheming), amid his destitution and suffering, and despite the fact that he feels persecuted and wounded by "the hand of God," Job makes an act of faith that seems to be without any human support:

> I know that I have a living Avenger (Go'el) and that at the end he will rise above the dust. After they pull my flesh from me, and I am without my flesh, I shall see God; I myself shall see him, and not as a stranger, my own eyes will see him. [19:25–27]

This famous and much scrutinized passage opens new perspectives. Job's experience of the Lord is becoming more profound. In a first phase, while rhetorically denying the possibility of an arbiter in his case against God, Job nonetheless called for such an arbiter to be present; he then drew a sketch of a mediator. Here this personage is called a *Go'el*, an avenger or defender. His advocate before God will be God.

A similar splitting of God can be seen in a passage of an author who had a keen awareness of human suffering and is representative in so many ways of the suffering people of Latin America. I am referring to César Vallejo, whose witness has helped me to understand the Book of Job and relate it more fully to my own experience. Shortly before his death, Vallejo dictated these dramatic and trust-filled lines to his wife Georgette: "Whatever be the cause I must defend before God after death, I myself have a defender: God." In the language of the Bible he had a *go'el*. This was a God whose fleeting presence he had felt at certain moments in his life. On this occasion, in a decisive hour of his life, he sees this God at his side as he faces the judgment that his life has merited from the same God.

AT THE WORLD'S THRESHOLD WAS GRATUITOUSNESS

Job passionately longed for God to speak to him; now, despite Elihu's skepticism, God does address him. Tapping his deepest poetical vein, the author puts the heart of his message into the mouth of God. The claim has been made that God's words do not make reference to concrete problems and therefore do not respond to Job's distress and questions. This is not correct. The divine discourse takes up the theme of God's own greatness, to which Job had referred (while adding, to be sure, some complaints) and which Elihu had made one of the main ideas of his peroration.

The author, who begins once again to call God "Yahweh," as he had at the beginning of his book, shows God challenging Job: "Who is this, obscuring my intentions with his ignorant words?" (38:2). His first discourse is devoted specifically to setting forth the foundations of his plan for creation. God will overwhelm Job with a broadside of questions, but his real purpose is to show that his freely given, unmerited love is the foundation of the world: "Where were you when I laid the earth's foundation?" [38:4]. . . .

Yahweh goes directly to the source of all existing things, to the place and time when everything began. The friends, and to some extent Job himself, thought that the world had been made in order to be immediately useful to human beings and to be of service in temporal retribution: a reward for the just, a punishment for sinners. This they regarded as the ultimate reason for God's works; therefore his action in history is foreseeable: "Have you an inkling of the extent of the earth? Tell me all about it if you have" [38:18].

The questions are beyond the ability of our protagonist to answer. Yet, always in ironical tones, God tries to get Job to answer. Thus the series of questions ends with this statement: "Surely you know, for you were born then, and the number of your days is great!" (38:21).

Other questions now follow, which make clearer what the Lord seeks to reveal. These questions play a key part in his discourse:

Who bores a channel for the downpour or clears the way for the rolling thunder so that rain may fall on lands where no one lives, and the deserts void of human dwelling, to meet the needs of the lonely wastes and make grass sprout on the thirsty ground? [38:25–27]

Rainfall in the desert may seem useless to Job and his friends, but God is not a prisoner of their ways of thinking. Rain in the wastelands is beautiful, and this beauty is its "usefulness." The Lord sends rain because God freely desires to do so; because it pleases God to see the rain. The gratuitousness of God's love, and not retribution, is the hinge on which the world turns.

The same idea is further emphasized when God speaks of God's own freedom, which is mirrored in the freedom of animals, which human beings cannot tame [39:5–12]. . . .

Is everything that exists in the natural world really meant to be domesticated by human beings and subjected to their service? God's speeches are a forceful rejection of a purely anthropocentric conception of creation. The idea of the human person as "lord of creation" has paradoxically caused us to forget the meaning of creation and the respect we owe it. Anything nonhuman seems to lie outside the history of salvation. The poet-theologian who wrote the Book of Job reacts against such a view. In his eyes, the world of nature expresses the freedom and delight of God in creating. The divine freedom refuses to be limited to the narrow confines of the cause-effect relationship.

Job is conquered, but not convinced. He takes note of what God has said to him, and he withdraws; he will not speak again: "I feel my littleness: what reply shall I give?" [40:4].

Job now knows more about God, but he does not yet know enough. The light has still not fully dawned for him. His struggle has been too extensive and too honest for him to change his opinion easily. The questions he had remain and continue to disturb him. Yahweh knows this and, consequently, does not appear satisfied with this first result. Moved, perhaps, by Job's persistence, God begins a new discourse. This time the theme will not be God's plan that springs from gratuitous love, but rather God's just government of the world. This was what Job had questioned, but if God was to deal with it in a fruitful way, God had first to situate it (as in the first speech) within the overall plan of creation and of the gratuitous love that motivates creation.

This time, despite the sarcastic tone, the Lord explains shyly and tenderly that he cannot simply destroy the wicked with a glance. He wants justice indeed, and desires that divine judgment reign in the world, but he cannot impose it, since he must respect what he has created. His power is limited by human freedom, for without freedom justice would not be present in history [40:9–14]. . .

BETWEEN GRATUITOUSNESS AND JUSTICE

Not everything, but certainly a great deal, is now clear to Job. His second answer to God is quite different in tone from the first. His attitude has changed: "I once knew you only by hearsay, now my eyes have seen you; therefore I repudiate and repent of dust and ashes" [42:5–6].

Job's former knowledge of God was indirect, gotten through others (for example, through his friends). It is different now. In his worst suffering he had cried out: "I shall see God; I myself shall see him" (19:26–27). This hope has been fulfilled. The encounter is a logical step for a man with the outlook of Job, of Job the man of prayer. At the same time, however, the closeness to God that he now experiences is beyond all his hopes: "Now my eyes have seen you." We are in the presence of profound contemplation.

The experience leads Job not to withdraw his words, but to set aside his lamentations and sadness; this is what is meant by "repenting of [changing his mind about] dust and ashes." Certain emphases in his protest had been due to the doctrine of retribution, which despite everything had continued to be his theological point of reference. Now that the Lord has overthrown that doctrine by revealing the key to the divine plan, Job realizes that he has been speaking of

God in a way that implied God was a prisoner of a narrow way of understanding the doctrine. It is this position that Job now says he is abandoning.

What is it that Job has understood? That justice does not reign in the world God has created? No. The truth that he has grasped and that has lifted him to the level of contemplation is that justice alone does not have the final say about how we are to speak of God. Only when we have come to realize that God's love is freely bestowed do we enter fully and definitively into the presence of the God of faith. Grace is not opposed to the quest for justice nor does it play it down; on the contrary, it gives it its full meaning. God's love, like all true love, operates in a world not of cause and effect but of freedom and gratuitousness. That is how persons successfully encounter one another in a complete and unconditional way: without payment of any kind of charges and without externally imposed obligations that pressure them into meeting the expectations of the other.

We saw earlier how in the debate with his friends Job came to see that he must transcend his individual experience. The dialogue brought home to him that his situation was not exceptional but was shared by the poor of this world. The new awareness in turn showed him that solidarity with the poor was required by his faith in a God who has a special love for the disinherited and exploited of human history. This preferential love is the basis for what I have been calling the prophetic way of speaking about God.

But the prophetic way is not the only way of drawing near to the mystery of God, nor is it sufficient by itself. Job has just experienced a second shift: from a penal view of history to the world of grace that completely enfolds and permeates him. In the first major step that Job had taken, he was not required to deny his personal suffering but to open himself to the suffering of others as well and to commit himself to its elimination. So in this second stage the issue is not to discover gratuitousness and forget the duty of establishing what is right and just, but to situate the quest for justice within the framework of God's gratuitous love. Only in the perspective of the latter is it possible to understand God's predilection for the poor.

This special love does not have for its ultimate motive the virtues and merits of the poor but the goodness and freedom of God, a God who is not simply the guardian of a rigid moral order. This preference for the poor—Job now realizes—is a key factor in authentic divine justice. Consequently there is no opposition between gratuitousness and justice, but there is indeed an opposition between gratuitousness and a conception of justice that can be translated into demands made of God by human beings and that renders God a prisoner of our deeds or our cultic actions. There is indeed a contradiction between the free, gratuitous, and creative love of God and the doctrine of retribution that seeks to pigeonhole God.

Inspired by the experience of his own innocence, Job bitterly criticized the theology of temporal retribution as maintained in his day and expounded by his friends. And he was right to do so. But his challenge stopped halfway and, as a result, except at moments when his deep faith and trust in God broke through, he could not escape the dilemma so cogently presented by his friends: if he was innocent, then God was guilty. God subsequently rebuked Job for remaining prisoner of this either-or mentality (see 40:8). What he should have done was to leap the fence set up around him by this sclerotic theology that is so dangerously close to idolatry, run free in the fields of God's love, and breathe an unrestricted air like the untamable animals described in God's argument. The world outside the fence is the world of gratuitousness; it is there that God dwells and there that God's friends find a joyous welcome.

The world of retribution—and not of temporal retribution only—is not where God dwells; at most he visits it. The Lord is not prisoner of the "give to me and I will give to you" mentality. Nothing, no human work however valuable, merits grace, for if it did, grace would cease to be grace. This is the heart of the message of the Book of Job. Paul will repeat it no less forcefully.

26. THE KINGDOM IS AT HAND

The words of Mark 1:15 might sound heartlessly cynical when spoken in Latin America: "This is the time of fulfillment; the kingdom of God is at hand." What can "fulfillment," "kingdom," and "at hand" mean in such a context? In the following passage from The God of Life *(1991; 98–103), Gutiérrez explains how God's gift of the kingdom presents those who receive it with the challenge of turning it into historical reality.*

At the beginning of his Gospel, Mark gives us a summary of the preaching of Jesus: "After John had been arrested, Jesus came to Galilee proclaiming the gospel of God: 'This is the time of fulfillment. The kingdom of God is at hand. Repent, and believe in the gospel'" (Mark 1:14–15). . . . With Jesus' witness, "the time of fulfillment" has come. The day of the Lord has arrived.

The Bible uses mainly two Greek words for time: *chronos* and *kairos.* The first, in addition to being the name of a Greek divinity, came to signify the quantitative, measurable, controllable aspects of time. The reference was to temporal succession as a dimension of things that was dependent on the movement of the stars. The reality meant could be measured by the calendar and the clock: "on this date, at this hour." This is the aspect of time to which we are most accustomed and which we have made part of our everyday lives; it is chronological time. Our appointment books remind us of it, sometimes painfully.

The second Greek word for time refers to something more complex. *Kairos* corresponds to a more qualitative outlook. It refers, that is, not so much to an hour or a date as to the element of human density, or, in other words, to historical significance, which is here in question. Something of this aspect of time also shows up in our everyday language, as, for example, "everyone's time comes," or when the military spoke of "D-Day" just before the Allied invasion of Europe during the Second World War. In the Bible, *kairos* signifies a propitious moment, a favorable day, a time when the Lord becomes present and manifests himself. "Behold, now is a very acceptable time" (2 Cor. 6:2; see also 1 Tim. 6:15; Heb. 1:7).

In the first chapter of Mark, the author refers to this understanding of time and speaks therefore of *kairos* and not of *chronos*. In the sentence, "This is the time of fulfillment," the meaning is that a *kairos* has arrived and not simply that a date set in advance has been reached. The implication of *kairos* is that God is now being revealed in a special way in the history in which Jesus has involved himself. The revelation is the revelation of the kingdom. Nor is the kingdom something purely interior that occurs in the depths of our souls. No, it is something planned by God that occurs at the heart of a history in which human beings live and die and welcome or reject the grace that changes them from within. The reality of the kingdom manifests itself by way of a difficult process to which Jesus alludes with his mention of John and which, more importantly, is present today in the person of Jesus the Messiah. The kingdom of love and justice is God's plan for human history; it speaks, therefore, to the whole person.

Being a Christian means being attentive to this *kairos,* this special moment of God's self-manifestation in our here and now. It means discerning the signs of the times, as John XXIII called upon us to do on the eve of the Second Vatican Council. At issue here is the authentically prophetic dimension of all Christian life. The *kairos* calls upon us to heed the judgment of God on the situation in which the great majority of people live in Latin America and in our own country [Peru]. It calls upon us to be aware that a reaction against a state of things contrary to the kingdom of life is being signaled today by gestures of solidarity among the poor, by the testimony of Christian communities that are arising among the poor and marginalized people of this world, by expressions of respect for all dimensions of the human person, by the joy and hopefulness of the poor amid their suffering, by the way men and women are learning profound prayer amid the struggle for liberation. All these phenomena are signs of the presence of the kingdom in our own history.

The kingdom is a gift, a *grace* of God, but also a *demand* made upon us. Its nearness makes these two dimensions of it all the more urgent. The two together constitute what Mark elsewhere calls "the mystery of the kingdom of God"(4:11). "Mystery," here, does not mean something enigmatic and hidden, but an enveloping reality that cannot be manipulated and within which we define the character and meaning of our lives.

The kingdom, which is the object of God's free and unmerited plan, is a dynamic reality that, for the followers of Jesus, gives history its final meaning.

"Final meaning," however, does not mean that the kingdom is located *chrono-logically* at the end of the historical process. Rather, it is something that is, if I may coin a word, "kairologically" at hand and in process of being brought to completion. This twofold aspect is captured in the term "eschatology," which refers both to the future and to the historical present or, in other words, to an event that is *already* present but has *not yet* attained its full form. There is at work here a dynamic vision of history as set in motion by the gift of the kingdom.

On the other hand, and closely connected with the point just made, the kingdom of God brings with it the demand for certain kinds of behavior. The disciples of Jesus who accept the gift of the kingdom respond to it by a specific conduct. This is the ethical dimension of the kingdom. "Repent" is the demand that accompanies the gift of the kingdom and leads to a new kind of activity in relation to God and one's brothers and sisters. Repentance, or conversion, supposes a break, but above all it means entering upon a new, and indeed constantly new, way: "Believe in the gospel." To believe is to say "Amen" to God; it is to declare our fidelity and our acceptance of the kingdom and its demands. The acceptance finds expression both in thanksgiving to God and in deeds done for our brothers and sisters. It is in this dialectic that the meaning of the kingdom emerges. The kingdom requires us to change our present reality, reject the abuses of the powerful, and establish relationships that are fraternal and just. With this way of acting we accept the gift of the Lord's presence.

The "eschatologicist" perspective (understood simply as a reference to future realities) strips ethics of its historical density and leaves it occupied with formalities that have no concrete meaning in relation to others. Here an apparently exclusive concern with God in our lives masks a forgetfulness of the demands that the God of the Bible makes upon us in relation to our brothers and sisters. This was precisely Jesus' objection to the conception of the law represented by the Pharisees, those who at that time, as today, "strain out the gnat and swallow the camel" (Matt. 23:24). The "Pharisees" are, for practical purposes, those who claim to comply with formally religious demands while at the same time exploiting and marginalizing the poor; who say they love God but do not take the side in history of those who are the privileged members of God's kingdom: the dispossessed and the needy. St. John calls them liars (see 1 John 4:20)—that is, deniers of the Lord who told us that he is "the truth" (John 14:6).

A moralist approach, meanwhile, puts the emphasis on the rights that works give in relation to God. This is a position that can at best lead to a moral humanism again alien to the teaching of Jesus, for whom thanksgiving for the gift of the Father's love is at the center of his disciples' lives and expands their vision of history. Only when the gratuitousness of this love has been grasped is it possible to understand the imperious demand for works in behalf of the neighbor.

Accepting the kingdom of God means refusing to accept a world that promotes or tolerates the premature and unjust deaths of the poor. It means rejecting the hypocrisy of a society that claims to be democratic but violates the most elementary rights of the poor. It means rejecting the cynicism of the powerful of this world. To be a disciple means proclaiming the liberation of captives and the evangelization of the poor (Luke 4:18–19) and lifting the hopes of a people that suffers age-old injustice. To accept the kingdom is to turn Mark's proclamation that "this is the time of fulfillment; the kingdom of God is at hand" into an initial historical reality. It is to find God in the dynamism that this *kairos* infuses into human history.

27. BETWEEN GIFT AND DEMAND

For Gutiérrez, Matthew's version of the Beatitudes is the church's Magna Carta, the dynamic law of Christian discipleship that requires both obedience and imaginative adaptation. The following text is found in chapter 7 of The God of Life, *"The Ethics of the Kingdom" (1991; 118–20).*

Discipleship is a central theme in the Gospel of Matthew, the nucleus around which many of the actions and sayings of Jesus crystallize. With different touches, words of encouragement, and warnings, Matthew sketches a portrait of those who follow the Lord. In my view, this perspective of his Gospel is key to understanding the meaning of his version of the Beatitudes. The difference between his version and Luke's (which is regarded by scholars as closer to the words of Jesus) is commonly attributed to his effort to "spiritualize" the Beatitudes, in the sense that he allegedly takes statements that in Luke were a concrete, historical expression of the coming of the Messiah and turns them into purely interior, unincarnated dispositions.

I do not think that this was the case. One reason, among others: it is undeniable that the Gospel of Matthew is especially insistent on the need of concrete, "material" actions toward others and especially the poor (see Matt. 5:13–16; 7:15–22; and, beyond a doubt, 25:31–46). The least that can be said is that this insistence is incompatible with an alleged Matthean "spiritualism." The apparent contradiction between these two approaches would seem to be the result of applying to the first Gospel categories inconsistent with the originality of its perspective. Let us try to enter into this perspective.

The Beatitudes open the section of the Gospel known as the Sermon on the Mount, a lengthy, polemical presentation of the new law in its relationship to the old. The sermon sets down the main ethical demands a Christian must meet. It does not limit itself to a wearisome reminder of the law in which "it was said" (see Matt. 5:21, 27, 31, 33, 38, 43), but puts the disciples on notice that they must continually seek new forms of loving others—that is, that they must fulfill the new law: "I say to you." Continuity, therefore, and newness. The Lord speaks here with the full authority with which he is invested. An ethics that has its roots in the gratuitousness of God's love is always creative. Christian Duquoc is right when he says that in the sermon "justice is linked to the order of gift and gratuitousness."

The justice in question, which "surpasses that of the scribes and Pharisees" (Matt. 5:20), is not limited to obeying precepts but draws its inspiration from an ever new and imaginative love. It leads us to the kingdom and makes the kingdom present even now in history. Kingdom and justice (gift and task) are the two key words that enable us to see the basic structure of the carefully constructed text that is the Beatitudes. The first and last of these speak of the promise of the kingdom here and now (the other six Beatitudes use the future tense). Each block of four Beatitudes (containing thirty-six words in the original Greek text) ends with the mention of justice:

to the poor in spirit	belongs the kingdom of heaven
the meek	will inherit the earth
they who mourn	will be comforted
they who hunger and thirst for justice	will be satisfied
the merciful	will be shown mercy
the clean of heart	will see God
the peacemakers	will be called children of God
to them who are persecuted for the sake of justice	belongs the kingdom of heaven

The kingdom is the center of Jesus' message, the utopia that sets history in motion for Christians. As everyone knows, Matthew speaks of "the kingdom of heaven" in order to avoid mentioning the name of God, out of a respect that is inborn in the Jewish mind. Justice is a theme closely connected with that of the kingdom.

Matthew retains the richness and complexity of the term "justice" in the Bible. Justice is the work of God and for this very reason must also be the work of those who believe in God. It implies a relationship with the Lord—namely, holiness; and at the same time a relationship with human beings—namely, recognition of the rights of each person and especially of the despised and the oppressed, or, in other words, social justice. In various ways, even when he is not using the word justice, Matthew reminds us of this demand of the kingdom: to do what is right and just. In a pithy summarizing statement, which comes right in the middle of the sermon, Matthew says forcefully: "Seek first the kingdom of God and his righteousness" (6:33).

The kingdom and its six specific descriptions are the reason for the happiness to which the Beatitudes bear witness; in all of them this reason is clearly asserted: the people described are blessed or happy "because" the promise is fulfilled now and will be in the future. The gift of the Lord produces happiness in those who dispose themselves to receive it and who act accordingly. The Beatitudes are clearly located in the dialectic of gift and demand.

28. THE WAY OF WORKS

In Gutiérrez brilliant intellect and graceful prose combine to illuminate the insistent challenge of the gospel. The following passages, taken from the concluding section of chapter 7 of The God of Life, *"The Ethics of the Kingdom" (1991; 128–32, 136–39), set forth the sometimes harsh demands of love with a humility born of personal experience and a boldness rooted in faith in God. The demands of love made upon the disciples of Jesus are themselves the product of the Lord's love for them and for all. Love for God and love for neighbor are in fact one and the same love expressed differently.*

Christ, who is also "the truth and the life," is the disciples' way to the Father (John 14:6). The Lord's life in us finds expression in works; these are the fruit of the presence of the Spirit. As Samuel Rayan says: "The followers of Jesus, those who are open to the Spirit, to the values of God and to an appreciation of life, those who are committed to affirming life in all its human fullness, whatever be their grasp of their faith, are bringers of life for the world." Works express this life, mark out the way, and "do the truth" (John 3:21)—that is, the love of God in history.

BRINGERS OF LIFE

Chapter 8 of the Book of Zechariah concerns the day of Yahweh. A few verses further on, Zechariah places the following exhortation on the lips of Yahweh: "These then are the things you should do: Speak the truth to one another; let there be honesty and peace in the judgments at your gates, and let none of you plot evil against another in his heart, nor love a false oath. For all these things I hate, says the Lord" (Zech. 8:16–17).

"The things you should do": there is here an ethical requirement that is to be concretized in a certain kind of behavior. If human beings speak the truth to one another, they will create a climate of credibility and will make Jerusalem truly a "faithful city" (Zech. 8:3). The next part of the sentence brings together two key words: *mishpat* (judgment) and *shalom* [with its] rich and complex meaning of [peace]. The reference is to judgments that are capable of establishing peace, harmony between persons, happiness, and life. It is to this end that behavior is directed that is in keeping with the gift of the day of Yahweh. Evil plots against others are contrary to *shalom* and opposed to the will of Yahweh.

A little earlier in his book, Zechariah himself gives us a very brief but meaningful code of ethics that is drawn up in the same perspective. "Thus says the Lord of hosts: Render true judgment, and show kindness and compassion toward each other. Do not oppress the widow or the orphan, the alien or the poor; do not plot evil against one another in your hearts" (Zech. 7:9–10).

On the positive side, true, genuine judgment, and the practice of love and mercy. The passage then describes in negative terms the behavior of believers in

Yahweh. The verb used here for "oppress" (*'shq*) has the connotation of economic exploitation. Believers are not to violate the rights of the poor or take from them the necessities of life. This is what is meant. Widows and orphans are among the weak and uncared for members of society; the compassionate love prescribed in the preceding verse must be shown especially to them. The foreigners often found living in the midst of the Jews were temporary workers, hired day by day. Having no permanent jobs and owning no property in a country that was not their own, they were a pool of cheap labor and open to exploitation (see Deut. 24:14). Widows, orphans, and foreigners are the great trilogy often used in the Old Testament to designate the poor. Rarely, however, do we find what we see here: the prophet adding the redundant word "poor" (here: *'ani*) to the list. By adding it, he reinforces and summarizes his references to those who are abused and unimportant and without legal protection.

Acceptance of the gift of the day of Yahweh, which Zechariah announces, implies actions done for others, especially the most needy. To the prophets, the establishment of justice means respecting the rights of all and especially the needs of the poor. Acceptance of God's merciful love requires that we commit ourselves to others; our acceptance of life from God should motivate us to create justice and peace, happiness and life, or, in a word, *shalom*, around us.

On the other hand, to oppress the poor means to take away their life, to murder them. Biblical texts on this point are very numerous. I shall cite a few from the New Testament:

> Behold, the wages you withheld from the workers who harvested your fields are crying aloud, and the cries of the harvesters have reached the ears of the Lord of hosts. You have lived on earth in luxury and pleasure; you have fattened your hearts on the day of slaughter. You have condemned and murdered the just one who does not resist you. [James 5:4–6]

Injustice is murder; the oppressor is a murderer. The passage echoes Sirach 34:18–22. It is not clear to what James is referring when he speaks of the "day of slaughter." The common view is that he is speaking of the "day of judgment" on which the rich will be punished; he may also, however, be rebuking those who feast and amuse themselves while oppressing the poor and shedding their blood. The words are harsh but well-aimed. Unfortunately, they fit situations that have recurred throughout the history of Christianity, including our own day. The Letter of James allows no loopholes or excuses. Bread is bread, and wine, wine. The Christian message seeks to overcome the conflict; therefore it does not deny its existence.

[I have argued elsewhere] that the Beatitudes pinpoint the attitudes proper to disciples. The verses that follow upon the Beatitudes in the Gospel of Matthew are completely integrated with them and thus form with them a single text that ought to be interpreted as a whole:

You are the salt of the earth. But if salt loses its taste, with what can it be seasoned? It is no longer good for anything but to be thrown out and trampled underfoot. You are the light of the world. A city set on a mountain cannot be hidden. Nor do they light a lamp and then put it under a bushel basket; it is set on a lampstand, where it gives light to all in the house. Just so, your light must shine before others, that they may see your good deeds and glorify your heavenly Father. [Matt. 5:13–16]

Verses 11–12, which are an explication of the eighth Beatitude, shift from the third person plural to the second, and the text now continues to refer to the second person plural. The disciples are said to be ("you are") the salt of the earth and the light of the world; the images embody a call for an identity and a visibility. Salt gives flavor and must do this permanently; if it becomes itself tasteless, it loses its specific function and can only be thrown out. The task of the disciples is to make known the message of Jesus; this is knowledge [*saber*] that must be presented with flavor [*con sabor*] so that the teaching will be valued and deepened. If the followers of Jesus do not put the commandments of their master into practice, they lose their identity and betray their mission; they become fools.

The visibility that light creates is reinforced by the images of the city on a mountain and the lamp that cannot be hidden. The phrase "light of the world," which is parallel to "salt of the earth," brings out the universal scope of the responsibility disciples have. The followers of Jesus cannot hide or conceal the message they bring. Only a personal and Christian identity will allow a genuine dialogue with others ("the earth," "the world").

Disciples are therefore called upon to bear witness through concrete actions. The entire opening section of Matthew 5 is directed toward verse 16, and the evangelist emphasizes the movement by connecting the verse with what has gone before: "Just so"—marked by the identity and visibility of true disciples—their conduct is to shine before others. "Good deeds" refer to concrete behavior that is in accord with God's will; they refer especially to works of mercy, a classical list of which is given in Matthew 25:31–46.

Reference is also made to good deeds in the first Letter of Peter: "Maintain good conduct among the Gentiles, so that if they speak of you as evil-doers, they may observe your good works and glorify God on the day of visitation" (1 Pet. 2:12).

The witness, here as in Matthew, is not in the service of self-glorification but is to be given for the glory of God, as Jesus did who was "eager to do what is good" (Titus 2:14). This is the ultimate meaning of the disciple's commitment: through disciples people must be led to the Father. To glorify the Father means to acknowledge the primacy of God's love, to adhere to his will, and to be faithful to his plan for the human race.

The works of the disciples are a way to the Father; by doing them, the disciples make the way of Christ their own. The passage that begins in Matthew 5:1

and ends at verse 16 may be regarded as the introduction to the Sermon on the Mount; it shows us the part played by deeds in the attitudes befitting a disciple. "Blessed are the poor in spirit," and so on, means "blessed are the disciples." Disciples are those who practice justice through life-giving works of love and thereby glorify the Father.

The focus seen here makes it possible to connect chapter 5 of Matthew, with which the preaching of Jesus begins, and chapter 25, with which this preaching concludes. [Elsewhere] I have pointed out its links with the passage on the final judgment. The proclamation of the kingdom begins with the promise made to the poor in spirit and ends with the gift of the kingdom to those who come to the aid of the materially poor. The disciples are said to be blessed, or happy, *because* they give life by giving food to the hungry and drink to the thirsty, by clothing the naked and visiting prisoners, or, in other words, by concrete actions; in this way they proclaim the kingdom and enter into it. This is what St. James calls "the law of the kingdom" (2:8). . . .

The life of disciples runs its course between gratuitousness and demand, investiture as witnesses and mission. In his version of the Beatitudes Matthew emphasizes the need of behavior oriented to others. This is a requirement that flows from the gift of the kingdom. Nothing makes greater demands for solidarity with others than the gratuitousness of God's love. . . .

WHERE ARE THE POOR TO SLEEP?

The Gospel of Matthew reports a conversation of Jesus with a Pharisee who puts a question to him with the intention of testing him:

> "Teacher, which commandment in the law is the greatest?" He said to him, "You shall love the Lord, your God, with all your heart, with all your soul, and with all your mind. This is the greatest and the first commandment. The second is like it: You shall love your neighbor as yourself. The whole law and the prophets depend on these two commandments." [Matt. 22:36–40]

By "the law and the prophets" Jews meant the entire Bible. Matthew uses the phrase here because he is writing in a Jewish setting. The two loves referred to in the two citations from the Old Testament (Deut. 6:5 and Lev. 19:18) sum up the commandments of God. In the parallel passage in Luke, the person who refers to the two loves is the same scholar of the law who asks the question, while Jesus limits himself to saying at the end: "You have answered correctly; do this and you will live" (Luke 10:8). The practice of these two commandments is the way to life and brings us near to the kingdom (Mark 12:34).

Love of God and love of neighbor are the two basic dimensions of the gospel of Christ. Some of the tensions we experience in the church are due to the skewed way in which we interpret the relation between these two demands. There are those who emphasize love of God in a way that makes it appear that our relation to our neighbor is something secondary, added on to what is truly important. Given this perspective, it is difficult to show the relevance of Christians' work in history and of the demands made on them by the orphan, the widow, and the foreigner.

On the other hand, there are those who imply that Christian existence finds its almost exclusive manifestation in commitment to and solidarity with others. The pressures of inhuman and deeply unjust situations seem to lead them to act, rather than to think, in this way. But then prayer, celebration, the knowledge of God's word and a taste for it—all of them vital expressions of the world of gratuitous love in which our relationship with the Lord has its setting—lose their full meaning and are narrowed in their scope.

We are not dealing here with two forms of service: one of God, the other of wealth, such as characterizes those who are "of two minds." No, there is but a single love, the different expressions of which cannot be separated, because when we clothe the naked we clothe the Lord himself. Only the clean of heart, those who live out their faith in an integral way, can grasp this identification of Christ and the poor.

It is important to note, moreover, that those who claim to find God while being uninterested in their neighbor will not find the God of the Bible. They will perhaps find a God who is first mover of all being or the explanation of creation, but they do not find the God whom Jesus Christ proclaimed, for he is inseparable from his kingdom—that is, from his will to love and justice for all human beings. Recognizing God as Father inevitably implies forming true fellowship among ourselves. Those who, for their part, limit themselves in practice solely to a commitment to others run the risk of seeing these others, who are beings of flesh and blood and not abstractions, slip through their fingers. Gratuitousness is the framework not only of our encounter with God but also of reciprocal recognition among human beings.

There is no middle ground. If we try to stop at one of these two loves, we lose both. When this kind of choice is made, there is not in fact a reduction of one of them to the other, but rather the disappearance of both. "Whoever is not with me is against me," says the Lord. To choose between the two dimensions of Christian life is to be against God.

One thing is certain: the tension between these two requirements exists more at the practical level than the conceptual. At the level of ideas it is perhaps possible to reach agreement on the unity to be maintained. The difficulty is greater in the sphere of our actions, and actions determine our real orientation.

A simple question in Exodus calls upon us to make a very concrete choice. It reminds us of what we must be concerned about: "This cloak of [your neighbor's] is the only covering he has for his body. What else has he to sleep in?" (Exod. 22:26). Are we concerned in this way? Are we anxious to know how the poor of our country will cover themselves and where they will spend the night? What happens within the intimacy of each home expresses, perhaps better than any other indicator, the deep differences there are among us. Will they sleep beneath a roof? On the ground, on a mat, or on a bed? One, two, five, six to a room? In housing from which they shall soon be evicted?

Those who would be Christians in present-day Latin America must be concerned about where the poor are to sleep. Given this kind of concrete problem, does it make sense to get into intellectual discussions about priorities or about the balance between love of God and love of neighbor? Precisely because it is concrete, this demand makes us realize what we have right in our own hands: the inseparable connection between the two loves. The question of where the poor are to sleep is important to God, as we are told in the same passage of Exodus: "If he cries out to me, I will hear him; for I am compassionate"' (Exod. 22:26). Therefore it ought to be important to us as well. The Lord wants acts toward the poor to have the value of an encounter with him.

The challenges posed by concrete human situations take us to the sources of Christian life. Conceptual distinctions and theological developments do not there disappear, as a pedantic anti-intellectualism would have it; on the contrary, they take on meaning and vitality. A concern for where the poor are to sleep will make us realize that it is in fact not possible to separate love of God and love of neighbor; that is, that we must live both aspects as intertwined with each other. When we experience things at their root, we are helped in seeing that the unity of our life is not created by a fine, balanced formulation of ideas, but by taking the path of practicing love of God and love of neighbor in one and the same act. This alone will lead us to life. The journey is a costly one but also full of hope, because on it we gradually become compassionate as the God in whom we believe is compassionate. "Compassionate" means to be capable of "feeling with" God and other human beings. Feeling, and not just thinking. When we situate ourselves at the sources, we seek unity as something new and creative, and not as a nicely balanced synthesis.

A final thought. There are those who feel a certain uneasiness when they hear: "Love your neighbor *as yourself*"—a command also found in the passage that has served as my guiding thread in these last few pages. They think they see in this admonition little radicalness in the demand or perhaps an excessive self-regard. These dangers do exist, but they do not exhaust the interpretation of the statement.

The gospel clearly calls upon us, in many passages, to forget our own interests as we commit ourselves to others. At the same time, the passage of Matthew, with its Old Testament roots, reminds us of something fundamental: we must also know how to love ourselves. We can undoubtedly distort this requirement and make it the justification for a more or less subtle self-centeredness. We may ask ourselves, nonetheless, whether mistreating ourselves on the grounds that we are serving others allows this commitment to be, as it should, joyful and friendly, a service done by people who do not seek compensation in it for what they have denied to themselves. Justice must be practiced joyfully (see Isa. 64:4).

I am not here rejecting the traditional ascetical call for a necessary moderation in all areas of Christian life. Rather I am trying to convey an understanding that solidarity with others is not achieved through an imbalance in personal life. We must love "Brother Body," we are told by Francis of Assisi, an eminently evangelical saint. Going astray here is possible, of course, but the truth is that there is also such a risk in the opposite direction.

Love of God and commitment to the poor (including love of ourselves) are central elements in the experience of those who believe in the God of life. The coordination of these elements turns our faith into a journey of solidarity in the following of Jesus.

Four

RETHINKING SOTERIOLOGY: LIBERATION, FREEDOM, AND COMMUNION

*Recognition of the inadequacy of the prevailing theory of salvation has often led to breakthroughs in the history of Christian theology. The rise of liberation theology is no exception. While the Second Vatican Council unequivocally affirmed that God's offer of salvation is universal, the Council did not spell out how this offer is made by God or accepted by human beings. Gutiérrez's interest, both intellectual and pastoral, in the soteriological question is evident in his earliest writings and gave rise to his well-known reinterpretation of salvation as a threefold process of human liberation. For Gutiérrez, salvation is "the communion of human beings with God and among themselves," and salvation "orients, transforms, and guides history to its fulfillment" (*Theology of Liberation, 86).*

29. THE PROCESS OF LIBERATION

The following selection from Theology of Liberation *(16–25) represents an early expression of Gutiérrez's view of history as "a process of human liberation" and of freedom as "a historical conquest." Concern for the liberation of the whole person and of all persons guides his nuanced discussion of the momentous and complex process of liberation underway in the 1960s in many parts of the world. Drawing on the thought of the intellectual architects of modernity such as René Descartes, Immanuel Kant, G. W. F. Hegel, Karl Marx, Sigmund Freud, and Herbert Marcuse as well as the teachings of the recently completed Second Vatican Council and the current pope, Paul VI, Gutiérrez sketched "three reciprocally interpenetrating levels of meaning" of the term "liberation": liberation from oppressive socioeconomic structures, emancipation from oppressed consciousness, and redemption from sinful self-centeredness. By attending to social, psychological, and spiritual liberation, Gutiérrez warned against restricting the notion to just one of its dimensions.*

FROM THE CRITIQUE OF DEVELOPMENTALISM
TO SOCIAL REVOLUTION

The term *development* has synthesized the aspirations of poor peoples during the last few decades. Recently, however, it has become the object of severe criticism due both to the deficiencies of the development policies proposed to the poor countries to lead them out of their underdevelopment and also to the lack of concrete achievements of the interested governments. This is the reason why *developmentalism (desarrollismo)* a term derived from *development (desarrollo)*, is now used in a pejorative sense, especially in Latin America.

Much has been said in recent times about development. Poor countries competed for the help of the rich countries. There were even attempts to create a certain development mystique. Support for development was intense in Latin America in the 1950s, producing high expectations. But since the supporters of development did not attack the roots of the evil, they failed and caused instead confusion and frustration.

One of the most important reasons for this turn of events is that development—approached from an economic and modernizing point of view—has been frequently promoted by international organizations closely linked to groups and governments which control the world economy. The changes encouraged were to be achieved within the formal structure of the existing institutions without challenging them. Great care was exercised, therefore, not to attack the interests of large international economic powers nor those of their natural allies, the ruling domestic interest groups. Furthermore, the so-called changes were often nothing more than new and underhanded ways of increasing the power of strong economic groups.

Developmentalism thus came to be synonymous with *reformism* and modernization, that is to say, synonymous with timid measures, really ineffective in the long run and counterproductive to achieving a real transformation. The poor countries are becoming ever more clearly aware that their underdevelopment is only the by-product of the development of other countries, because of the kind of relationship which exists between the rich and the poor countries. Moreover, they are realizing that their own development will come about only with a struggle to break the domination of the rich countries.

This perception sees the conflict implicit in the process. Development must attack the root causes of the problems and among them the deepest is economic, social, political, and cultural dependence of some countries upon others—an expression of the domination of some social classes over others. Attempts to bring about changes within the existing order have proven futile. This analysis of the situation is at the level of scientific rationality. Only a radical break from the status quo, that is, a profound transformation of the private property system, access to power of the exploited class, and a social revolution that would break this dependence would allow for the change to a new society, a socialist society—or at least allow that such a society might be possible.

In this light, to speak about the process of *liberation* begins to appear more appropriate and richer in human content. Liberation in fact expresses the inescapable moment of radical change which is foreign to the ordinary use of the term *development*. Only in the context of such a process can a policy of development be effectively implemented, have any real meaning, and avoid misleading formulations.

HUMAN BEINGS; AGENTS OF THEIR OWN DESTINY

To characterize the situation of the poor countries as dominated and oppressed leads one to speak of economic, social, and political liberation. But we are dealing here with a much more integral and profound understanding of human existence and its historical future.

A broad and deep aspiration for liberation inflames the history of humankind in our day, liberation from all that limits or keeps human beings from self-fulfillment, liberation from all impediments to the exercise of freedom. Proof of this is the awareness of new and subtle forms of oppression in the heart of advanced industrial societies, which often offer themselves as models to the underdeveloped countries. In them subversion does not appear as a protest against poverty, but rather against wealth. The context in the rich countries, however, is quite different from that of the poor countries: we must beware of all kinds of imitations as well as new forms of imperialism—revolutionary this time—of the rich countries, which consider themselves central to the history of humankind. Such mimicry would only lead the revolutionary groups of the Third World to a new deception regarding their own reality. They would be led to fight against windmills.

But, having acknowledged this danger, it is important to remember also that the poor countries would err in not following these events closely since their future depends at least partially upon what happens on the domestic scene in the dominant countries. Their own efforts at liberation cannot be indifferent to that proclaimed by growing minorities in rich nations. There are, moreover, valuable lessons to be learned by the revolutionaries of the countries on the periphery, who could in turn use them as corrective measures in the difficult task of building a new society.

What is at stake in the South as well as in the North, in the West as well as the East, on the periphery and in the center, is the possibility of enjoying a truly human existence, a free life, a dynamic liberty which is related to history as a conquest. We have today an ever-clearer vision of this dynamism and this conquest, but their roots stretch into the past. The fifteenth and sixteenth centuries are important milestones in human self-understanding. Human relationship with nature changed substantially with the emergence of experimental science and the techniques of manipulation derived from it. Relying on these achievements, humankind abandoned its former image of the world and itself. Etienne Gilson expresses this idea in a well-known phrase: "It is because of its physics that metaphysics grows old." Because of science humankind took a step forward and began to regard itself in a different way. This process indicates why the best philosophical tradition is not merely an armchair product; it is rather the reflective and thematic awareness of human experience of human relationships with nature and with other persons. And these relationships are interpreted and at the same time modified by advances in technological and scientific knowledge.

René Descartes is one of the great names of the new physics which altered human relationship to nature. He laid the cornerstone of a philosophical reflection which stressed the primacy of thought and of "clear and distinct ideas," and so highlighted the creative aspects of human subjectivity. Immanuel Kant's "Copernican Revolution" strengthened and systematized this point of view. For him our concept ought not to conform to the objects but rather "the objects . . . must conform to my conceptions." The reason is that "we only cognize in things *a priori* that which we ourselves place in them. Kant was aware that this leads to a "new method" of thought, to a knowledge which is critical of its foundations and thus abandons its naïveté and enters an adult stage.

G. W. F. Hegel followed this approach, introducing with vitality and urgency the theme of history. To a great extent his philosophy is a reflection on the French Revolution. This historical event had vast repercussions, for it proclaimed the right of all to participate in the direction of the society to which they belong. For Hegel one is aware of oneself "only by being acknowledged or 'recognized'" by another consciousness. But this being recognized by another presupposes an initial conflict, "a life-and-death struggle," because "solely by risking life that freedom is obtained."

Through the master-slave dialectic (resulting from this original confrontation), the historical process will then appear as the genesis of consciousness and therefore of the gradual liberation of humankind. Through the dialectical process humankind constructs itself and attains a real awareness of its own being; it liberates itself in the acquisition of genuine freedom which through work transforms the world and educates the human species. For Hegel "world history is the progression of the awareness of freedom." Moreover, the driving force of history is the difficult conquest of freedom, hardly perceptible in its initial stages. It is the passage from awareness of freedom to real freedom. "It is Freedom in itself that comprises within itself the infinite necessity of bringing itself to consciousness and thereby, since knowledge about itself is its very nature, to reality." Thus human nature gradually takes hold of its own destiny. It looks ahead and turns toward a society in which it will be free of all alienation and servitude. This focus will initiate a new dimension in philosophy: social criticism.

Karl Marx deepened and renewed this line of thought in his unique way. But this required what has been called an "epistemological break" (a notion taken from Gaston Bachelard) with previous thought. The new attitude was expressed clearly in the famous *Theses on Feuerbach*, in which Marx presented concisely but penetratingly the essential elements of his approach. In them, especially in the First Thesis, Marx situated himself equidistant between the old materialism and idealism; more precisely, he presented his position as the dialectical transcendence of both. Of the first he retained the affirmation of the objectivity of the external world; of the second he kept the transforming capacity of human nature. For Marx, to know was something indissolubly linked to the transformation of the world through work. Basing his thought on these first intuitions, he went on to construct a scientific understanding of historical reality. He analyzed capitalistic society, in which were found concrete instances of the exploitation of persons by their fellows and of one social class by another. Pointing the way toward an era in history when humankind can live humanly, Marx created categories which allowed for the elaboration of a science of history.

The door was opened for science to help humankind take one more step on the road of critical thinking. It made humankind more aware of the socioeconomic determinants of its ideological creations and therefore freer and more lucid in relation to them. But at the same time these new insights enabled humankind to have greater control and rational grasp of its historical initiatives. (This interpretation is valid unless of course one holds a dogmatic and mechanistic interpretation of history.) These initiatives ought to assure the change from the capitalistic mode of production to the socialistic mode, that is to say, to one oriented toward a society in which persons can begin to live freely and humanly. They will have controlled nature, created the conditions for a socialized production of wealth, done away with private acquisition of excessive wealth, and established socialism.

But modern human aspirations include not only liberation from *exterior* pressures which prevent fulfillment as a member of a certain social class, country, or society. Persons seek likewise an interior liberation, in an individual and intimate dimension; they seek liberation not only on a social plane but also on a psychological. They seek an interior freedom understood, however, not as an ideological evasion from social confrontation or as the internalization of a situation of dependency. Rather it must be in relation to the real world of the human psyche as understood since Freud.

A new frontier was in effect opened up when Sigmund Freud highlighted the unconscious determinants of human behavior, with repression as the central element of the human psychic make-up. Repression is the result of the conflict between instinctive drives and the cultural and ethical demands of the social environment. For Freud, unconscious motivations exercise a tyrannical power and can produce aberrant behavior. This behavior is controllable only if the subject becomes aware of these motivations through an accurate reading of the new language of meanings created by the unconscious. Since Hegel we have seen conflict used as a germinal explanatory category and awareness as a step in the conquest of freedom. In Freud, however, they appear in a psychological process which ought also to lead to a fuller liberation of humankind.

The scope of liberation on the collective and historical level does not always and satisfactorily include psychological liberation. Psychological liberation includes dimensions which do not exist in or are not sufficiently integrated with collective, historical liberation. We are not speaking here, however, of facilely separating them or putting them in opposition to one another. "It seems to me," writes David Cooper,

> that a cardinal failure of all past revolutions has been the dissociation of libera-
> tion on the mass social level, i.e., liberation of whole classes in economic and
> political terms, and liberation on the level of the individual and the concrete
> groups in which he is directly engaged. If we are to talk of revolution today, our
> talk will be meaningless unless we effect some union between the macro-social
> and micro-social, and between "inner reality" and "outer reality."

Moreover, alienation and exploitation as well as the very struggle for libera-
tion from them have ramifications on the personal and psychological planes which it would be dangerous to overlook in the process of constructing a new society and a new person. These personal aspects—considered not as excessively privatized, but rather as encompassing all human dimensions—are also under consideration in the contemporary debate concerning greater participation of all in political activity. This is so even in a socialist society.

In this area, Herbert Marcuse's attempt, under the influence of Hegel and Marx, to use the psychoanalytical categories for social criticism is important. Basing his observations on a work which Freud himself did not hold in high regard, *Civilization and Its Discontents*, Marcuse analyzes the *over-repressive character* of the affluent society and envisions the possibility of a non-repressive soci-
ety, a possibility skeptically denied by Freud. Marcuse's analyses of advanced industrial society, capitalistic or socialistic, lead him to denounce the emergence of a one-dimensional and oppressive society. In order to achieve this non-repres-
sive society, however, it will be necessary to challenge the values espoused by the society which denies human beings the possibility of living freely. Marcuse labels this the Great Refusal: "the specter of a revolution which subordinates the development of the productive forces and higher standards of living to the requirements of creating solidarity for the human species, for abolishing poverty and misery beyond all national frontiers and spheres of interest, for the attain-
ment of peace."

We are not suggesting, of course, that we should endorse without question every aspect of this development of ideas. There are ambiguities, critical observations to be made, and points to be clarified. Many ideas must be reconsidered in the light of a history that advances inexorably, simultaneously confirming and

rejecting previous assertions. Ideas must be reconsidered too in light of praxis, which is the proving ground of all theory, and in light of socio-cultural realities very different from those from which the ideas emerged. But all this should not lead us to an attitude of distrustful reserve toward these ideas; rather it should suggest that the task to be undertaken is formidable. And the task is all the more urgent because these reflections are attempts to express a deeply-rooted sentiment in today's masses: the aspiration to liberation. This aspiration is still confusedly perceived, but there is an ever greater awareness of it. Furthermore, there are many persons who, beyond this or that nuance or difference, have made this aspiration—in Vietnam or Brazil, New York or Prague—the norm for their behavior and a sufficient reason to offer their lives for others. Their commitment is the backbone which validates and gives historical viability to the development of the ideas outlined above.

To conceive of history as a process of human liberation is to consider freedom as a historical conquest; it is to understand that the step from an abstract to a real freedom is not taken without a struggle against all the forces that oppress humankind, a struggle full of pitfalls, detours, and temptations to run away. The goal is not only better living conditions, a radical change of structures, a social revolution; it is much more: the continuous creation, never ending, of a new way to be human, a *permanent cultural revolution*.

In other words, what is at stake above all is a dynamic and historical conception of the human person, oriented definitively and creatively toward the future, acting in the present for the sake of tomorrow. Pierre Teilhard de Chardin has remarked that humankind has taken hold of the reins of evolution. History, contrary to essentialist and static thinking, is not the development of potentialities preexistent in human nature; it is rather the conquest of new, qualitatively different ways of being a human person in order to achieve an ever more total and complete fulfillment of the individual in solidarity with all humankind.

THE CONCEPT OF LIBERATION THEOLOGICALLY CONSIDERED

Although we will consider liberation from a theological perspective more extensively later, it is important at this time to attempt an initial treatment in the light of what we have just discussed.

The term *development* is relatively new in the texts of the ecclesiastical magisterium. Except for a brief reference by Pius XII, the subject is broached for the first time by John XXIII in the encyclical letter *Mater et magistra. Pacem in terris* gives the term special attention. *Gaudium et spes* dedicates a whole section to it, though the treatment is not original. All these documents stress the urgency of eliminating the existing injustices and the need for an economic development geared to the service of humankind. Finally, *Populorum progressio* discusses development as its central theme. Here the language and ideas are clearer; the adjective *integral* is added to development, putting things in a different context and opening new perspectives.

These new viewpoints were already hinted at in the sketchy discussion of Vatican Council II on dependence and liberation. *Gaudium et spes* points out that "nations on the road to progress . . . continually fall behind while very often their *dependence* on wealthier nations deepens more rapidly, even in the economic sphere" (no. 9). Later it acknowledges that "although nearly all peoples have gained their independence, it is still far from true that they are free from excessive inequalities and from every form of *undue dependence*" (no. 85).

These assertions should lead to a discernment of the need to be free from dependence, to be liberated from it. The same *Gaudium et spes* on two occasions touches on liberation and laments the fact that it is seen exclusively as the fruit of human effort: "Many look forward to a genuine and total *emancipation* of humanity wrought solely by human effort. They are convinced that the future rule of man over the earth will satisfy every desire of his heart" (no. 10). Or it is concerned that liberation be reduced to a purely economic and social level: "Among the forms of modern atheism is that which anticipates the *liberation* of man especially through his economic and social emancipation" (no. 20). These assertions presuppose, negatively speaking, that liberation must be placed in a wider context; they criticize a narrow vision. They allow, therefore, for the possibility of a "genuine and total" liberation.

Unfortunately, this wider perspective is not elaborated. We find some indications, however, in the texts in which *Gaudium et spes* speaks of the birth of a "new humanism, one in which man is defined first of all by his responsibility toward his brothers and toward history" (no. 55). There is a need for persons who are makers of history, "who are truly new and artisans of a new humanity" (no. 30), persons moved by the desire to build a really new society. Indeed, the conciliar document asserts that beneath economic and political demands "lies a deeper and more widespread longing. Persons and societies thirst for a full and free life worthy of man—one in which they can subject to their own welfare all that the modern world can offer them so abundantly" (no. 9).

All this is but a beginning. It is an oft-noted fact that *Gaudium et spes* in general offers a rather irenic description of the human situation; it touches up the uneven spots, smoothes the rough edges, avoids the more conflictual aspects, and stays away from the sharper confrontations among social classes and countries.

The encyclical *Populorum progressio* goes a step further. In a somewhat isolated text it speaks clearly of "building a world where every person, no matter of race, religion, or nationality, can live a fully human life, freed from servitude imposed on him by other people or by natural forces over which he has not sufficient control" (no. 47). It is unfortunate, however, that this idea was not expanded in the encyclical. From this point of view, *Populorum progressio* is a transitional document. Although it energetically denounces the "international imperialism of money," "situations whose injustice cries to heaven," and the growing gap between rich and poor countries, ultimately it addresses itself to the great ones of this world urging them to carry out the necessary changes. The outright use of the language of liberation, instead of its mere suggestion, would have given a more decided and direct thrust in favor of the oppressed, encouraging them to break with their present situation and take control of their own destiny.

The theme of liberation appears more completely discussed in the message from eighteen bishops of the Third World, published as a specific response to the call made by *Populorum progressio*. It is also treated frequently—almost to the point of being a synthesis of its message—in the conclusions of the Second General Conference of Latin American bishops held in Medellín, Colombia, in 1968, which have more doctrinal authority than the eighteen bishops' message. In both these documents the focus has changed. The situation is not judged from the point of view of the countries at the center, but rather of those on the periphery, providing insiders' experience of their anguish and aspirations.

The product of a profound historical movement, this aspiration to liberation is beginning to be accepted by the Christian community as a sign of the times, as a call to commitment and interpretation. The biblical message, which presents the work of Christ as a liberation, provides the framework for this interpretation. Theology seems to have avoided for a long time reflecting on the conflictual character of human history, the confrontations among individuals, social classes, and countries. St. Paul continuously reminds us, however, of the paschal core of Christian existence and of all of human life: the passage from the old to the new person, from sin to grace, from slavery to freedom.

"For freedom Christ has set us free" (Gal. 5:1), St. Paul tells us. He refers here to liberation from sin insofar as it represents a selfish turning in upon oneself. To sin is to refuse to love one's neighbors and, therefore, the Lord himself. Sin— a breach of friendship with God and others—is according to the Bible the ultimate cause of poverty, injustice, and the oppression in which persons live. In describing sin as the ultimate cause we do not in any way negate the structural reasons and the objective determinants leading to these situations. It does, however, emphasize the fact that things do not happen by chance and that behind an unjust structure there is a personal or collective will responsible—a willingness to reject God and neighbor. It suggests, likewise, that a social transformation, no matter how radical it may be, does not automatically achieve the suppression of all evils.

But St. Paul asserts not only that Christ liberated us; he also tells us that he did it in order that we might be free. Free for what? Free to love. "In the language of the Bible," writes Dietrich Bonhoeffer, "freedom is not something man has for himself but something he has for others. . . . It is not a possession, a presence, an object . . . but a relationship and nothing else. In truth, freedom is a relationship between two persons. Being free means 'being free for the other,' because the other has bound me to him. Only in relationship with the other am I free." The freedom to which we are called presupposes the going out of oneself, the breaking down of our selfishness and of all the structures that support our selfishness; the foundation of this freedom is openness to others. The fullness of liberation—a free gift from Christ—is communion with God and with other human beings.

CONCLUSION

Summarizing what has been said above, we can distinguish three reciprocally interpenetrating levels of meaning of the term *liberation*, or in other words, three approaches to the process of liberation.

In the first place, *liberation* expresses the aspirations of oppressed peoples and social classes, emphasizing the conflictual aspect of the economic, social, and political process which puts them at odds with wealthy nations and oppressive classes. In contrast, the word *development*, and above all the policies characterized as developmentalist *(desarrollista)*, appear somewhat aseptic, giving a false picture of a tragic and conflictual reality. The issue of development does in fact find its true place in the more universal, profound, and radical perspective of liberation. It is only within this framework that *development* finds its true meaning and possibilities of accomplishing something worthwhile.

At a deeper level, *liberation* can be applied to an understanding of history. Humankind is seen as assuming conscious responsibility for its own destiny. This understanding provides a dynamic context and broadens the horizons of the desired social changes. In this perspective the unfolding of all the dimensions of humanness is demanded—persons who make themselves throughout their life and throughout history. The gradual conquest of true freedom leads to the creation of a new humankind and a qualitatively different society. This vision provides, therefore, a better understanding of what in fact is at stake in our times.

Finally, the word *development* to a certain extent limits and obscures the theological problems implied in the process designated by this term. On the contrary the word *liberation* allows for another approach leading to the biblical sources which inspire the presence and action of humankind in history. In the Bible, Christ is presented as the one who brings us liberation. Christ the Savior liberates from sin, which is the ultimate root of all disruption of friendship and of all injustice and oppression. Christ makes humankind truly free, that is to say, he enables us to live in communion with him; and this is the basis for all human fellowship.

This is not a matter of three parallel or chronologically successive processes, however. There are three levels of meaning of a single, complex process, which finds its deepest sense and its full realization in the saving work of Christ. These levels of meaning, therefore, are interdependent. A comprehensive view of the matter presupposes that all three aspects can be considered together. In this way two pitfalls will be avoided: first, *idealist* or *spiritualist* approaches, which are nothing but ways of evading a harsh and demanding reality, and second, shallow analyses and programs of short-term effect initiated under the pretext of meeting immediate needs.

30. CHRIST THE LIBERATOR

The following text is the conclusion to chapter 9 of A Theology of Liberation, *"Liberation and Salvation" (102–105), and represents a further elaboration of ideas sketched by Gutiérrez in 1969 at Cartigny, Switzerland, in his presentation "Notes on Theology of Liberation." Rejecting a "naïve optimism which denies the role of sin in the historical development of humanity," he asserts the inadequacy of understanding sin simply as "an individual, private, or merely interior reality." On the contrary, sin is also "a social historical fact, the absence of fellowship and love in relationships among persons, the breach of friendship with God and with other persons, and as a consequence, an interior, personal division" (102–103). It is Christ who, by his death and resurrection, has liberated us from sin, the fundamental alienation and root of all injustice. Christ's gift of the Spirit allows us to enter into communion with God and others.*

Our approach [to political liberation] opens up for us—and this is of utmost importance—unforeseen vistas on the problem of sin. Indeed, an unjust situation does not happen by chance; it is not something branded by a fatal destiny: there is human responsibility behind it. The prophets knew how to put it clearly and energetically and we are rediscovering their words now. This is the reason why the Medellín Conference refers to the state of things in Latin America as a "situation of sin," as a "rejection of the Lord." This characterization, in all its breadth and depth, not only criticizes the individual abuses on the part of those who enjoy great power in this social order; it calls into question their uses of power, that is to say, it is a repudiation of the whole existing system—to which the church itself belongs.

In this approach we are far, therefore, from that naïve optimism which denies the role of sin in the historical development of humanity. This was the criticism, one will remember, of the Schema of Ariccia [at Vatican II] and it is frequently made in connection with Teilhard de Chardin and all those theologies enthusiastic about human progress. But in the liberation approach sin is not considered as an individual, private, or merely interior reality—asserted just enough to necessitate "spiritual" redemption which does not challenge the order in which we live. Sin is regarded as a social, historical fact, the absence of fellowship and love in relationships among persons, the breach of friendship with God and with other persons, and, therefore, an interior fracture—a personal one. When it is considered in this way, the collective dimensions of sin are rediscovered. This is the biblical notion that José Maria González Ruiz calls the "hamartiosphere," the sphere of sin: "a kind of parameter or structure which objectively conditions the progress of human history itself." Moreover, sin does not appear as something added, which one has to mention so as not to stray from tradition or leave oneself open to easy attack. Nor is this a matter of escape into a disincarnate spiritualism. Sin is found in oppressive structures, in the exploitation of humans by humans, in the domination and slavery of peoples, races, and social classes. Sin arises, therefore, as the fundamental alienation, the root of a situation of injustice and exploitation. It is the fundamental alienation that, for that very reason, cannot be encountered in itself, but only in concrete situations, in particular alienations. It is impossible to understand the one without the other. Sin requires a radical liberation, but this necessarily includes a political liberation. Only by participating in the historical process of liberation will it be possible to show the fundamental alienation present in every partial alienation.

This radical liberation is the gift which Christ offers us. By his death and resurrection he redeems us from sin and all its consequences, as [Medellín] says very well: "It is the same God who, in the fullness of time, sends his Son so that, in the flesh, he might come to liberate all men from *all* forms of slavery to which sin has subjected them: ignorance, hunger, misery, ignorance, and oppression, in a word, that injustice and hatred which have their origin in human selfishness." This is why the Christian life is a passover, a passage from sin to grace, from death to life, from injustice to justice, from the subhuman to the human. Indeed, Christ introduces us by the gift of his Spirit into communion with God and with all human beings. More precisely, it is *because* he introduces us into this communion, into a continuous search for its fullness, that he conquers sin— which is the negation of love—and all its consequences.

In dealing with the notion of liberation, I distinguished three levels of meaning: political liberation, liberation in the course of history, and liberation from sin and entrance to communion with God. In the light of [what I said above,] we can now study this question again. These three levels mutually affect each other, but they are not the same. One is not present without the others, but they are distinct: they are all part of a single, all-encompassing salvific process, but they are to be found at different levels. Not only is the growth of the kingdom not reduced to temporal progress; because of the Word accepted in faith, we see that the fundamental obstacle to the kingdom, which is sin, is also the root of all misery and injustice; we see that the very meaning of the growth of the kingdom is also the ultimate precondition for a just society and a new human person. One reaches this root and this ultimate precondition only through the acceptance of the liberating gift of Christ, which surpasses all expectations. But, inversely, all struggle against exploitation and alienation, in a history which is fundamentally one, is an attempt to vanquish selfishness, the negation of love. This is the reason why any effort to build a just society is liberating—part of a liberation that affects, indirectly but effectively, the fundamental alienation. It is a salvific work, although it is not all of salvation. As a human work it is not exempt from ambiguities, any more than what is considered to be strictly "religious" work. But this does not weaken its basic orientation or its objective results.

Temporal progress—or, to avoid this aseptic term, let us say, liberation of the person—and the growth of the kingdom both are directed toward complete communion of human beings with God and among themselves. They have the same goal, but they do not follow parallel roads, not even convergent ones. The growth of the kingdom is a process which occurs historically *in* liberation, insofar as liberation means a greater fulfillment of the human person—the precondition for the new society, but is not exhausted by it. While the kingdom is implemented in liberating historical events, it censures their limitations and ambiguities, proclaims their fulfillment, and impels them effectively toward total communion. This is not an identification. Without liberating historical events, there would be no growth of the kingdom. But the process of liberation will not have conquered the very roots of human oppression and exploitation without the coming of the kingdom, which is above all a gift. Moreover, we can say that the historical, political liberating event *is* the growth of the kingdom and *is* a salvific event; but it is not *the* coming of the kingdom, not *all* of salvation. It is the historical realization of the kingdom and, therefore, it also proclaims its fullness. This is what establishes the difference. It is a distinction made from a dynamic viewpoint, which has nothing to do with the one which holds for the existence of two juxtaposed "orders," closely connected or convergent, but at bottom exterior from each other.

All this is required, in short, by the very radicalness and totality of the salvific process. Nothing escapes this process, nothing is outside the pale of the action of Christ and the gift of the Spirit. This gives human history its profound unity. Those who reduce the work of salvation are indeed those who limit it to the strictly "religious" sphere and are not aware of the universality of the process. It is those who think that the work of Christ touches the social order in which we live only indirectly or tangentially, and not in its roots and basic structure. It is those who in order to protect salvation (or to protect their interests) remove salvation from where the pulse of history beats, where men and women and social classes struggle to liberate themselves from the slavery and oppression to which other individuals and social classes have subjected them. It is those who refuse to see that the salvation of Christ is a radical liberation from all misery, all despoliation, all alienation. It is those who by trying to "save" the work of Christ will "lose" it.

In Christ and by the spirit, the all-comprehensiveness of the liberating process reaches its fullest sense. His work encompasses the three levels of meaning which we mentioned above. A Latin American text on the missions seems to us to summarize this assertion accurately:

> All the dynamism of the cosmos and of human history, the movement toward the creation of a more just and fraternal world, the overcoming of social inequalities among persons, the efforts—so urgently needed on our continent—to liberate human beings from all that depersonalizes them—physical and moral misery, ignorance and hunger—as well as the awareness of human dignity (*Gaudium et spes,* no. 22)—all these originate, are transformed, and reach their

perfection in the saving work of Christ. In him and through him salvation is present at the heart of human history, and there is no human act which, in the last instance, is not defined in terms of it.

31. ESCHATOLOGY AND POLITICS

First presented in his address at Cartigny (1969), Gutiérrez's ideas on the relationship between the New Testament's eschatological promises and the political engagement of Christians in history were more fully developed in chapter 11 of Theology of Liberation, *"Eschatology and Politics." In the first part of the chapter, "To Account for Hope," he notes both the contributions and limitations of modern European theologies such as the theology of hope and political theology. For Gutiérrez, neither theology sufficiently roots hope in the death and resurrection of Christ experienced in the historical present—that is, in the struggle for liberation.*

In the final section of chapter 11, entitled "Faith, Utopia, and Political Action," Gutiérrez sets forth the threefold meaning of the term "liberation." It is a schema to which he has explicitly returned several times, most notably in The Truth Shall Make You Free *(1986), and which informs his entire theological vision. The strength of his proposal, indeed, its whole point, lies in the unity he claims for the complex process of liberation (salvation). At the same time, he is careful to distinguish the three levels. The key to establishing a proper link between faith in God and political activity in history—a classical problem for theology— lies in the middle term "utopia" which mediates the two. For Gutiérrez, utopia corresponds to that level of liberation which brings into being a qualitatively new kind of human person and a new kind of human society. As he explains, the utopian imagination has little to do with fantasy, idealization, or wishful thinking; indeed it is manifest in the transformation of those who participate in the socio-political movements of marginalized people in his own country (the* movimiento popular*). At the core of such "new persons" stands hope, a grace from God. And "to hope in Christ is . . . to believe in the adventure of history [with its] infinite field of possibilities for love and action. . . ." (140).*

The commitment to the creation of a just society and, ultimately, to a new human being, presupposes confidence in the future. This commitment is an act open to whatever comes. What is the meaning of this *new* reality in the light of faith? It has often been stressed that a characteristic of contemporary persons is that they live in terms of tomorrow, oriented toward the future, fascinated by what does not yet exist. The spiritual condition of today's person is more and more determined by the model of the person of tomorrow. Human self-awareness is made up to a large degree of the awareness that we will go beyond what presently exists and that we are entering into a new era, a world "to the second power," fashioned by the hands of human beings. We await the epiphany of the person, an "anthropophany." History is no longer as it was for the Greeks, an *anamnesis*, a remembrance. It is rather a thrust into the future. The contemporary world is full of latent possibilities and expectations. History seems to have quickened its pace. The confrontation of the present with the future makes men and women impatient.

But are we not painting an idealized picture, valid perhaps for other places, but not for Latin America? It is, indeed, inaccurate to regard this sketch as a complete description of the contemporary life-experience of this continent. Large numbers of Latin Americans suffer from a fixation on the past which leads them to overvalue it. This has been correctly interpreted by Paulo Freire. It is one of the elements of what he has called a precritical consciousness, that is, the consciousness of human beings who have not taken their lives into their own hands. Nevertheless, it is necessary to recall that the revolutionary process now under way in one way or another is generating the kind of person who critically analyzes the present situation, takes control of personal destiny, and is oriented toward the future. This kind of person, whose actions are directed toward a new society yet to be built, is in Latin America more of a motivating ideal than a reality already realized or widespread. But things are moving in this direction. A profound aspiration for the creation of a new human being energizes the process of liberation which the continent is undergoing. This is a difficult creation which will have to overcome conflicts and antagonisms. Rightly does Medellín comment that "[w]e are on the threshold of a new epoch in the history of our continent, a time full of yearning for total emancipation, for liberation from every form of servitude, for personal maturation, and for collective integration. In these signs we perceive the first indications of the painful birth of a new civilization."

Latin America faces a complex situation which does not allow for a simple acceptance or rejection of this orientation toward the future which we noted as characteristic of contemporary men and women. But this situation does lead us to recognize the existence of other realities, of a transitional situation, and to specify that this thrust toward the future occurs *above all* when one participates in the building up of a just society, qualitatively different from the one which exists today. Going deeper into the matter, one moreover gets the impression that many in the developed countries do not have an intense experience, in political matters, of this typical characteristic of the contemporary human person, because they are so attached—in both the East and the West—not to the past, but rather to an affluent present which they seek to preserve and defend in any way they can.

Here we have two approaches. For some, especially in the developed countries, the openness toward the future is an openness to the control of nature by science and technology with no questioning of the social order in which they live. For others, especially dependent and dominated peoples, it will be a future of conflicts and confrontations in which they will have to free themselves from the powers which enslave individuals and exploit social classes. For these persons the development of productive forces, in which scientific and technological advances do indeed play an important part, dialectically demands however that the established order be questioned. Without such a challenge, there is no true thrust into the future.

Be that as it may, the intensification of revolutionary ferment, which is to be found in varying degrees in the modern world, is accentuating and accelerating this thrust toward what is to come. All this creates a complex reality which challenges the Christian faith. The idea of eschatology as the driving force of a future-oriented history attempts to provide a response. But this opening of eschatology to the future is inseparably joined with its historical contemporaneity and urgency. This notion of eschatology is diametrically opposed to that which "eschatologist" theologians upheld some twenty years ago in opposition to the "incarnationalists." The eschatologist tendency expressed the wish for a disengagement of the Christian faith from the powers of this world, but the basis for this was a lack of interest in terrestrial tasks and a historical pessimism which discouraged any attempt at great works. This school was also easy prey to all kinds of conciliatory juxtapositions.

The current eschatological perspective has overcome these obstacles. Not only is it not an evasion of history, but also it has clear and strong implications for the political sphere, for social praxis. This is what some recent reflections on hope, on the political reach of the gospel message, and on the relationship between faith and historical utopia are convincingly demonstrating. . . .

TO ACCOUNT FOR HOPE

To hope does not mean to know the future, but rather to be open, in an attitude of spiritual childhood, to accepting it as a gift. But this gift is accepted in the negation of injustice, in the protest against trampled human rights, and in the struggle for peace and fellowship. Thus hope fulfills a mobilizing and liberating function in history. Its function is not very obvious, but it is real and deep. Péguy has written that "little Hope," which seems to be led by her two older sisters, Faith and Charity, actually leads them. But this will be true only if hope in the future roots itself in the present, if it takes shape in daily events with their joys to experience but also with their injustices to eliminate and their enslavements from which to be liberated. In another context Albert Camus said "true generosity toward the future consists in giving everything to the present."

The somewhat overwhelming emergence of reflection both on eschatology and on its implications on the level of social praxis has put the theology of hope in the forefront. In former years, one had the impression that a theology centered on the love of God and neighbor had replaced a theology concerned especially with faith and the corresponding orthodoxy. The primacy of faith was followed by the "primacy of charity." This permitted the recovery of the notion of love of neighbor as an essential element of Christian life. But paradoxically, at the same time this was also partially responsible for the fact that for some the relationship with God was obscured and became difficult to live out and understand. Today, due partly perhaps to such impasses, the perspective of a new primacy seems to be emerging—that of hope, which liberates history because of its openness to the God who is coming. If faith was reinterpreted by charity, both are now being reinterpreted by hope. All this is very sketchily drawn; we are also, of course, confronted here with a question of emphasis. Christian life and theological reflection must integrate these various dimensions into a profound unity. But the history of the Christian community continuously demonstrates how, at a particular time, one element is stressed over another. New syntheses follow. It is possible that the evolution which we have recalled is leading us to one of these syntheses.

Be this as it may, it might be interesting to trace a parallel between this evolution of theology and the evolution we find in the thought of three men of great influence on our times whose association with theology was not insignificant: G. W. F. Hegel, Ludwig Feuerbach, and Karl Marx. We will do this briefly, and only suggestively, but with the suspicion that a deeper study of this parallel would illuminate our theological reflection.

Feuerbach strongly contrasted love with faith: "Faith is the opposite of love." For him faith was a way of opposing the person to God. Indeed, the essence of the human person is human nature, and this essence is concretely achieved by love, the expression of the need one human being has for another. God is nothing more than this essence projected outside the human being, outside reality. "Knowledge of God is self-knowledge." To find itself again, humankind must abandon faith in this nonexistent being. Human love is "the truth" (in the Hegelian sense of the word) of Christianity. Faith begins with the affirmation of God, while love begins with the affirmation of men and women. Faith separates; love unites. Faith particularizes; love universalizes. Faith divides the person within; love unifies the person. Faith oppresses; love liberates. For Feuerbach, the Hegelian system was based on faith, hence its strongly Christian character, its rigidity, its authoritarian and repressive characteristics. Attempting to place himself in diametrical opposition to Hegelian thought, Feuerbach seeks to center his doctrine on love, going so far as to formulate it as a "religion of love."

Marx, who accepts many of Feuerbach's criticisms of Hegel—especially those directed against religion—comments ironically on the religion of love of the so-called "true socialists," who find their inspiration in Feuerbach. Moreover, he takes Feuerbach to task for overlooking the need for a revolution, due to his erroneous way of relating theory and praxis. In a well-turned phrase, Marx said: "Insofar as Feuerbach is a materialist he does not deal with history, and insofar as he deals with history, he is not a materialist." Marx's idea of praxis is different; it is based on his dialectical conception of history—necessarily advancing, with eyes fixed on the future and with real action in the present, toward a classless society based on new relationships of production.

The theology of hope, on which Marxian thought exercises a certain amount of influence through the work of Ernst Bloch, is a response to the "death of God" approach, in which the presence of Feuerbach's thought is evident. . . .

FAITH, UTOPIA, AND POLITICAL ACTION

The term *utopia* has once again been employed within the last few decades to refer to a historical plan for a qualitatively different society and to express the aspiration to establish new relations among human beings. Numerous studies have been and continue to be made on utopian thought as a dynamic element in the historical becoming of humanity. We must not forget, however, that what really gives utopian thought relevance and highlights its fecundity is the revolutionary experience of our times. Without the support of the lives—and deaths—of many men and women who, rejecting an unjust and alienating social order, throw themselves into the struggle for a new society, the subject of a utopia would never have left the realm of academic discussion.

The main lines of utopian thought were essentially established by Thomas More's famous *Utopia*. Later, the term degenerated until it became in common language synonymous with illusion, lack of realism, irrationality. But because today there is emerging a profound aspiration for liberation—or at least there is a clearer consciousness of it—the original meaning of the expression is again gaining currency. Utopian thought is taking on, in line with its initial intention, its subversive character and its character as a driving force of history. Three elements characterize the notion of utopia as we shall develop it in the following pages: its relationship to historical reality, its verification in praxis, and its rational nature.

Utopia, contrary to what current usage suggests, is characterized by its *relationship to present historical reality*. The literary style and subtle humor exhibited by More have deceived some and distracted others toward accidentals, but it has been demonstrated that the background of his work was the England of his time. The fiction of the country of Utopia in which the common good is paramount, where there is no private property, no money or privileges, was the opposite of his own country, in whose politics he was involved. More's Utopia is a city of the future, something to be achieved, not a return to a lost paradise. This is the characteristic feature of utopian thought in the perspective from which we are speaking here. But this relationship to historical reality is neither simple nor static. It appears under two aspects which mutually require each other. This makes for a complex and dynamic relationship. These two aspects, in Paulo Freire's words, are "denunciation" [condemnation] and "annunciation" [proclamation].

Utopia necessarily means a condemnation of the existing order. Its deficiencies are to a large extent the reason for the emergence of a utopia. It is a matter of a complete rejection which attempts to get to the root of the evil. This is why utopia is revolutionary. As Eric Weil says, "Revolutions erupt when man is discontent with his discontent" (discontent with his reformism?). This condemnation of an intolerable state of affairs is what Marcuse has called—in the context of the affluent societies in which his thought moves—the "Great Refusal." This is the retrospective character of utopia.

But utopia is also a proclamation, an annunciation of what is not yet, but will be; it is the forecast of a different order of things, a new society. It is the field of creative imagination which proposes the alternative values to those rejected. The condemnation is to a large extent made in function of the proclamation. But the proclamation in its turn presupposes this rejection, which clearly delimits it retrospectively. It defines what is not desired. Otherwise, although we might seem to be advancing, we could be going subtly backward. Utopia moves forward; it is a pro-jection toward the future, a dynamic factor which moves history. This is the prospective character of utopia.

According to Paulo Freire, between the condemnation and the proclamation is the time for building, for historical *praxis*. Moreover, condemnation and proclamation can be achieved only *in* praxis. This is what we mean when we talk about utopia as setting history in motion and subverting the existing order. If utopia does not lead to action in the present, it is an evasion of reality. The utopian thesis, writes Paul Ricoeur, is efficacious only "in the measure in which it gradually transforms historical experience," and he specifies, "Utopia is deceiving when it is not concretely related to the possibilities offered to each era." A rejection will be authentic and profound only if it is made within the very act of creating more human living conditions—with the risks that this commitment implies today, particularly for dominated peoples. Utopia must necessarily lead to a commitment in support of the emergence of a new social consciousness and new relationships among persons. Otherwise, the condemnation will remain at a purely verbal level and the proclamation will be only an illusion. Authentic utopian thought postulates, enriches, and supplies new goals for political action, while at the same time it is verified by this action. Its fruitfulness depends upon this relationship.

In the third place, utopia, as I am using it here, belongs to the *rational* order. This claim has been vigorously defended by Paul Blanquart, who notes perceptively that utopia "is not irrational except in respect to a superseded state of reason (the reason of conservatives), since in reality it takes the place of true reason." Utopias emerge with renewed energy at times of transition and crisis, when the stage at which science finds itself has reached its limits in its explanation of social reality, and when new paths open up for historical praxis. Utopia, so understood, is neither opposed to nor outside of science. On the contrary, it constitutes the essence of its creativity and dynamism. It is the prelude of science, its proclamation. The theoretical construct which allows us to know social reality and which makes political action efficacious demands the mediation of the creative imagination: "The transition from the empirical to the theoretical presupposes a jump, a break: the intervention of the imagination." And Blanquart points out that imagination in politics is called utopia.

This is the difference between utopia and ideology. The term *ideology* has a long and turbulent history and has been understood in very different ways. But we can basically agree that ideology does not offer adequate and scientific knowledge of reality; rather, it masks it. Ideology does not rise above the empirical, irrational level. Therefore, it spontaneously fulfills a function of preservation of the established order. Therefore, also, ideology tends to dogmatize all that has not succeeded in separating itself from it or has fallen back under its influence. Political action, science, and faith do not escape this danger. Utopia, however, leads to an authentic and scientific knowledge of reality and to a praxis which transforms what exists. Utopia is different from science but does not thereby stop being its dynamic, internal element.

Because of its relationship to reality, its influence on praxis, and its rational character, utopia is a factor in moving history and in radicalizing transformation. Utopia, indeed, is on the level of the cultural revolution which attempts to forge a new kind of person. Freire is right when he says that in today's world only the oppressed human being, class, and country can condemn and proclaim. Only they are capable of working out revolutionary utopias and not conservative or reformist ideologies. The oppressive system's only future is to maintain its present of affluence.

The relationship between faith and political action could, perhaps, be clarified by appealing to the clarifications I have just made with respect to the historical plan designated by the term *utopia*. In trying to understand the notion of liberation, I said that we were dealing with a single process. Yet it is a complex, differentiated unity, which encompasses—without confusing—distinct levels of meaning: economic, social, and political liberation; liberation which leads to the creation of new men and women in a society of solidarity; and liberation from sin and entrance into communion with God and with all others. The first corresponds to the level of scientific rationality which supports real and effective transforming political action; the second stands at the level of utopia, of the historical project, with the characteristics we have just considered; the third is on the level of faith. These different levels are profoundly linked; one does not occur without the others. On the basis of the clarifications we have just made, we can perhaps go one step further toward understanding the bond which unites them. It is not, however, our intention to reduce to an easy schematization what we have said regarding the complex relationship which exists between the kingdom and historical events, between eschatology and politics. However, to shed light on the subject from another angle may be helpful.

To assert a direct, immediate relationship between faith and political action too easily encourages one to seek from faith norms and criteria for particular political options. To be really effective, these options ought to be based on rational analyses of reality. Thus confusions are created which can result in a dangerous politico-religious messianism which does not sufficiently respect either the autonomy of the political arena or that which belongs to an authentic faith, liberated from religious baggage. As Blanquart has pointed out, politico-religious messianism is a backward-looking reaction to a new situation which the messianists are not capable of confronting with the appropriate attitude and means. This is an "infrapolitical movement" which "is not in accord with the Christian faith either."

On the other hand, to assert that faith and political action have nothing to say to each other is to claim that they move on juxtaposed and unrelated planes. If we begin with this assertion, either we will have to engage in verbal gymnastics to show—without succeeding—how faith should become concrete in a commitment to a more just society; or faith ends up coexisting in a most opportunistic manner with any political option.

Faith and political action will not enter into a correct and fruitful relationship except through the project of creating a new type of person in a different society, that is, except through utopia, to use the term we have attempted to clarify in the preceding paragraphs. This project provides the background for the struggle for better living conditions. Political liberation appears as a path toward the utopia of freer, more human persons, protagonists of their own history. Che Guevara has said: "Socialism currently, in this stage of the construction of socialism and communism, has not as its only purpose to have shining factories; it is intended for the whole person; human beings must be transformed at the same time as production increases, and we would not be doing our job well if we produced only things and not at the same time persons." It follows that for him the important thing for the building up of a new society is simultaneously "a daily increase in both productivity and consciousness."

Utopia so understood, far from making political fighters into dreamers, radicalizes their commitment and helps them keep their work from betraying their purpose—their desire to achieve a real encounter among all persons at the heart of a free society without social inequalities. "Only utopia," comments Ricoeur, "can give economic, social, and political action a human focus." The loss of utopia makes us fall into bureaucratism and sectarianism, into new structures which oppress the human being. The process, apart from understandable ups and downs and deficiencies, is not liberating if the project for new men and women in a freer society is not held to and concretized. This project is not for later, when political liberation will have been attained. It must accompany, from the beginning and permanently, the struggle for a more just society. Without this critical and rational element of historical dynamism and creative imagination, science and political action see a changing reality slip out of their hands, and they easily fall into dogmatism. And political dogmatism is as worthless as religious dogmatism; both represent a step backward toward ideology. But for utopia validly to fulfill this role, it must be verified by social praxis; it must become effective commitment, without intellectual purisms and without inappropriate demands; it must be revised and concretized constantly.

The historical project, the utopia of liberation as the creation of a new social consciousness and as a social appropriation not only of the means of production, but also of the political process, and, definitively, of freedom, is the proper arena for the cultural revolution. That is to say, it is the arena of the permanent creation of a new person in a different society characterized by solidarity. Therefore, that creation is the place of encounter between political liberation and the communion of all persons with God, a communion which passes through liberation from sin, the ultimate root of all injustice, all dispossession, all divisions among persons. Faith proclaims that the human fellowship which is sought through the abolition of exploitation of some by others is something possible, that efforts to bring it about are not in vain, that God calls us to it and assures us of its complete fulfillment, and that what is definitive reality is being constructed within what is provisional. Faith reveals to us the deep meaning of the history which we forge with our own hands: it teaches us the value of communion with God—of salvation—which every human act oriented toward the construction of a more just society has, and inversely it teaches that all injustice is a breach with God.

In human love there is a density which the human being does not suspect: in human love the encounter with the Lord takes place. If utopia gives a human face to economic, social, and political liberation, this human face—in the light of the gospel—reveals God. If doing justice leads us to a knowledge of God, finding God in turn requires a commitment to doing justice. The mediation of the historical project of the creation of a new human being assures that liberation from sin and communion with God in solidarity with all persons—which affects political liberation and is enriched by its contributions-does not fall into idealism and evasion. But, at the same time, this mediation prevents this impact from becoming translated into any kind of Christian ideology of political action or a politico-religious messianism. Christian hope opens us, in an attitude of spiritual childhood, to the gift of the future promised by God. It keeps us from any confusion of the kingdom with any one historical stage, from any idolatry toward unavoidably ambiguous human achievement, from any absolutizing of revolution. In this way hope makes us radically free to commit ourselves to social praxis, moved by a liberating utopia and with the means which the scientific analysis of reality provides for us. And our hope not only frees us for this commitment; it simultaneously demands and judges it.

The gospel does not provide a utopia for us; this is a human work. The Word is a free gift of the Lord. But the gospel is not alien to the historical project; on the contrary, the human project and the gift of God imply each other. The Word is the foundation and the meaning of all human existence; this foundation is attested to and this meaning is concretized historically through human actions. For those who live by them, faith, charity, and hope are a radical source of spiritual freedom and historical creativity and initiative.

In this way, the claim that "the victory which has conquered death is our faith" will be lived, inescapably, at the very heart of history, in the bosom of a single process of liberation which leads that history to its fulfillment in the definitive encounter with God. To hope in Christ is at the same time to believe in the adventure of history, which opens up an infinite field of possibilities for the love and action of the Christian.

32. JESUS AND THE POLITICAL WORLD

Although Gutiérrez has not (to date) produced a thoroughgoing Christology, there can be no doubt about the place Jesus Christ occupies in his consideration of nearly every theological problem. For Gutiérrez, history is "christo-finalized" (see the first selection of this section), "Christ makes humankind truly free," (Theology of Liberation, *25), and "Christ is the truth, a truth that sets us free"* (Truth, *105). In theology as in pastoral practice, his purpose is to advance the saving work of Christ. A question arises, of course: which Christ? In the following passage from chapter 11 of* Theology of Liberation, *"Eschatology and Politics" (130–35), entitled "Jesus and the Political World," Gutiérrez locates Jesus' subversive character in the evangelical message of love he preached and courageously lived out, and for which he was put to death by the political authorities. Preaching the good news of God's* universal *love inevitably means condemning all "injustice, privilege, oppression, or narrow nationalism" (135). Such radicality cannot be politically disinterested; at the same time it transcends mere revolutionary politics (such as the activity of the Zealots in Jesus' day). Instead, the life and preaching of Jesus imply (among other things) personal transformation and social justice, that is, "the unceasing search for a new kind of person in a qualitatively different society" (134).*

The current concern about the liberation of the oppressed, about the social revolution which is to transform the present order, about the counterviolence opposed to the violence which the existing order produces—and with which it defends itself—have all led many Christians to ask themselves about the attitude of Jesus regarding the political situation of his time. The question may surprise us. If so, it is because we take it for granted that Jesus was not interested in political life: his mission was purely religious. Indeed we have witnessed a process which José Comblin terms the "iconization" of the life of Jesus. . . . The life of Jesus is thus placed outside history, unrelated to the real forces at play. Jesus and those whom he befriended, or whom he confronted and whose hostility he earned, are deprived of all human content. They are there reciting a completed script. It is impossible not to experience a sensation of unreality when presented with such a life of Jesus.

To approach the man Jesus of Nazareth, in whom God was made flesh, to penetrate not only his teaching, but also his life, what it is that gives his word an immediate, concrete context, is a task which more and more needs to be undertaken. One aspect of this work will be to examine the alleged apoliticism of Jesus, which would not coincide with what I have pointed out regarding the biblical message and Jesus' own teaching. Hence, a serious reconsideration of this presupposition is necessary. But it has to be undertaken with a respect for the historical Jesus, not forcing the facts in terms of our current concerns. If we wished to discover in Jesus the least characteristic of a contemporary political activist, we would not only misrepresent his life and witness and demonstrate a lack of understanding on our part of politics in the present world; we would also deprive ourselves of what his life and witness have that is deep and universal and, therefore, valid and concrete for today.

The more recent studies on the life of Jesus related to the political problems of his time, although they have not reached a consensus on all matters, have highlighted some aspects of the question which had been somewhat neglected until now. I will concentrate on three of them which we can consider indisputable: the complex relationship between Jesus and the Zealots, his attitude toward the leaders of the Jewish people, and his death at the hands of the political authorities.

It is becoming clearer that the *Zealot movement* is very important for an understanding of the New Testament and especially of the life and death of Jesus. To situate Jesus in his time implies an examination of his connection with this movement of religious and political resistance to the Roman oppressors. Zealots (from the Greek *zelos*, "zeal") were part of the circle of Jesus' closest associates. He exercised a great attraction over these people who loved the Law, who were strong nationalists, who fiercely opposed Roman domination, and who ardently awaited the impending arrival of the kingdom which was to end this situation. Oscar Cullmann has proved that some of the direct disciples of Jesus were Zealots or had some connection with them; he concludes his study with this assertion: "One of the Twelve—Simon the Zealot—*certainly* belonged to the Zealots; others *probably* did, like Judas Iscariot, Peter, and *possibly* the sons of Zebedee." But there is more. We find many points of agreement between the Zealots and the attitudes and teachings of Jesus, for example, his preaching of the proximity of the kingdom and the role he himself plays in its advent, the assertion—whose interpretation is debated—that "the kingdom of Heaven has been subjected to violence and the violent are seizing it" (Matt. 11:12), his attitude toward the Jews who worked for the Romans, his action of purifying the temple, his power over the people who wanted to make him king. For these reasons, Jesus and his disciples were often related to the Zealots (cf. Acts 5:37; 21:38; cf. also Luke 13:1).

But at the same time, Jesus kept his distance from the Zealot movement. The awareness of the universality of his mission did not fit with the somewhat narrow nationalism of the Zealots. Because they disdainfully rejected the Samaritans and pagans, the Zealots must have been shocked by Jesus' behavior toward them. The message of Jesus is addressed to all; the justice and peace he advocated know no national boundaries. In this he was even more revolutionary than the Zealots, who were fierce defenders of literal obedience to the Law; Jesus taught an attitude of spiritual freedom toward it. Moreover, for Jesus the kingdom was, in the first place, a gift. Only on this basis can we understand the meaning of the active participation of all in its coming; the Zealots tended to see it rather as the fruit of their own efforts. For Jesus, oppression and injustice were not limited to a specific historical situation; their causes go deeper and cannot be truly eliminated without going to the very roots of the problem: the breakdown of fellowship and communion among human beings. Besides, and this will have enormous consequences, Jesus is opposed to all politico-religious messianism which does not respect either the depth of the religious realm or the autonomy of political action. Messianism can be efficacious in the short run but the ambiguities and confusions which it entails frustrate the ends it attempts to accomplish. This idea was considered as a temptation by Jesus; as such, he rejected it. The liberation which Jesus offers is universal and integral; it transcends national boundaries, attacks the foundation of injustice and exploitation, and eliminates politico-religious confusions, without thereby being limited to a purely "spiritual" plane.

It is not enough, then, to say that Jesus was not a Zealot. There are those who seek, in good faith but uncritically, to cleanse Jesus from anything which could provide grounds for speaking of a political attitude on his part. But Jesus' stance precludes all oversimplification. To close one's eyes to this complexity amounts to letting the richness of his testimony on this score escape.

During all his public life, Jesus confronted the *groups with power* within the Jewish people. Herod, a man employed by the Roman oppressor, was called "the Fox" (Luke 13:32). The publicans, whom the people considered collaborators with the dominant political power, were placed among the sinners (Matt. 9:10; 21:31; Luke 5:30; 7:34). The Sadducees were conscious that Jesus threatened their official and privileged position. Jesus' preaching strongly attacked their skepticism in religious matters; they were in the majority in the Great Sanhedrin which condemned him. His criticism of a religion made up of purely external rules and observances also brought him into violent confrontation with the Pharisees. Jesus turned to the great prophetic tradition and claimed that worship is authentic only when based on profound personal dispositions, on the creation of true fellowship, and on real commitment to others, especially the neediest (cf., for example, Matt. 5:23–24; 25:31–45). To this criticism Jesus added a head-on opposition to the rich and powerful and a radical option for the poor; one's attitude toward them determines the validity of all religious behavior; it is above all for them that the Son of man has come. The Pharisees rejected Roman domination, but they had structured a complex world of religious precepts and norms of behavior which allowed them to live on the margin of the situation. They certainly accepted coexistence. The Zealots were well aware of this, thus their opposition to the Pharisees despite many other points of agreement with them. When Jesus attacked the very foundation of their arrangement, he unmasked the falsity of their position and appeared in the eyes of the Pharisees as a dangerous traitor.

Jesus *died at the hands of the political authorities,* the oppressors of the Jewish people. According to the Roman custom, the title on the cross indicated the reason for the sentence; in the case of Jesus this title denoted political guilt: King of the Jews. Cullmann can therefore say that Jesus was executed by the Romans as a Zealot leader, and he finds an additional proof of this affirmation in the episode of Barabbas who was undoubtedly a Zealot. . . . The Sanhedrin had religious reasons for condemning a man who claimed to be the Son of God, but it also had political reasons: the teachings of Jesus and his influence over the people challenged the situation of privilege and power of the Jewish leaders. These political considerations were related to another which affected the Roman authority itself: the claim to be Messiah and King of the Jews. His trial closely combined these different reasons. . . . From the moment he started preaching, the die was cast for Jesus: "I have spoken openly to all the world" (John 18:20), he tells the High Priest. For this reason [Heinrich Schlier holds that] John's Gospel presents the life of Jesus as a case "brought, or intended to be brought, against Jesus by the world, represented by the Jews. This action reached its public, judicial decision before Pontius Pilate, the representative of the Roman state and holder of political power."

What conclusions can we draw from these facts about the life of Jesus? For Cullmann—one of the authors who has studied this matter most seriously and carefully—the key to the behavior of Jesus in political matters is what he calls "eschatological radicalism," which is based on the hope of an *imminent* advent of the kingdom. Hence it follows that "for Jesus, *all* the realities of this world necessarily had to be *relativized* so that his position goes beyond the alternatives of the 'existing order' or 'revolution.'" Jesus was not uninterested in action in this world, but because he expected an imminent end of history, he "was concerned only with the conversion of the individual and was not interested in a reform of the social structures." According to Cullmann, the attitude of Jesus cannot therefore be transposed to our times without qualification. From the moment that the development of history shows us that the end of the world is not imminent, it becomes clear that "more just social structures also promote the individual change of character required by Jesus." Henceforward, then, we must postulate "a reciprocal influence between individual conversion and the reform of structures."

In interpreting the behavior of Jesus in political matters, Cullmann gives the expectation of the imminent end of time a definitive role. What has been called "consequent eschatology," in the perspective opened by Albert Schweitzer, already held that Jesus had erroneously announced and awaited the imminent coming of the kingdom. This is a difficult and controversial exegetical question. For this very reason, it does not provide a sufficiently sound basis for an understanding of Jesus' attitude regarding political life. The interpretation is based on Jesus' words but tends to remove or weaken the tension between the present and the future which characterizes his preaching of the kingdom.

Moreover, Cullmann uses this belief of Jesus to support his insistence on personal conversion as opposed, in a certain sense, to the need for the transformation of structures; the latter would appear only when the waiting is prolonged. But, in fact, when he preached personal conversion, Jesus pointed to a fundamental, permanent attitude which was primarily opposed not to a concern for social structures, but to purely formal worship, devoid of religious authenticity and human content. In this, Jesus was only turning to the great prophetic line which required "mercy and not sacrifice," "contrite hearts and not holocausts." Now for the prophets this demand was inseparable from the denunciation of social injustice and from the vigorous assertion that God is known only by doing justice. To neglect this aspect is to remove from the call to personal conversion its social, vital, and concrete context. To attribute the concern for social structures—except for the nuances operative today—to the prolongation of the waiting period impoverishes and definitely distorts the matter.

What then are we to think of Jesus' attitude in these matters? The facts we have recalled vigorously ratify what we know of the universality and totality of his work. This universality and totality touch the very heart of political behavior, giving it its true dimension and depth. Misery and social injustice reveal "a situation of sin," a breakdown of fellowship and communion; by freeing us from sin, Jesus attacks the very root of an unjust order. For Jesus, the liberation of the Jewish people was only one aspect of a universal and permanent revolution. Far from showing no interest in this liberation, Jesus rather placed it on a deeper level, with fruitful consequences.

The Zealots were not mistaken in feeling that Jesus was simultaneously near and far away. Neither were the powerful of the Jewish people mistaken in thinking that their position was imperiled by the preaching of Jesus, nor the oppressive political authorities when they put him to death as a rebel. They were mistaken (and their followers have continued to be mistaken) only in thinking that it was all accidental and transitory, in thinking that with the death of Jesus the matter was closed, in supposing that no one would remember it. The gospel entails heavy human responsibility and social transformation which are permanent and essential because it destroys the narrow limits of particular historical situations and goes to the very root of human existence: relationship with God in solidarity with other persons. The gospel does not get its political dimension from one or another particular option, but from the very nucleus of its message. If this message is subversive, it is because it takes on Israel's hope: the kingdom as, [in Wolfhart Pannenberg's words], "the end of domination of person over person; it is a kingdom in contradiction to the established powers and on behalf of humankind." And the gospel gives Israel's hope its deepest meaning; indeed it calls for a new creation: The life and preaching of Jesus postulate the unceasing search for a new kind of person in a qualitatively different society. Although the kingdom must not be confused with the establishment of a just society, this does not mean that it is indifferent to this society. Nor does it mean that a just society constitutes a "prior condition" for the arrival of the kingdom nor that they are closely linked, nor that they converge. More profoundly, the proclamation of the kingdom reveals to society itself the aspiration for a just society and leads it to discover unsuspected dimensions and unexplored paths. The kingdom is realized in a society of fellowship and justice; and, in turn, this realization shines forth in promise and in hope of complete communion of us all with God. The political is grafted into the eternal.

This does not impoverish the gospel proclamation; rather it enriches the political sphere. On the other hand, the life and death of Jesus are no less evangelical because of their political connotations. His testimony and his message acquire this political dimension precisely because of the radicalness of their salvific character: preaching the universal love of the Father goes inevitably against all injustice, privilege, oppression, or narrow nationalism.

33. THE PATH OF LIBERATION

In the context of the critical evaluation of liberation theology underway at various levels of the church in the 1980s, Gutiérrez clarified themes with which he had previously dealt and took up new questions as well. Key sections of the following selection (found in Truth, *105–141) were first presented as lectures in the early 1980s during Lima's "summer course" in theology and were published in a 1984 essay called "Por el camino de la pobreza" (roughly, "Taking the Road of Poverty"). In his redaction for the second part of the lengthy essay "The Truth Shall Make You Free" (1986), Gutiérrez first examines the radically individualistic notion of freedom prevalent in the West and reveals the "underside" of its historical development. He then notes the usefulness of the "Chalcedonian principle" (distinguishing elements in order to unite them) in understanding the single, yet complex, process of liberation "which finds its deepest sense and its full realization in the saving work of Christ." Finally, he reformulates the three levels of liberation (social liberation, interior freedom, and full communion with God and others) with exemplary precision and concreteness. Throughout the essay he pays particular attention to the two "Instructions" on liberation theology drawn up by the Vatican's Sacred Congregation for the Doctrine of the Faith,* Libertatis nuntius *(1984) and* Libertatis conscientia *(1986).*

Christ is the truth, but a truth that sets us free. The liberation he gives is an integral one that embraces all dimensions of human existence and brings us to full communion with God and among ourselves. This liberation is therefore one that begins within history, which thus becomes a way to a fullness that lies beyond it.

An examination of the historical vicissitudes of freedom will bring to light the different perspectives on God and on the poor found in them. In this area, the basic datum of our faith is Christ's lordship over the development of the human race (of which St. Paul was especially conscious). This basic datum enables us to understand that liberation—within which we can distinguish different levels—is a route toward communion. Communion, however, is a gift of Christ who sets us free in order that we may be free, free to love; it is in this communion that full freedom resides (see Gal. 5:1 and 13).

FAR FROM GOD . . . AND FROM THE POOR

Libertatis conscientia (1986; hereafter *LC*) begins with an important discussion and critique of the movement for modern freedoms in Europe. This phase of history is heavy with consequences for that continent and the contemporary world generally, as well as for the task of the church in our time. It is useful to recall the main lines of this stage of European history and bring to light the ruptures which took place in the poor countries in relation to this development.

THE MOVEMENT FOR THE MODERN FREEDOMS

The question of human freedom has always been a challenge to the Christian conscience. Christianity preaches a truth that saves, but this truth must be accepted by free beings. Truth and freedom thus stand in a fruitful tension. Christian life is a dialogue between a God who calls and human beings who respond; their response must be free, just as the gift is free that God wants to make of God's self.

Truth and Freedom. The question of freedom arose even in the first centuries. Faced with the hostility of the Roman Empire, which sought to impose its will, Christians firmly claimed the rights they associated with their religious faith. They found the ultimate basis for this claim in sacred scripture, but the historical situation in which they were living made them keenly, and increasingly, conscious of it. Tertullian and Lactantius are two great witnesses from this period. Both clearly assert that freedom of religion is a right of every human being and that political authorities have no jurisdiction in this area. Both of these assertions are based on a profound conviction—namely, that freedom is a condition for attaining to truth.

From the fourth century on, the situation of Christianity in the empire changed. The basic insights in the matter of religious freedom lost something of their urgency, for a new factor now had to be taken into account: the existence of a political authority that placed itself at the service of the Christian religion. True enough, the essential point in the claim of religious freedom persisted, but it took a different form. The claim now was that the act of faith is free; in other words, any imposition of Christian truth was rejected; no one could be forced to accept the faith. This was a problem unknown to the earlier centuries when Christianity was being persecuted in the Roman Empire. The very fact that the new question could be raised proves that the historical situation in which Christianity found itself had indeed changed. There was an even greater change from the earlier refusal to allow political authorities any competence in religious matters. From the sixth century on, the emphasis was rather on the service that the temporal power should render to religious truth, although this service ought never take the form of imposing the faith. This ministerial conception of political power in relation to religion was to be reaffirmed throughout the Middle Ages, to the extent, at times, of seriously endangering freedom in these matters.

The question of religious freedom was posed anew in connection with the Protestant Reformation and Renaissance humanism. But, as *LC* says, "it was above all in the age of the Enlightenment and at the French Revolution that the call to freedom rang out with full force" (no. 6). The call was for freedom for the human person in various areas, one of these—and a very important one—being the area of religion. Down to our own day, modernity, with its lights and shadows, has influenced European society and has had repercussions in other parts of the world.

Everyone is aware of the attitude of rejection that the church adopted toward this movement for the modern freedoms. If we read the documents of the popes from Pius VI to Pius IX, it is easy to see that a single major concern, expressed in different ways, motivated this rejection: that these freedoms would endanger the salvation of human beings. According to these documents, the abolishment of Catholicism as the state religion and the proclamation of civil equality for other forms of worship are the results of an indifferentism that puts truth and error on the same level.

The confrontation that went on throughout the nineteenth century was painful and erosive for the church. Its institutional influence decreased in European society, and in Latin America today is not what it was in earlier centuries. On the other hand, with the passage of time the elements that initially seemed to form a monolithic block were separated out. Needed distinctions were gradually made, misunderstandings were cleared up, and the representatives of both liberalism and the church came to speak more calmly. It came to be realized that many claims of modernity had a Christian source. Some Christian circles ("liberal Catholicism") accepted the new perspectives, rejecting at the same time what could be in opposition to their faith. Their attitude was one of magnanimity and readiness for dialogue; this did not, however, exclude the ambivalence to be seen in every historical process. Their position, though vigorously rejected by the popes in the beginning (cf. the condemnations of Gregory XVI and Pius IX), was enriched with new perspectives and has gradually been spreading.

The position taken by the popes gradually changed during the twentieth century; then came Vatican II. The "Declaration on Religious Freedom," which is cited often in the first chapter of *LC*, was one of the most keenly debated documents of the Council, for the burden of the bitter and painful discussion that had gone on for over a century was still too great to cast aside easily. The so-called conciliar minority believed that to defend religious freedom would be to undermine the papal magisterium of the previous century. The victory finally went, however, to the principle that distinguishes between the legitimacy of the demand for modern freedoms, especially religious freedom, and the ideological and antireligious wrappings in which the claim was initially made by some.

Distance from God. *LC* adopts the perspective of the "Declaration on Religious Freedom" and fervently defends religious freedom and other human freedoms. The Instruction honestly acknowledges the "errors of judgment and serious omissions for which Christians have been responsible in the course of the centuries" (no. 20) in this area. There were indeed errors and omissions. I have mentioned only what happened with the matter of religious freedom, but there are other cases.

These mistakes inflicted a great deal of suffering; above all, however, they were an obstacle to the vital presence of the gospel in today's world. Much of what we now criticize in modern society is due to the fact that we Christians did not know how to be critical and involved in its construction, attentive to what is valid in its demands, and able to share our own message. History has taught us a painful but rewarding lesson here. We should therefore welcome with joy the resolute defense in *LC* of religious freedom and of human freedoms generally.

The greatest mistake was to think that the assertion of religious freedom would be at the expense of Christian truth. Truth and error were hypostasized, and it was said that truth alone has rights, when in fact only the human person is a subject of rights over against the civil power. The Christians of the first centuries realized from experience and reflection that truth and freedom were not opposed, that the latter was the necessary condition for attaining the former. Their historical context made this vision of things easier for the early Christians; our task is to renew the vision in our own situation, which is certainly much more complex.

The conciliar "Declaration on Religious Freedom" takes this point into account and begins with a resolute affirmation regarding the truth that saves (no. 1, a text based on a draft edited by Yves Congar), in order then to maintain, no less resolutely, that "the human person has a right to religious freedom" (no. 2). The Council does not go into the theological twists and turns of the subject but provides what might be called a necessary mental hygiene in regard to it and prepares the way for entering more deeply into it.

Libertatis conscientia vigorously defends the permanent values of religious freedom as well as its present necessity in face of the totalitarian threats in today's world. The present situation causes the Vatican Congregation to reread the history of recent centuries with its successes, but also with its errors that still prevail today. The situation also allows the Congregation to reevaluate the relation between the church and freedom. While acknowledging past "errors of judgment," it asserts, with good reason, that much of the church's criticism of the modern world "has often been misunderstood. . . . With the passage of time, however, it is possible to do greater justice to the church's point of view" (no. 20).

The 1986 Instruction has some relevant remarks on this reaction of the modern world, and it criticizes as unacceptable the opposition that some facets of the modern mentality set up between God and the human person: "For many . . . , it is God who is the specific alienation of humankind. There is said to be a radical incompatibility between the affirmation of God and of human freedom. By rejecting belief in God, they say, humankind will become truly free" (no. 18). Unbelief or skepticism in religious matters and distance from God are in fact characteristic of important portions of modern consciousness.

THE AMBIGUITIES OF A PROCESS

The intellectual and philosophical side of the movement for modern freedoms—the movement we know as the Enlightenment—set goals and raised aspirations that very soon began to be disappointed. The initial optimism quickly faded. The most clearsighted representatives of the movement saw the internal contradictions in the process they themselves were promoting. Hegel could already speak of the "unsatisfied Enlightenment." From the very first decades of the period, people were also aware of the paradoxical possibility of totalitarianism in the assertion of freedoms.

Modern Individualism. LC takes up and continues this criticism first made from within the historical process that went on mainly in Europe but also reached certain intellectual and political minorities in Latin America. In this same critique, in addition to its consequences in the area of religion, is the main line of the document's stance toward that phase in the history of the Western world known as modernity with its claims in the areas of reason and freedom. *LC* aptly says that "in the field of social and political achievements, one of the fundamental ambiguities of the affirmation of freedom in the age of the Enlightenment had to do with the concept of the subject of this freedom as an individual who is fully self-sufficient and whose finality is the satisfaction of its own interests in the enjoyment of earthly goods" (no. 13).

In fact, the chief characteristic of the modern mentality is its radical individualism. In the area of economics this outlook finds clear expression in the declaration of human rights as enunciated by the French revolution: "Every man is free to use his muscles, his skills, and his capital as appears good and useful to himself. He can make what pleases him and what seems good to him." There is no other objective than one's own will and interests. This outlook gave rise to an exaggerated view of the legitimate right of private property as the setting in which responsible personal freedom was to be exercised. The liberal historian Guido de Ruggiero has rightly said: "Freedom in work is a child of modern individualism and even its favorite child."

The individual is an absolute principle not only in economic activity but also in the building of society, for society is simply the sum total of the individual decisions that establish what J. J. Rousseau called a "social contract." Social life is thus entirely in the hands of individuals and their interests. The perspective of the common good carries less weight in social life.

The individualistic root is also found in the area of knowledge. Nothing is to be accepted as true that has not been submitted to the judgment of critical reason. Individual reason is sovereign and acknowledges no authority above itself, just as it does not recognize any authority in economic matters or even in social life.

Radical individualism is the expression of the self-sufficiency which *LC* criticizes. We must recognize the existence of this individualism if we are to understand the contribution but also the enormous limitations of the modern mentality. If we keep this individualism in mind, we will not be surprised at what *LC* has to say about the situation created in the poor countries during the period of history in which the wealth of countries guided by social groups representative of the modern ideology was affirmed. The 1986 Instruction says that in this way a situation was created which "favored the unequal distribution of wealth at the beginning of the industrial era to the point that workers found themselves excluded from access to the essential goods that they had helped to produce and to which they had a right. Hence the birth of powerful liberation movements from poverty caused by industrial society" (no. 13).

The Underside of History. The point made by *LC* is important; here again, however, it is necessary to go deeper and develop further the critique of the modern mentality. This will help to understand a theology done from "the underside of history."

In his encyclical on human work *(Laborem exercens;* henceforth *LE)* John Paul II speaks as follows of the social consequences of the modern mentality: "In the modern period, from the beginning of the industrial age, the Christian truth about work had to oppose the various currents of *materialistic* and *economistic* thought" (no. 7, italics added). For these currents, capital took precedence over labor. The pope goes on to speak of what happened in the last century as a consequence of the industrial age: "a just social reaction and . . . the impetuous emergence of a great burst of solidarity between workers, first and foremost industrial workers" [*LE*, no. 8].

This response, which is described a little further on as an "ethically just social reaction," was provoked by the affirmation of capitalism as "an economic and social system" (*LE*, no. 7). The reaction sprang from the real poverty and injustice created by an advancing industrialization that paid no heed to the human rights of workers.

This complex historical relationship is also to be found in the majority of the population of Third World countries. The present situation of the poor sectors and countries of the world has in large measure resulted from the predominance of the modern individualist spirit, which is alert to its own interests but myopic when it comes to the claims of others in both the social and the economic areas. At the opening of the Puebla Conference in Mexico, John Paul II spoke of the mechanisms "that lead on the international level to the ever-increasing wealth of the rich at the expense of the ever-increasing poverty of the poor." He thereby denounced a situation that is the result of a historical process of universal scope. The issue is not simply economic and social; it is human. That is why *LE* speaks of an "ethical" reaction.

For the same reason—and this is of utmost importance—the liberation movement that proceeds from "the underside of history" is not purely and simply a continuation of the movement for modern freedoms. Far from it. The discontinuities and oppositions between the two have theoretical significance and therefore very extensive practical consequences. There are also, of course, threads of continuity between the two, as there always are in this kind of historical process. But if we do not see the breaks and contrasts, we will end up attributing both movements to the same impulse and classifying them under the same heading; in that case, we will lose sight of what is specific to each and become confused about the challenges to be met. *Libertatis conscientia* does not appear to perceive this sufficiently.

The human and ethical level of which I have been speaking is the specific terrain of theological reflection that springs from the faith experience of the poor. Our interlocutors here are those who are not looked upon as persons in the present social order, those whose human dignity, is systematically trampled down, those who are regarded as less important than the fruit of their work.

The interlocutors of modern theology are different, and it is only right to take this fact into account. Modern theology is called upon to answer the questions raised by the modern consciousness and perceptively expressed by the Enlightenment. For if theology is done in the service of evangelization, then it must find the language needed for the Christian message to be effectively present in the modern world, the world in which the church, too, is living. Modern theology is therefore a necessary theology that has to meet the challenges of unbelievers and counteract the secularizing influence these challenges exert in the Christian world.

The theology being done in Latin America (and in other areas of the poor world) has a different point of departure. It is a reflection arising from "the underside of history," to which I referred earlier—that is, from the place where the historical results of the process carried through by the rich countries are to be seen. Theology is, of course, first of all an understanding illumined by faith, and its ultimate criteria of truth are derived from the *depositum fidei*. But our thinking as human beings is always affected by the world in which we live and by the questions that world puts to us; this means that our theological discourse must relate to the faith as lived in and by the church in the historical phase through which it is passing.

Liberation theology, therefore, is not (as some seem to think) the radical wing of European progressivist theology. The latter is facing challenges that are not ours, or at least are not primary for us. This point must be kept clearly in mind if there is to be any fruitful theological dialogue. For there is a magnanimous tendency in some European circles to extend their internal debates to include theologies they persist in regarding as simple appendices, less scientific and more politically radicalized, to what is going on in the Old World.

I am obviously not claiming that, simply because we here are attempting to do our reflection within our own reality of poverty and within the life of our church, others must accept everything we do under pain of being otherwise considered bad Christians or oppressors. That would be inadmissible. What we do ask, in the name of openness to the Spirit that breathes where it will and in the name of respect for our people, is that others acknowledge the standpoint we adopt and the questions we are trying to answer. Everything else must be an object of theological discussion and meet the requirements, which all must respect, of doctrinal orthodoxy and scientific work.

The Right of the Poor to Think. Theological discourse that is immersed in the life of the poor and accepts all the consequences this immersion entails cannot ignore the faith of the people. The people of Latin America are both exploited and Christian. A failure to be attentive to both dimensions would mean a distortion of this complex reality; furthermore, each leaves its stamp on theological work.

While the modern world may think of itself as distant from God, the same is not true of the world of the poor. This matter is profound and decisive. In sacred scripture contempt for the poor implies contempt for God; passages to this effect are beyond counting. It is not surprising, therefore, that the blindness of the modern spirit to the poor, a blindness resulting from the economic and social order that spirit inspires, should also find expression in distance from the God of Jesus Christ and the demands God makes of human beings.

Libertatis conscientia criticizes modern individualism for its aloofness from God; to this aloofness must be added its remoteness from the poor and their just demands. These are but two sides of the same coin, a fact that accounts for the constant criticism of the modern world (whose good points, however, are also recognized) in the kind of theological thinking done from the viewpoint of those whom James Cone calls "the victims of history." By the same token, and in a reversal of that historical development, sensitivity to the rights of the poor brings us closer to the God of life. [As I wrote in 1977], "The spiritual . . . is not opposed to the social. The real opposition is between bourgeois individualism and the spiritual in the biblical sense."

Liberation theology is anything but the spearhead of a secularizing approach or of "bourgeois Christianity" in Latin America. We think rather that a clear rejection, inspired by Christian faith, of the inhuman poverty existing in Latin America will militate against the negative side of secularism and the modern spirit. We are convinced that our thinking starts from a social, cultural, and religious reality differing from that of Europe and that this situation offers a completely new historical possibility that we must explore and develop. Not to do so would be an infidelity to the gospel and a betrayal of the poor of Latin America. Liberation theology contributes to a sound and profound Christian identity that in turn makes possible a fruitful relationship with those Latin Americans who do not share the Christian faith but are committed to the poor and honestly sensitive to the Christian dimension in the life of the Latin American peoples.

The defense of life and the struggle for justice in Latin America bear the mark of faith in the God of life. At the very beginning of the evangelization of Latin America, Bartolomé de Las Casas preached a God who is alive amid the situation of death that was evident even then. The process of liberation has been watered by the blood of humble peasants and settlers who have endeavored to bear witness to their Christian faith through solidarity with their poorer brothers and sisters. The same is true of outstanding churchmen such as Bishops Enrique Angelelli and Oscar Romero, who, in addition, made clear their acceptance of this pastoral and theological perspective.

While the movement for the modern freedoms displayed aspects of distance from God and from the poor, the process of liberation that is now going on in Latin America is pregnant with new forms of closeness to the God of life and to the poor in their situation of death. Any effort to assimilate these two movements is not only historically inaccurate but, above all, would be a serious mistake in face of the demands laid upon us by our duty to bear witness and proclaim the reign of God.

There is no question of denying the ambivalences that mark every historical development; on the contrary, we must be attentive to them. But this ought not prevent us from being sensitive to their human and Christian possibilities. To thwart them out of fear that history may repeat itself would be to display too narrow an analysis of the situation and a lack of hope in the God who makes all things new (see Rev. 21:5).

Libertatis conscientia is accurate when it says that "a new phase in the history of freedom is opening before us" (no. 24). In this phase, lessons learned from the past are as important as the possibilities and special features of the present.

CHRIST, THE LORD OF HISTORY

Integral liberation in Christ is the primary datum for thinking about the theme of liberation. The work of Christ is an efficacious call to full communion with the Father and for that reason has repercussions even now within history. Liberation is the way to freedom and beyond freedom to communion with God, to the Pauline "face to face." This it is that gives meaning and profound unity to a process in which it is possible and necessary to distinguish levels in order to understand better the free and unmerited gift of God's love.

SALVATION AND HISTORY

The central focus of the Lord's message is the kingdom of God: a kingdom of life, love, truth, peace, justice, and freedom. "The kingdom is at hand," Jesus tells us at the beginning of his preaching (Mark 1:15; Matt. 4:17). And, in a passage that John Paul II describes as "the first messianic program" (encyclical *Rich in Mercy*, no. 3), Luke specifies the content of Jesus' preaching: "The Spirit of the Lord is upon me, because he has anointed me to preach good news to the poor. He has sent me to proclaim release to the captives and recovery of sight to the blind, to set at liberty those who are oppressed, to proclaim the acceptable year of the Lord" (Luke 4:18–19).

Salvation in Christ gives human history as a whole its ultimate meaning and elevates it beyond itself. But for that very reason this salvation is already present in history—God's saving action is working upon history from within. History will be judged in terms of God's will as expressed in the kingdom. The relation between kingdom and history is a major theme of theology, but my concern here is only with two points having to do with the integral character of liberation in Jesus Christ. The two points find expression in themes and passages of the Bible on the one hand and the magisterium on the other. These themes and passages help us grasp the deep unity of history, but the assertion of unity in no way means that we do not perceive and establish distinctions needed in order to avoid confusions and indeed to appreciate the meaning of the basic unity being affirmed.

An Experience of God the Liberator. Both *Libertatis nuntius* (1984) and *Libertatis conscientia* emphasize the part played by the Exodus in our effort to grasp the meaning of liberation in the Bible. That saving event shows clearly the global scope of God's liberating action. "The major and fundamental event of the Exodus . . . has a meaning that is both religious and political" (*LC,* no. 44). Both aspects are in fact present in the experience; the latter cannot, therefore, be reduced to only one of them.

The one aspect does not negate the other; rather they are at different levels of depth. This is the important point to be kept in mind, for otherwise the message is mutilated. The ultimate meaning of the event is to be found in God's call to the people, inviting all of them to enter into full communion with God. This process takes place within a concrete history. . . . This is a point about which we must remain clear: priority belongs to the religious element, to the covenant with Yahweh, because it is this that gives the entire movement its deeper meaning. On the other hand—and this should be obvious—when we remind ourselves of the fact that the Exodus of the Jewish people was also a social and political liberation, we are not thereby laying greater emphasis on this aspect than on the proper goal and ultimate meaning of the entire movement. The point of the reminder is rather to indicate the comprehensive character and broad scope of the covenant in the liberating event that was the Exodus.

It is because of this comprehensiveness that the event of the Exodus can be called paradigmatic for biblical faith. The term "paradigm" is often used in the biblical sciences, and does not mean that the event must be repeated as such in the history of the Christian community. Instead, it points to its deeper meaning, namely, the liberating intervention of God.

This presence of the Lord, together with his gift of full communion, gives unity to a process of liberation whose several aspects (and the differences between them) we may not overlook. From this point of view, the Exodus truly plays an important part in liberation theology. Its importance should not be exaggerated, however, since other themes and other passages of the Bible also have a decisive role in this theological approach.

More Human Conditions. There is a passage in the writings of Paul VI that played a decisive role in my approach to human history as a complex unity. The passage is no. 21 of the encyclical *Populorum progressio,* and it deals with integral development. This passage helped me to establish the distinction between the three levels of a single process of liberation.

Integral development is seen here as a passage from less human to more human living conditions. The pope says: "Less human conditions: the lack of material necessities for those who are without the minimum essential for life, the moral deficiencies of those who are mutilated by selfishness. Less human conditions: oppressive structures, whether due to the abuses of ownership or to the abuses of power, to the exploitation of workers or to unjust transactions." The pope is speaking of an infrahuman situation that must be rejected in a movement toward more human conditions. He goes on to say:

> Conditions that are more human: the passage from misery toward the possession of necessities, victory over social scourges, the growth of knowledge, the acquisition of culture. Additional conditions that are more human: increased esteem for the dignity of others, the turning toward the spirit of poverty, cooperation for the common good, the will and desire for peace. Conditions that are still more human: the human acknowledgment of supreme values, and of God as their source and their finality.

The elimination of misery and the right to have the necessities of life are fundamental requirements for a human and just society. But this is not enough; other values must also be promoted: human dignity, the desire for peace, ethical sensitivity, an openness to God.

"Conditions that, finally and above all, are more human: faith, a gift of God accepted by human good will, and unity in the charity of Christ, who calls us all to share as sons and daughters in the life of the living God, the Father of all." Here the process advances toward a human plenitude. The pope describes several things as "more human . . . above all": faith, charity, and adoption as God's children, insofar as these divine gifts are freely accepted by human beings. This does not, of course, mean that the grace of God is being reduced to the purely human level. The pope is simply reminding us of an ancient Christian theme: complete human fulfillment comes only through elevation to the order of grace.

This important passage shows the different phases to be parts of a profound continuity and unity. Paul VI thus threw significant light on the problems that we were facing at that time in our pastoral activity.

The unified approach that liberation theology was beginning to take was confirmed by another important document of the magisterium. I am referring to the well-known passage in Medellín's document on justice: "It is the same God who in the fullness of time sent the Son in order that he might become flesh and save all human beings from *all the forms of enslavement* to which sin keeps them in subjection: ignorance, hunger, misery, and oppression, or, in short, the injustice and hatred that spring from human selfishness."

Liberation from sin by Christ (a central theme in liberation theology) attacks the ultimate root of all injustice and thus links together, though without confusing them, the several dimensions of liberation. In the passage just cited, the bishops gathered at Medellín were acknowledging the social significance of liberation in Christ: an aspect given little attention at that time. Clear reference is made to this same aspect *LC:* "The work of salvation is thus seen to be indissolubly linked to the task of improving and raising the conditions of human life in this world" (no. 80).

The passages I have cited were and still are central for an understanding of salvation in human history. The Bible and the magisterium are at one in showing us a perspective, forestalling dangers, and, above all, reminding us how all-embracing is God's free and gratuitous will that the human race in its historical course should experience life.

THE CHALCEDONIAN PRINCIPLE

The idea that, [as I wrote in *A Theology of Liberation*], "there are three levels of meaning of a single, complex process, which finds its deepest sense and its full realization in the saving work of Christ" is fundamental to my perspective and has its basis in a classic theological viewpoint. Also to be kept in mind is the fact that with this distinction (not separation) in mind, liberation theology was the first to speak of "total and integral liberation," a phrase much used nowadays. The passage from Paul VI on integral development, which I cited above, played a role here.

As I said, in order to avoid all kinds of confusion we must distinguish three levels of meaning in the liberation process. The three must then be conjoined, but as parts of "a single, complex process." The word "complex" is deliberately used in order to stress that we must avoid confusions and simplistic identifications.

These different "levels of meaning mutually imply each other"; that is, we are dealing with different things. At work here is the old Scholastic principle of which Jacques Maritain so perceptively reminded us all in recent decades: we must "distinguish in order to unite," and not in order to separate or confuse. "These three levels mutually condition each other, but they are not confused. One is not present without the others, but they are distinct: they are all part of a single, all-encompassing salvific process, but they are to be found at different levels.

The complex unity comes, in the final analysis [as I said in *A Theology of Liberation*], from "Christ the savior," who "liberates the human being from sin, which is the ultimate root of all disruption of friendship and of all injustice and oppression [first level]. Christ makes humankind truly free [second level], that is to say, he enables us to live in communion with him; and this is the basis for all human fellowship [third level]."

The stress, therefore, is on the third level: the work of Christ that liberates us from sin and brings us into communion with him. The changes that may take place in the social sphere are important, but they are also inadequate from the Christian viewpoint. For "a social transformation, no matter how radical, it may be, does not automatically bring with it the suppression of all evils."

The issue is to distinguish in order to unite—a unity that is not simply the sum of the parts but one that has an orienting and ultimately decisive focal point. The theological approach here is inspired by the Council of Chalcedon, which defined that in Christ there are two natures, the human and the divine, which are distinct but neither confused nor separated. Furthermore, the profound unity given by the divine person in virtue of being the Son does not suppress the human nature of Christ. My treatment of "total or integral liberation" is inspired by this Chalcedonian principle.

This idea of unity without confusion was also emphasized at Medellín. Their document on catechesis (no. 4) clearly shows the mind of the Latin American bishops:

> While avoiding confusions or simplistic identifications, [catechetical teaching] must always make clear the profound unity that exists between God's plan of salvation realized in Christ, and human aspirations; between the history of salvation and human history; between the church, the people of God, and the temporal communities; between the liberating action of God and the experience of human beings; between the supernatural gifts and charisms and human. Thus excluding all dichotomy or dualism in the Christian, catechesis prepares the progressive actualization of the People of God in the direction of its eschatological completion—which even now is expressed in the liturgy.

The unified approach arises from the conviction that the gratuitous gift of God's love is all-embracing. That which comes from God cannot affect only one sector of human life; that would be too narrow a conception of God's work. The challenge is to maintain the distinctions that allow us to understand the various levels of gratuitousness, while at the same time not separating human life into watertight compartments, as if there were areas of life into which the love of God, which is always free and unmerited, does not enter. *LC* says:

> It is of course important to make a careful distinction between earthly progress and the growth of the kingdom, which do not belong to the same order. Nonetheless, this distinction is not a separation; for the human vocation to eternal life does not suppress but confirms the task of using human energies and means received from the creator for developing temporal life [no. 60].

The ultimate terms of the process are God's call and the free response of human beings marked with the consistency proper to the freedom that the Lord wants them to have. . . .

CONTEMPORARY THEOLOGY AND THE UNITY OF HISTORY

This unified view of history is not the private possession of liberation theology, but common in contemporary theology. Among other sources, it emerged from discussions on the relationship of grace to nature that went on in the first half of the present century among such theologians as Yves de Montcheuil, Henri de Lubac, Karl Rahner, Hans Urs von Balthasar, Juan Alfaro, and others. The end result was unequivocal: a retrieval of the traditional approach (which St. Augustine so strongly emphasized), which says that in the concrete, human history is permeated at every point by the opposition between grace and sin. Juan Alfaro has shown that this was also St. Thomas' real position. The distinctions his philosophical tools (Aristotelianism) enabled him to make with greater clarity (but which became inflexible in the later Scholasticism of Cajetan and others) did not alter this approach; they were simply that: needed distinctions.

Adopting this historical perspective, I wrote in *A Theology of Liberation:* "Historically and concretely we know humanity only as actually called to meet God." The basic statement here is that from the viewpoint of faith "the history of salvation is the very heart of human history." Consequently, "the historical evolution of humanity must be placed definitively in the salvific horizon." At issue here is the primacy of grace and of God's action in history.

From this standpoint I have criticized the "distinction of planes model," but this by no means signifies a critique of the distinction between nature and grace. What I question is a particular theology (a very fruitful theology, as I pointed out a number of times in *A Theology of Liberation*) which sees things differently from the theology of "New Christendom" and which furnishes a clear framework for dealing with questions of interest to the theology of liberation. (It was, moreover, the theological position I had taken up many years before.) What I reject—on theological grounds, not on grounds of faith—is, as I wrote, "the existence of two juxtaposed 'orders,' intimately linked or convergent," because the two are regarded "at bottom [as] external to each other."

The productive theological discussion of these themes that went on in the church made it possible to conclude that "in the concrete there is only one vocation: freely given communion with God. In fact there is no pure nature and there never has been; there is no one who is not invited to communion with the Lord, no one who is not marked by grace." The viewpoint adopted here is that of how, in the concrete, the economy of salvation works. This not only does not hinder, but it even necessarily demands the distinction between nature and grace for a proper understanding of this unity in the concrete. For this reason, *A Theology of Liberation* rejects any monolithic unity and speaks always of a "complex unity." For the same reason, it posits a distinction of levels, which is taken over from the "distinction of planes" model but lays greater stress on the concrete unity of the economy of salvation.

In reality, all of this flows from a single, but fundamental, biblical datum: all things were created and have now been redeemed in Christ (a theme often found in St. John and St. Paul). A profound unity comes from him, but the distinction between creation and redemption is not abolished.

This relationship is clearly shown in Ephesians 1:4: "[God the Father] chose us in [Christ] before the foundation of the world." The choice, or election, was to make us adoptive sons and daughters, and, contrary to the picture we sometimes draw for ourselves, it took place before creation. The "before" does not indicate a chronological precedence but a precedence of meaning and finality; we live, as I've said, in "a 'christo-finalized' history."

Let me repeat: Christ, who is both God and human, is the basis of a unity that does not do away with distinctions but does prevent confusions and separations. It is from this standpoint that we speak of creation as a "saving act."

Within the basic affirmations required by the faith (nature and grace), theologians have continued to develop this subject—because there are no finished formulas in this field—with the desire to be ever more faithful to the Word of the Lord and the teachings of the church.

For this reason, after saying (in *A Theology of Liberation*) that "historically and concretely we know humanity only as actually called to meet God," I go on to add: "But an even more precise formulation has been sought in an effort to be faithful both to the gratuitousness of God's gift as well as to its unique and all-embracing character." The caution implicitly urged here is repeated a number of times; here is another passage:

> It seems, however, that contemporary theology has not yet fashioned the categories that would allow us to think through and express adequately this unified approach to history. We work, on the one hand, under the fear of falling back again into the old dualisms, and, on the other, under the permanent suspicion of not sufficiently safeguarding divine gratuitousness or the uniqueness of Christianity.

The same concern led me to be more nuanced in my criticism of a dualist approach; at the end of it I referred to a passage in which Hans Urs von Balthasar points out, "ironically but perceptively," the oversimplifications into which persons can fall when they reject every kind of distinction. The truth is, we are dealing here with a disputed theological question which is still not worked through completely.

The reader should be clear, then, that when I reject the existence of two histories, I am saying that *in the actual order* of the economy of salvation there is not a history of nature and another history of grace, one of fellowship and another of filiation. Rather, the relationship between grace and nature, between God's call and the free response of human beings, is located within a single christofinalized history. *LC* affirms in this respect that "the distinction between the supernatural order of salvation and the temporal order of human life must be seen in the context of God's singular plan to recapitulate all things in Christ" (no. 80).

FREEDOM AND COMMUNION

There is, then, a total liberation, the unity of which comes in the final analysis from communion with God and others, and in which three levels of meaning are distinguishable. This is a claim made in liberation theology from its very beginnings; it is often heard today when the subject is raised, whether in theological studies or in documents of the magisterium.

This approach closely links liberation, freedom, and communion: three concepts to which I shall be referring in the following pages [and which I set forth in *A Theology of Liberation*]:

> The freedom to which we are called presupposes the going out of oneself, the breaking down of our selfishness and of all the structures that support our selfishness; the foundation of this freedom is openness to others. The fullness of liberation—a free gift from Christ—is communion with God and with other human beings. [Thus], we can distinguish three reciprocally interpenetrating levels of meaning of the term liberation, or, in other words, three approaches to the process of liberation.

At Puebla a similar formulation occurs at the beginning of a lengthy discussion of the three planes of liberation and their reciprocal relationships: "Freedom always implies the capacity we all possess in principle to be our own persons so that we can go on fashioning communion and participation which must be embodied in definitive realities, on three inseparable planes: our relationship to the world as its master, to other persons as brothers or sisters, and to God as God's children" (no. 322).

It is important to look at these levels or planes in detail, in order to get beneath the surface of each and to show how they imply one another within the controlling context of God's saving action.

SOCIAL LIBERATION

Medellín spoke very clearly of the situation of "distressing poverty, which in many cases becomes inhuman wretchedness" (*Poverty*, no. 1). It also said that the situation was not inevitable: "misery, as a collective fact, is an injustice that the heavens protest" (*Justice*, no. 1); that is, it has causes for which human beings are responsible . . ., "a situation of injustice which can be called institutionalized violence" (*Peace*, no. 16).

Libertatis conscientia echoes this denunciation of "institutionalized violence" which provoked—and still provokes—such controversy:

> In the systematic recourse to violence presented as the only way to liberation, it is necessary to denounce a destructive illusion, which leads to new servitudes. It must be condemned with the same vigor as the *violence* exercised by landowners against the poor, police arbitrariness, and every form of *violence* set up as a system of government [no. 76, emphasis added].

From this reality, "a muffled cry breaks out, from millions of human beings, begging their pastors for a liberation that does not come to them from anywhere" (*Poverty*, no. 2). Some years later, Puebla states that this cry "may have seemed muffled at that time, but now it is clear, growing, impetuous, and, on occasion, threatening" (no. 89). "It is the cry of a people suffering, demanding justice, freedom, respect for the fundamental rights of the person and of peoples" (no. 87).

These texts, among many others, set the terms for liberation at this level: an inhuman state of affairs, an unjust order—the principal cause of poverty that must be changed, and a cry for liberation that comes from millions of the poor. *LC* begins with a reference to these needed changes:

> Awareness of human freedom and dignity, together with the affirmation of the inalienable rights of individuals and peoples, is one of the major characteristics of our time. But freedom demands conditions of an economic, social, political, and cultural kind, which make possible its full exercise. A clearer perception of the obstacles that hinder its development and offend human dignity is at the source of the powerful aspirations to liberation which torment the world today [no. 1; see also nos. 17 and 61].

The Political Sphere. The passage from *LC* makes it clear that there is a situation here from which we may not turn away if we want to be faithful to the God of life and in solidarity with our brothers and sisters, especially the poor. For the sake of a better knowledge of this social reality and its causes and in the interests of commitment to those living in that situation, we may look to the social sciences for help. The problems and challenges entailed in this recourse to social analysis are dealt with in the article "Theology and the Social Sciences" [see selection no. 5 in this volume].

The field of society and politics is always tricky and challenging. It will be useful, therefore, to note some clarifications regarding it [which I first set forth in *A Theology of Liberation*]. Two meanings of "political" must be distinguished: a broader or more inclusive use, and a more specific one. In the broader use of the term, the political sphere "is the sphere for the exercise of a critical freedom won in the course of history. It is the global influence and the collective arena for human fulfillment." The second use is understood in reference to the first: "Only within this broad meaning of the political sphere can we situate the more precise notion of 'politics' as an orientation to power. For Max Weber this orientation constitutes the characteristics typical of political activity."

The first—and wider—meaning of the term "political" indicates the field in which "a person emerges as a free and responsible being, as a person in relationship with other persons, as someone who takes up a task in history." The word "political" must therefore not be understood exclusively in its second meaning, which refers to a more technical and partisan terrain. Only the broad meaning allows us to say, for example, that in the historical life of a human being "nothing lies outside the political sphere understood in this way. Everything is politically colored." (The words "understood in this way" refer to what I gave as the broad meaning; to remove the words would change the meaning of the statement.)

Just as the political sphere is one dimension of human existence, so too liberation in that sphere is one level within an all-embracing process that takes its meaning from liberation from sin and communion with God and other human beings. Because sin is the breaking of friendship with God and neighbor, it is "the ultimate root" of all injustice (as the two Vatican Instructions put it). I shall return to this point; for the moment I wish only to repeat the perceptive and critical observation of G. Thils concerning *Libertatis nuntius:* "If one sees sin as the 'ultimate root' of injustices and oppressions, one is also implicitly recognizing that these can, at the same time, have more or less the same explanation."

Social and political liberation aims at eliminating the proximate causes of poverty and injustice. This is required by the situation in which the vast majority of Latin Americans live. But let me repeat that "to affirm that all human reality has a political dimension in no way means, as the term itself indicates, to reduce everything to this dimension." "Dimension," after all, is a term from spatial geometry; a body has three dimensions but is not reducible to one of them. The term is applied to human existence in order to bring out its complexity and richness; so too it is applied to the process of liberation.

Social Conflict. Social liberation is necessary if any attempt is to be made to build a society based on respect for others, especially the weakest and least important. In other words, a society based not on the modern individualism but on a proper social understanding—a society in which the hunger for bread will disappear, as a deeply moved John Paul II said in an emotional impromptu response to the words of the people of Villa San Salvador, during his visit to Peru.

These observations indicate one reason why I often speak of a "qualitatively different" society. It will be qualitatively different because other persons will be normative in a society in which the needs of the poor are more important than the power of the privileged—qualitatively different, too, because it is not a matter of incorporating more individuals into a consumer society but changing the way in which human beings are viewed. But this takes us to the second level of liberation.

To conclude this point, let me say only that this necessary social liberation for which Medellín and Puebla call and which liberation theology emphasizes does not exhaust the human aspiration for liberation. A change at this level is important but not sufficient; more than that, it is ambiguous, especially if not followed by other, deeper changes. This approach led me, twenty years ago, to say very clearly: "Christian hope opens us, in an attitude of spiritual childhood, to the gift of the future promised by God. It keeps us from any confusion of the kingdom with any one historical stage, from any idolatry toward unavoidably ambiguous human achievement, from any absolutizing of revolution."

THE FREEDOM OF THE HUMAN PERSON

A radical change of the socioeconomic order that creates poverty in Latin America is something we must demand, as human beings and as Christians. The criteria we apply in making judgments must not stop short at isolated facts but must "concern economic, social, and political systems" (*LC*, no. 74). This desire to make changes is based on a conviction that social structures do not arise from "an alleged determinism of history" but "depend on the responsibility of human beings, who can alter them" (ibid.).

This conviction brings me to what I have been calling the second dimension of liberation, a dimension in which human freedom plays a key role. We are now at a deeper level, involving "an understanding of history as a process of human liberation in which humankind is consciously taking responsibility for its own destiny. This understanding broadens the horizon of desired changes and places that horizon in a dynamic context. In this perspective the changes we seek are seen as required by the unfolding of all the dimensions of the human person."

While the social dimension is of the utmost importance, it is only one side of liberation. Awareness of the different human possibilities and the assumption of historical responsibility are one manifestation of what Vatican II called a *new* humanism: "We are witnessing . . . the birth of a new humanism, where humankind is defined before all else by responsibility to one's fellow human beings and at the court of history" (*Gaudium et spes*, no. 55).

Here we have the idea of the "new human being," an expression current in political philosophy and historical approaches intended to stress the point that new social structures are not enough. For structures always depend on concrete persons, and the latter must be involved if we want real change. This is true for every type of society, for society must be based not only on justice but also on freedom. That is why I wrote: "These personal aspects—considered not as excessively privatized, but rather as encompassing all human dimensions—are also under consideration in the contemporary debate concerning greater partic-ipation of all in political activity, including in the bosom of a socialist society." The requirement is a universal one that knows no exceptions.

A change of social structures can help to bring about this personal change but does not automatically bring it about. On the other hand, there are also alleged transformations of persons that have no consequences in the social sphere. We must avoid falling victim to facile generalizations that do not adequately respect the autonomy proper to each level: "It is no more 'mechanistic' to think that a structural change automatically makes for a new humanity, than to think that a 'personal' change guarantees social transformations. Any mechanistic approach is unreal and naïve."

In the approach I am taking, there is no room for a historical analysis based on economic determinism; the very assertion of freedom in all dimensions of the human already rejects this kind of determinism that impoverishes human histo-ry. Structural change is necessary, but it is not everything. Human freedom has an interior dimension that is sometimes neglected due to the urgent demands of the commitment to justice. But, to offset that tendency, it is important to bear in mind that "people today aspire not only to a liberation from *exterior* pressures, which prevent fulfillment as members of a certain social class, country, or soci-ety. Persons likewise seek an *interior* liberation, in an individual and intimate dimension; they seek liberation not only on a social plane but also on a psycho-logical plane." This outlook is inconsistent with one that does not take the inte-rior freedom of human beings into account, for this interior freedom is also the object of a powerful human aspiration. . . .

In my view, a society that is mindful of this interior liberation and the dif-ferent dimensions of the human being can likewise be called "qualitatively dif-ferent." It is with this in mind that I have spoken on some occasions of "a social appropriation . . . of freedom." My intention in using this expression is to dis-tance myself from the individualist viewpoint which characterizes the modern world and which many propose as a model for Latin America. I use it also in order to bring out the need of freedom for all. As was said during the discussions on religious freedom, freedom is indivisible. It is not possible to defend freedom for some and to deny it in practice to the majority. But this is what happens in even the best democratic phases in the life of our countries. Personal freedom must extend to the whole of society. Nor is the issue to secure freedom for the majority; no, the need is to ensure the freedom of all. This is the challenge we face in Latin America in the present process of liberation.

All that has been said makes it clear that the second level of liberation, which postulates the necessity of constructing a new human being, is located on the plane of history and is a human effort. The meaning of "new human being" here is not the meaning St. Paul gives the term when he opposes the new person or self to the old. The new human being of which St. Paul speaks is produced by the forgiveness of sin and the unmerited gift that makes men and women God's adoptive children. That is still another level of liberation in Christ, and it is the most decisive level. If I mention Paul here, it is because he "continuously reminds us . . . of the paschal core of Christian existence and of all of human life; the passage from the old to the new person, from sin to grace, from slavery to freedom. 'For freedom Christ has set us free' (Gal. 5:1), St. Paul tells us. He refers here to liberation from sin insofar as it represents a selfish turning in upon oneself." But that, as I said, points us toward the third level of liberation.

Let me end this section by saying that at this second level are located the plans for a *new* society, the utopia that spurs action in history. In this sense it can be said that "political liberation appears as the path toward the utopia of a freer, more human humankind, the protagonist of its own history." At the same time, however, the journey must be made with respect for personal freedom, for this is not only the goal of the journey but the necessary condition for any authentic political liberation. *LC* reminds us of this: "Only a process of liberation that has been achieved can create better conditions for the effective exercise of freedom. Indeed a liberation that does not take into account the personal freedom of those who fight for it is condemned to defeat in advance" (no. 31; see no. 26).

But for the very reason that this dimension of liberation is not restricted to what is usually understood by "the political sphere," it enables us to connect political liberation with liberation from sin, without either identifying or juxtaposing the two.

TOWARD FULL COMMUNION

Both *Libertatis nuntius* and *Libertatis conscientia* firmly assert that the saving work of Christ is primarily a deliverance from sin, which is "the most radical form of slavery" (*LN*, IV, 2), "the most radical evil" (*LC*, no. 3) and the source of other slaveries and other evils. It is a question of what *LC* calls a "soteriological liberation."

As everyone knows, liberation from sin is a dominant theme in liberation theology and in my own contribution to it. I say this in all simplicity but also firmly. In the treatment of some other themes, readers may find that one or another statement of liberation is unclear or needs to be put more carefully, but on this point there can be no doubt. Because sin is a breaking of friendship with God and others, it is the ultimate root of all injustice and all division among human beings; God's grace alone can overcome sin.

We have here reached the third level of liberation and can see what gives it its radicality and makes it so all-embracing. "In the Bible, Christ is presented as the one who brings us liberation. Christ the Savior liberates humankind from sin, which is the ultimate root of all disruption of friendship and of all injustice and oppression. Christ makes humankind truly free, that is to say, he enables us to live in communion with him; and this is the basis for all human fellowship." It is the grace of Christ that liberates us from sin and enables us to live in communion. Let us look at these two points.

The Concept of Sin. Sin is a rejection of the gift of God's love. The rejection is a personal, free act. It is a refusal to accept God as Father and to love others as the Lord loved us. Only the action of God can heal human beings at the root of the egotism that prevents them from going out of themselves.

There was a period (not that of the fathers of the church nor of the great medieval theologians) when the predominant type of theology neglected the social dimension of sin. In recent decades a growing awareness of the social problem has brought a return to the true perspective with its profound biblical roots; in addition, Medellín brought it to mind when it spoke of "a sinful situation."

Some were disturbed by this. But just before the Puebla Conference the pope summed up current thinking on this matter and insisted on the point by using, for example, the expression "sinful structure." As a result, the theme received special emphasis at Puebla (see nos. 28, 70, 73, 92, 185, 186, 281, 452, 482, 487, 515, 1032, 1258, 1269). *LC,* for its part, observes: "In the light of the gospel, many laws and structures seem to bear the mark of sin and prolong its oppressive influence in society" (no. 54).

This is the setting for what liberation theology has to say on the subject. The emphasis on the social dimension of sin is due to the fact that this dimension was so little present to Christian consciousness at that time. But the emphasis is thus placed chiefly because this perspective, based on the faith, enables us to understand better what has happened and is still happening in Latin America. This also accounts for the presence of the theme at Medellín and Puebla. The concern is fundamentally pastoral: "Faced with the situation of sin, the church has a duty to engage in denunciation. Such denunciation must be objective, courageous, and evangelical. Rather than condemning, it seeks to save both the guilty party and the victim" (Puebla, no. 1296).

This emphasis, however, by no means signifies a forgetfulness of the personal dimension of sin. The breaking of friendship with God is the action of a free will. Moreover, [as I wrote in *A Theology of Liberation*], "behind an unjust structure there is a personal or collective will responsible—a desire to reject God and neighbor." Again, "because sin is a personal and social intrahistorical reality, a part of the daily events of human life, it is also, and above all, an obstacle to life's reaching the fullness we call salvation." Or, looking at it from a different angle, "sin is regarded as a social, historical fact, the absence of fellowship and love in relationships among persons, a breach of friendship with God and with other persons, and therefore, an interior, personal fracture."

As these passages show, the importance of the social consequences of sin—highlighted in documents of the magisterium—does not mean forgetting that sin is always the result of a personal, free act. Thus *LC* says that "the sin at the root of unjust situations is, in the proper and primordial sense, a voluntary act that has its source in the freedom of individuals. Only in a derived and secondary sense is it applicable to structures, and only in this sense can one speak of 'social sin'" (no. 75). "Derived," because the reference is to the consequences of acts for which some person is responsible. Society as such does not perform free acts (these are the prerogative of persons), but it is affected by what flows from sin, as the texts I have cited show.

John Paul II writes, therefore:

> To speak of social sin means in the first place to recognize that, by virtue of a human solidarity that is as mysterious and intangible as it is real and concrete, each individual's sin in some way affects others. . . . Consequently, one can speak of a communion of sin. . . . In other words, there is no sin, not even the most intimate and secret one, the most strictly individual one, that exclusively concerns the person committing it. All sin has repercussions, with greater or lesser intensity, with greater or lesser damage, on the whole of the ecclesial body and on the whole human family. [*Reconciliatio et penitentia no. 16*]

In my own approach to theology, sin occupies a central place. This breaking of friendship with God and others is a rejection of that, "communion with the Lord and with all humans [which] is more than anything else a gift." For this reason, "to sin is to refuse to love, to reject communion and fellowship, to reject even now the very meaning of human existence."

Francisco Moreno has brought out the christological perspective in which sin is treated in liberation theology. Here is what he says of sin's role in this theology: "If Latin American theology has given a privileged place to the discussion of sin, it is out of theological honesty and faithfulness vis-à-vis a situation in which real sin cries to heaven; it is also due to the consistency and adaptability of a theological method that is especially sensitive to and capable of capturing this dimension of reality."

Collaboration in the building of a just society is an act of solidarity and love; it demands resistance to that which is a negation of love: sin. But it is also clear that because sin is radical evil, it can be conquered only by the grace of God and the radical liberation that the Lord bestows. This grace of God is present in every act of authentic human love. The relationship between grace and sin is played out in the inmost depths of the human person.

Communion in Love. Liberation from sin is one side of the coin; the other is communion with God and others. According to a classic distinction, *freedom from* is directed toward *freedom for*. It is to this *freedom for* that Christ's saving work is also directed. By nailing sin to the cross, Jesus opened the way for us to full communion with the Father. [As I wrote,] this communion discloses the meaning of our lives:

> The knowledge that at the root of our personal and community existence lies the gift of the self-communication of God, the grace of God's friendship, fills our life with gratitude. It allows us to see our encounters with others, our loves, everything that happens in our life, as a gift. There is a real love only

when there is free giving—without conditions or coercion. Only gratuitous love goes to our very roots and elicits true love.

The entire process of liberation is directed toward communion. Some pages back, I stated my agreement (a long-standing agreement, in fact) with an important theme in *LC*—that liberation is a way to freedom. But we must go further, for freedom is not an end in itself, but must be ordered to love and service. In Galatians 5:1 Paul reminds us that Christ has set us free for freedom, and in 5:13 he speaks of true freedom as love. In the final analysis, freedom shows itself as openness to God and others. Although *LC* has some passages along this line, it does not have any full development of the idea of communion as the ultimate purpose of liberation; it would have been helped here by a more biblical perspective.

The question that arises at this point is the connection between this grace of communion (and liberation from sin) and the first two levels of liberation. Puebla found an excellent formulation of the connection:

> Authentic communion and participation can exist in this life only if they are projected on to the very concrete plane of temporal realities, so that mastery, use, and transformation of the goods of this earth and those of culture, science, and technology find embodiment in humanity's just and fraternal lordship over the world—which would include respect for ecology. Confronted with the realities that are part of our lives today, we must learn from the gospel that in Latin America we cannot truly love our fellow human beings, and hence God, unless we commit ourselves on the personal level, and in many cases on the structural level as well, to serving and promoting the most dispossessed and humiliated human groups and social classes, with all the consequences that will entail on the plane of temporal realities (no. 327).

What we have here is not simply a theological formulation. This teaching of the magisterium proved to be a call that, together with the teaching of Medellín, inspired the activity, life, and death of many Latin American Christians: men and women who dared to live their communion with God in solidarity with the poor, the least of our society, and who accepted "all the consequences" that that solidarity entailed.

To distinguish these levels, which are located at different degrees of depth is not to separate them. There is no question, [as I have written,] of "three parallel or chronologically successive processes. . . . There are three levels of meaning of a single, complex process, which finds its deepest sense and its full realization in the saving work of Christ." This saving work is what gives the whole process its meaning:

> These levels of meaning, therefore, mutually imply each other. A comprehensive view of the matter presupposes that they are not to be separated. In this way two pitfalls will be avoided: first, idealist or spiritualist approaches, which

are nothing but ways of evading a harsh and demanding reality, and second, shallow analyses and programs of short-term effect initiated under the pretext of meeting immediate needs.

The grace of God is a gift, but it also sets a task. The process by which we are saved is marked by both the gratuitous initiative of God and the free response of human beings. Our acceptance of the gift of adoptive filiation must find expression in the building of authentic brotherhood and sisterhood in history. Nothing is more demanding than gratuitousness, nothing calls for greater commitment. The elderly Paul tells Philemon that he expects him to "do even more than I say" (v. 21). Thereby he opens the door to the possibility of limitless work on Philemon's part in the service of his brother, who, in this case, is a man who is not acknowledged to be a human being with all human rights. Christians must in one or other fashion daily "invent" their life of love and commitment.

Five

LIBERATING EVANGELIZATION: CHURCH OF THE POOR

Despite his unremitting attention to the church's mission in a world of both dehumanizing oppression and courageous struggles for liberation, Gutiérrez has not to date set forth a comprehensive ecclesiology. Still, the church functions in nearly all his writings as a paramount theological source and locus, a fundamental hermeneutical principle, and the primary beneficiary of his theological work. Called by God to be the sacrament (that is, the "fulfillment and the manifestation of [God's] salvific plan," Theology of Liberation, 146) of a liberating evangelization, the church can best carry out its prophetic mission by becoming the "church of the poor," a phrase Gutiérrez traces to Pope John XXIII. The texts which follow indicate why the views of Gutiérrez have assumed such importance in the postconciliar ecclesiological debate, both Catholic and Protestant. They also make plain his great love for the church, which he unquestionably considers his home.

34. CREATING A NEW ECCLESIAL PRESENCE

The following text first appeared as the second part of Gutiérrez's prologue to Signos de renovación: Recopilación de documentos post-conciliares de la Iglesia en América Latina (1969), *a documentary history of the Latin American church between 1966 and 1969. In nearly all of his early writings Gutiérrez expressed concern about the efficacy of the church's praxis and posed the alternatives ("options") faced by the Christian community. This essay illustrates not only his own ecclesial consciousness but also the role of ecclesiological concerns in the birth and evolution of the theology of liberation. The text is found in* The Power of the Poor in History, *30–35.*

At Vatican II the church affirmed a desire to render service. The concrete forms that this pledge takes are—and must necessarily be—based on the world in which the Christian community is present.

THE CHURCH'S INADEQUACIES

A better knowledge of the harsh realities in Latin America goes hand in hand with a clearer realization that the church's structures are inadequate for the world in which it lives. They appear as outdated and lacking dynamism in the face of new questions, and in one way or another seem to be tied up with the unjust order we wish to abolish. This situation is the chief source of the misunderstandings, frictions, crises, and desertions [from the church] that we witness.

Those who want to shape their lives to the demands of the gospel find it increasingly difficult to accept vague, lyrical appeals to "fellowship" and "Christian unity" that do not take account of the causes underlying the present state of affairs, or of the concrete conditions required for the construction of a just society. Such vague appeals forget that the catholicity, the universality, of the church is not something attained once for all time, or something to be maintained at any price. It must be won by courageous, costly, and open-eyed struggle. Consciously or not, these appeals seem designed to palliate the real tensions that do and should exist, and ultimately to maintain the status quo. The frank and decisive stands taken by the hierarchy and other sectors of the church in the last few years have been welcome breaths of fresh air. They will undoubtedly help to separate the wheat from the chaff among those who call themselves Christians.

Vatican II proclaims that the church, like Christ, must carry out its work of redemption "in poverty and under oppression" [*LG* 8]. But this is not the image presented by the Latin American church as a whole. Quite the contrary. Once upon a time we may not have been clearly aware of this, but that time is past. Today in the church with anguish we live out the drama of feeling disloyal to the gospel and out of step with the real situation in Latin America.

This has given rise to letters, declarations, new forms of commitment, and even "protest movements" in the church—all easily sensationalized. But altogether apart from their transitory news value, their sometimes ambiguous doctrinal roots, and the misleading commentaries they provoke, they challenge us to discover their much deeper significance. They betoken the concern many Christians have with the form that the church's presence in Latin America now takes. They reveal a hidden vitality, a spirit that refuses to be a prisoner of the law. If we do not pay heed to the message they contain, we may one day find ourselves in an atmosphere of general indifference, longing wistfully for those "hotheads" who had used unconventional means to express their desire to change the church and their painful fidelity to the gospel.

The most dynamic sectors of the people of God in Latin America are thus, from this point of view, committed to a search for two things: (1) the theological bases that will encompass the whole of their activity on a continent caught up in a process of liberation; and (2) new ecclesial structures that will allow them to live a true life of faith in accordance with Latin Americans' awareness of their own specific historical destiny.

A THEOLOGY OF HUMAN LIBERATION

Would a concern for the specifically political dimensions of an authentic presence in Latin America mean that the church is falling into an aberrant temporalism and abandoning its spiritual mission? After all, this is what frightens many persons of good (and ill) will.

The gospel, these persons say, is first and foremost a message of eternal salvation; building the earth is a task for human beings on this earth. The first task belongs to the church, the second task belongs to temporal society. The most they will admit is that the church may lay down certain ethical dictates for the work of building the earthly city—so long as they do not openly contradict the interests of those who hold the reins of economic and political power.

But a closer look at reality has wrought a profound change in the life and outlook of the church. Although I cannot discuss the process in detail here, I can point out that the church has restored its ties with the most ancient Christian tradition and has rediscovered that salvation embraces all of humanity and the entire human person. It will be worth our while to spell out briefly the theological notions that form the basis for this new outlook in the church—"new" in the sense of "I give you a new commandment."

Concrete reflection on human existence has carried contemporary theology far beyond the scholastic and essentialist outlook that was based on distinguishing various orders and levels. At the same time that it was being renewed through contact with biblical sources, theology was moving toward the notion that humankind has but one vocation; or, to put it more exactly, that all human beings share the same single vocation. Thus we do not have two juxtaposed histories, one sacred and the other profane. There is only one single process of human development, irreversibly assumed by Christ, the Lord of history. His salvific work embraces all the dimensions of human existence. Two major biblical themes clearly illustrate this: the relationship between creation and salvation, and the messianic promises.

In the rather simplistic catechetics of the past, creation was presented as the explanation for the existing world. This is not incorrect, but it is incomplete. In the Bible, creation is not a stage prior to the work of salvation; it is the first salvific activity. "Before the world was made, he chose us in Christ" (Eph. 1:4). Creation is inserted in the salvation process, in God's self-communication. The religious experience of Israel is primarily history, but this history is simply the prolongation of the creative act. That is why the Psalms praise Yahweh simultaneously as Creator and Savior (see Ps. 136). The God who transformed chaos into cosmos is the same as the one who acts in salvation history. The redemptive work of Christ, in turn, is presented in the context of creation (see John 1). Creation and salvation have a christological import; in Christ everything has been created and everything has been saved (see Col. 1:15–20).

Thus when we say that men and women actualize themselves by carrying on the work of creation through their own labors, we are asserting that they are operating within the framework of God's salvific work from the very first. Subduing the earth, as Genesis bids them do, is a salvific work. To work, to transform the world, is to save. Inasmuch as it is a humanizing factor that transforms nature, work normally tends to build a society that is more just and more worthy of humankind through the transformation of nature—as Karl Marx clearly saw. The Bible helps us to appreciate the deeper reaches of this effort. Building the earthly city is not simply a humanizing phase prior to evangelization, as theology put it until recently. Building the earthly city actually immerses human beings in a salvation process that touches the whole person. Every offense, every humiliation, and every alienation from human work is an obstacle to the work of salvation.

A second major theme of the Bible echoes this same thinking. The messianic promises, the events that announce and accompany the coming of the Messiah, are not an isolated theme but, like the first, a theme which runs through the whole Bible. It is vitally present in the history of Israel, and thus has its proper place in the historical development of God's people.

The prophets proclaim a reign of peace. But peace implies the establishment of justice, the defense of the rights of the poor, the punishment of oppressors, and a life free from the fear of enslavement by others. A poorly understood spiritualization has often caused us to forget the human responsibility, and the power which can transform unjust social structures, which the messianic promises entail. The conquest of misery and the abolition of exploitation are signs of the Messiah's arrival. According to the Book of Isaiah, the kingdom will become a reality when "they shall not build for others to live in, or plant for others to eat"—when they profit "from their own labor" (Isa. 65:22). To fight for a just world where there is no servitude, oppression, or alienated work is to proclaim and signify the advent of the Messiah. The messianic promises establish a close tie between the kingdom of God and living conditions that are worthy of human beings. God's kingdom and social injustice are incompatible.

The message to be gleaned from these two biblical themes is clear. Salvation embraces the whole human person, as *Populorum progressio* (21) reminds us. Preaching the gospel message is not preaching escape from the world. On the contrary, the Word of God leads us to deepen and to radicalize our commitment in history. Concretely, this involvement means solidarity with the oppressed of Latin America and participation in their struggle for emancipation, realizing that salvation history is a liberation in process. It is through encounters with human beings, especially the poor and the exploited, that we shall encounter the Lord (see Matt. 25:31 ff.). To be a Christian in our day is to involve oneself creatively in the different stages of humanity's liberation process. Faith opens up infinite horizons to our human effort, giving dynamic vitality to our actions in history.

These are some of the theological notions that implicitly or explicitly under-lie the new Christian statements coming from Latin America. Only against this backdrop can we understand the efforts of certain Christian groups to be authentically present in the world of Latin America. Theirs is not a suspect tem-poralism; theirs is a desire, though undoubtedly flawed and imperfect, to be wholly loyal to the Word of the Lord.

NEW ECCLESIAL STRUCTURES

There was a time when the vitality or weakness of the Latin American church was measured by the number of its priests. You simply calculated the number of faithful per priest (the experts further darkened the picture by adding the factor of distance between priests and faithful) and made your projections on that basis. The scarcity of vocations seemed to be the major obstacle to be overcome if the underdeveloped church of Latin America were to "take off." Today, few still view the matter that way. The problem of priests has other, more delicate, facets. Everything seems to indicate that the lifestyle of the priest, which had remained static for centuries, is about to undergo a profound transformation in the near future. But even more important is the fact that it is merely one symptom of the broader and graver crisis afflicting the Christian community.

The older approach to this whole problem had a markedly clerical cast, which tended to minimize the problematical nature of the situation. Its gravest error was undoubtedly the type of solution it suggested for the church's prob-lems. It was felt we could move out of the past by making efforts to modern-ize certain ecclesiastical structures or to inaugurate certain pastoral adapta-tions. Basically it is that whole approach that is today being called into question.

From now on we shall have to attack this issue with greater boldness, with the courage that Scripture enjoins on Christ's disciples (see Acts 4:31). That courage must lead us not to halfway reforms that badly gloss over our fears and trepida-tions, but to a transformation of what we know today. The times demand of us a creative spark that will allow us to think up and create new ecclesial structures and new ways for the Christian community to be present to the world. The alarm which seems visible in some sectors of the church in the face of the ques-tions raised by the signs of the times is no solution.

For the Latin American church a main line in this quest must be the asser-tion of its own distinctive personality. We have lived in a state of dependence that has not allowed us to fully develop our own qualities up to now. As a church, we have been a mirror image rather than a fountainhead, in the terms of Father de Lima Vas. We have been mirroring the European church—uncritical-ly borrowing our theology, institutions, canon law, lifestyle, and spirituality. We have not been a creative fountainhead for new attitudes toward a society in revolution, for ecclesial structures that would be appropriate for a Third World church, or for ideas that would allow us to strike deep roots in our own reality. Working free of the colonial mentality is undoubtedly one of the major tasks confronting the Christian community of Latin America. It will also be one way in which we can contribute to the authentic enrichment of the universal church.

Another main line will be our commitment to genuine poverty. This is an area where Christians offer ample witness to the contrary. We often confuse making a vow of poverty with living a life of poverty. We often confuse possession of absolute essentials with comfortable ensconcement in the world. We often confuse instruments for service with power leverage. We need an honest, clear-headed reform that will put an end to the discrepancy between our preaching and our practice. Living honestly as a church that is not only open to the poor but poor itself will substantially change the face which the Christian community presents today.

In this sense, the episcopal conference at Medellín may represent for the Latin American church what Vatican II was for the whole church. It was not an end point but a point of departure. It was not only a forum for documents that take up the ecclesial community's present awareness of this moment in history, but also a stimulus to push on further, a spirit to enliven the letter of the law. All this will not be done without difficulty. We shall always feel light-headed impulses that will prompt us to sensation-seeking postures rather than deep commitments. But the greatest threat will be the temptation to immobility and a preference for changes that at bottom perpetuate the existing situation. We are more bound to the old structures than we realize.

Vatican II, and, one hopes, the Medellín conference, opened up the floodgates, and long-dammed waters have flowed freely and continue to rise. When the flood is over, we shall realize that it has done more cleansing than destroying. Right now, however, our task is not to anxiously protect the texts of Vatican II and Medellín from erroneous interpretations, or to provide erudite commentaries. The important thing for us is to expound them in our deeds—to verify their truth in our daily Christian life.

The church is experiencing the effects of living in a world that is undergoing profound and decisive changes. The church itself must set out on uncharted roads, turn down new byways, without knowing what risks and obstacles will be encountered. It is not easy to accept the idea that the Spirit will "lead [us] to the whole truth" (John 16:13) without first consulting us about the route to be taken. But today that is what the Christian community in Latin America must do.

Some may well complain that the positions expressed here do not offer any responses or solutions. That may be true. But we must not forget that, as has been said, those who change the course of history are usually not those who offer solutions but those who pose a new set of questions.

241

35. THE CHURCH: SACRAMENT OF HISTORY

Concern about an effective proclamation of the gospel and the church's role in Latin American society guided Gutiérrez's theological investigations from the time of his return to Peru from studies in Europe in 1959 to the present. In Theology of Liberation *he employed the central symbol of the Council's theology of the church, namely sacrament (see* Lumen gentium *1, 9, and 48;* Gaudium et spes *45;* Sacrosanctum concilium *5 and 26), to argue that "the church must be the visible sign of the presence of the Lord within the aspiration for liberation and struggle for a more human and just society" (148). Such a mission requires that the church link its "first task," the celebration of the Eucharist, to the task of proclaiming and forging genuine human fellowship in a world fractured by injustice. The following passages are excerpted from chapter 12 of* Theology of Liberation, *"The Church: Sacrament of History."*

Because the church has inherited its structures and its lifestyle from the past, it finds itself today somewhat out of step with the history which confronts it. But what is at stake is not simply a renewal and adaptation of pastoral methods. It is rather a question of a new ecclesial consciousness and a redefinition of the task of the church in a world in which it is not only *present*, but of which it *forms a part* more than it suspected in the recent past. In this new consciousness and redefinition, intraecclesial problems take second place.

UNIVERSAL SACRAMENT OF SALVATION

The unqualified affirmation of the universal will of salvation has radically changed the way of conceiving the mission of the church in the world. It seems clear today that the purpose of the church is not to save in the sense of "guaranteeing heaven." The work of salvation is a reality which occurs in history. This work gives to the historical becoming of humankind its profound unity and its deepest meaning. It is only by starting from this unity and meaning that we can establish the distinctions and clarifications which can lead us to a new understanding of the mission of the church. The Lord is the Sower who arises at dawn to sow the field of historical reality before we establish our distinctions. Distinctions can be useful for what Liege calls "the new initiatives of God in human history," but as he himself says, "Too great a use of them, however, threatens to destroy the sense of a vocation to a single fulfillment toward which God has not ceased to lead the world, whose source he is." The meaning and the fruitfulness of the ecclesial task will be clear only when they are situated within the context of the plan of salvation. In doing this we must avoid reducing the salvific work to the action of the church. In short, all our ecclesiology will depend on the kind of relationship that we establish between the two.

A NEW ECCLESIOLOGICAL PERSPECTIVE

The perspective we have indicated presupposes an "uncentering" of the church, which ceases considering itself as the exclusive place of salvation and orients itself toward a new and radical service of people. It also presupposes a new awareness that the action of Christ and his Spirit is the true hinge of the plan of salvation.

Indeed, the church of *the first centuries* lived spontaneously in this way. Its minority status in society and the consequent pressure that the proximity of the non-Christian world exercised on it made it quite sensitive to the action of Christ beyond its frontiers, that is, to the totality of his redemptive work. This explains why, for example, the great Christian authors of that time affirmed without qualification human liberty in religious matters as a human and natural right and declared that the state is incompetent to intervene in this area. Because they had confidence in the possibility of salvation at work in everyone, they saw liberty not so much as a risk of wandering from the path as the necessary condition for finding the path and arriving at a genuine encounter with the Lord.

The situation of the Christian community changed in *the fourth century.* Instead of being marginated and attacked, Christianity was now tolerated (Edict of Milan, 313 c.e.) and quickly became the religion of the Roman state (Decree of Thessalonica, 381 c.e.). The proclamation of the gospel message was then protected by the support of political authority, and the Christianization of the world of that time received a powerful impulse. This rapid advance of Christianity brought about a change in the manner of conceiving the relationship of humankind to salvation. It began to be thought that there were only two kinds of people: those who have accepted faith in Christ and those who have culpably rejected it. The Fathers continued to teach the doctrine of the universal will of salvation and held that this could not occur without free acceptance on the part of human beings. But they asserted that there was no longer any excuse for ignorance of the Savior, for thanks to the ministry of the church, the voice of the gospel had come in one way or another to all humans. Neither Jews nor gentiles had any excuse. These ideas, which were presented with hesitation and even anguish in the fourth and fifth centuries, gradually gained ground. By the Middle Ages, when the church was coextensive with the known world of that time and deeply pervaded it, Christians had the vital experience of security and tranquillity that "outside the church there is no salvation." *To be for or against Christ came to be fully identified with being for or against the church.* Therefore it is not strange that there was no longer any mention of bits of truth which could be found beyond the frontiers of the church; there was no longer any world outside the church. The church was regarded as the sole repository of religious truth. In a spontaneous and inevitable fashion, then, there arose an ecclesiocentric perspective which centered more and more on the life and reflection of the church—and continues to do so even up to the present time.

From that time on, therefore, there was a subtle displacement of religious liberty as "a human and natural right" of all humans by "the liberty of the act of faith"; henceforth, the right to freedom in religious matters would be synonymous with the right not to be coerced by the forced imposition of the Christian faith. In a parallel fashion there occurred another important displacement: no longer was it a question of the "incompetence" of political power in religious matters; rather it was a question of the state's "tolerance"—which presupposed an "option" for the truth—toward religious error. The reason for these two displacements is the same: the position of strength of a church which had begun to focus on itself, to ally itself with civil power, and to consider itself as the exclusive repository of salvific truth.

This condition of the church began to change in the *modern period*, with the internal rupture of Christendom and the discovery of new peoples. But at the beginning of this period the ecclesiocentric perspective persisted, apart from a few new touches. In the matter of religious liberty, which we have focused on here, it was the period of "religious tolerance": what Thomas Aquinas considered valid for the Jews was extended to the descendants of Christians who had "culpably" separated themselves from the church. In the nineteenth century religious tolerance gave rise to the by-product of the theory of thesis and hypothesis; this theory sought to respond to the ideas born in the French Revolution, thereby taking the idea of tolerance a step further. But fundamentally the position continued being the same: salvific truth could be found only in the church. It is for this reason that "modern freedoms" endangered the eternal destiny of humankind.

The effects of the new historical situation in which the church found itself began to be felt more strongly in the nineteenth century and even more so in recent decades. Vatican II did not hesitate to place itself in the line of a frank affirmation of God's universal saving will and to put an end to the anachronistic theological and pastoral consequences deduced from the ecclesiocentrism which we have already mentioned. This explains the change of attitude regarding religious liberty. The declaration dedicated to this subject tried to achieve a consensus by placing itself simply on the level of the dignity of the human person. But this position in fact implies a change of position with regard to fundamental theological questions having to do with the role of the church in the encounter between God and humankind.

We might speak here of a return to the posture of the church in the first centuries. Without being inexact, however, this affirmation tends to schematize the process. There is never a pure and simple regression. The process which began in the fourth century was not simply an "accident." It was a long and laborious learning experience. And that experience forms part of the contemporary ecclesial consciousness; it is a factor which explains many kinds of behavior today. It also cautions us against what might happen again. What was spontaneously and intuitively expressed in the first centuries must manifest itself today in a more reflective and critical fashion.

SACRAMENT AND SIGN

Thanks to the process which we have just reviewed, Vatican II was able to set forth the outlines of a new ecclesiological perspective. And it did this almost surprisingly by speaking of the church as a sacrament. This is undoubtedly one of the most important and permanent contributions of the Council. The notion of sacrament enables us to think of the church within the horizon of salvific work and in terms radically different from those of the ecclesiocentric emphasis. The Council itself did not manage to place itself totally in this line of thinking. Many of the texts still reveal the burden of a heavy heritage; they timidly point to a way out from this turning in of the church on itself, without always accomplishing this. But what must be emphasized is that in the very midst of a council over which an ecclesiocentric problematic hovered, new elements arose which had to permit a break with this problematic and allow for thinking more in accord with the real challenges to the Christian faith of today.

In theology the term *sacramentum* has two closely related meanings. Initially it was used to translate the Greek word *misterion*. According to Paul, *mystery* means *the fulfillment and the manifestation of the salvific plan*: "the secret hidden for long ages and through many generations, but now disclosed" (Col. 1:26). The gospel is, therefore, "that divine secret kept in silence for long ages but now disclosed . . . made known to all nations, to bring them to faith and obedience" (Rom. 16:25–26). This mystery is the love of the Father, who "loved the world so much that he gave his only Son" (John 3:16) in order to call all humans, in the Spirit, to communion with God. All are called—together, as a community and not as separate individuals—to participate in the life of the trinitarian community, to enter into the circuit of love that unites the persons of the Trinity. This is a love which "builds up human society in history" (see *Ad gentes* 1–5). The fulfillment and the manifestation of the will of the Father occur in a privileged fashion in Christ, who is called therefore the "mystery of God" (Col. 2:22; see also Col. 1:27, 4:3; Eph. 3:3; 1 Tim. 3:16). For the same reason Sacred Scripture, the church, and the liturgical rites were designated by the first Christian generations by the term *mystery*, and by its Latin translation, *sacrament*. In the sacrament the salvific plan is fulfilled and revealed; that is, it is made present among humans and for humans. But at the same time, it is through the sacrament that humans encounter God. This is an encounter *in* history, not because God comes *from* history, but because history comes from God. The sacrament is thus the efficacious revelation of the call to communion with God and to the unity of all humankind.

This is the primordial meaning of the term *sacrament* and it is in this way that it is used in the first centuries of the church. At the beginning of the third century, however, Tertullian introduced a nuance which gradually gave rise to a second meaning derived from the first. This African Father began to use the term *sacrament* to designate the rites of Baptism and the Eucharist. Gradually the two terms, *mystery* and *sacrament*, became distinct. The first referred more to the doctrinal mysteries; the second designated what we commonly call sacraments today. The theology of the Middle Ages recovered the meaning of sacrament, in the strict sense, in the formula *efficacious sign of grace*. The sign marks the character of visibility of the sacrament, by means of which there occurs an effective personal encounter of God and the human person. But the sign refers to a reality from beyond itself, in this case the grace of communion, which is the reason for and the result of this encounter. This communion is also an intrahistorical reality.

To call the church the "visible sacrament of this saving unity" (*LG* 9) is to define it in relation to the plan of salvation, whose fulfillment in history the church reveals and signifies to the human race. A visible sign, the church refers to the reality of "communion with God and of unity among all humankind" (*LG* 1). The church can be understood only in relation to the reality which it proclaims to humankind. Its existence is not "for itself," but rather "for others." Its center is outside itself, it is in the work of Christ and his Spirit. It is constituted by the Spirit as "the universal sacrament of salvation" (*LG* 48); outside of the action of the Spirit which leads the universe and history toward its fullness in Christ, the church is nothing. Even more, the church does not authentically attain consciousness of itself except in the perception of this total presence of Christ and his Spirit in humanity. The mediation of the consciousness of the "other"—of the world in which this presence occurs—is the indispensable precondition of its own consciousness as community-sign. Any attempt to avoid this mediation can only lead the church to a false perception of itself—to an ecclesiocentric consciousness.

Through the persons who explicitly accept his Word, the Lord reveals the world to itself. He rescues it from anonymity and enables it to know the ultimate meaning of its historical future and the value of every human act. But by the same token the church must be converted to the world, in which Christ and his Spirit are present and active; the church must allow itself to be inhabited and evangelized by the world. [As O. Clement has pointed out], a theology of the church in the world should be completed by "a theology of the world in the church." This dialectical relationship is implied in the emphasis on the church as sacrament. This puts us on the track of a new way of conceiving the relationship between the historical church and the world. The church is not a non-world; it is humanity itself attentive to the Word. It is the People of God which lives in history and is orientated toward the future promised by the Lord. It is, as Teilhard de Chardin said, the "reflectively Christified portion of the world." The church-world relationship thus should be seen not in spatial terms, but rather in dynamic and temporal ones.

As a sacramental community, the church should signify in its own internal structure the salvation whose fulfillment it announces. Its organization ought to serve this task. As a sign of the liberation of the human being and of history, the church itself in its concrete existence ought to be a place of liberation. A sign should be clear and understandable. If we conceive of the church as a sacrament of the salvation of the world, then it has all the more obligation to manifest in its visible structures the message that it bears. Since the church is not an end in itself, what matters is its capacity to signify the reality in function of which it exists. Outside of this reality the church is nothing; it makes the church live under the sign of provisionality; and it is toward the fulfillment of this reality that the church is oriented: this reality is the kingdom of God which has already begun in history. The break with an unjust social order and the search for new ecclesial structures—in which the most dynamic sectors of the Christian community are engaged—have their basis in this ecclesiological perspective. We are moving toward forms of presence and structure of the church the radical newness of which can barely be discerned on the basis of our present experience. This trend, at its best and healthiest, is not a fad; nor is it due to professional nonconformists. Rather it has its roots in a profound fidelity to the church as sacrament of the unity and salvation of humankind and in the conviction that its only support should be the Word which liberates.

We must recognize, nevertheless, that the ecclesiocentric point of view is abandoned more rapidly in the realm of a certain theological reflection than in the concrete attitudes of the majority of the Christian community. This presents not a few difficulties, for what is most important is what happens at this second level. Spending too much time on intraecclesial problems—as often happens with certain forms of protest in the church, especially in the developed countries—is to pass over the richest lode for a true renewal of the church. For this renewal cannot be achieved in any deep sense except on the basis of an effective awareness of the world in which the church lives and a real commitment to it. Changes in the church will be made on this basis. To seek anxiously after changes themselves is to pose the question in terms of survival. But this is not the question. The point is not to survive, but to serve. The rest will be given.

In Latin America the world in which the Christian community must live and celebrate its eschatological hope is the world of social revolution; the church's task must be defined in relation to this. Its fidelity to the gospel leaves it no alternative: the church must be the visible sign of the presence of the Lord within the aspiration for liberation and the struggle for a more human and just society. Only in this way will the message of love which the church bears be made credible and efficacious.

EUCHARIST AND HUMAN FELLOWSHIP

The mission of the church is found where the celebration of the Lord's Supper and the creation of human fellowship are indissolubly joined. This is what it means in an active and concrete way to be the sacrament of the salvation of the world.

"IN MEMORY OF ME"

The first task of the church is to celebrate with joy the gift of the salvific action of God in humanity, accomplished through the death and resurrection of Christ. This is the Eucharist: a memorial and a thanksgiving. It is a memorial of Christ which presupposes an ever-renewed acceptance of the meaning of his life—a total gift of self to others. It is a thanksgiving for the love of God which is revealed in these events. The Eucharist is a feast, a celebration of the joy that the church desires and seeks to share. The Eucharist is done within the church, and simultaneously the church is built up by the Eucharist. In the church "we celebrate," writes Schillebeeckx, "that which is achieved outside the church edifice, in human history." This work, which creates a profound human fellowship, gives the church its reason for being.

In the Eucharist we celebrate the cross and the resurrection of Christ, his Passover from death to life, and our passing from sin to grace. In the gospel the Last Supper is presented against the background of the Jewish Passover, which celebrated the liberation from Egypt and the Sinai Covenant. The Christian Passover takes on and reveals the full meaning of the Jewish Passover. Liberation from sin is at the very root of political liberation. The former reveals what is really involved in the latter. But on the other hand, communion with God and others presupposes the abolition of all injustice and exploitation. This is expressed by the very fact that the Eucharist was instituted during a meal. For the Jews a meal in common was a sign of fellowship. It united the diners in a kind of sacred pact. Moreover, the bread and the wine are signs of fellowship which at the same time suggest the gift of creation. The objects used in the Eucharist themselves recall that fellowship is rooted in God's will to give the goods of this earth to all persons so that they might build a more human world. The Gospel of John, which does not contain the story of the Eucharistic institution, reinforces this idea, for it substitutes the episode of the washing of the feet—a gesture of service, love, and fellowship. This substitution is significant: John seems to see in this episode the profound meaning of the Eucharistic celebration, the institution of which he does not relate. Thus the Eucharist appears inseparably united to creation and to the building up of a real human fellowship. . . .

The basis for fellowship is full communion with the persons of the Trinity. The bond which unites God and humanity is celebrated—that is, effectively recalled and proclaimed—in the Eucharist. Without a real commitment against exploitation and alienation and for a society of solidarity and justice, the Eucharistic celebration is an empty action, lacking any genuine endorsement by those who participate in it. This is something that many Latin American Christians are feeling more and more deeply, and they are thus more demanding both of themselves and of the whole church. "To make a remembrance" of Christ is more than the performance of an act of worship; it is to accept living under the sign of the cross and in the hope of the resurrection. It is to accept the meaning of a life lived to the point of death—at the hands of the powerful of this world—for love of others.

CONDEMNATION AND PROCLAMATION

The primary task of the church, as we have said, is to celebrate with joy the salvific action of the Lord in history. In the creation of fellowship implied and signified by this celebration, the church—taken as a whole—plays a role which is unique, but varies according to historical circumstances.

In Latin America to be church today means to take a clear position regarding both the present state of social injustice and the revolutionary process which is attempting to abolish that injustice and build a more human order. The first step is to recognize that in reality a stand has already been taken: the church is tied to the prevailing social system. In many places the church contributes to creating "a Christian order" and to giving a kind of sacred character to an alienating situation and to the worst kind of violence—a situation which pits the powerful against the weak. The protection which the church receives from the social class which is the beneficiary and the defender of the prevailing capitalist society in Latin America has made the institutional church into a part of the system and the Christian message into a part of the dominant ideology. Any claim to non-involvement in politics—a banner recently hoisted by conservative sectors—is nothing but a subterfuge to keep things as they are. The mission of the church cannot be defined in the abstract. Its historical and social coordinates, its here and now, have a bearing not only on the adequacy of its pastoral methods. They also should be at the very heart of theological reflection.

The church—with variations according to different countries—has an obvious social influence in Latin America. Without overestimating it, we must recognize that numerous facts have demonstrated this influence, even up to the present day. This influence has contributed, and continues to contribute, to supporting the established order. But this is no longer the entire picture. The situation has begun to change. The change is slow and still very fragile, but growing and active minorities of the Latin American Christian community are involved in this change. The process is not irreversible, but it is gradually gaining strength. It is still afflicted with many ambiguities, but the initial experiences are beginning to provide the criteria by which these ambiguities can be resolved. Within these groups—as might have been expected—there has arisen a question; on its answer will depend to a large degree the concrete path to be followed. The question is: Should the change consist in the church's putting its current social influence on the side of necessary transformations? Some fear a kind of "Constantinianism of the Left," and believe that the church should divest itself of every vestige of political power. This fear is opportune because it points out a genuine risk which we must keep in mind. But we believe that the best way to achieve this divestment of power is precisely through resolute solidarity with the oppressed and the exploited in the struggle for a more just society. The groups that control economic and political power will not forgive the church for this. They will withdraw their support, which is the principal source of the ambiguous social prestige which the church enjoys in Latin America today. Indeed, this has already begun. Moreover, formulated in this way the question is somewhat artificial. Indeed, how can the church preach the Word, incarnated where the pulse of Latin American history throbs, without putting this social influence at stake? How can it make a situation disappear which—with all its ambiguities—is the church's own doing? How can it denounce the unjust order of the continent and announce the gospel outside of the concrete position which it has today in Latin American society? The truth is that it is not a question of whether the church should or should not use its influence in the Latin American revolutionary process. Rather, the question is in what direction and for what purpose is it going to use its influence: for or against the established order, to preserve the social prestige which comes with its ties to the groups in power or to free itself from that prestige with a break from these groups and with genuine service to the oppressed? It is a question of social realism, of becoming aware of an already given situation, to start from it, and to modify it; it is not a question of creating that situation. The situation is already there and is the concrete, historical framework within which the task proper to the Latin American church will be determined.

Within this framework the Latin American church must make a prophetic *condemnation* of every dehumanizing situation, which is contrary to fellowship, justice, and liberty. At the same time it must criticize every sacralization of oppressive structures to which the church itself might have contributed. Its condemnation must be public, for its position in Latin American society is public. This condemnation may be one of the few voices—and at times the only one—which can be raised in the midst of a country subjected to repression. In this critical and creative confrontation of its faith with the historical present—a task whose roots must be in the hope in the future promised by God—the church must go to the very causes of the situation and not be content with pointing out and attending to certain of its consequences. Indeed, one of the most subtle dangers threatening a "renewed" church in Latin America is to allow itself to be assimilated into a society which seeks certain reforms without a comprehensive critique. It is the danger of becoming useful to the system all over again, only this time to a system which tries to modernize and to suppress the most outrageous injustices without effecting any deep changes. In Latin America this denunciation must represent a radical critique of the present order, which means that the church must also criticize itself as an integral part of this order. This horizon will allow the church to break out of its narrow enclosure of intraecclesial problems by placing these problems in their true context—the total society and the broad perspective of commitment in a world of revolutionary turmoil.

It has been pointed out, and rightly so, that this critical function of the church runs the risk of remaining on a purely verbal and external level and that it should be backed up with clear actions and commitments. Prophetic denunciation can be made validly and truly only from within the heart of the struggle for a more human world. The truth of the gospel, it has been said, is a truth which must be done. This observation is correct and necessary. Having presupposed that, however, we should recall that given the concrete conditions in which the church finds itself in Latin American society, a precise and opportune denunciation on the part of the church is not only a "word" or a "text"; it is an action, a stand. The church's social influence itself means that its words—if they are clear and incisive—will not be hollow. When the church speaks, it can cause the old underpinnings of the established order to fall, and it can mobilize new energies. This is so much the case that simply because of their "speaking" or "making statements," certain organisms of the church and many Christians have undergone severe attacks and serious difficulties at the hands of the representatives of the established order—including the loss of liberty and even the loss of life. I do not at all want to overestimate the word and so to diminish the value of concrete actions; but we need to remember, out of simple realism that at times the word is also an important gesture of commitment. In this regard, the critical function of the church finds in Latin America—given its historical and social coordinates—the preconditions for its exercise and possibilities for action in relation to the process of liberation which are not found elsewhere. Therefore, its responsibility is all the greater.

The condemnation, however, is achieved by confronting a given situation with the reality which is *proclaimed:* the love of the Father which calls all persons in Christ and through the action of the Spirit to union among themselves and communion with him. To announce the gospel is to proclaim that the love of God is present in the historical becoming of humankind. It is to make known that there is no human act which cannot in the last instance be defined in relation to Christ. To preach the Good News is for the church to be a sacrament of history, to fulfill its role as a sign-community, a sign of the convocation of all by God. It is to announce the coming of the kingdom. The gospel message reveals, without any evasions, what is at the root of social injustice: the rupture of the fellowship based on our being offspring of the Father; the gospel reveals the fundamental alienation which lies below every other human alienation. In this way, evangelization is a powerful factor in personalization. Because of it persons become aware of the profound meaning of their historical existence and live an active and creative hope in the full achievement of the fellowship that they seek with all their strength.

Moreover, the personalization stimulated by the proclamation of the gospel can take on—in cases like Latin America—very particular and demanding forms. If a situation of injustice and exploitation is incompatible with the coming of the kingdom, the Word which proclaims this coming ought normally to point out this incompatibility. This means that the people who hear this message and live in these conditions by the mere fact of hearing it should perceive themselves as oppressed and feel impelled to seek their own liberation. Very concretely, they should "feel their hunger" and become aware that this hunger is due to a situation which the gospel repudiates. The proclamation of the gospel thus has a conscienticizing function, or in other words, a politicizing function. But this is made real and meaningful only by living and proclaiming the gospel from within a commitment to liberation, only in concrete, effective solidarity with exploited persons and social classes. Only by participating in their struggles can we understand the implications of the gospel message and make it have an impact on history. The preaching of the Word will be empty and ahistorical if it tries to avoid this dimension. It will not be the message of the God who liberates, of "the One who returns to life," as José María Arguedas says.

Some years ago, a pope who is beyond any suspicion of "horizontalism," Pius XII, then Cardinal Pacelli, said that the church civilizes by evangelizing. And this assertion was accepted without opposition. In the contemporary Latin American context it would be necessary to say that the church should politicize by evangelizing. Will this expression receive the same acceptance? Probably not. To many it will seem shocking; they will perhaps accuse it of "humanizing" the gospel message or of falling into a deceitful and dangerous "temporalism." This reaction can be explained in part by the fact that there are still many who—lacking a realistic and contemporary conception of the political sphere—do not wish to see the gospel "brought down" to a level which they believe is nothing more than partisan conflict. But the more severe attacks will doubtless come from those who fear the upsurge of a true political consciousness in the Latin American masses and can discern what the contribution of the gospel to this process might be. When it was a question of "civilizing," they had no objection, because this term was translated as the promotion of ethical, cultural, and artistic values and at the most as a very general and uncommitted defense of the dignity of the human person. But "to politicize," "to conscienticize"—these terms have today in Latin America a deeply subversive meaning. Can we say that the struggle against the "institutionalized violence" endured by the weak and the struggle for social justice are therefore less human, less ethical, less "civilizing" than the promotion of moral, cultural, and esthetic values which are bound to a given social system? Girardi is correct when he says that "institutionalized violence generally goes along with institutionalized hypocrisy."

When we affirm that the church politicizes by evangelizing, we do not claim that the gospel is thus reduced to creating a political consciousness in persons or that the revelation of the Father—which takes on, transforms, and fulfills in an unsuspected way every human aspiration—is thereby nullified. We mean that the annunciation of the gospel, precisely insofar as it is a message of total love, has an inescapable political dimension, because it is addressed to people who live within a fabric of social relationships, which, in our case, keeps them in a subhuman condition. But did those who think in this way believe that Pius XII was reducing the gospel to a civilizing work? If they did not believe it before, why do they think so now? Let us openly say why: to "civilize" does not seem to challenge their privileged situation in *this* world; to conscienticize, to politicize, to make the oppressed become aware that they are human beings—do challenge that privilege.

This conscienticizing dimension of the preaching of the gospel, which rejects any aseptic presentation of the message, should lead to a profound revision of the pastoral activity of the church. Among other things, this activity should be directed effectively and primarily to those who are oppressed in the oppressed nations and not—as is presently the case—to the beneficiaries of a system designed for their own benefit. Or still better, the oppressed themselves should be the agents of this pastoral activity. The marginated and the dispossessed still do not have their own voice in the church of him who came to the world especially for them. The issue is not accidental. Their real presence in the church would work a profound transformation in its structures, its values, and its behavior. The owners of the goods of this world would no longer be the "owners" of the gospel.

It would be naïve, nevertheless, to claim that the revolutionary exigencies in Latin America do not bring with them the danger of oversimplifying the gospel message and making it a "revolutionary ideology"—which would definitively obscure reality. But we believe that the danger is not averted simply by noting its presence. It is not evaporated by a climate of alarm. It is necessary to look at it face to face and lucidly to analyze its causes as well as the factors which make it important for Christians committed to the social struggle. Are we not in this position because we have tried to hide the real political implications of the gospel? Those who—without stating so—neutralized these implications or oriented them for their own benefit are those who now have the least authority for giving lessons in evangelical "purity." We cannot expect the true and opportune counsel today to come from those who are "verticalists" in theory and "horizontalists" in practice. The problem exists, but the solution can come only from the very roots of the problem. It is where the proclamation of the gospel seems to border on submersion into the purely historical realm that there must be born the reflection, the spirituality, and the new preaching of a Christian message which is incarnated—not lost—in our here and now. To evangelize, M.-D. Chenu has said, is to incarnate the gospel in time. This time today is difficult and sinister only for those who ultimately do not know, or hesitate to believe, that the Lord is present in it.

The concrete measures for effecting the denunciation and the annunciation will be discerned little by little. It will be necessary to study carefully in a *permanent* fashion the signs of the times (*GS* 4), responding to specific situations without claiming to adopt at every step positions valid for all eternity. There are moments in which we will advance only by trial and error. It is difficult to establish ahead of time—as we have perhaps long thought we could—the specific guidelines which ought to determine the behavior of the church, taken as a whole, in these questions. The church should rise to the demands of the moment with whatever lights it has at that moment and with the desire to be faithful to the gospel. Some chapters of theology can be written only afterwards.

But the degree of incertitude and apprenticeship involved in this task should not lead us to disregard the urgency and necessity of taking stands or to forget what is permanent—that the gospel proclamation opens human history to the future promised by God and reveals God's present work. On the one hand, this proclamation will show that in every achievement of fellowship and justice among humans there is a step toward total communion. By the same token, it will show the incomplete and provisional character of any and every human achievement. The gospel will fulfill this function based on a comprehensive vision of the human being and of history and not on partial focuses, which have their own proper and effective instruments of criticism. The prophetic character of the Christian message, [as L. Gera says,] "always works from an eschatological option and affirmation. According to it, history will not achieve its total maturity as long as it has not achieved its eschatological end. Therefore every historical period always has new possibilities before it." On the other hand, by affirming that human fellowship is possible and that it will indeed be achieved, the proclamation of the gospel will inspire and radicalize the commitment of the Christian in history. In history and only in history is the gift of the love of God believed, loved, and hoped for. Every attempt to evade the struggle against alienation and the violence of the powerful and for a more just and more human world is the greatest infidelity to God. To know God is to work for justice. There is no other path to reach God.

36. COMMUNITY: OUT OF SOLITUDE

The last chapter of We Drink from Our Own Wells *(1983; 128–35) is devoted to a consideration of the communitarian nature of Christian discipleship, an early and consistent theme in the theology of Gutiérrez and, indeed, essential to his theological method. Not only is his intellectual work interdisciplinary in the usual sense; like his pastoral approach, it is also the product of teamwork. Such, indeed, is the modus operandi of the Instituto Bartolomé de Las Casas, which he founded in Lima in 1971.*

Especially notable in the following text, as in so many of his writings, is Gutiérrez's willingness to acknowledge certain hazards in the construction of a "church of the poor." Here he faces up to the dangers posed to all, believers and non-believers alike, who participate in movements for social change, namely, loneliness, isolation, and despair at the slow and costly process. But he notes a particular danger facing Christians involved in such movements: the neglect of the personal dimension of Christian faith. The following text represents a substantial alteration of the original English translation.

The development of the community dimension of faith is a characteristic of Christian life in our day. Vatican II contributed a great deal to this development. In Latin America one way in which this trend has found expression is in the rise of the basic ecclesial communities, which, in the judgment of Puebla, "are one of the causes of joy and hope for the church" (no. 96). We are also dealing here with another essential aspect of the following of Jesus Christ—the communal experience of encounter with him.

Here I should like to bring out the fact that for many Latin American Christians this community dimension is not something added simply and with joy to the Christian outlook already in place. In fact, the journey toward life in community frequently takes an unexpected turn: a passage through a painful experience of profound solitude or loneliness. This is, moreover, a classical theme in the history of spirituality.

The experience of the solitude of the desert is a profound aspect of the encounter with God. Passage through this desert is a journey of pure faith, with God alone for support and guidance. In solitude the Lord speaks to us "tenderly" (Hos. 2:14), calls us to fidelity, and consoles us. Being all alone with God, who enriches us with the gift of happiness in the innermost depths of our being, is an irreplaceable and ineffable experience, that is, largely incommunicable. The writings of the great mystics make this very clear.

But this experience of solitude takes on special features in our present situation. It leads to an urgent realization of the importance of the Christian community, not as a group of which we deign to be a part (as though we might just as well have made the opposite choice), but as a basic ecclesial dimension of walking according to the Spirit.

THE DARK NIGHT OF INJUSTICE

For those who make the commitment to liberation there is understandably a very keen sense of the situation of the vast majorities, as well as of their role in historical change. In other words, those involved take very seriously the scope of love as expressed in the famous words of M.-D. Chenu: "The masses, my neighbor." This fact, added to what I have just been saying about the community dimension of faith, may lead us to think that there is little room left for the personal dimension, including solitude, in human existence and in the experience of faith. All energies would be poured out into scattered commitment and an unmitigated activism.

There is no doubt that this danger exists. But it is no more than that: a risk; the essential and most fruitful substance of the experience is not to be found there. The passage through what has been called "the dark night of injustice" is part of the spiritual journey in Latin America. [As J. Hernández Pico says,] on this journey "of an entire people toward its liberation through the desert of structural and organized injustice that surrounds us . . . , it is very important to persevere in prayer, even if we hardly do more than stammer groans and cries, while in this struggle the image of God in us is purified in an extraordinary 'dark night.'"

The crossing of the desert takes place only in "a deep and vast solitude," as John of the Cross said. Many of those who seek to be in solidarity with the poor Latin American masses experience this solitude. There is no authentic acceptance of that commitment that does not involve great difficulties. I know this from the experience of many. . . . There are problems with those who see their privileges being challenged; there is isolation due to the unwanted nature of the consequences of making the world of the poor one's own; there is distrust and even hostility from many who share the same faith.

However, what renders these difficulties even more intense is the situation of poverty and exploitation in which the poor live. It is a situation that seems to have no end; it is like living halfway through a tunnel. The interests that the poor are challenging, both within each country and at the international level, are very powerful (think of what is happening in Central America in these years). There is, in addition, the great—and unwanted—human cost of an effort at liberation in which no successful outcome can even be glimpsed. It is what allows us to measure what García Márquez expressively calls "the size of our solitude."

All this gives rise to moments of great suffering and deep loneliness. Juan Alsina, another murdered priest, wrote as follows on the evening before he was found dead:

> We have come to the end of the road; we cut a path but now we are among the rocks . . . we shall continue on, those of us who remain. How long? . . . "None of those who dipped their bread in the fleshpots of Egypt will see the Promised Land without passing through the experience of death.". . .Who is at the other end of the phone? Who is knocking on the door at this hour? The difficulty is not to know what I will do but what they will do, and the most painful question of all: Why? This is the source of the uncertainty and the consciousness of uncertainty, the fear.

Yes, the fear, and why not? The fear not only of dying, which itself is no small matter, but also of weakening, of thinking more about oneself than is right. Of beginning to consider other and less costly forms of commitment.

When they find themselves alone—and there are many kinds of solitude—many persons would like to rewrite their lives; they wish they had not done or said this or that. Not all wishes at such a moment are dictated by a healthy self-criticism; weariness plays a part, as does cowardice and even despair at the thought of the many obstacles and misunderstandings that must be overcome. There are also moments for great decisions in which nothing is clear, but a decision must nonetheless be made. There are no fixed points of reference. All that remains is the conviction that one is doing the Father's will and serving a people which is poor, but even this occurs in a dryness that, despite one's conviction, makes one's tongue cleave to the roof of the mouth (Ps. 137:6).

In all these circumstances there is a new encounter with oneself and, above all, a new face-to-face encounter with the Lord who is testing and consoling us. John of the Cross speaks of the "frightful night" through which one must pass, but he also says that the desert is "the more delightful, delicious, and loving, the deeper, vaster, and more solitary it is." Such is the twofold experience of the Christian who wishes to be faithful to the Lord even in the blackest depths of "the dark night of injustice." Trust in God and in the ecclesial community is present, then, even though the light of day has still not dawned. . . .

These are the simple experiences of followers of the Lord. They are echoes, reverberating down through the history of the Christian community, of the cry of Jesus himself: "My God, my God, why have you abandoned me?" (Mark 15:34). But in these experiences Christians do not fail to realize that Jesus' expression of heartrending solitude comes on the threshold of the most tremendous and most radical communion possible: communion in the life and joy of the resurrection.

LIVING IN COMMUNITY

The passage through the experience of solitude leads to a profound community life. The solitude of which I am speaking is something quite different from individualism. In individualism there is a large measure of intentional and self-interested withdrawal in order to ensure a life of quiet privacy. Others may come and knock on the door, but if the individualist opens to them, it is as one who does a favor, as one who graciously adds, so to speak, a community dimension to a Christian life that is self-sufficient without it.

The experience of solitude, on the other hand, gives rise to a hunger for communion. There is an aloneness with oneself and with God that, however hard it may be to endure at certain times, is a requirement for authentic community.

God, in other words, does not call us to live in the desert but to cross it, and to emerge from it in order to reach the promised land. The journey through solitude creates a community flowing with the milk and honey of the fellowship of those who recognize God as their Father [see Ps. 133].

There is, however, no question here of two stages: first solitude and *then* community. Rather it is within community that one experiences solitude. The successive levels of depth prove disconcerting, even to those who experience them.

This is what happened to Archbishop Romero. His experience of solitude and the communion to which it calls us are described by Bishop Sergio Méndez Arceo (Cuernavaca, Mexico):

> He sought communion and proclaimed it, but solitude encircled him and he was left alone before his enemies. Today this operation continues. I could sum up in a widely-repeated phrase the strategy used to isolate him: "he was a good man, but mistaken." This is said so that his voice will not continue moving his people, nourishing his people.
>
> Brothers and sisters, the task of all of us who are united in his memory is to not leave him alone, to not allow him to remain alone. . . . Brothers and sis

ters, everyone, of whatever station in life, listen to my invitation: let us not leave him alone. Let us not permit anyone to isolate him. He died on behalf of the people, for the people—that is, he died on behalf of God, for God. That is why our work is a Christian work; it is a service to the God of Jesus Christ. It is not opposition to anyone; it is service.

The support of the community is essential for the crossing of the desert. So true is this that only in community can one travel this road. . . . Life in community welcomes and proclaims God's reign; in this reception and proclamation a community builds itself up as a community. [As the parishioners of my parish Christ the Redeemer in Lima, Peru, put it,] "Only in community can we hear, accept, and proclaim the gift and grace of the Lord, the privileged call to overcome everything that destroys fraternal communion (oppression, injustice, marginalization, discrimination, etc.)—because at the same time it is a break with God—and to struggle to implant the values of the kingdom that Jesus proclaims."

The community is also the place where we remember the death and resurrection of the Lord. Paul speaks with realism of our membership in the body of Christ. It implies liberation of our own bodies from the forces of death: sin, the root of all injustice. From the midst of the poverty and exploitation in which the majority of Latin Americans live, from within their emaciated, often massacred, bodies, the Spirit makes us penetrate deeper into the meaning of the Eucharist as an act of thanksgiving to the Father for sharing with us the body of the dead and resurrected Christ. Communion with the Lord's body and blood commits us to communion with the meaning he wanted to give his life and death, the meaning confirmed by the Father in resurrecting him: the testimony of love for every person and in particular for the poorest.

The breaking of the bread is at once the starting-point and goal of the Christian community. In it we express a profound communion in human sorrow and recognize with joy the Risen One who gives life to and raises the hope of those assembled in *ecclesia* by his words and deeds [cf. Luke 24:30–31]. As an old patristic theme puts it, the church creates the Eucharist and the Eucharist creates the church. That is why, in the words of the Fourth International Ecumenical Congress of Theology (1980),

> The Eucharist, or Lord's Supper, should hold the central place in our communities, together with the sharing of the Word of God. When they are celebrated among the poor and oppressed, they are both a promise of, and demand for, the justice, freedom, and the fellowship for which the peoples of the Third World are fighting.

The Eucharist, the sacrament which is the source of abundance, is a celebration of reconciliation, thanksgiving, and fraternal communion. Many have experienced the depth and creativity of celebrations among the poor. To a firm conviction of faith that is rooted in an ecclesial and personal tradition there is added an increasingly clear realization that the Eucharist celebrates a hope. The act of thanksgiving that is the Eucharist expresses a confidence that the communion of life that does not yet exist among us can become a reality, a communion where there would be "food for all and God's love," as Antonio Cisneros put it. This "anticipation," if I may so put it, is not an evasion; rather it moves people to commitment now. It represents an acknowledgment that the gift of life given by the risen Christ concerns every moment and every area of human existence.

This celebration is carried out in community—but a community that extends beyond the confines of the near and the local, because it is both the expression and the task of the entire church. . . . In the church we experience moments of solitude as well as times of community sharing. We are a messianic people on pilgrimage through history and we are, of course, exposed to the vicissitudes of that process in its varied forms; nonetheless it is in and with the people that we make our way. The ecclesial outlook is one of the dominant notes of the spirituality now coming to birth in Latin America.

"In the end, Lord, I die a daughter of the church," said the great Teresa of Avila who nevertheless knew many painful misunderstandings in her lifetime. It is in the church, the sacrament of the kingdom of life in history, that the committed Christians of Latin America are living—and dying.

37. THE LIBERATING MISSION OF THE CHURCH

In the third and final part of his 1986 essay "The Truth Shall Make You Free," Gutiérrez outlined in three stages the church's "liberating mission" in the world. The first section of this part, presented below, sets forth the theological warrants for a "liberating evangelization." The second section considers the biblical roots of the preferential option for the poor and describes the "church of the Beatitudes" (the latter is found in selection 24 above). The third section traces the emergence of the notion of the "church of the poor"—and in particular its christological foundation—from John XXIII (1962) to the second "Instruction" of the Sacred Congregation for the Doctrine of the Faith (1986). The idea of a church of the poor was, to be sure, already present in Pauline tradition (cf. 1 Cor. 1:26–31). Among the thorny problems confronted by Gutiérrez in the passage below are the relationship between evangelization and liberation and the requirements of social justice and personal freedom. The fact that Gutiérrez takes up these matters within a discussion of the church's mission must not be overlooked. The source is The Truth Shall Make You Free *(1986; 141–55).*

The truth that liberates is Jesus himself. The task imposed on those whom he sets free (see John 8:36) is to proclaim the saving truth that he came to bring us. The salvation in question I have been calling integral liberation, because, with liberation from sin as its starting point, it extends to all dimensions of the human.

The mission of the church, as the community of Jesus' disciples, is to communicate and bear witness to this total liberation of the human being. The liberation has, indeed, aspects that have a degree of autonomy (social liberation,

liberation of the human person), but these are not watertight compartments into which the saving grace of Christ does not reach. The church must respect the inner coherence proper to each of these several areas; it does not have a right to give directives in fields that are the proper objects of human efforts. On the other hand, it does have a duty to show the connection of these areas with the kingdom of God and its ethical demands.

Furthermore, the church must remind human beings of the ultimate meaning and destiny of every human work. For as a profound passage in *Gaudium et spes* of Vatican II says:

> When we have spread on earth the fruits of our nature and our enterprise— human dignity, brotherly communion, and freedom—according to the command of the Lord and in his Spirit, we will find them once again, cleansed this time from the stain of sin, illuminated and transfigured, when Christ presents to his Father an eternal and universal kingdom "of truth and life, a kingdom of holiness and grace, a kingdom of justice, love, and peace." Here on earth the kingdom is mysteriously present; when the Lord comes it will enter into its perfection [no. 39].

At stake here is the very identity of the church and of its being and activity. The dialogue with the world presupposes that the church is aware of its difference from the world, not in order to distance itself from the world but precisely in order that it may be truly close to the world. For the church, of him who came to set up his tent in our midst (see John 1:14), consciousness of its identity does not mean a defensive turning in upon itself. Neither does it mean that the church is not to be humbly but resolutely conscious of having a message that must be transmitted; it does not mean that the church is to be dissolved into the movement of history under the pretext of serving that movement.

It is not an easy task to find the appropriate and fruitful way of manifesting this identity; but this is one of the most important demands made of the church at the present time. It is also the best way of showing fidelity to the Second Vatican Council, which laid special emphasis on the mystery of the church and its mission. Romano Guardini spoke of our age as "the time of the church"; the prophecy will be fulfilled to the extent that the church seeks "first the kingdom of God and its justice," because everything else will be given to it as well (Matt. 6:33).

LIBERATING EVANGELIZATION

"The church's essential mission, following that of Christ, is a mission of evangelization and salvation. It draws its zeal from the divine love. Evangelization is the proclamation of salvation, which is a gift of God" (*Libertatis conscientia*, 1986, 63). Due to the pastoral experiences and theological reflections that I have been presenting, this task of the church has in recent times been increasingly referred to as one of "liberating evangelization." In this regard, the episcopal conference at Medellín and the theology being done in Latin America have been an important influence. The apostolic exhortation *Evangelii nuntiandi* (henceforth, *EN*) then established the terms in which the evangelizing task of the church was to be described, and Puebla took the question up again in the Latin American context. Along the same lines *LC* gives the title "The Liberating Mission of the Church" to its fourth chapter.

The church's mission is, as I said, to proclaim an integral liberation, because nothing is left untouched by the saving work of Christ:

> The love that impels the church to communicate to all persons a sharing in the grace of divine life also causes it, through the effective action of its members, to pursue the true temporal good of persons, help them in their needs, provide for their education, and promote an integral liberation from everything that hinders the development of individuals. The church desires the good of humankind in all its dimensions [*LC* 63].

Proclamation of the message springs from contemplative experience that is characterized by joy in the Lord's gift. [As I wrote in *The Power of the Poor in History*]:

> To know that the Lord loves us, to accept the free gift of his love, is the deep source of the joy and gladness of a person who lives by the Word of God. Evangelization is the communication of this joy. It is the communication of the good news of the love of God that has changed our life. It is a free, gratuitous proclamation, just as the love in which it originates is free and gratuitous. In the point of departure of the task of evangelization, then, there is always an experience of the Lord—a living experience of the Father's love, the love that makes us God's daughters and sons, the love that transforms us, making us more fully human, more fully brothers and sisters to all.

The joy that the love of God produces in us should characterize our proclamation of the divine will that we be set free.

At the same time, to proclaim the gospel is to call human beings together as a church. [As I've said elsewhere], "To proclaim the gospel is to announce the mystery of filiation and fellowship . . . 'a mystery hidden for generations and centuries and . . . revealed' in Christ. Hence to proclaim the gospel is to summon persons together, summon them into *ecclesia*, to call them together into the assembly." This assembly is the sign of the kingdom in history.

KINGDOM AND HISTORY

The Second Vatican Council chose the church as the focal point of its thinking. In doing so, it made its own a decades-long effort to think through the mystery of the church, its role in the contemporary world, the relationship between the different Christian confessions, and the attitude to be adopted toward other religions. Vatican II refused to offer a definition of the church and sought rather to enter into the mystery of the church. The category of "sacrament" seemed appropriate for this purpose, for it made it possible to bring together many aspects of the reality that is the church.

The idea of "sacrament" implies the idea of "sign," but the sign in this case is an efficacious sign. When the church is called "the universal sacrament of salvation" (*LG* 48), what is meant is that it transforms the life of human beings. The power of the Spirit is present in the church. [As I wrote in *A Theology of Liberation*],

> In the sacrament the salvific plan is fulfilled and revealed; that is, it is made present among humans and for humans. But at the same time, it is through the sacrament that humans encounter God. This is an encounter in history, not because God comes from history, but because history comes from God. The sacrament is thus the efficacious revelation of the call to communion with God and to the unity of all humankind.

The church is the sacrament of God's saving plan—that is, of the kingdom. It mediates an encounter inasmuch as God comes forth in search of human beings; the initiative belongs to God who, as we saw earlier, is not reducible to human history but is revealed in it. The revelation that the sacrament gives is efficacious and creative—provided human freedom consents of communion with God and the unity of the human race. The church is the sacrament of this communion and unity (see *LG* 1).

The nature or being of the church is the basis of its evangelizing activity. "The church can be understood only in relation to the reality that it announces to human beings. Its existence is not 'for itself,' but rather 'for others.' Its center is outside itself; it is in the work of Christ and his Spirit." The power of the Spirit who "will guide you into all the truth" (John 16:13) is the driving force in the church's evangelizing mission.

The church proclaims a fullness and a life that will not be fully realized except beyond history, but that already affect the progress of humanity. The necessity of attending to the life of persons living today, in the context of a proclamation that looks beyond history, compels *LC* to say:

> When the church speaks about the promotion of justice in human societies or when it urges the faithful laity to work in this sphere according to their own vocation, it is not going beyond its mission. It is, however, concerned that this mission not be absorbed by concerns which involve the temporal order or reduced to such concerns. Hence it takes great care to maintain clearly and firmly both the unity and the distinction between evangelization and human promotion: unity, because it seeks the good of the whole person; distinction, because these two tasks enter in different ways into its mission [no. 64].

This matter must be looked at in the light of what I said earlier about the connection between the several levels of liberation. There must be both unity and distinction, as the passage just cited says. At the beginning of my work on liberation theology I said, at the end of a lengthy section devoted to this point: "Not only is the growth of the kingdom not reduced to temporal progress; because of the word accepted in faith, we see that the fundamental obstacle to the kingdom, which is sin, is also the root of all misery and injustice; we see that the very meaning of the growth of the kingdom is also the ultimate precondition for a just society and a new humanity."

I went on to explain:

We are not faced with an identification. Without liberating historical events, there would be no growth of the kingdom. But the process of liberation will not have conquered the very roots of human oppression and the exploitation of human beings by human beings without the coming of the kingdom, which is above all a gift. Moreover, we can say that the historical, political liberating event is the growth of the kingdom and is a salvific event; but it is not the coming of the kingdom, not all of salvation. It is the historical realization of the kingdom and, therefore, it also proclaims its fullness.

"Complete communion" controls the entire process, and this communion is first and foremost a gift, a grace from the Lord. In this communion the human being reaches his or her full liberation. For the Christian, "the cross and the resurrection are the seal of our liberty."

From the perspective of faith we may not reduce the kingdom to any historical embodiment, however human and just we think it to be. We are in a different order of things here. This point is at the heart of the Christian message. The fundamental statements in this area are clear, but the concrete ways of expressing the connection between the Christian message and human liberation are always a quarry open to theological excavation.

A few years back, Yves Congar asked about the connection between "Christian salvation and the irrepressible movement for human liberations," and he suggested an interesting approach. After surveying the theme of the church as sacrament of salvation, he turned to another major idea of the Council—one with an ancient biblical and patristic lineage—in order to make the question more specific. The church, which is the sacrament of salvation, is (Congar said) the people of God, the messianic people, in its totality; it is not simply the institution, though that is what the word "sacrament" might suggest to some.

This gives a historical dynamism to the expression "universal sacrament of salvation," while at the same time the messianic character of this people points to Christ the messiah and to the way in which he conceived his task in regard to human liberations.

The eschatological justice that Christ proclaims inspires a critique of "situations and actions that God's plan for the human person condemns"; at the same time, it seeks "translation into human forms," which, however, it leaves "on their proper level and in their proper order." These considerations make it possible, says Congar, to raise the question of "faith and the political order," without succumbing to confusions. He concludes: "Always the Chalcedonian rule: no separation, no confusion" (this is the final sentence of his book).

At an earlier point, he had said: "What is the sacrament of salvation? The people of God. Where and how? In all its life, in all its history, which it lives within the history of the world. This is why God [the Lord Jesus] has given us the Holy Spirit who spoke through the prophets." The idea of the historical journey that the church must make as sacrament, underscored by its identification with the people of God, seems to me especially fruitful in connection with the subject I am treating here.

The mission of the Holy Spirit, which Congar emphasizes, is the central theme of a book by Jürgen Moltmann. I am interested here only in what relates to the question with which I am concerned at the moment. The German theologian regards as important but inadequate the christological foundation that both Karl Barth and Karl Rahner give to the idea of sacrament (he thinks their approaches are convergent, even though they start from different premises). In fact, the sacramentality of the church has been seen primarily in relation to Christ as the primordial sacrament. Adopting an ecumenical perspective, Moltmann goes so far as to ask: "Granted the remaining difference in the Protestant-Catholic convergence, . . . could this not be overcome through the trinitarian understanding of the eschatological gift of the Holy Spirit as the sacrament?"

To this end he appeals to the idea of mystery (*sacramentum*) as the revelation of God in history (an idea to which I referred earlier) and says that this can be understood only in an eschatological perspective. Thus viewed, "the use of the word 'mystery' spreads beyond Christology and flows into pneumatology, ecclesiology, and the eschatology of universal history."

The conclusion is inescapable and pregnant with consequences: "the sending of the Holy Spirit" is "the sacrament of the kingdom" and leads "the church beyond its own present existence into the world and drives it toward the perfected kingdom of God." This foundation makes possible a better understanding of the role the church must play, on its historical journey, as it confronts whatever is out of harmony with the values of the kingdom.

These varying approaches show that reflection on these topics is very much alive. Within the framework of the basic affirmations of faith on these topics, we must consider how the approaches look when seen in the Latin American context. What is at stake is our fidelity to the Word of God and our rejection of all the forms of oppression which the peoples of Latin America suffer. As John Paul II said in his address to the episcopal conference at Puebla: "It is . . . not out of opportunism or a thirst for novelty that the church, the 'expert in humanity' [as Paul VI put it to the United Nations in 1965], is a defender of human rights. It is prompted by an authentically evangelical commitment, which, like that of Christ, is primarily a commitment to those most in need."

Evaluating what had been accomplished in Latin America, Puebla was therefore able to say:

> We are pleased to note many examples of efforts made to live out liberative evangelization in all its fullness. One of the chief tasks involved in continuing to encourage Christian liberation is the creative search for approaches free of ambiguity and reductionism (*EN* 32) and fully faithful to the Word of God. Given to us in the church, that word stirs us to offer a joyful proclamation to the poor as one of the messianic signs of Christ's kingdom [no. 488].

The proclamation of the good news to the poor is a sign of the presence of Christ the messiah in human history.

THE MYSTERY OF EVANGELIZATION

Medellín said that the church must be "poor, *missionary*, and paschal" (emphasis added). The missionary perspective was very much present in Vatican II; it can even be said to have been the major inspiration of its documents. The Council was concerned that the church move outside itself in service to the world and, in the final analysis, to the Lord of history, as *Gaudium et spes* says.

This missionary inspiration is well expressed in *Ad gentes,* which is one of the most richly theological documents of the Council. In it mission is presented, in light of its trinitarian foundation, not as one among many activities of the church, but as a main trait of the Christian community as a whole. Medellín adopts the same perspective, but in terms of a church that has hitherto existed in a situation that might be described as "Christendom."

Puebla repeats the call to mission that was uttered at Medellín and speaks of "a missionary church that joyously proclaims to persons today that they are children of God in Christ; that commits itself to the liberation of the whole human being and all human beings . . . and that in solidarity immerses itself in the apostolic activity of the universal church" (no. 1304).

I should like to emphasize two things that have been characteristic of the Latin American church in this area.

The Poor Are Evangelized. Vatican II referred to this profound and demanding theme of the gospel, and Medellín made it central in its own reflections. There it supplied the context for the preferential option for the poor that inspired the principal documents of that conference and that has characterized the life of the Latin American church in the years since then. Many experiments have been undertaken and many commitments made in an effort to proclaim the message to the most disinherited. In proceeding along this line, the church has found itself in tune with the deep longing the poor of Latin America have, for liberation.

All this has brought with it an extensive renewal in the church's way of acting. The call to mission always entails a going out of its own world and an entering into a different world. This is what sizable sectors of the Latin American church have experienced as they have embarked upon the evangelization of the poor and the oppressed: they have begun to discover *the world of the poor.* That world is more alien to the church than it has been accustomed to think. It is a world that has deficiencies and limitations but also possibilities and riches. To be poor is to survive rather than live; it is to be subject to exploitation and injustice; it is also, however, to possess a special way of feeling, thinking, loving, believing, suffering, and praying. The proclamation of the gospel to the poor requires entering their world of misery and of hope.

The church in Latin America has only entered upon this road. It has made a beginning, however, of what is one form of openness to the world as called for by the Council; in this case, openness to the world of poverty. The commitment has not been without its defects; nonetheless there is a definite will to solidarity with the real poor: "Those who are oppressed by poverty are the object of a love of preference on the part of the church, which ever since its origin and in spite of the failings of many of its members, has not ceased to work for their relief, defense, and liberation" (*LC* 68).

This is not the first passage in which the 1986 Instruction acknowledges these failures in the historical course taken by the Christian community; the acknowledgment only enhances its emphasis on what ought to be, and in fact is, the mission of the church. Part of this mission is to meet the immediate needs of the poor, while at the same time promoting "structural changes in society so as to secure conditions of life worthy of the human person."

The efforts [to be present among the poor] are only beginnings, but they are real . . . But this closeness to the poor also brings new challenges to which no response is possible apart from a deepening Christian maturity in the Spirit.

The Evangelizing Potential of the Poor. Puebla, like Medellín, emphasized the importance for the church of evangelizing the poor; this is a basic and abiding requirement of the gospel. At the same time, however, the years that had elapsed between the two conferences had made it possible to study the call to evangelization more thoroughly and discover new aspects of it.

They had been years of commitment "to defend the rights of the poor and oppressed according to the gospel commandment" (Medellín, *Peace* 22); years, too, in which basic ecclesial communities were established as "the first and fundamental ecclesiastical nucleus, which . . . must make itself responsible for the richness and expansion of the faith" (Medellín, *Joint Pastoral Planning* 10). These ecclesial experiences "have helped the church to discover the evangelizing potential of the poor" (Puebla 1147).

The poor, the privileged (not exclusive) addressees of the message of the kingdom, are also its *bearers*. One way in which they carry out this role is through the basic ecclesial communities that Puebla hails as one of the most important developments in the life of the Latin American church and as an embodiment of "the church's preferential love for the common people" (no. 643). In these communities, moreover, the poor "are given a concrete opportunity to share in the task of the church and to work with commitment for the transformation of the world" (ibid.).

One of the most interesting statements in *LC* is undoubtedly the one referring to this very important aspect of the church's life in Latin America:

The new basic communities or other groups of Christians that have arisen to be witnesses to this evangelical love are, a source of great hope for the church. If they really live in unity with the local church and the universal church, they will be a real expression of communion and a means, for constructing a still deeper communion. Their fidelity to their mission will depend on how careful they are to educate their members in the fullness of the Christian faith through listening to the Word of God, fidelity to the teaching of the magisterium, to the hierarchical order of the church, and to the sacramental life. If this condition is fulfilled, their experience, rooted in a commitment to the complete liberation of humankind, becomes a treasure for the whole church [no. 69].

At the same time, we should like to have seen in the Instruction a fuller development of this new presence of the poor both in Latin American society and in the Christian community.

The base ecclesial communities are undoubtedly one of the most fruitful forces at work in the Latin American church. They have their place in the broad channel cut out by the Council in its reflections on the people of God and, its historical journey. They are a manifestation of the people of God as existing in the world of poverty but at the same time they are profoundly marked by Christian faith. They reveal the presence in the church of the "nobodies" of history or, to use another expression of the Council, of a "messianic people." They are, in other words, a people journeying through history and continually bringing about the messianic reversal—"the last shall be first"—that is a key element in every truly liberating process.

A CHRISTIAN PRAXIS

[Elsewhere] I have discussed the meaning and scope of the term "praxis." *LC* (and *EN* as well) uses the word several times and in its final chapter relates it to the church's social teaching. Especially interesting in this chapter are the frequent citations of John Paul II's encyclical on human work, which has brought a new vision to many aspects of this field. For the encyclical does not limit itself to pointing out one or another social problem but shows that in this area we are dealing with a real *economic and social system* that is built on the priority of capital over labor.

The deepest meaning of praxis is love and justice. *LC* speaks of praxis as "the putting into practice of the great commandment of love. This is the supreme principle of Christian social morality, founded upon the gospel and the whole of tradition since apostolic times and the age of the fathers of the church up to and including the recent statements of the magisterium" (no. 71).

The issue is indeed social morality and not political programs. The latter are not the church's business: "The political and economic running of society is not a direct part of its mission" (*LC* 61). The church's social teaching "has established itself as a doctrine by using the resources of human wisdom and the sciences. It concerns the ethical aspect of this life. It takes into account the technical aspects of problems but always in order to judge them from the moral point of view" (72).

It is very interesting to see how this teaching is always presented in a way that is open to new questions. Rightly so, for the ground on which it is located is especially changeable. *LN* therefore says: "This teaching is by no means closed. It is, on the contrary, open to all the new questions that are so numerous today. In this perspective, the contribution of theologians and other thinkers in all parts of the world to the reflection of the church is indispensable today" (XI,

12). *LC* takes up the idea in very clear terms: "being essentially oriented toward action, this teaching develops according to the changing circumstances of history. This is why, together with principles that are always valid, it also involves contingent judgments. Far from constituting a closed system, it remains open to new questions that continually arise; it requires the contribution of all charisms, experiences, and skills" (72).

The texts are clear and significant. We are dealing with matters undergoing change, and factual judgments are therefore contingent; the important thing is to proceed in fidelity to the permanent ethical requirements of the kingdom of life and to the concrete life of persons in society.

The right to property provides a clear example of the approach taken by a social morality that is always open to new situations. The nature of the present essay does not allow me to review the teachings of the church on this subject. I shall simply remind the reader that the treatment of the subject by the fathers of the church is dominated by consideration for the right of the poor—that is, the right to life, which is God's gift. In Thomas Aquinas we find in more technical form distinctions that had begun to emerge centuries before. [As Yves Calvez put it],

> The institution of private property is legitimate, but only by a secondary natural right and not by a primary natural right as such. In other words, St. Thomas justified private property in a relative way, combining the idea of every human being's natural right of *dominium* over things with considerations on the appropriateness of a distribution of property among human beings with the intention that it also be correctly administered for the good of all.

This passage describes the level at which the right to private property is located. In the social teaching of the church private property has always been looked upon as the material setting for the exercise of personal freedom. But this freedom itself implies relationships. Therefore because private property derives from the right of all to the goods of this world and because it is meant as an aid to a freedom that, as socially exercised, implies bonds with other persons, private property too will always have a social function. This is a classic element in the teaching of the church, but in recent years John XXIII and Paul VI have laid special stress on it.

As early as the Puebla Conference, John Paul II referred to "the church's teaching, which says that there is a *social mortgage* on all private property." He subsequently returned often to this theme. His most forceful statement on the subject is his encyclical on human work. Here the primacy of human beings over the fruits of their work makes possible a strong and penetrating critique of every type of liberalism and collectivism that repudiates, in fact or in principle, the value of the human person.

There is no need to insist on the danger of an individualist conception that regards profit as the driving force of economic activity or on that of a totalitarian vision that disregards the freedom of each person. The statements in my writings on the social appropriation of the means of production (which does not necessarily mean state ownership, although this may be the form it takes in some cases) are intended as a response to the first danger. In like manner my statement about the social appropriation of freedom was meant to counteract an individualist approach, but also to meet the second danger just mentioned—that is, the failure to allow for the personal freedom of *all* members of a society.

Justice and freedom are two requirements of a human society. In this realm of ideas, many think that a healthy balance between private ownership, social ownership, and state ownership can be a good way of meeting and promoting these two requirements. But here we are certainly in the presence of what *LC* calls "contingent judgments." It is important, for this reason, to be always open to "the new questions that continually arise." The concrete forms may vary, but we will always have to maintain the right to life that finds expression in the right to use the goods of this world, together with all that flows from them, and the right to personal freedom.

Given the present situation in Latin America, the social aspect is very important for liberation theology. But it is precisely that: *one* aspect in a theological approach that covers other fields. Because liberation theology is a reflection on the faith, it must be attentive to many other aspects of the Christian message. Furthermore, [as I wrote in *On Job*] it must always bear in mind [that]

> Emphasis on the practice of justice and on solidarity with the poor must never become an obsession and prevent our seeing that this commitment reveals its value and ultimate meaning only within the vast and mysterious horizon of God's gratuitous love. Furthermore, the very building of a just society requires a stimulus and an enveloping atmosphere that gratuitousness alone can supply.

The social teaching of the church deals with the ethical implications of social problems and is the work of the magisterium. Liberation theology, like every theology, is a discourse on the entire Christian message and does not have the authority of the church's magisterium. It is not a matter, therefore, of choosing one or the other.

38. THEOLOGY: AN ECCLESIAL FUNCTION

At the heart of the widespread discussion in the post-conciliar church about the proper task, method, scope, and sources of theology has been the question of theology's—and the theologian's—link to the church itself. In a 1994 article published in Páginas, *"La teología: una función eclesial," Gutiérrez set forth the modest yet significant contribution theologians are called to make to the "primary task" of the church, namely the proclamation of the gospel of Jesus Christ. Perhaps as much as the argument he makes, the* tone *of his words—confident and bold yet filled with humility—expresses Gutiérrez's view of the essentially ecclesial character of all theological work. This article also demonstrates his singular proficiency in finding language with which to speak to the entire church at once—the magisterium, fellow theologians, and the faithful. It is from* Paginás *130 (1994): 10–17 and is published here in English translation for the first time. The translation is by the present editor.*

I would like to present here some thoughts about how I see the present role and future tasks of theological reflection in the life of the church present in Latin America and the Caribbean. My intention is to elucidate what I have stated on other occasions and thus to clarify certain concepts in a sphere where it is easy to fall into oversimplifications and even erroneous ways of understanding theological work. The role of theology is not in fact to forge an ideology which would justify social and political positions already taken but rather to help believers to let themselves be judged by the Word of the Lord. Theology cannot therefore give up the critical function of faith vis-à-vis every historical realization. I begin from the conviction that the theological task is a vocation which arises and is exercised in the heart of the ecclesial community. Indeed, its starting point is the gift of faith in which we welcome the truth of the Word of God, and its contributions are at the service of the evangelizing mission of the church.

This ecclesial location gives theology its raison d'être, determines its scope, nurtures it with the sources of revelation—Scripture and Tradition—enriches it with the recognition of the charism of the magisterium and dialogue with the magisterium, and puts it in contact with other ecclesial functions.

EVANGELIZATION AND THEOLOGY

What is the role of theology in the evangelizing responsibility which is incumbent upon the whole church? "Theology," says the "Instruction on the Ecclesial Vocation of the Theologian" of the Congregation for the Doctrine of the Faith, "makes its contribution so that faith may be communicable to Christians, of course—thus theology plays an important role within the church—but also (and in a special way) to "those who do not yet know Christ." The missionary perspective, anxious about the aspirations and concerns of those who are far from, or do not share, the Christian faith, gives the deepest meaning to the effort to understand faith.

Within this dynamism—the dynamism of a "truth which tends toward being communicated"—lies the theological task. Theology is a task which is carried out in the church convoked by the Word. From *there*, from "within the church," [as the Instruction puts it,] the truth which frees (cf. John 8:32) is proclaimed—salvation in Jesus Christ—and theological reflection is carried out. This is what the Latin American bishops called "the prophetic ministry of the church" when they gathered in Santo Domingo in 1992: to this ministry belongs the service which theologians must offer (no. 33). Its content is the proclamation of Christ and of his integral liberation, the proclamation which must be made in a language faithful to the message and which can speak to our contemporaries. This is the very point of the theological contribution; this is why it must enter into dialogue with the mentality of the culture of those who listen to the Word. In this way it will be able to contribute efficaciously to a pastoral practice which motivates those to whom it is directed to follow the witness and teachings of Jesus.

In this task "the theologian, without ever forgetting that he or she is a member of the People of God, must respect it and commit himself or herself to give them a teaching which does not injure in any way the doctrine of the faith." Otherwise theologians runs the risk that the pressing needs of the moment may make it hard to see the requirements of the message in its entirety. They will not fulfill their function of service to the evangelizing of the church and its pastors. Indeed, "the freedom proper to theological reflection is exercised within the faith of the church."

Theology is a speaking about God in the light of faith, a language about one who is, in truth, its only theme. We ought to approach the mystery of God with respect and humility; but in a biblical perspective, mystery does not signify something which should remain secret. Rather, mystery should be spoken and communicated. To be revealed belongs to the very essence of mystery (cf. Rom. 16:25–26). Theology, then, becomes a "science of Christian revelation."

At the same time theologians must be aware that their efforts cannot exhaust the significance of the Word contained in Scripture and transmitted by the living tradition of the church in which the charism of the magisterium is located. Furthermore, "the deposit of faith" present in the church is not limited to answering our queries; it also raises new questions and constantly requires of us an examination of our faith. On the other hand, speaking about God takes place in a constantly changing historical reality in which the ecclesial community lives. No dimension of human existence—which itself is lived in the midst of complex social situations—escapes the condition of being a disciple of Jesus. From this reality arise constant challenges to the discourse on faith. For this reason, the episcopal conference at Santo Domingo—locating itself in its own Latin American environment—speaks of a theological labor which would promote "work in favor of social justice, human rights, and solidarity with the poorest" (33). These are urgent necessities among us.

For these reasons theological language contains much that is approximate; it must therefore always be open to renovation from new perspectives, further precision of concepts, and the correction of formulations. Similarly, there is the permanent emergence of new paths in our speech about God which seeks to express revealed truth in appropriate terms. All this is required along with the clear conviction that—according to a traditional affirmation—no theology can be identified with the faith. Theological pluralism within the unity of faith is an old fact in the church. In this context different theologies are useful and important efforts but on condition that they do not consider themselves unique or indispensable and that they be aware of their role of modestly serving the primary tasks of the church.

A MOMENT FOR LATIN AMERICA

When Christian faith—received and lived out in the church—experiences new challenges to its communication to others, theology asks itself (as it is always called to do) about the relevance of its reflection on the revealed message. There are numerous historical witnesses to this fact. It is the moment to renew this reflection, going once again to the inexhaustible sources of faith which feed the life of the church.

Poverty is a theme of the gospels and a challenge which has always been present throughout the church's history. But the denunciations of Medellín ("inhuman misery"), Puebla ("poverty opposed to the gospel"), and Santo Domingo ("intolerable extremes of misery"), made the situation of poverty which the great majority of the population of Latin America and the Caribbean suffers appear in all its harshness before our eyes. It was a matter of a secular reality but one which pounded the human and Christian conscience in a new way and which for the same reason raised demanding questions for the ecclesial task. The "others" of a society which marginalizes and excludes them became present, demanding solidarity. The root question—how to say to the poor, to the least of society, that God loves them?—has demonstrated its fruitfulness in the pastoral action of the church and in the theological path undertaken to respond to it.

In the face of unjust and premature death which poverty implies, "the noble combat for justice" (Pius XII) acquires dramatic and urgent characteristics. To be aware of this is a question of clarity and honesty. It is necessary, moreover, to overcome the mentality which places these facts in an exclusively political field in which faith has little or nothing to say; this attitude expresses the "divorce between faith and life" which Santo Domingo sees still today as capable of "producing clamorous situations of injustice, social inequality, and violence" (24). However, to recognize social conflicts as a fact must not in any way signify that social conflict is being promoted as a method of change in society. Thus we cannot accept "the programmed class struggle" (John Paul II, *Laborem exercens* 11).

We are without a doubt on controversial and slippery terrain. The risk of reductionism (or of expressions which can be interpreted as reductionistic) is thus limiting and threatening. It is easy to be absorbed by the emotional aspects of the situation, to experience a certain fascination with something new, or to overestimate the value of the social sciences. The social sciences are necessary if we are to understand socioeconomic reality but they represent efforts still in the beginning stages. In view of this to speak of a scientific understanding of the social universe cannot be considered something definitive or apodictic, nor as something completely free of ideological connections.

As for the distinction among three levels in the notion of liberation, Puebla therefore alerts us that "the unity of these three planes" implies that "the mystery of the death and resurrection of Jesus Christ must be lived out on the three planes . . . without making any one of them exclusive" (326). This is the integral liberation in Christ which leads us to full communion with God and others (cf. *LG* 1). Social and political liberation should not in any way hide the final and radical significance of liberation from sin which can only be a work of forgiveness and of God's grace. It is important then to refine our means of expression in order to avoid confusion in this matter.

We must pay attention to these dangers and reaffirm the proper and direct level of the gospel; its content is the reign but the reign must be accepted by people who live in history and consequently the proclamation of a reign of love, peace, and justice impinges on life together in society. Nevertheless, the demands of the gospel go beyond the political project of building a different society. Society will be just, and in a certain sense new, to the degree that it places the dignity of the human person at its center—a dignity that for a Christian has its ultimate foundation in the condition of being the "image of God" which Christ saves by reestablishing the friendship between human beings and God.

Conflictive social realities cannot make us forget the requirements of a universal love that does not recognize boundaries of social class, race, or gender. The affirmation that the human person is the agent of his/her own destiny in history must be made in such a way that the gratuitous initiative of God in the salvific process—the ultimate meaning of the historical evolution of humanity—may be clearly seen. Indeed, the gift of God "who loved us first" (1 John 4:19) frames and gives rise to human action as a free response to that love.

It is possible to go astray in these matters, and in fact this has happened. Nor have misunderstandings been lacking in the face of new themes and new languages. In this way a debate over the theology of liberation arose which even flowed beyond the world of the church and into the wide and stormy world of the media. Nevertheless, beyond appearances and arduous discussions, a profound process was taking place in those years, characterized by a serious and respectful confrontation, well-founded objections, requests for necessary refinements from those who have authority in the church to do so, recognition of the value of being sensitive to the sign of the times which the aspiration to liberation signifies, a legitimate presentation of doubts, and interest in a theology close to the base Christian communities.

All this leads us to see that the effort to capture new realities theologically has to be constantly clarified. Imperfections of language must be overcome, and inexact formulations must be corrected by concepts which do not give rise to errors in matters concerning the doctrine of the faith. Indeed, theological reflection always carries the imprint of the moment and of the circumstances in which it is formulated. This is true in particular for the effort undertaken in Latin America in these years when it was necessary to confront difficult situations, respond to unheard of challenges to the understanding of the faith, and be able to reach—with the missionary spirit proper to theology—those who do not perceive the significance of the gospel for these realities and for their lives.

It is important above all to be clear about these risks and limitations, to listen with humility to divergent opinions. This attitude follows—it is appropriate to note it—from understanding the meaning of theological work as a service to the evangelizing mission of the entire church to which I have already referred. In theology it is necessary to be ever ready, [in the words of John Paul II], to "modify one's own opinions" in function of one's service to "the community of believers." This is the meaning of theological work; this is why it may rightly be affirmed, [as the "Letter on the Formation of Future Priests" puts it], that theology "cannot prescind from the doctrine and lived experience in the sphere of the church in which the magisterium authentically watches over and interprets the deposit of faith."

TO PROCLAIM THE REIGN TODAY

For all these reasons, and because the process has been complex and difficult but simultaneously rich, a fundamental perspective has opened up a path which carries with it the best of the ecclesial experience of this period. I refer to the preferential option for the poor which, born of the experience and practice of the Latin American Christian communities, was first expressed at Medellín and then explicitly embraced at Puebla. As we know, this focus is today part of the universal magisterium of the church, as numerous texts of John Paul II and of diverse non-Latin American episcopacies attest. If something should remain from this period of Latin American and church history, it is precisely this option as a demanding commitment, an expression of a love which is always new, and the axis of a new evangelization of the continent.

A series of economic, political, and ecclesial events, as much worldwide as Latin American or national, make people think that the stage in which the theological reflection recalled a few pages ago came to be born is now coming to an end. The years which have passed were, on the one hand, stimulating and creative, but tense and conflictive on the other. In the face of new situations (the worsening of poverty and the end of certain political projects, for example), many earlier discussions do not respond to current challenges.

Everything would seem to indicate that a different period is beginning. The collaboration of all in facing the enormous questions which the reality of Latin America presents us becomes more and more necessary. There is a reconstitution of the social fabric within which we had sought to place the proclamation of the reign of God, a reconstitution which requires new liberating practices. These must be careful not to fall into the "verticalism of a disembodied spiritual union with God or into a simple existential personalism . . . nor, even less, into socioeconomic-political horizontalism" (Puebla 329). Both deviations, each in its own way, distort at the same time the transcendence and the immanence of the reign of God.

The summoning tone of the Santo Domingo texts responds to this requirement and thus makes an energetic call to all to participate in the *new evangelization* of the continent. This concern was present since the preparations for
Medellín, but it took on new strength with the vigorous call of John Paul II in
Haiti (1983), the poorest and most forgotten country of Latin America. Directing himself to CELAM, the pope spoke of "a new evangelization—new in its
zeal, in its methods, in its expression." Santo Domingo made this perspective
one of its central themes and one its primary pastoral directions. The theological reflection formulated in the Latin American context finds here fertile ground
in its collaboration with the evangelizing task of the church. Making use of successes and avoiding failures of previous years, our discourse on the faith should
help us to find the route and the language to proclaim to "the poor of this continent" the need for the "gospel of radical and integral liberation"; not to do so,
adds John Paul II, would be to cheat and disillusion the poor.

Santo Domingo takes up a second theme from which it deduces an important pastoral direction: *human promotion.* This is not something foreign or
extrinsic to evangelization. In recent years numerous texts of the magisterium
have vigorously reminded us that to promote human dignity is part of the evangelizing task. It is a dignity called into question by "the most devastating and
humiliating scourge which Latin America and the Caribbean are experiencing"
and constituted by "the growing impoverishment" of millions of Latin Americans—the consequence in large part of the "policies of the neoliberal type"
which predominate in the continent (Santo Domingo 179).

The depth of the problem is such that it calls the entire church—with no
exceptions—to face it. Biblical reflection on poverty and the experiences of solidarity of previous years are of great usefulness here, but this must not hide what
is distinct or delicate in the present situation. The renovation of the church's
social teaching energetically undertaken by John Paul II not only offers guidelines for an authentic and contemporary social harmony and for the construction of a just and new society with total respect for human life and dignity, but
will also enrich the theological task and provide a fertile field of study pertinent
to the social and historical context of Latin America. These texts remind us that
the values of peace, justice, and liberty are not only goals of a social commitment
but that they ought to inspire, beginning now, the methods we employ for
achieving a human society which respects the rights of all.

The new evangelization will have to be an *inculturated evangelization.* "Inculturation" is a new term for designating an old reality which, for the Christian,
carries resonances of incarnation. The Word must incarnate itself in diverse
worlds, situations, and cultures. Despite this, its transcendence is not affected;
rather, it is reaffirmed. This perspective has put a finger right on the wound in
a continent of such great racial and cultural diversity. The cultures and values of
the different indigenous peoples and of the black population of Latin America
constitute a great treasure which must be appreciated and respected by those

who have the responsibility for proclaiming the gospel. We are face-to-face with an immense and urgent task which has scarcely been initiated, and a stimulating challenge to theological reflection.

There are, then, three themes, three primary pastoral directions (cf. Santo Domingo, nos. 287–301), and thus three spheres of theological reflection which, as I have pointed out, seek to be at the service of the proclamation of the "gospel of liberation."

To take up these perspectives is to renew "the evangelical and preferential option for the poor, following the example and the words of the Lord Jesus" (Santo Domingo, no. 180). Christ is, indeed, the ultimate foundation of this option and of the pastoral directions mentioned. As the "living Son of God," he is "the unique reason for our life and the source of our mission" (Santo Domingo, no. 296).

For this reason the preferential option for the poor not only demands that we seek to know, seriously and responsibly, the reality and the causes of poverty; not only does such an option lead us to make our pastoral action more effective and to deepen our theological reflection. It also ought to mark our spirituality—that is, our following of Jesus Christ who is "the way, the truth, and the life" (John 14:6). His life, his death, and his resurrection put their imprint on the course in history taken by the church and by every Christian.

Like every believer, the theologian must undertake the discipleship of Jesus. For this purpose, she (or he) will, like Mary, have to preserve "all these things in her heart" (Luke 2:51); that is, the deeds and words in which God is revealed. Whatever the historical context may be in which we live, no matter how tense the situations which must be faced, this discipleship signifies leading a life nourished—as John frequently says—by the will of the Father. The contemplative dimension, the practice of prayer, is essential to the Christian life.

In concrete and beautiful terms Puebla invited us "to discover in the suffering faces of the poor the face of the Lord" (nos. 31–39). Santo Domingo reiterates this call and proposes that we extend further the list of those suffering faces who populate our continent (cf. nos. 178 and 179). This discovery and this solidarity are the privileged way in history by which the Spirit leads us to the Father through Jesus Christ.

39. SHAME

From the beginning of his theological career, Gutiérrez has made crystal-clear the principal tasks he envisions for theology as well as those he judges beyond its competence. Chief among the former, of course, is to seek an adequate language for speaking about God. Yet in view of the profoundly inhuman conditions in which the majority of human beings today struggle to survive and the church's mission to make the Word of God efficacious in history, theology cannot avoid speaking about concrete historical situations. Gutiérrez himself has offered examples of the boldness and restraint proper to the theologian. Among his infrequent but penetrating analyses of particularly difficult moments in Peru's political history of the past thirty years stands an article which appeared in the Lima daily La República of June 18, 1995. An intense political and moral crisis was generated by the hasty passage in Peru's Congress of a law granting immunity from prosecution to members of national security forces responsible for several notorious massacres in the previous ten years. It brought the following response from the country's best-known priest and theologian. The Spanish text may be found in Páginas 134 (1995): 6–10 (translation here by the present editor).

Shame, a deep and uncontrollable shame, is what we Peruvians are experiencing these days. Words of great human and Christian import, such as reconciliation and forgiveness, have been invoked to legalize and justify immunity from punishment for grave but common crimes, including wicked assassinations. With clear verbal excess, to say the least, these crimes have been characterized as "excesses" committed in the exercise of certain functions, functions which consist (though it sounds sarcastic to recall it) in protecting the life and rights of all citizens.

EVERYTHING IS POSSIBLE

Not long ago a rumor circulated that a proposal of this kind was about to be put before the Peruvian Congress. The prospect seemed so unreal that many of us asked ourselves if it were not simply the idea of some outlandish politician (the kind who wanders outside all ethical considerations) wanting to make political points. Or if we were dealing with something motivated, and invented, by special interests in the political struggle.

On Tuesday morning we woke to a terrible and unbelievable reality; from restful sleep we passed to a nightmare. It was not just a trial balloon or an empty and malicious speculation. It was something premeditated and fiercely carried through. The shock produced by the content of this plan, and by the way in which it was presented, allowed for twenty-four hours of desperate hope that the law would not be promulgated. But injustice was not long in being legalized; immunity was disguised as reconciliation. A so-called pardon has opened the door to new and abominable abuses and crimes. To this we must add the ambiguity of poor legislative drafting, intentional or innocent, which allows for the most arbitrary interpretations.

Though it might be painful to acknowledge, anything seems possible in Peru today. The deliberate plan to confuse, as Cardinal Vargas Alzamora has observed, by lumping alleged "offenses of opinion" in the same category as deeds too horrible to name (already tried or in process), lends credence to this view. The conflation is without a doubt an offense against honorable and respectable persons. But we cannot forget that the most serious thing is to try in this way to justify assassinations carried out "in the heat of battle"—assassinations which in most cases affect people (some of them children) who belong to the world of the poor and the socially insignificant. "There is no justice for the poor," a witness to the events of the Barrios Altos said categorically. Let us not be detained here in minute analysis of this assertion; it comes from a profound feeling and is expressed with a scream. One thing is certain: the poor have supplied the first and the largest number of victims of the different types of violence we have experienced in this country.

ETHICS AND POLITICS

Any attempt to remove ethics from politics goes against politics itself. In point of fact, politics takes place in the arena of the social life of free and responsible beings and is oriented toward the common good. One of the essential aspects of the common good is respect for human rights, beginning with the first right of all: respect for life, a respect wounded by the law I am challenging. The ethical dimension is, then, constitutive of the person and his or her life in society. And with this reprehensible affair, we are fully involved in an ethical question even beyond political decisions. There is no way to mask this reality; certain attitudes during the debate in the Congress were significant in this respect. That was the reason for the indignation that people and institutions who have legitimate political differences among themselves on a number of subjects have begun to express. With this kind of tactic perhaps dark and petty political and personal interests may benefit, but not society as a whole. If someone were seeking to poison the life of the country in the present circumstances and to close off its future, they could not have chosen a better way to do it.

Not long ago an enormous surge of public opinion, the macabre appearance of mutilated and burned human remains, and the tenacity and courage of certain people overcame the resistance to investigate and bring charges against those responsible for the murders of La Cantuta. It was thought that this would make it possible to find out what happened in Barrios Altos and in so many other cases (without forgetting about the prisons), and thus lead to trial and punishment for those responsible. Those deaths leave tombs empty which, according to the present law, must also be covered with earth. They will nevertheless not cease being witnesses to the absence of sanity, of human sensitivity, and of the most elemental principles of morality, which we cannot help but lament and reject.

Let no one appeal to the bloody terrorism we have endured these past years to justify such acts. Among other reasons, it is an insult to the memory of those civilians and those in uniform who gave their lives fighting crime dressed in political clothing or who were its victims. Precisely because they matter to us, we reject methods similar to those which their assassins employed. It is often said that terrorism, despite signs of life here and there (or of death, if we want to be exact), has been substantially defeated. We can only hope this is the case. No one wants to relive what we experienced for over a decade. But, for that very reason, we regret that to the destruction of human lives and material goods, the sufferings and damages provoked by terrorism, there is now being added what we could call (forgive the barbarous expression) a mental "senderization" of many Peruvians [Sendero Luminoso: Peruvian terrorist group]. I am referring to the attitude which leads people to think that violence alone, a firm hand no matter who goes down in the process, and treacherous murder can settle difficult situations. If this mentality takes hold of us and becomes a behavior we tolerate or justify, terrorist violence will have achieved its greatest and most perverse victory. We must block such an eventuality.

With this conduct we will not be opening channels by which the water destined to give life to the earth, and to those nourished by the earth, can flow. Rather we shall be opening common graves in which unburied corpses will be piled up. I am concerned that these measures might increase alienations, fears, and even hatreds among Peruvians and might provoke the terrible feeling of shame at belonging to a society which ignores the most elemental human values. With what moral authority are we going to ask for disclosure and sanctions in cases of corruption that preoccupied the media during the last few weeks?

The constitutional right of the Congress to grant amnesty (within the constitution's limits, of course) is not in question. What is in question is the moral capacity for sanctioning forgetfulness—wiping the slate clean—to erase not political deeds but crimes of the magnitude we all know about.

IF THE COUNTRY MATTERS TO US. . .

If the country matters to us, that is, if every one of the people who live in it is of concern to us, then we cannot resign ourselves to what seeks to look like a *fait accompli*, inevitable, and with which we must all comply, period. Laws are of human origin and can be revoked. It is the job of lawmakers to show us the ways to do it, but the need for a change is clear. Naturally there are also political and economic reasons, domestic and foreign, to take the road of justice in our legal order. People with greater competence than I will see to providing them.

For my part I am interested in emphasizing that, as the bishops of the permanent commission of the Peruvian Bishops' Conference have just reminded us, "only on the basis of the truth, justice, and mercy which God has put in the heart of human beings can we pour the foundations for an authentic reconciliation" (press release of June 16). Reconciliation and forgiveness are two great human and Christian terms and themes. For that very reason we cannot trifle with them and besmirch them, grounding them in lies and injustice. If we do so, in the present instance, we will be supporting "a social countervalue: death and scorn for life" (ibid.)—the life of everyone but in particular the life of the poorest and most vulnerable.

Indeed, this is what is at stake: the value which we give to human life, to life in general, in the Peru of today. The same thing which leads us to reject from the very core of our being the crimes of terrorism prevents us now from endorsing the legalization of exemption from punishment in the face of other forms of assassination.

Let it be clear that I am alluding to cases which were tried, or should have been, with complete accountability. The rights that any person has to a defense were respected and the punishments were set with the respect due the inalienable human dignity of every person. I believe that in a society which respects itself persons cannot take justice into their own hands. So, too, no one can mistreat a person legally found guilty; guilt does not remove his or her condition as a person. In saying this, I am thinking of all those who—to all appearances a minority of those who participated in punishable acts—have been found responsible and have received a sentence; I am thinking too of course of those who have just been exempted. Homicide is reprehensible not only because it is committed against an innocent person (this of course increases its gravity) but against a human person and, for a believer, a child of God. To the legal system, and to it alone, falls the responsibility of trial and sentencing.

National reconciliation is certainly a challenge. But it is also a process; it must be built by just and firm steps. To begin with, it requires a broad consensus based on a demanding democratic style in our shared life and not on inopportune means which block the road and move the goal even further away from realization. With such means we do not advance; instead, we go backward. We take a step back too when we try to put the law of remorse (which excluded precisely cases of assassination) on the same level as the present amnesty law. People need to be told the reasons why laws about life in society are passed with respect for justice and equity. Otherwise, reactions to privileges granted by force or other forms of power are poisoned by a resentment of a situation already charged with unjust and historical inequalities.

Reconciliation not only must be seen as a process of the convergence of wills in their respect for the rights of all. It requires time, but it also requires going to the roots of our social ills. The immense poverty of the Peruvian people does not justify in any way terrorist violence, but it is a breeding ground which must be eliminated because it can give rise to dangerous outbursts. National reconciliation happens through the effective recognition of the right of all to life, bread, housing, health, respect, and a dignified existence.

Let us hope that this painful and difficult episode in the life of the country shakes consciences up. We need a great national movement which would demand the repeal of the law whose passage gives rise to these words, but let it go beyond that. May the healthy forces in the country, which have begun to react to these deeds and which come from diverse points in national life go lucidly to the prime causes of our problems. It is a matter of reconstructing national life which requires the peaceful effort of all, civilians and members of the armed forces alike. Exclusions are mutilations which we cannot allow ourselves.

We need pacification, but above all we need peace. And we know that there is no true peace if it is not cemented in truth and in justice. To set out to procure it is to begin to lose the stifling feeling of shame that threatens to paralyze us.

40. "AND THEY SAID THEY WOULD SEE TO IT. . ."

In the Conclusion to his monumental study of Bartolomé de Las Casas's theological evolution (Las Casas, 455–60), Gutiérrez maintains that what was ultimately at stake in the Americas in the sixteenth century was the lives of the hemisphere's inhabitants. Today the lives of the majority of the world's people still hang in the balance. It was, and is, that simple—and that scandalous. Those who claim to follow Christ today must make a decision. Will they join the Council of the Indies, turn away from the sight of the poor, and repeat those empty—and death-dealing—words: "We'll see to it"? Or will they join Las Casas and others in attempting to "transform this time of dissipation and death into a time of vocation and grace"?

Las Casas's reflections lead us down to the most profound levels of the history of the peoples caught up in the whirlwind of sixteenth-century events. They thrust us beyond the conjunctural. They help us not to become enmired in the anecdotal or lost amidst the peaks and valleys of the age. They set us inexorably before the high stakes of the Indies: the life and death of their inhabitants. It is that simple and that scandalous. Here, according to Bartolomé, is the ground on which Jesus' resurrection—life's definitive victory over death—is to be proclaimed.

At that time, many considered that the Indians lacked any values of their own. As Columbus himself had said, they were a *tabula rasa,* a clean slate. Consequently, their lot was to toil for the newcomers and ultimately to be assimilated by them. By contrast with those who thought and acted in this manner, Bartolomé de Las Casas, and certain others with him, saw in the Indians the *other*—the one who was different from Western culture. The route to this genuine discovery was longer and more hazardous than the one Columbus had undertaken across uncharted seas. Not without sluggishness, not without limitations, these persons, whose cultural distance from the Indians was so great, gradually divested themselves of their spontaneous sense of superiority and sought to move to the viewpoint of the dispossessed. This effort enabled them to read history in a different way and to understand the meaning of the swift and violent events of those years from the other side of that history.

The attitude was necessary also in order to avoid evangelization becoming just another way of subjugating the Indian nations. This is precisely what happens whenever the gospel is unduly linked to a particular culture, whenever the evangelizer fails to follow the path of what we call today the inculturation of the faith. The word is new, but the reality is old. For believers it rings of incarnation and of a presence of God that is respectful of the human condition. Thus, for Las Casas the "only way" to evangelize is by persuasion and dialogue. Seeing things "as if we were Indians"—that is, from the viewpoint of the race, customs, cultures, and religious practices of the Indians—makes us more sensitive to the injustice of the treatment being inflicted on the autochthonous population, as well as to the rejection of evangelical values that this violation of their rights implies.

Bartolomé had another penetrating intuition. He saw in the Indian, in this "other," this one-different-from-the-Westerner, the poor one of the gospel, and ultimately Christ himself. This is without a doubt the very key to the Lascasian spirituality and theology. It sketches Bartolomé's "intelligence of faith" with original strokes, giving its own physiognomy among other theological reflections of the age. The right to life and liberty, the right to be different, the perspective of the poor—these are intimately connected notions in the experience our friar has of the God of Jesus Christ, in whom he believes with all his strength, a strength he therefore places at the service of the liberation of the Indian. Despite the obvious distance between historical contexts, Bartolomé's commitment constitutes a challenge for us today. In our times, too, the rights of the poor and oppressed must be defended according to the guidelines of the Medellín Conference. We are called on to defend these persons' values—and in a way, to defend their very existence, inasmuch as they continue to be treated as if they were "nonpersons."

In view of all of this, Las Casas's witness is particularly important for the self-discovery that the peoples of Latin America must make today. The sixteenth century was decisive in our history. Things happened and options were made then that marked the centuries to come. From the Christian viewpoint, Bartolomé sees it as the "time of vocation" and calling of the Indian nations, the time when God "decided to open the treasures of the divine mercies." But greed and arrogance transformed that time into a "time of tribulation, a time of drought, of revenge, of rage, of affliction and dissipation, a cruel, deadly time." That age became an age when not only the bread that feeds the body was denied and withheld from the Indian, but also "the bread that feeds souls, which is the teaching of Jesus Christ." The text we cite, which expresses a lucid historical intelligence and a faith sensitive to persons' daily lives, concludes with a painful, acute question: "And when, in another time, was death ever so sorely, or at any rate so speedily, sovereign?"

How often we have asked ourselves the same question, in this, the hour of Latin America and Peru! Why indeed does death continue to be so sovereign among us? Ours is a time of drought and tribulation, but also, in terms of the rich Lascasian focus, of calling and mercy. These two times frame, and urge, our freedom, our projects, our hopes. When we have transformed the one into the other, we shall have embraced the ultimate meaning of Las Casas's life and work: to be a witness of the God who is "rich in mercy" (Eph. 2:4) in the Indies. This witness cost some missioners their lives in Bartolomé's day, as it has other Christians in our era. In between, how many dear, beloved friends have fallen as well—our companions along our way, with whom we have shared concerns and perplexities, joys and sorrows, projects and leisure, Eucharist and silence! It is certain that their death has left an indelible trace on our lives. This martyrdom is the wealth, a sorrowful wealth, of the church of yesterday and today on this continent.

We have no intention of positing facile equations between eras endowed each with its own coordinates and personality. But neither must we fail to perceive the points of contact between them or the teachings that we can gather from the past. The present acquires density and substance when it is nourished by the memory of a journey, which the courage is found to identify unsolved problems and wounds not yet healed. Here are gaping maws that hunger still and voraciously consume so many energies today. The historical view gains effect and luminosity when maintained from the present. This has its risks, of course, and consequently must be done with great respect for a far-off age so different from our own.

Part of this memory means acknowledging our responsibility in what the poor have always had to suffer. The Christian manner of assuming this responsibility is to beg humble forgiveness from God and the victims of history for our complicity, explicit or tacit, past and present, as individuals and as a church. To ask to be forgiven expresses a will to change in our behavior and reasserts the obligation of being an efficacious sign in the history of the reign of love and justice. It is not a fixation on the past. It is a step toward the future.

Only historical honesty can deliver us from the prejudices, narrow interpretations, paralyzing ignorance, and the deceptions foisted on us by private interests, which lay our history on us like a permanent mortgage instead of transforming it into a thrust to creativity. The recovery of our memory will inspire us to fling to the trash heap as inadequate, and consequently useless, the so-called white legend and black legend of what occurred in the sixteenth century. A concealment of the complexity of what occurred in those years for fear of the truth, in order to defend current privileges, or—at the other extreme—a frivolous, irresponsible use of offensive expressions, condemns us to historical sterility.

At the same time, our interest in and revulsion for much of what occurred with the various Indian nations and cultures in the sixteenth century must not incline us to ignore the intricate process of later centuries, with the arrival of new races and cultures, or the situation of injustice and dispossession in which the poor of today find themselves on this continent. In view of current problems, it would be a grave error to allow concerns aroused by the fifth centenary to confine us to the sixteenth century. In our day, as well, we have a destruction of persons and cultures, and we continue to hear "the just cries, which everywhere have mounted to heaven," as Túpac Amaru said, in accents identical with those of the Bible. Latin American reality is variegated, and cannot be explained through summary, immature analyses.

One of the major challenges of Latin America and Peru is our cultural plurality. Here a wealth becomes a stumbling-block when its enormous possibilities go unrecognized and undeveloped. Many different racial, cultural, and spiritual families live in these lands, but they have not yet learned to live together. None of them must arrogate to itself alone the representation of the continent, none must be marginalized or despised. All should participate on an equal basis in the building of a just and democratic society. Racism is an assault on human dignity and Christian conscience.

In the quest for this life of social harmony, the proclamation of the Christian message—in deed and word—has a role to fulfill, inasmuch as that message can be fittingly proclaimed only in profound respect for the cultural values of peoples and the freedom of persons. Rightly have Medellín and John Paul II so insistently called for the undertaking of a "new evangelization," one that will take into account the unprecedented aspects of the current situation, a situation as new as the commandment of love is ever new (John 13:34). The special bearers of this evangelization—as Puebla demanded—must be the poor, the members of the races, cultures, and social classes that our society marginalizes.

The witness of martyrdom, to which we referred a moment ago, demonstrates that those members of the people of God on pilgrimage in Latin America were speaking very seriously in these lands when, more than twenty-five years, they provided the church with the impulse for a preferential option for the poor. Thus did they lay the foundations for a new evangelization. And thus did they blaze a trail to a new set of social relations in Latin America.

In this task, the example of Bartolomé, a "witness of the gospel before the eyes of the poor," as M.-D. Chenu described him, has much to teach us. It requires a great deal of effort to find new avenues for the transmission of the gospel message. It requires a dogged attention to a changing situation to find an evangelization for our times. Creativity and tenacity were precisely two characteristics of that prophet of his time that Las Casas was. And both were maintained by a great sensitivity to the human suffering that makes Juan Gonzalo Rose say, with poetic intuition:

> Ah, militant of Christian love!
> In the name of my people I baptize thee:
> friar human being,
> friar friend,
> friar sibling.
>
> ["Epístola a Bartolomé de Las Casas"]

Here is a human being who defended the equality of all human beings, a friend of God who is in turn the "friend of life" (see Wis. 11:26) and the brother of all those in whom he read the face of Christ, our elder Brother. Las Casas, who could not recount "without tears" what was occurring in the Indies, who seemed to have been born "to mourn for others' griefs", is one of those who have not appeared before the Lord with dry cheeks and who therefore have received the tender consolation of which the prophet tells: "The Lord God will wipe away the tears from all faces; the reproach of his people he will remove from the whole earth" (Isa. 25:8).

Toward the end of his life, Las Casas dispatched a memorandum to the Council of the Indies in which he summarized the position he had adopted throughout his life in matters of the Indies. His poor state of health prevented him from presenting his petition personally, and his close followers and friends took up the relays. One of them, the great theologian Alonso de Veracruz, has left us with a revealing testimonial. "And this is the truth," writes Veracruz, honestly adding a note that seems sad and ironical to us today: "[The Council members] gave no interim ruling on this matter. Instead they said that they would see to it." This is the answer the poor continue to hear on this continent. We are still "seeing to" the memorandum they have been formulating for centuries in defense of human beings' most elementary demand: the right to God's gift of life.

A response to the call of the poor requires that we pose ourselves a question in all honesty. How can we make faith in the God who "has a very fresh and living memory of the smallest and most forgotten" the inspiration of our lives? How can we transform this time of dissipation and death into a time of calling and grace? In other words, how can we make our own today the counsel the great apostle Paul received from the "pillars" of the church—to be "mindful of the poor" (Gal. 2:9, 10)?

Neither Las Casas nor Guamán Poma [the controversial Peruvian Indian and Christian who early in the seventeenth century, wrote the king of Spain a book about the dispossession of the Indians] shows us the way. This is our charge and responsibility. They do give us the impassioned witness of their own quest, which they carried forward with determination and hesitancy, in success and failure, right on target and missing the mark, amid light and darkness—but ever with hope and with love, in the footsteps of Christ's poor. Rather than fixate on the past, we are called by them—each of us from his or her own cultural world—to make the present our own and forge the time which is coming.

They both challenge us to hurry to write our names, with urgency and with concrete proposals, on the pages of that history of long duration that is the coming of the reign of life proclaimed by Jesus.

Six

DISCIPLESHIP:
WALKING ACCORDING
TO THE SPIRIT

Though Gutiérrez's understanding of Christian discipleship—the following of Jesus Christ—is the theme of Chapter Six, it could easily have been placed first. Certainly the meaning and practice of discipleship were the center of his initial speeches and writings in the early 1960s. But more importantly, discipleship, as he has repeatedly pointed out, is also methodologically prior *to theological reflection. As he put it in 1988 in "Expanding the View," "in liberation theology the route to rational talk about God is located within a broader and more challenging course of action: the following of Jesus"* (Theology of Liberation, *xxxii). Furthermore, because there is no difference between discipleship and spirituality for Gutiérrez, "all authentic theology is spiritual theology"* (We Drink, *37).*

If spirituality was at the center of Gutiérrez's first writings, it has remained at the core of his pastoral and intellectual work ever since. An evolution in his thought cannot be denied and exemplifies his early conviction that "theology is a progressive and, in a certain sense, variable understanding" ("Notes for a Theology of Liberation," Theological Studies *31 (1970), 245). At the same time, any attempt to divide his written corpus as a whole, or any one of his works individually, into rigid compartments of "theology," "political analysis," or "spirituality," would be artificial and misleading. In truth,* all *of his writings are theological* and *political* and *spiritual, for reflection on the mystery of Love cannot be otherwise.*

41. A SPIRITUALITY OF LIBERATION

Gutiérrez's first sketches of a "spirituality of liberation" already included nearly all the principal elements of later, more developed treatments, for example, the priority of an encounter with God, conversion to the neighbor, and an awareness of love's gratuitousness experienced in prayer. The theological foundations of "following the Lord" were laid in two early essays. In "Caridad y amor humano" ("Charity, or Love of God, and Human Love") published in 1966, he argued that all love comes from God and that only by loving others can one love God. In "Libertad religiosa y diálogo salvador" ("Religious Liberty and the Saving Dialogue") he declared that "God speaks in fact to human beings through human beings, and from the time that God became a human being, the relation of human being to human being mediates the relation between the human being and God." See Gustavo Gutiérrez, Juan Luis Segundo, et al., Salvación y construcción del mundo *(Barcelona: Nova Terra, 1968), 15.*

The following brief selection, the conclusion of chapter 10 of Theology of Liberation, *"Encountering God in History" (116–20), presents a remarkably complete outline of ideas later developed in such works as* We Drink from Our Own Wells *and* The God of Life.

To place oneself in the perspective of the kingdom means to participate in the struggle for the liberation of those oppressed by others. This is what many Christians who have committed themselves to the Latin American revolutionary process have begun to experience. If this option seems to separate them from the Christian community, it is because many Christians, intent on domesticating the Good News, see them as wayward and perhaps even dangerous. If they are not always able to express in appropriate terms the profound reasons for their commitment, it is because the theology in which they were formed—and which they share with other Christians—has not produced the categories necessary to express this option, which seeks to respond creatively to the new demands of the gospel and of the oppressed and exploited peoples of this continent. But in their commitments, and even in their attempts to explain them, there is a greater understanding of the faith, greater faith, greater fidelity to the Lord than in the "orthodox" doctrine (some prefer to call it by this name) of reputable Christian circles. This doctrine is supported by authority and much publicized because of access to social communications media, but it is so static and devitalized that it is not even strong enough to abandon the gospel. It is the gospel which is disowning it.

But theological categories are not enough. We need a vital attitude, all-embracing and synthesizing, informing the totality as well as every detail of our lives; we need a "spirituality." Spirituality, in the strict and profound sense of the word is the dominion of the Spirit. If "the truth will set you free" (John 8:32), the Spirit "will guide you into all the truth" (John 16:13) and will lead us to complete freedom, the freedom from everything that hinders us from fulfilling ourselves as human beings and offspring of God and the freedom to love and to enter into communion with God and with others. It will lead us along the path of liberation because "where the Spirit of the Lord is, there is liberty" (2 Cor. 3:17).

A spirituality is a concrete manner, inspired by the Spirit, of living the gospel; it is a definite way of living "before the Lord," in solidarity with all human beings, "with the Lord," and before human beings. It arises from an intense spiritual experience, which is later explicated and witnessed to. Some Christians are beginning to live this experience as a result of their commitment to the process of liberation. The experiences of previous generations are there to support it, but above all, to remind them that they must discover their own way. Not only is there a contemporary history and a contemporary gospel; there is also a contemporary spiritual experience which cannot be overlooked. A spirituality means a reordering of the great axes of the Christian life in terms of this contemporary experience. What is new is the synthesis that this reordering brings about, in stimulating a deepened understanding of various ideas, in bringing to the surface unknown or forgotten aspects of the Christian life, and above all, in the way in which these things are converted into life, prayer, commitment, and action.

The truth is that a Christianity lived in commitment to the process of liberation presents its own problems which cannot be ignored and meets obstacles which must be overcome. For many, the encounter with the Lord under these conditions can disappear by giving way to what he himself brings forth and nourishes: love for humankind. This love, however, does not know the fullness of its potential. This is a real difficulty, but the solution must come from the heart of the problem itself. Otherwise, it would be just one more patchwork remedy, a new impasse. This is the challenge confronting a spirituality of liberation. Where oppression and human liberation seem to make God irrelevant— God filtered by our longtime indifference to these problems—there must blossom faith and hope in him who came to root out injustice and to offer, in an unforeseen way, total liberation. This is a spirituality which dares to sink roots in the soil of oppression-liberation.

A spirituality of liberation will center on a *conversion* to the neighbor, the oppressed person, the exploited social class, the despised ethnic group, the dominated country. Our conversion to the Lord implies this conversion to the neighbor. Evangelical conversion is indeed the touchstone of all spirituality. Conversion means a radical transformation of ourselves; it means thinking, feeling, and living as Christ—present in exploited and alienated persons. To be converted is to commit oneself to the process of the liberation of the poor and oppressed, to commit oneself lucidly, realistically, and concretely. It means to commit oneself not only generously, but also with an analysis of the situation and a strategy of action. To be converted is to know and experience the fact that, contrary to the laws of physics, we can stand straight, according to the gospel, only when our center of gravity is outside ourselves.

Conversion is a permanent process in which very often the obstacles we meet make us lose all we had gained and start anew. The fruitfulness of our conversion depends on our openness to doing this, our spiritual childhood. All conversion implies a break. To wish to accomplish it without conflict is to deceive oneself and others: "No one is worthy of me who cares more for father or mother than for me." But it is not a question of a withdrawn and pious attitude. Our conversion process is affected by the socioeconomic, political, cultural, and human environment in which it occurs. Without a change in these structures, there is no authentic conversion. We have to break with our mental categories, with the way we relate to others, with our way of identifying with the Lord, with our cultural milieu, with our social class, in other words, with all that can stand in the way of a real, profound solidarity with those who suffer, in the first place, from misery and injustice. Only thus, and not through purely interior and spiritual attitudes, will the "new person" arise from the ashes of the "old."

Christians have not done enough in this area of conversion to the neighbor, to social justice, to history. They have not perceived clearly enough yet that to know God *is* to do justice. They still do not live *in one sole action* with both God and all humans. They still do not situate themselves in Christ without attempting to avoid concrete human history. They have yet to tread the path which will lead them to seek effectively the peace of the Lord in the heart of social struggle.

A spirituality of liberation must be filled with a living sense of *gratuitousness*. Communion with the Lord and with all humans is more than anything else a gift. Hence the universality and the radicalness of the liberation which it affords. This gift, far from being a call to passivity, demands a vigilant attitude. This is one of the most constant biblical themes: the encounter with the Lord presupposes attention, active disposition, work, fidelity to God's will, the good use of talents received. But the knowledge that at the root of our personal and community existence lies the gift of the self-communication of God, the grace of God's friendship, fills our life with gratitude. It allows us to see our encounters with others, our loves, everything that happens in our life as a gift. There is a real love only when there is free giving—without conditions or coercion. Only gratuitous love goes to our very roots and elicits true love.

Prayer is an experience of gratuitousness. This "leisure" action, this "wasted" time, reminds us that the Lord is beyond the categories of useful and useless. God is not of this world. The gratuitousness of God's gift, creating profound needs, frees us from all religious alienation and, in the last instance, from all alienation. The Christian committed to the Latin American revolutionary process has to find the way to real prayer, not evasion. It cannot be denied that a crisis exists in this area and that we can easily slide into dead ends. There are many who—nostalgically and in "exile," recalling earlier years of their life—can say with the psalmist: "As I pour out my soul in distress, I call to mind how I marched in the ranks of the great to the house of God, among exultant shouts of praise, the clamor of the pilgrims" (Ps. 42:4). But the point is not to backtrack; new experiences, new demands have made heretofore familiar and comfortable paths impassable and have made us undertake new itineraries on which we hope it might be possible to say with Job to the Lord, "I knew of thee then only by report, but now I see thee with my own eyes" (42:5). Dietrich Bonhoeffer was right when he said that the only credible God is the God of the mystics. But this is not a God unrelated to human history. On the contrary, if it is true, as we recalled above, that one must go through humankind to reach God, it is equally certain that the "passing through" to that gratuitous God strips me, leaves me naked, universalizes my love for others, and makes it gratuitous. Both movements need each other dialectically and move toward a synthesis. This synthesis is found in Christ; in the God-Man we encounter God and humankind. In Christ humankind gives God a human countenance and God gives it a divine countenance. Only in this perspective will we be able to understand that the "union with the Lord," which all spirituality proclaims, is not a separation from others; to attain this union, I must go through others, and the union, in turn, enables me to encounter others more fully. Our purpose here is not to "balance" what has been said before, but rather to deepen it and see it in all its meaning.

The conversion to one's neighbors, and in them to the Lord, the gratuitousness which allows me to encounter others fully, the unique encounter which is the foundation of communion of persons among themselves and of human beings with God, these are the source of Christian joy. This joy is born of the gift already received yet still awaited and is expressed in the present despite the difficulties and tensions of the struggle for the construction of a just society. Every prophetic proclamation of total liberation is accompanied by an invitation to participate in eschatological joy: "I will take delight in Jerusalem and rejoice in my people" (Isa. 65:19). This joy ought to fill our entire existence, making us attentive both to the gift of integral human liberation and history as well as to the detail of our life and the lives of others. This joy ought not to lessen our commitment to those who live in an unjust world, nor should it lead us to a facile, low-cost conciliation. On the contrary, our joy is paschal, guaranteed by the Spirit (Gal. 5:22; 1 Tim. 1:6; Rom. 14:17); it passes through the conflict with the great ones of this world and through the cross in order to enter into life. This is why we celebrate our joy in the present by recalling the passover of the Lord. To recall Christ is to believe in him. And this celebration is a feast (Apoc. 19:7), a feast of the Christian community, those who explicitly confess Christ to be the Lord of history, the liberator of the oppressed. This community has been referred to as the small temple in contradistinction to the large temple of human history. Without community support neither the emergence nor the continued existence of a new spirituality is possible.

The Magnificat expresses well this spirituality of liberation. A song of thanksgiving for the gifts of the Lord, it expresses humbly the joy of being loved by him: "Rejoice, my spirit, in God my Savior; so tenderly has he looked upon his servant, humble as she is. . . . So wonderfully has he dealt with me, the Lord, the Mighty One" (Luke 1:47–49). But at the same time it is one of the New Testament texts which contains great implications both as regards liberation and the political sphere. This thanksgiving and joy are closely linked to the action of God who liberates the oppressed and humbles the powerful. "The hungry he has satisfied with good things, the rich sent empty away" (vv. 52–53). The future of history belongs to the poor and exploited. True liberation will be the work of the oppressed themselves; in them, the Lord saves history. The spirituality of liberation will have as its basis the spirituality of the *anawim*.

Living witnesses rather than theological speculation will point out—are already pointing out—the direction of a spirituality of liberation. This is the task which has been undertaken in Latin America by those referred to above as a "first Christian generation."

42. POVERTY: SOLIDARITY AND PROTEST

The ideas found in the final chapter of Theology of Liberation, *"Poverty: Solidarity and Protest," were first presented in a course on "The Church and the Problems of Poverty" given by Gutiérrez at the University of Montréal in July, 1967. The adoption of his threefold understanding of the term "poverty" at Medellín in 1968 (see "Poverty of the Church" 4) and Puebla in 1979 (see nos. 1134–65) alone ensured Gutiérrez's stamp on the subsequent history of the Roman Catholic Church and its theology. More recently, Gutiérrez has pointed out the correspondence between the three meanings of poverty and the three components of the expression "preferential option for the poor." "The poor" designates those who live in privation and marginalization; "preferential" points to the disciple's openness to, and trust in, the God of life; and "option" means choosing to live in solidarity with the poor and, in them, with God. This selection is from* Theology of Liberation, *162–73.*

For some years now we have seen in the church a growing demand for a more authentic and radical witness of poverty. At first this occurred within various recently-founded religious communities. It quickly went beyond the narrow limits of "religious poverty," however, reaching other sectors of the church with demands and questions. Poverty has become one of the central themes of contemporary Christian spirituality and indeed has become a controversial question. From the concern to imitate more faithfully the poor Christ, there has spontaneously emerged a critical and militant attitude regarding the countersign that the church as a whole presents in the matter of poverty.

This perspective—with John XXIII leading the way—knocked insistently at the doors of Vatican II. In an important message in preparation for the opening of the Council, John opened up a fertile perspective, saying, "For underdeveloped countries, the church presents herself as she is and as she wants to be—as the church of all and especially the church of the poor." Indeed, from the first session of the Council the theme of poverty was in the air. Later there was even a "Schema 14," which on the issue of poverty went beyond "Schema 13" (the draft for *Gaudium et spes*). The final results of the Council, however, did not correspond to the expectations. The documents allude several times to poverty, but it is not one of the major thrusts.

Later, *Populorum progressio* is somewhat more clear and concrete with regard to various questions related to poverty. But it will fall to a church which lives on a continent of misery and injustice to give the theme of poverty its proper importance: *it is a witness on which the authenticity of the preaching of the gospel message depends.*

The theme of poverty has been dealt with in recent years, especially in the field of spirituality. In the contemporary world, fascinated by a wealth and power established upon the plunder and exploitation of the great majorities, poverty emerged as an inescapable precondition to sanctity. This is why the greatest efforts focused on meditating on biblical texts which recall the poverty of Christ and thus on an identification with him in this witness.

More recently a properly theological reflection on poverty has been undertaken, based on ever richer and more precise exegetical studies. From these first attempts there stands out clearly one rather surprising result: poverty is a notion which has received very little theological treatment and in spite of everything is still quite unclear. Lines of interpretation overlap; certain exegeses still carry weight today, even though they were developed in very different contexts which no longer exist; certain aspects of the theme function as static compartments which prevent a grasp of its overall meaning. All this has led us to slide onto unstable ground which we are trying to leave more by intuition than by clear and well-formulated ideas.

AMBIGUITIES IN THE TERM "POVERTY"

"Poverty" is an equivocal term. But this terminological ambiguity does nothing more than express the ambiguity of the notion or notions themselves which are involved. To try to clarify what we understand by "poverty," we must clear the path and examine some of the sources of the ambiguity. This will also permit us to indicate the meaning we will give to various expressions which we will use later.

The term "poverty" designates in the first place *material poverty*, that is, the lack of economic goods necessary for a human life worthy of the name. In this sense poverty is considered degrading and is rejected by the conscience of contemporary persons. Even those who are not—or do not wish to be—aware of the root causes of this situation believe that poverty should be struggled against. In Christian circles, however, there is often a tendency to give material poverty a positive meaning, to see it almost as a human and religious ideal. It is seen as an ideal of austerity and indifference to the things of this world and a precondition for a life in conformity with the gospel. This places the demands of Christianity at cross-purposes with the great aspiration of men and women today who want to free themselves from subjection to nature, to eliminate the exploitation of some persons by others, and to create wealth for everyone. This double and contradictory meaning of "poverty" allows for superimposing one language on the other and is a frequent source of ambiguities. The matter becomes even more complex if we take into consideration that the concept of material poverty is in constant evolution. Not having access to certain cultural, social, and political values, for example, is today part of the poverty that persons hope to abolish.

Would material poverty as an "ideal" of Christian life also include lacking these things?

On the other hand, poverty has often been thought of and experienced by Christians as part of the condition—seen with a certain fatalism—of isolated individuals, of "the poor," who are an object of our mercy. But things are no longer like this. Social classes, nations, and entire continents are becoming aware of their poverty, and when they see its root causes, they rebel against it. We are facing a collective poverty which creates bonds of solidarity among those who suffer it and leads them to organize to struggle against this situation and against those who benefit from it.

Material poverty is located, then—and so I will consider it here—on the level of the subhuman. As we shall see later, the Bible also considers it this way. Concretely, to be poor means to die of hunger, to be illiterate, to be exploited by others, not to know that you are a human being. It is in relation to this poverty—material and cultural, collective and militant—that evangelical poverty will have to be defined.

The notion of *spiritual poverty* is even less clear. Often it is seen simply as an interior attitude of unattachment to the goods of this world. "The poor," therefore, are not so much those who have no material goods but those who are not attached to them—even if they do possess them. This view allows us to say, for example, that a rich person can be spiritually poor and that, conversely, a poor person can be rich at heart. But this is to work with extreme cases that distract attention toward the exceptional and the accessory. Claiming to be based on the Beatitude of Matthew concerning "the poor in spirit," this approach in the long run leads to comforting and tranquilizing conclusions.

This spiritualistic perspective rapidly leads to dead ends and to affirmations that the interior attitude must necessarily be incarnated in a testimony of material poverty. But if this is so, questions arise: What kind of poverty are we talking about? The poverty that the contemporary conscience considers subhuman? Is it in such poverty that spiritual poverty should be incarnated? Some would answer that it is not necessary to go to such extremes, and they attempt to distinguish between destitution and poverty. It would be a matter in this case of taking on the second kind of poverty, not the first. But then, as I mentioned, we are not referring to poverty as it is lived and perceived by people today, but rather to a different kind of poverty, one that is abstract and made to fit the specifications of our spiritual poverty. This is to play with words—and with human beings.

The distinction between evangelical counsels and precepts creates other ambiguities. According to it, evangelical poverty would be a counsel appropriate to a particular vocation and not a precept obligatory for all Christians. This distinction kept evangelical poverty confined incommunicado for a long time within the narrow limits of religious life, which focuses on "the evangelical counsels." Today the distinction is only another source of misunderstandings.

All these ambiguities and uncertainties have prevented us from touching solid ground and have made us take an unsure path where it is difficult to advance and easy to wander. They have also led us to a very vague terminology and a kind of sentimentalism which in the last analysis justifies the status quo. In situations like the present one in Latin America this is especially serious. We see the danger, for example, in various commentaries on the writings of Bossuet regarding "the eminent dignity of the poor in the church"; or in symbolism like that which considers the hunger of the poor as "the image of the human soul hungering for God"; or even in the expression "the church of the poor," which—in spite of the indisputable purity of intention of John XXIII—is susceptible to an interpretation smacking of paternalism.

Clarification is needed. In the following pages we will attempt to sketch at least the broad outlines. We will try to keep in mind that—as one spiritual writer has said—the first form of poverty is to let go of the idea we already have of poverty.

BIBLICAL MEANING OF POVERTY

Poverty is a central theme both in the Old and the New Testaments. It is treated both briefly and profoundly; it describes social situations and expresses spiritual experiences communicated only with difficulty; it defines personal attitudes, a whole people's attitude before God, and the relationships of persons with each other. It is possible, nevertheless, to try to unravel the knots and to clear the horizon by following the two major lines of thought that seem to stand out: poverty as a scandalous situation and poverty as spiritual childhood. The notion of evangelical poverty will be illuminated by a comparison of these two perspectives.

POVERTY: A SCANDALOUS SITUATION

In the Bible poverty is a scandalous situation inimical to human dignity and therefore contrary to the will of God.

This rejection of poverty is seen very clearly in the vocabulary used. In the Old Testament the term which is used least to speak of the poor is *rash*, which has a rather neutral meaning. As Gelin says, the prophets preferred "designations which photograph the concrete, living poor person." The poor person is, therefore, *ébyôn*, the one who desires, the beggar, the one who is lacking something and who awaits it from another. He is also *dal*, the weak one, the frail one; the expression "the poor of the land" (the rural proletariat) is found very frequently. The poor person is also *ani*, the bent over one, the one laboring under a weight, the one not in possession of his whole strength and vigor, the humiliated one. And finally he is *anaw*, from the same root as the previous term but having a more religious connotation—"humble before God." In the New Testament the Greek term *ptokom* is used to speak of the poor person. *Ptokus* means one who does not have what is necessary to subsist, the wretched one driven into begging.

Indigent, weak, bent over, wretched are terms which well express a degrading

human situation. These terms already insinuate a protest. They are not lim[
to description; they take a stand. This stand is made explicit in the vigo[
rejection of poverty. The climate in which poverty is described is one of in[
nation. And it is with the same indignation that the cause of poverty is indi[
ed: the injustice of oppressors. This is how a text from Job expresses it:

> The wicked jostle the poor out of the way; the destitute
>   huddle together, hiding from them.
> The poor rise early like the wild ass, when it scours the
>   wilderness for food;
> But though they work till nightfall, their children go
>   hungry. [Job 24:4–6]

Poverty is not caused by fate; it is caused by the actions of those whom t[
prophet condemns:

Thus says Yahweh:

> For crime after crime of Israel I will grant them no reprieve because they sell
> the innocent for silver and the destitute for a pair of shoes. They grind the
> heads of the poor into the earth and thrust the humble out of their way. [Amos
> 2:6–7]

There are poor people because there are people who are the victims of other
people. "Shame on you," it says in Isaiah,

> you who make unjust laws and publish burdensome decrees, depriving the
> poor of justice, robbing the weakest of my people of their rights, despoiling
> the widow and plundering the orphan [10:1–2].

The prophets condemn every kind of abuse, every form of keeping the poor
in poverty or of creating new poor people. There are not merely allusions to situations; the finger is pointed at those who are to blame. Fraudulent commerce
and exploitation are condemned (Hos. 12:8; Amos 8:5; Mic. 6:10–11; Isa. 3:14;
Jer. 5:27; 6:12), as well as the hoarding of lands (Mic. 2:1–3; Ezek. 22:29; Hab.
2:5–6), dishonest courts (Amos 5:7; Jer. 22:13–17; Mic. 3:9–11; Isa. 5:23,
10:1–2), the violence of the ruling classes (2 Kings 23:30, 35; Amos 4:1; Mic.
3:1–2; 6:12; Jer. 22:13–17), slavery (Neh. 5:1–5; Amos 2:6; 8:6), unjust taxes
(Amos 4:1; 5:11–12), and unjust functionaries (Amos 5:7; Jer. 5:28). In the
New Testament oppression by the rich is also condemned, especially in Luke
(6:24–25; 12:13–21; 16:19–31; 18:18–26) and in the Letter of James (2:5–9;
4:13–17; 5:1–6).

But it is not simply a matter of denouncing poverty. The Bible speaks of positive and concrete measures to prevent poverty from becoming established
among the People of God. In Leviticus and Deuteronomy there is very detailed
legislation designed to prevent the accumulation of wealth and the consequent
exploitation. It is said, for example, that what remains in the fields after the har-
vest and the gathering of olives and grapes should not be collected; it is for the

alien, the orphan, and the widow (Deut. 24:19–21; Lev. 19:9–10). Even more, the fields should not be harvested to the very edge so that something remains for the poor and the aliens (Lev. 23:22). The Sabbath, the day of the Lord, has a social significance; it is a day of rest for the slave and the alien (Exod. 23:12; Deut. 5:14). The triennial tithe is not to be carried to the temple; rather it is for the alien, the orphan, and the widow (Deut. 14:28–29; 26:12). Interest on loans is forbidden (Exod. 22:25; Lev. 25:35–37; Deut. 23:20). More important measures include the Sabbath year and the jubilee year. Every seven years the fields will be left to lie fallow "to provide food for the poor of your people" (Exod. 23:11; Lev. 25:2–7), although it is recognized that this duty is not always fulfilled (Lev. 26:34–35). After seven years the slaves were to regain their freedom (Exod. 21:2–6) and debts were to be pardoned (Deut. 15:1–18). This is also the meaning of the jubilee year of Lev. 25:10 ff. . . .

Behind these texts we can see three principal reasons for this vigorous repudiation of poverty. In the first place, poverty contradicts the very meaning of *the Mosaic religion*. Moses led his people out of the slavery, exploitation, and alienation of Egypt so that they might inhabit a land where they could live with human dignity. Moses' liberating mission closely linked the religion of Yahweh and the elimination of servitude [see Exod. 16:6–8]. . . .

The worship of Yahweh and the possession of the land are both included in the same promise. The rejection of the exploitation of some by others is found in the very roots of the people of Israel. God is the only owner of the land given to people (Lev. 25:23, 38); God is the one Lord who saves the people from servitude and will not allow them to be subjected to it again (Deut. 5:15; 16:22, Lev. 25:42; 26:13). And thus Deuteronomy speaks of "the ideal of a fraternal people where there should be no poor people." In their rejection of poverty, the prophets, who were heirs to the Mosaic ideal, referred to the past, to the origins of the people; there they sought the inspiration for the construction of a just society. To accept poverty and injustice is to fall back into the conditions of servitude which existed before the liberation from Egypt. It is to retrogress.

The second reason for the repudiation of the state of slavery and exploitation of the Jewish people in Egypt is that it goes against *the mandate of Genesis* (1:26; 2:15). Men and women are created in the image and likeness of God and are destined to dominate the earth. They fulfill themselves only by transforming nature and thus entering into relationships with other persons. Only in this way do persons come to a full consciousness of themselves as subjects of creative freedom which is gained through work. The situation of exploitation and injustice which poverty implies make work into something servile and dehumanizing. Alienated work, instead of liberating persons, enslaves them even more. And so it is that when just treatment is asked for poor persons, slaves, and foreigners, it is recalled that Israel also was alien and enslaved in Egypt (Exod. 22:21; 23:9; Deut. 10:19; Lev. 19:34).

And finally, men and women not only have been made in the image and like-

ness of God; they are also *the sacrament of God*. We have already recalled this profound and challenging biblical theme. The other reasons for the biblical rejection of poverty have their roots here: to oppress the poor is to attack God; to know God is to act for justice among human beings. We meet God in our encounter with other persons; what is done for others is done for the Lord.

In a word, the existence of poverty reflects a rupture of solidarity among persons and also of communion with God. Poverty is an expression of a sin, that is, of a negation of love. This is why it is incompatible with the coming of the kingdom of God, a kingdom of love and justice.

Poverty is an evil, a scandalous situation, which in our times has taken on enormous proportions. To eliminate it is to bring closer the moment of seeing God face to face, in union with other persons.

POVERTY: SPIRITUAL CHILDHOOD

There is a second line of thinking concerning poverty in the Bible. The poor person is the "client" of Yahweh; poverty is "the ability to welcome God, an openness to God, a willingness to be used by God, a humility before God," [as Gelin put it].

The vocabulary used here is the same as that used to speak of poverty as an evil. In fact the terms used to designate the poor person receive an ever more demanding and precise religious meaning. This is the case especially with the term *anaw*, which in the plural (*anawim*) is the privileged designation of the spiritually poor person.

Repeated infidelity to the Covenant of the people of Israel led the prophets to elaborate the theme of the "tiny remnant" (Isa. 4:3; 6:13). Made up of those who remained faithful to Yahweh, the remnant would be the Israel of the future. From its midst there would emerge the Messiah and consequently the first fruits of the New Covenant (Jer. 31:31–34; Ezek. 36:26–28). From the time of Zephaniah (seventh century B.C.E.), those who awaited the liberating work of the Messiah were called "poor." "But I will leave in you a people afflicted and poor, and the survivors in Israel shall find refuge in the name of the Lord" (Zeph. 3:12–13). In this way the term acquired a spiritual meaning. From then on poverty was presented as an ideal: "Seek the Lord, all in the land who live humbly by his laws, seek righteousness, seek a humble heart" (Zeph. 2:3). Understood in this way poverty is opposed to pride, to an attitude of self-sufficiency; on the other hand, it is synonymous with faith, with abandonment and trust in the Lord. This spiritual meaning will be accentuated during the historical experiences of Israel after the time of Zephaniah. Jeremiah calls himself poor (*ébyôn*) when he sings his thanksgiving to God (20:13). Spiritual poverty is a precondition for approaching God. "All these things my hand has made, and so all these things are mine, says the Lord. But this is the one to whom I will look, to the humble and contrite in spirit, who trembles at my word" (Isa. 66:2). The Psalms can help us to understand more precisely this religious attitude.

To know Yahweh is to seek him (9:11; 34:11), to abandon and entrust oneself to him (10:14; 34:9, 37:40), to hope in him (25:3–5, 21; 37:9), to fear the Lord (25:12, 14; 34:8, 10), to observe his commandments (25:10); the poor are the just ones, the whole ones (34:20, 22; 37:17–18), the faithful ones (37:28; 149:1). The opposite of the poor are the proud, who are the enemy of Yahweh and of the helpless (10:2; 18:28; 37:10; 86:14).

Spiritual poverty finds its highest expression in the Beatitudes of the New Testament. The version in Matthew—thanks to solid exegetical studies—no longer seems to present any great difficulties in interpretation. The poverty which is called "blessed" in Matt. 5:1 ("Blessed are the poor in spirit") is spiritual poverty as understood since the time of Zephaniah: to be totally available to the Lord. This is the precondition for being able to receive the Word of God. It has, therefore, the same meaning as the gospel theme of spiritual childhood. God's self-communication is a gift of love; to receive this gift it is necessary to be poor, a spiritual child. This poverty has no direct relationship to wealth; in the first instance it is not a question of indifference to the goods of this world. It goes deeper than that; it means to have no other sustenance than the will of God. This is the attitude of Christ. Indeed, it is to him that all the Beatitudes fundamentally refer.

In Luke's version ("Blessed are you who are poor" [6:20]) we are faced with greater problems of interpretation. Attempts to resolve these difficulties follow two different lines of thinking. Luke is the evangelist who is most sensitive to social realities. In his Gospel as well as in Acts, the themes of material poverty, of goods held in common, and of the condemnation of the rich are frequently treated. This has naturally led to thinking that the poor whom he blesses are the opposite of the rich whom he condemns; the poor would be those who lack the necessities. In this case the poverty that he speaks of in the first Beatitude would be *material poverty.*

But this interpretation presents a twofold difficulty. It would lead to the canonization of a social class. The poor would be the privileged of the kingdom, even to the point of having their access to it assured, not by any choice on their part but by a socioeconomic situation which had been imposed on them. Some commentators insist that this would not be evangelical and would be contrary to the intentions of Luke. At the opposite extreme are those who hope to get around this obstacle without losing the sociological and concrete meaning of poverty in Luke. Situating themselves in the perspective of wisdom literature, they say that the first Beatitude opposes the present world to the world beyond; the sufferings of today will be compensated for in the future life. Extraterrestrial salvation is the absolute value which makes the present life insignificant. But this point of view implies purely and simply that Luke is sacralizing misery and injustice and is therefore preaching resignation to it.

Because of these impasses, an explanation is sought from another perspective:

Matthew's. Like Matthew, Luke would be referring to *spiritual poverty*, or to openness to God. As a concession to the social context of Luke there is in this interpretation an emphasis on real poverty insofar as it is, [as Gelin says], "a privileged path toward poverty of soul."

This second line of interpretation seems to us to minimize the sense of Luke's text. Indeed, it is impossible to avoid the concrete and "material" meaning which the term "poor" has for this evangelist. It refers first of all to those who live in a social situation characterized by a lack of the goods of this world and even by misery and indigence. Even further, it refers to a marginated social group, with connotations of oppression and lack of liberty.

All this leads us to retrace our steps and to reconsider the difficulties—which we have recalled above—in explaining the text of Luke as referring to the materially poor.

"Blessed are you who are poor, for yours is the kingdom of God" does not mean, it seems to us: "Accept your poverty because later this injustice will be compensated for in the kingdom of God." If we believe that the kingdom of God is a gift which is received in history, and if we believe, as the eschatological promises—so charged with human and historical content—indicate to us, that the kingdom of God necessarily implies the reestablishment of justice in this world, then we must believe that Christ says that the poor are blessed *because* the kingdom of God has begun: "The time has come; the kingdom of God is upon you" (Mark 1:15). In other words, the elimination of the exploitation and poverty that prevent the poor from being fully human has begun; a kingdom of justice which goes even beyond what they could have hoped for has begun. They are blessed because the coming of the kingdom will put an end to their poverty by creating a world of fellowship. They are blessed because the Messiah will open the eyes of the blind and will give bread to the hungry. Situated in a prophetic perspective, the text in Luke uses the term "poor" in the tradition of the first major line of thought we have studied: poverty is an evil and therefore incompatible with the kingdom of God, which has come in its fullness into history and embraces the totality of human existence.

AN ATTEMPT AT SYNTHESIS: SOLIDARITY AND PROTEST

Material poverty is a scandalous situation. Spiritual poverty is an attitude of openness to God and spiritual childhood. Having clarified these two meanings of the term "poverty" we have cleared the path and can now move forward toward a better understanding of the Christian witness of poverty. We turn now to a third meaning of the term: poverty as a commitment of solidarity and protest.

We have laid aside the first two meanings. The first is subtly deceptive; the second partial and insufficient. In the first place, if *material poverty* is something to be rejected, as the Bible vigorously insists, then a witness of poverty cannot make of it a Christian ideal. This would be to aspire to a condition which is recognized as degrading to persons. It would be, moreover, to move against the current of history. It would be to oppose any idea of the domination of nature by humans and the consequent and progressive creation of better conditions of life. And it would equally mean—and this is no less serious—justifying, even if only involuntarily, the situation of injustice and exploitation which is the cause of poverty.

On the other hand, our analysis of the biblical texts concerning *spiritual poverty* has helped us to see that it is not directly or in the first instance an interior detachment from the goods of this world, a spiritual attitude which becomes authentic by incarnating itself in material poverty. Spiritual poverty is something more profound and all-encompassing. It is above all total availability to the Lord. Its relationship to the use or ownership of economic goods is inescapable, but secondary and partial. Spiritual childhood—the power to embrace, not passive acceptance—defines the total posture of human existence before God, persons, and things.

How are we therefore to understand the evangelical meaning of the witness of a real, material, concrete poverty? *Lumen gentium* invites us to look for the deepest meaning of Christian poverty *in Christ:* "Just as Christ carried out the work of redemption in poverty and under oppression, so the church is called to follow the same path in communicating to others the fruits of salvation. Christ Jesus, though he was by nature God . . . emptied himself, taking the nature of a slave (Phil. 2:6), and being rich, he became poor (2 Cor. 8:9) for our sake. Thus, although the church needs human resources to carry out her mission, she is not set up to seek earthly glory, but to proclaim humility and self-sacrifice, even by her own example" (no. 8). The Incarnation is an act of love. Christ became human, died, and rose from the dead to set us free so that we might enjoy freedom (Gal. 5:1). To die and to rise again with Christ is to vanquish death and to enter into a new life (cf. Rom. 6:1–11). The cross and the resurrection are the seal of our liberty.

The taking on of the servile and sinful condition of humanity, as foretold in Second Isaiah, is presented by Paul as an act of voluntary impoverishment: "For you know how generous our Lord Jesus Christ has been: he was rich, yet for your sake he became poor, so that through his poverty you might become rich" (2 Cor. 8:9). This is the humiliation of Christ, his *kenosis* (Phil. 2:6–11). Yet he does not take on the human sinful condition and its consequences to idealize it but rather out of love for, and solidarity with, those who suffer it. It is to redeem them from sin and to enrich them with his poverty. It is to struggle against human selfishness and everything that divides persons, against whatever results in rich and poor people, owners and non-owners, oppressors and oppressed.

Poverty is an act of love and liberation. It has a redemptive value. If the ultimate cause of human exploitation and alienation is selfishness; the deepest reason for voluntary poverty is love of neighbor. Christian poverty thus cannot have meaning except as a commitment of solidarity with the poor, with those who suffer misery and injustice in order to testify to the evil which these represent, the fruit of sin and a breach of communion. It is not a question of idealizing poverty, but on the contrary of taking it on as it is—an evil—to protest against it and to struggle to abolish it. As Paul Ricoeur says, you cannot really be with the poor unless you are struggling against poverty. Thanks to this solidarity—which must manifest itself in specific actions, a style of life, a break with one's social class—one can also help the poor and exploited to become aware of their exploitation and seek liberation from it. Christian poverty, an expression of love, is solidarity *with the poor* and is a protest *against poverty*. This is the concrete, contemporary meaning of the witness of poverty. It is a poverty lived not for its own sake, but rather as an authentic imitation of Christ; it is a poverty which means taking on the sinful human condition to liberate the human being from sin and all its consequences.

Luke presents the community of goods in the early church as an ideal. "All whose faith had drawn them together held everything in common" (Acts 2:44); "no one claimed private ownership of any possessions, but everything they owned was held in common" (Acts 4:32). They did this with a profound unity, "of one heart and soul" (ibid.). But as Dupont correctly points out, this was not a question of erecting poverty as an ideal, but rather of seeing to it that there were no poor: "There was not a needy person among them, for as many as owned lands or houses sold them and brought the proceeds of what was sold They laid it at the apostles' feet, and it was distributed to each as any had need" (Acts 4:34–35). The meaning of the community of goods is clear: to eliminate poverty because of love for of the poor person. Dupont rightly concludes, "If goods are held in common, it is not therefore in order to become poor for love of an ideal of poverty; rather it is so that there will be no poor. The ideal pursued is, once again, charity, a true love for the poor."

We must pay special attention to the words we use. The term "poor" might seem not only vague and churchy, but also somewhat sentimental and aseptic. The "poor" person today is the oppressed person, the one marginalized by society, the proletarian struggling for the most basic rights; the exploited and plundered social class, the country struggling for its liberation. In today's world the solidarity and protest of which we are speaking have an evident and inevitable "political" character insofar as they imply liberation. To opt for the oppressed is to opt against the oppressor. In our times and on our continent to be in solidarity with the "poor," understood in this way, means to run personal risks—even to put one's life in danger. Many Christians—and non-Christians—who are committed to the Latin American revolutionary process are running these risks. And so there are emerging new ways of living poverty which are different from the classic "renunciation of the goods of this world."

Only by rejecting poverty and by making itself poor in order to protest against it can the church preach something that is uniquely its own: "spiritual poverty," that is, the openness of the human being and history to the future promised by God. Only in this way will the church be able to fulfill authentically—and with any possibility of being listened to—its prophetic function of denouncing every injustice which attacks persons and of preaching the liberating message of a real human fellowship.

Only authentic solidarity with the poor and a real protest against the poverty of our time can provide the concrete, vital context necessary for a theological discussion of poverty. The absence of a sufficient commitment to the poor, the marginalized, and the exploited is perhaps the fundamental reason why we have no solid or actualized reflection on the witness of poverty.

For the Latin American church especially, this witness is today an inescapable and urgent sign of the authenticity of its mission.

43. ENCOUNTER WITH THE LORD

From his earliest writings Gutiérrez demonstrated a profound appreciation of the great Christian spiritualities of the past and a commitment to healing the breach between spirituality and theology, which began in the fourteenth century and continues today. He was also mindful of a new spirituality (whose birth he assisted) arising among the believing poor of Latin America and their allies. In the final section of chapter 10 of Theology of Liberation, *"Encountering God in History," Gutiérrez sketched what he called "a spirituality of liberation" by highlighting its principal elements: ongoing conversion to the neighbor, the experience of gratuitousness (prayer), and the joy of living and struggling for freedom in community. In the last chapter of the same book, "Poverty: Solidarity and Protest," he offered a detailed account of the biblical theme of poverty, fundamental to a spirituality of liberation.*

Though such a spirituality—understood as solidarity with the poor and in them with the God of life—constitutes the very soil in which liberation theology has grown, Gutiérrez's promise to offer a more complete and explicit treatment of the spirituality of liberation was fulfilled above all in We Drink from Our Own Wells: The Spiritual Journey of a People *(Spanish original, 1983). Written during an increasingly painful period of entrenched oppression, savage terrorism, and ferocious repression for the people of Peru, and of Latin America generally, the book is replete with contrasting images of darkness and light, enslavement and freedom, death and life. In these years attention to the ultimate consequence of sin—namely premature death in countless forms for countless human beings—led Gutiérrez to explore, with humility and sometimes anguish, the purposes of the Giver of life and the meaning of the gift.*

The following text is drawn from chapter 3 of We Drink from Our Own Wells *(35–51). Here Gutiérrez sets forth the principal elements of the spirituality of liberation.*

A spirituality is a walking in freedom according to the Spirit of love and life. This walking has its point of departure in an encounter with the Lord. Such an encounter is a spiritual experience that produces and gives meaning to the freedom of which I have been speaking. The encounter itself springs from the Lord's initiative. The Scriptures state this repeatedly: "This is why I told you that no one can come to me unless it is granted him by the Father" (John 6:65). "You did not choose me, but I chose you" (John 15:16).

A spiritual experience always stands at the beginning of a spiritual journey. That experience becomes the subject of later reflection and is proposed to the entire ecclesial community as a way of being disciples of Christ. The spirituality in question is therefore not, as is sometimes said, an application of a particular theology. Let me begin by clarifying this point.

SPIRITUALITY AND THEOLOGY

The adoption of a spiritual perspective is followed by a reflection on faith (a theology) as lived in that perspective. This sequence is clear from the historical course followed in all the great spiritualities.

I BELIEVE IN ORDER TO UNDERSTAND

Spiritual experience is the terrain in which theological reflection strikes root. Intellectual comprehension makes it possible to carry the experience of faith to a deeper level, but the experience always comes first and is the source. St. Anselm (1033–1109) reminds us of this in a well-known passage:

> Lord, I do not attempt to comprehend your sublimity because my intellect is not at all equal to such a task. But I yearn to understand some measure of your truth, which my heart believes and loves. For I do not seek to understand in order to believe but I believe in order to understand. For I am sure that if I did not believe, I would not understand.

I believe in order to understand. The level of the experience of faith supports a particular level of the understanding of faith. For theology is in fact a reflection that, even in its rational aspect, moves entirely within the confines of faith and direct testimony. "This is the disciple who is bearing witness to these things, and who has written these things; and we know that his testimony is true" (John 21:24). In the gospels themselves, then, the experience of faith is presented as the starting point of all testimony and reflection. . . .

As a matter of fact, in the early centuries every theology took the form of what we today call a "spiritual theology"—that is, it was a reflection carried on in function of the following of the Lord, the "imitation of Christ" (*imitatio Christi*). This integrated approach inspired the work of Thomas Aquinas who established a solid foundation for theology as a rationally organized body of knowledge. But toward the fourteenth century a divorce began to take place between theology and spirituality that was to be harmful to both.

The solidity and energy of theological thought depend precisely on the spiritual experience that supports it. This experience takes the form, first and foremost, of a profound encounter with God and God's will. Any discourse on faith starts from, and takes its bearings from, the Christian life of the community. Any reflection that does not help in living according to the Spirit is not a Christian theology. When all is said and done, then, all authentic theology is spiritual theology. This fact does not weaken the rigorously scientific character of the theology; it properly situates it.

SPIRITUAL EXPERIENCE

At the root of every spirituality there is a particular experience that is had by concrete persons living at a particular time. The experience is both proper to them and yet communicable to others. St. Bernard of Clairvaux says that in these matters all people should drink from their own well. The great spiritualities in the life of the church continue to exist because they keep sending their followers back to the sources.

The image of a well is used here because a spirituality is indeed like living water that springs up in the very depths of the experience of faith. John writes: "He who believes in me, as the Scripture has said, 'Out of his heart shall flow rivers of living water'" (7:38). The life signified in the image of water comes to us through encounter with the Lord: "Whoever drinks of the water that I shall give him will never thirst; the water that I shall give him will become in him a spring of water welling up to eternal life" (John 4:14). In these texts "living water" refers to the gift of the Spirit that Jesus makes to his disciples. Drinking from one's own well, then, is a "spiritual" experience in the fullest sense of the word. To have this experience is to live in the age of the Spirit and according to the Spirit.

What is going on today in Latin America makes it the place of an experience that is giving birth to a distinctive way of being Christian—that is, to a spirituality. This experience in turn is leaving its mark on the theological reflection that is springing out of all that is best in the Latin American church.

Such a statement does not in the least imply a forgetfulness of the task proper to a discourse on faith. All it does is make us aware that a theology that is not located in the context of an experience of faith is in danger of turning into a kind of religious metaphysics or a wheel that turns in the air without making the cart advance. Theological reflection takes on its full meaning only within the church and in the service of the life of the church and its action in the world.

This is what many Christians are now experiencing in Latin America. To be a follower of Jesus requires walking with, and being committed to, the poor; within such commitment Christians encounter the Lord who is simultaneously revealed and hidden in the faces of the poor (see Matt. 25:31–46, and the fine commentary in Puebla nos. 31–39). This is a profound and demanding spiritual experience, the starting point for one way of following Jesus and reflecting on his words and deeds.

SEE, TOUCH, FOLLOW

The gospels present to us the experience that the disciples had of Jesus, and they do so with all the intimacy implied in the verbs "see," "hear," and "touch." To encounter the Lord is first of all to be encountered by the Lord. "You did not choose me, but I chose you and appointed you that you should go and bear fruit" (John 15:16). In this encounter we discover where the Lord lives and what the mission is that he entrusts to us.

The here and now always puts its mark on this experience. And the experience calls for a testimony to it and a communication of it. "'Do not hold me,'" Jesus says to Mary, "'for I have not yet ascended to the Father; but go to my brethren and say to them, I am ascending to my Father and your Father, to my God and your God.' Mary Magdalene went and said to the disciples, 'I have seen the Lord'; and she told them that he had said things to her" (John 20:17–18). Here is the testimony of a decisive life that gives full meaning to a shared filiation, which in its turn is the basis for human fellowship. . . .

Encounter with the Lord is not restricted to the disciples, for the very nature of the event leads to communication, to witness. The former disciples of John the Baptist are fully conscious of the kind of encounter that has just taken place.

This is why they share the encounter with others, recognizing in Jesus, whom they have called Rabbi, the Messiah. That is, they recognize in him the One God has anointed to proclaim the good news of his reign. The community now beginning to take shape will be a messianic community destined to offer a specific witness in human history.

The following of Jesus is not an individual matter but a collective adventure. The journey of the people of God is set in motion by a direct encounter with the Lord, an encounter in community: "*We* have found the Messiah" (John 1:41).

BEARING WITNESS TO LIFE

Two other New Testament passages enable us to penetrate more deeply into the meaning of encounter with the Lord and the resultant following of him.

The Gospel to the Poor. Matthew and Luke, like John (1:35–42), tell us about an encounter of two disciples of John the Baptist with Jesus. . . . "Are you he who is to come, or shall we look for another?" (Matt. 11:3; cf. Luke 7:19). . . . Again as in John, Jesus' answer takes the form of concrete witness. This time he bids the disciples, not to come after him and see, but to return to John the Baptist and tell him what they have seen and heard. Jesus' works are to provide the answer to the question of his identity. They are works that match those foretold by Isaiah (61:1–2) in a passage that plays an important role in the gospels in defining the mission of the Messiah. Luke 4:16–20 makes use of the same passage in order to elicit from Jesus what has been called his "first messianic declaration."

Works done to benefit the poor and needy identify Jesus as the Messiah, the same Messiah whom (in the passage from John) the disciples claim to have met. Perhaps these disciples had witnessed such works when they accepted the invitation to live with the Rabbi. The Son of man who has no place to lay his head lives in these actions that manifest the breakthrough of the reign of God into the present age. That reign is meant first and foremost for the poor and then, through them, for every human person.

The cures of which the parallel passages in Matthew and Luke speak are an anticipation and pledge of that reign. The alleviation of the suffering of *some* of the poor in the time of Jesus is a sure promise that the good news of the reign of God is being proclaimed to *all* the poor of history. It is a proclamation through liberating words and liberating actions. The gospel is proclaimed to the poor by means of concrete deeds. When Jesus made human beings see and walk and hear and, in short, gave them life, he was giving an example for that time and a mandate to the Christian community throughout history. This is what is meant by "remembering the poor," and it is something we should be "eager to do" (Gal. 2:10). There is no authentic evangelization that is not accompanied by action on behalf of the poor.

The cures reported give full meaning to the good news for the poor that is promised in Isaiah and that becomes a reality through the messianic activity of Jesus. But this method of revealing his messiahship will not be readily understood, and this is why the passage ends in a Beatitude: "Blessed is the one who takes no offense at me."

It is in this messianic work that the Lord has his dwelling. In this work worship "in Spirit and truth" will be offered (John 4:23). Happy are they who do not take offense but instead accept the invitation to follow Jesus and live with him.

Life was Revealed. The second passage of which the meeting of the Baptist's disciples with Jesus reminds us comes from the Johannine writings and deals with the necessity of sharing with others the experience of the Lord (1 John 1:1–4). What we proclaim (says the writer) is what we have heard and seen and looked upon and touched with our hands. These are direct, unmediated experiences that are communicated in order that others too may have the joy of encountering the Lord. The gospels are full of such testimonies (Luke 2:16–17, 38; John 4:28; 20:17–18). What is revealed in this way is life. That is the content of the reign of the Father, the living God, who raises Jesus to life and thus overcomes death once and for all.

A follower of Jesus is a witness to life. This statement takes on a special meaning in Latin America where the forces of death have turned into a social system that marginalizes the poor person, the favorite in the kingdom of life. This context gives us a better understanding of what we nowadays call the spiritual life: life according to the Spirit, life lived in love. We know that in this same letter

John tells us the last word about God: "God is love" (1 John 4:8). The follower of Jesus must therefore not live in fear which, according to John, is the opposite of the love that sets us free (1 John 4:18).

Anyone who has met the Lord "has the Son" and "has life" (1 John 5:12). Witness must be borne to this.

ACKNOWLEDGING THE MESSIAH

To give witness to life implies passage through death. This experience, which marks the present Latin American situation, is an ineluctable consequence of the encounter with and acknowledgment of Jesus as the Messiah, of whom the texts of John and Matthew speak. But this is not something easy for a follower to accept (see Mark 8:27–35). . . .

The affirmation that Jesus of Nazareth is the Messiah, the Christ, is the nucleus of christological faith. The first sentence in Mark's Gospel reads: "The beginning of the gospel of Jesus Christ, the Son of God" (1:1); and John's Gospel ends: "These signs are written that you may believe that Jesus is the Christ, the Son of God, and that believing you may have life in his name" (20:31). According to Luke, this affirmation is a résumé of Peter's preaching to the Jews among the newer members of the community of believers: "Let all the house of Israel therefore know assuredly that God has made him both Lord and Christ, this Jesus whom you crucified" (Acts 2:36).

"This Jesus": indeed, to say *Jesus Christ* is to express a conviction. It is not a matter of a simple "compound name"; it is an authentic confession of faith. It is the assertion of an identity. the Jesus of history, the son of Mary, the carpenter of Nazareth, the preacher of Galilee, the one who was crucified, *is* the Anointed One of God, the Christ, the Messiah.

AN INTERROGATION

In Mark's text, the question does not come from his listeners or disciples to Jesus (as in John 1:38 and Matt. 11:3); it comes from the Lord himself (Mark 8:29). It is directed to those who have accompanied him for some time and have been witnesses of his words and deeds. The question is not, therefore, directed to persons who do not know him or who have had little contact with him. It is directed to those who have reason to know something about him because they have followed him. They are his disciples.

It is a question that looks for a profession of faith, though perhaps now the only answer it receives is an expression of doubt or perplexity. The language is direct and leaves no room for evasion. And it is not directed to one person, but to the disciples conjointly: "you" in the plural. It is a question directed to a group which in turn requires a collective answer. Profession of faith will be communal, as will also the expression of doubt or perplexity.

The interrogation presents a certain rhythm. It is made in two steps; in fact it is a double question. The *first* question is "Who do *people* say that I am?" His mission has been public; in that environment people can be expected to have—and certainly do have—an opinion about him. What is asked, then, is how the disciples receive and process that opinion, how they are affected by what people say. This is a question, then, about the faith of the disciples themselves because one aspect of our own faith is what others discover in it. Opinions about Jesus, then and now, do not rest only on what people see in *him*, but also on what they perceive in those who say they are his followers. Indeed, several chapters earlier Mark already narrated the sending of the disciples on an evangelical mission (6:6–13). The question is also, then, a way of asking, What testimony have all of you given of me?

This first question is not simply a stepping stone to the second question. It is a question in its own right, a question about the faith of his immediate interlocutors, because when we refer to what others think, we always show what we think: we accept their opinion, distance ourselves from it, or reject it.

This also can remind us that the answer to the question about Jesus is not something that belongs to us in some kind of private manner. Nor does it concern only the church. Christ is found beyond its boundaries and questions all of humanity, as Vatican II clearly reminded us. "Who do they say that I am?" is a question that, precisely because it escapes these bounds, retains its validity for the community of yesterday and today. It is important for ecclesial faith to know what others think about Jesus and about our witness as disciples. Knowing how to listen will lead us to make a better and more efficacious proclamation of our faith in the Lord vis-à-vis the world.

The text continues: "They answered him, 'John the Baptist; and others, Elijah; and still others, one of the prophets'" (8:28). Let us note in passing that the impression left by John the Baptist—a contemporary of Jesus and his disciples—must have been very strong if he was thought to still be alive. Nevertheless, it is significant that the crowds—at least according to the disciples—did not think that Jesus was the Messiah. It does not appear, then, that in the dialogue we are considering here, political messianism played a major role.

In a parallel text, Matthew adds the name of Jeremiah to that of Elijah. All the individuals mentioned are important in the religious history of the Jewish people. We are thus given an interpretation of the new (Jesus) on the basis of what is already known (persons of the past). This is a spontaneous procedure, often resorted to. And, in this case, it includes an evaluation, given the significance of the persons mentioned, although it does not evince a perception of the newness of Jesus' testimony. But it points to a fruitful path: they were all prophets. If Jesus is not sketched in all his singularity, what is implied is something freighted with consequences; Jesus is seen as standing in the prophetic line, as someone who speaks "in the name of God." Jesus in fact took great care to connect his preaching to the great prophetic perspective of Israel. But this is not enough for us to understand him.

The *second* question has more of a bite to it and goes much deeper: Who do *you* say that I am? You; not the others. As before, what is asked refers to an objective reality, something exterior to the disciples: "Who am I?" Diverse answers may be given, but they are all concerned with a single reality which is more than a matter of opinion: the person of the Lord. This removes us from our subjective world and, de-centering us, locates the reference point of our faith, and of our life, beyond ourselves, in the other.

The answer will have to have above all the seal of objectivity. But at the same time the question is directed to "you" in the plural, and its answer will be made by them and consequently will be shaped by their way of viewing Jesus. Firstly and most basically, the answer depends on what is asked; but it also depends on who is being asked. Knowing Jesus has an impact on all the aspects of our existence, and conversely all these aspects will figure in the response that we give.

The text continues with the clear confession of Peter in the name of the other apostles: "You are the Messiah" (8:29). Not simply a prophet, as the crowds thought, but the Anointed of God, the Christ, he in whom God's promises are fulfilled. Mark writes his gospel in the light of this acknowledgment which synthesizes the disciple's faith, yet insists once more: "He sternly ordered them not to tell anyone about him" (8:30).

DISCIPLESHIP AS A RESPONSE

What follows is decisive. Jesus reveals something new ("Then he began to teach them"), something which until now he had not done: his mission will be rejected by the leaders of his people (the elders, chief priests, and scribes, that is, the Sanhedrin) This rejection will lead to his death. Peter, who had just acknowledged Jesus to be the Messiah, refuses to accept the conflictual part of Jesus' mission. What shocks Peter is not necessarily failure, since Jesus speaks also of his resurrection "after three days"—though perhaps this proclamation did not at all seem clear to the disciples. What shocks Peter is the conflict and suffering that had to be endured.

Jesus' response to Peter's stance is radical: "Get behind me, Satan." The expression, *upage opiso mou*, "get behind me," could mean "take up again your post as a disciple and do not be an obstacle (Satan) in my way." The place for the disciple of Jesus is behind him, behind the Master. So interpreted, what seems a harsh reprimand is really a call to return to the path of discipleship. Thus Jesus' reprimand also expresses—although this angle of the text is not emphasized—confidence in Peter's capacity to realign himself with the followers of the Master. The disciple's refusal to accept the consequences that messiahship carries for Jesus and his followers is sharply rejected. Peter, even though he had made himself worthy of being compared to Satan, receives a call to order that includes a pardon. Jesus' reprimand even contains a note of tenderness.

We are here touching on a central point in belief in Jesus. This text has often been interpreted to mean that Peter's resistance stems from a political conception of the Messiah while here Jesus is revealing that his mission is spiritual.

There is undoubtedly a gradual clarification in this regard which takes place in the disciples (see Mark 10:35–45). But the truth of this interpretation must be placed within a broader and deeper perspective. There is in Jesus a clear rejection of the nationalist and zealot conception of the Messiah. Furthermore, Mark narrates his gospel from this perspective. But he and the other evangelists also make clear that the reasons for Jesus' confrontation with the powerful of his day are to be found in the proclamation of the good news of the Father's love for every human being, and, first of all, for the poor. This marks the character of Jesus' messiahship. What was rejected in him, and led to his death on the cross, was the very nucleus of his teaching: the kingdom of God.

Jesus' concrete form of proclaiming the gratuitous love of God and the kingdom had inevitable consequences for the religious, social, and economic order prevailing in his time. That is how those who searched for him and ordered his execution saw it (Mark 3:1–6). At bottom, the conflict and suffering that Peter feared (and which we fear too!) were provoked by the very mission. Hostility did not arise because the teaching of the Messiah was political (which it clearly was not, particularly in the strict sense of the term), but precisely because it was a religious proclamation which affected all human existence.

What prompted Peter's rejection was his reluctance to accept the consequences of acknowledging that Jesus is the Christ. Verses 34 and 35 spell out the requirements of the following of Jesus. This is what Peter balked at. It is not enough to recognize that Jesus is the Christ; it is necessary to accept all that that implies. To believe in Christ is also to take up his practice because a profession of faith without practice is incomplete, as stated in Matthew: "Not everyone who says to me 'Lord, Lord,' shall enter the kingdom of heaven, but he who does the will of my Father who is in heaven" (7:21). Orthodoxy, correct opinion, demands orthopraxis, that is, behavior in accord with the opinion expressed.

The practice of the following of Jesus will show what lies behind the recognition of the Messiah. It will show whether our thoughts are those of God or only our own (Mark 8:33)—the ideas we have of Jesus and of our discipleship. It is in our following in history—in making Jesus' path our own—that the final judgment on our faith in Christ will be made. The following of Jesus is the solid ground on which can be built a reflection on Jesus as the Christ, a Christology; otherwise it will be built on sand. In theology, as in all intellectual elaboration, critical thought is required. In this task we cannot ignore the critique that comes from practice—in this case the following of Jesus.

To the question "Who do you say that I am?" we cannot give a merely theoretical or theological answer. What answers it, in the final analysis, is our life, our insertion in history, our manner of living the gospel. Peter's affirmation, "You are the Christ," is fundamental. But what is demanded is that we make that affirmation the meaning of our life—accepting all the consequences, however hard they may be. Only in this way is our response valid, as honest and sincere as it may be without it. Our response to the question, "Who do you say that I am?" does not end with a profession of faith or a theological systemization. It is always a demanding question addressed to our life and that of the entire church. It permanently tests the Christian faith, leading it to its ultimate consequences.

The final verses of the text spell out the preconditions for following Jesus. "Taking up the cross" can be a rich metaphor, and it is often taken in that sense. But that is not its only meaning. It can also point to a cruel reality: condemnation to death on the cross. Jesus' contemporaries were well aware of this realism; they knew of crucifixions ordered and imposed on Jewish soil by the Roman occupiers. It would take place a little later for Jesus himself. The experience of martyrdom being lived in Latin America makes us see once again and with clarity the scope of this text.

The true disciple must, therefore, be prepared to confront a like situation. Such willingness is not an easy matter; we all carry within us—despite our profession of faith—Peter's reaction as an abiding possibility. It expresses itself in subtle and cunning ways. The testimony of numerous Latin American Christians manifests this difficulty, but it also makes us realize that there are more than a few who have determined to put themselves behind Jesus and follow him, paying the price of rejection, of calumny, or even of the surrender of their own lives. Those who lose their life for the Lord and the gospel will save it. The requirement posed for a disciple's following of Jesus is situated within the horizon of the Resurrection, the horizon of absolute life.

44. "I WILL NOT RESTRAIN MY TONGUE"

Drawn to the Book of Job by the enormous suffering of his own people—symbolized for him by the Andean city of Ayacucho and its agony of terrorism and counterterrorist repression in the 1980s—Gutiérrez uncovered in the Hebrew classic no "rational or definitive explanation of suffering" (On Job, 93). Yet the courage and integrity of Job made wisdom possible and led him to see that only a language that is both prophetic and mystical is adequate to the complex reality of human experience. Neither the condemnation of unjust affliction nor the contemplation of God's great goodness is complete apart from the other. In a special way the following passage, taken from the Conclusion of On Job (93–103), reveals the person of its author: in the face of injustice it is not Job alone who promises, "I will not restrain my tongue."

The movement of the Book of Job is twofold: a forward, linear movement, and a circling movement of deepening insight into the answer to the opening question: Is it possible to believe in God without expectation of reward, or "for nothing"? In an effort to answer this question the poet comes upon the doctrine of temporal retribution. This, he finds, does not take into account his own experience or the experience of so many others. He therefore looks for a correct way of talking about God within the most strained and knotty of all human situations: the suffering of the innocent.

TO SING AND TO LIBERATE

The Book of Job does not claim to have found a rational or definitive explanation of suffering; the poet is quite aware that the subject is a complex one. On the other hand, his faith prompts him to inquire into the possibility of finding an appropriate language about God that does justice to the situation of suffering. Not to make the effort is to risk succumbing to impotent resignation, a religion of calculated self-interest, a cynical outlook that forgets the suffering of others, and even despair.

Perhaps the author knew these attitudes from experience, for there are echoes of all of them in his work. But his profound sense of God and his keen sensitivity to the misfortunes of others kept him from yielding to these temptations. Despite everything, he remained resolutely disposed to look for and find a way of talking about God. He remains a deeply human and religious man who takes seriously the reality of unjust suffering and does not play down the difficulty of understanding it. His determination to seek and find—which is already a gift from the Lord—leads him through a battlefield in which, as one author puts it, the shots come at him from every side. He does not avoid them, despite the danger that they may put an end to him and his hope of finding a correct way of talking about God. His personal courage and his trust in God impel him to follow paths that are a challenge to the theology of his day. At once more traditional than those who boast of being such, and more innovative than the standards of the mediocre allow them to be, the poet of the Book of Job is guided by God's hand to discover ways of talking about God. . . .

As his experience of unjust suffering broadened, Job acquired a moving realization of the suffering of others. The ethical perspective—inspired by consideration of the needs of others and especially of the poor made him abandon a morality of rewards and punishments, and caused a reversal in his way of speaking about God. . . . After accepting adversity he rebelled and struggled with God but meanwhile kept hoping in God and, despite everything, finally surrendered to God's presence and unmerited love. But the two paths that [Job—and those who read the Book of Job—] travel should not be thought of as simply parallel; in fact, they cross and enrich each other, and finally converge to yield a correct way of talking about God.

For Job to leave his own world and enter into that of the poor already meant taking the path of gratuitousness and not simply that of concern for justice. On the other hand, all prophecy has as its starting point an encounter with the Lord and the Lord's unmerited love (see the theme of the prophetic vocation in Isa. 6; Jer. 1:4–10; Ezek. 2 and 3). The result is that two languages—the prophetic and the contemplative—are required; but they must also be combined and become increasingly integrated into a single language.

Prophetic language makes it possible to draw near to a God who has a predilection for the poor precisely because divine love refuses to be confined by the categories of human justice. God has a preferential love for the poor not because they are necessarily better than others, morally or religiously, but simply because they are poor and living in an inhuman situation that is contrary to God's will. The ultimate basis for the privileged position of the poor is not in the poor themselves but in God, in the gratuitousness and universality of God's *agapeic love*. Nothing can limit or contain this love, as Yahweh makes clear to Job in the revelation of what Yahweh has established as the fulcrum of the world. Belief in God and God's gratuitous love leads to a preferential option for the poor and to solidarity with those who suffer wretched conditions, contempt, and oppression, those whom the social order ignores and exploits. The God of utter freedom and gratuitousness who has been revealed to Job can alone explain the privileged place of those whom the powerful and the self-righteous of society treat unjustly and make outcasts. In the God of Christian revelation gratuitousness and preferential love for the poor go hand in hand; they are therefore also inseparable in our contemplation of God and our concern for the disinherited of this world.

The doctrine of retribution contained a valid principle: that to be a believer requires a certain ethical behavior. But even this idea became distorted when inserted into a narrow framework of rewards and punishments.

The language of the prophets took a different approach in emphasizing the connection between God and the poor. It acknowledged the demands of ethics but it transformed their meaning, because the fulfillment of these demands was not regarded as a form of personal insurance or as a way of gaining a hold on God. Obedience was rather a matter of freely giving what we have freely received (see Matt. 10:8).

As a result, prophetic language supports and reinforces language inspired by contemplation of God. At the very beginning of the Book of Job and at the level of popular faith we saw the proper tone to be used in speaking of the Lord's actions. But the tone weakened as Job's unjust situation was prolonged and as he listened to the criticisms of his friends. The language of mysticism restores vigor to the values of popular faith by strengthening them and enabling them to resist every attempt at manipulation. It thus prevents the distortion that turns these values into fruitless resignation and passivity in the face of injustice. But conversely the language of contemplation likewise becomes more vigorous and more community-minded to the extent that it is nourished by popular faith.

Mystical language expresses the gratuitousness of God's love; prophetic language expresses the demands this love makes. The followers of Jesus and the community they form—the church—live in the space created by this gratuitousness and these demands. Both languages are necessary and therefore inseparable; they also feed and correct each other. Jeremiah brings out the connection nicely: "Sing to the Lord; praise the Lord! For he has delivered the life of the needy from the hand of evil-doers" [20:13].

To sing and *to liberate:* thanksgiving for the liberation of the poor. Contemplation and practice, gratuitousness and justice. This is a central theme of the Bible (see Ps. 69:34–35; 109:30–31). After her people had been delivered from the Assyrian threat, Judith sang a song of thanksgiving (Jth. 16:2). The figure and theme of the suffering servant in Isaiah show numerous and very valuable points of contact with Job. In the first of the Isaian poems [Isa. 42:1–5] God presents the servant and describes his mission among the nations. . . . Anointed with the Spirit of the Lord, the servant has as his task to promote and bring forth justice (*mishpat*) on earth, to restore the full justice of God. A little further on, and in the context of the universalist vision of Second Isaiah, we are again urged to "sing a new song" to the Lord (Isa. 42:10). In this "new song" *liberation* supplies the words while *thanksgiving* provides the melody. Job likewise points to the combination of these two elements when he voices his hope that he will *see* his *go'el* (his avenger), the protector of the poor (19:25–27). The poet of the Book of Job gives the name "Yahweh" the guarantor of covenantal *justice*—to the God who "from the heart of the tempest" reveals to Job the plan of *unmerited love*.

Vision of God (final stage in Job's suit against God) and defense of the poor (a role he discovers for himself because of his own innocence) are thus combined in the experience of Job as a man of justice. They are two aspects of a single gift from the Lord and of the single road that leads to the Lord.

For the same reason, emphasis on the practice of justice and on solidarity with the poor must never become an obsession and prevent our seeing that this commitment reveals its value and ultimate meaning only within the vast and mysterious horizon of God's gratuitous love. Furthermore, the very building of a just society requires a stimulus and an enveloping atmosphere that gratuitousness alone can supply. The point here, is not to assign greater importance to the element of play and gratuitousness than to justice but to ensure that the world of justice finds its full meaning and source in the freely given love of God.

The world of unmerited love is not a place dominated by the arbitrary or the superfluous. Without the prophetic dimension the language of contemplation is in danger of having no grip on the history in which God acts and in which we meet God. Without the mystical dimension the language of prophecy can narrow its vision and weaken its perception of the God who makes all things new (Rev. 21:5). Each undergoes a distortion that isolates it and renders it inauthentic.

The journey of prophecy and the journey of contemplation are precisely that: a journey. The road must be traveled in freedom without turning from it because of its pitfalls, and without pretending ignorance of its ever new forms, for unjust human suffering continues to be heartrending and insatiable; it continually raises new questions and causes new dilemmas. It never ends; neither does protest, after the manner of Job. Although the way of talking about God has become clearer, it continues to be mysterious, as awesome and as alluring as ever.

Many difficult tasks remain to be done, many distressing questions to be answered; but an initial glimpse has been given of the path to full encounter with the loving and free God.

The language of contemplation acknowledges that everything comes from the Father's unmerited love and opens up "new horizons of hope" (Puebla §1165). The language of prophecy attacks the situation—and its structural causes—of injustice and deprivation in which the poor live, because it looks for "the suffering features of Christ the Lord" in the pain-ravaged faces of an oppressed people (Puebla §§31–39). Both languages arise, among the poor of Latin America as in Job, out of the suffering and hopes of the innocent. For poverty and unjust suffering are in fact the situation of the majority in Latin America. Our theological reflection thus starts from the experience of the cross and death as well as from the joy of the resurrection and life.

This twofold language is the language that Jesus, prefigured by Job, uses in speaking of the Father's love. The author of the Book of Job stammers out what Christ will say unhesitatingly. He starts from the experience of unjust human suffering, which Jesus in turn will share on the "two sticks" of which Gonzalo Rose speaks to us with such tenderness. The author of Job reminds us of the call for justice that issues from God the liberator. The Messiah will make that same call his own as a central element in the message of love that sums up "the ten commandments of God," which fit into our hands "like ten more fingers," to cite Gonzalo Rose once again. The author of Job directs us toward that gratuitousness of the Father's love that will be the heart of the proclamation and witness of Jesus Christ. He seeks a way; he offers himself as "the way" (John 14:6).

A CRY OF LONELINESS AND COMMUNION

Jesus speaks to us of the Father, and in his discourses language about God achieves its greatest expressiveness. The Son of God teaches us that talk of God must be mediated by the experience of the cross. He accepts abandonment and death precisely in order to reveal God to us as love. Universal love and preference for the poor distinguish the message of the divine reign that both purifies human history and transcends it. Sin, which is the refusal to accept the message, brings Jesus to his death; the cross is the result of the resistance of those who refuse to accept the unmerited and demanding gift of God's love.

The final words of Jesus—"My God, my God, why hast thou forsaken me?" (Matt. 27:46; Mark 15:34)—speak of the suffering and loneliness of one who feels abandoned by the hand of God. But when he cries out his feeling of abandonment in the opening words of Psalm 22, he also makes the rest of the psalm his own. The whole of the psalm must therefore be taken into account if we are to understand the meaning of his lament.

Psalm 22 expresses the cruel loneliness experienced by a man of deep faith. In the midst of this experience he turns to his God (vv. 1–3). But in the Bible complaint does not exclude hope; in fact, they go together. We saw this to be so in the case of Job. The confidence of the psalmist grows as he recalls that this is a God who has delivered the people of Israel from slavery and deprivation . . ., referring to the deliverance from Egypt and to Exodus 3:7. This was the experience on which biblical faith was based. All the more reason, then, for him to describe his own pitiful situation in all its bleakness. This man who laments knows that God does not regard suffering as an ideal. His complaint is filled with a longing for life (vv. 6–8, 14–17).

The person speaking in this psalm tells of his misfortune and abandonment, but he makes no reference to personal faults which would have merited such adversity. This is a case of an innocent person who has been treated unjustly. This fact makes it easier for the evangelists to apply the text to Jesus at various moments in their accounts of his death.

The psalmist sinks deeper into suffering and loneliness. His situation is due to those who harass him and mock his faith in a God who can deliver him. But he remains steadfast; he knows that his God is bent on justice, and hears and protects the poor [vv. 24, 26].

The God who could hear the cry of the Israelites when they were oppressed in Egypt does not disdain "the destitution of the destitute," the poverty of the poor and the least of human beings. Verse 26 is an allusion to Deuteronomy 14:29, which says that "the sojourner, the orphan, and the widow"—the biblical triad used in referring to the poor and helpless—shall all "eat and be filled."

This solidarity with the poor and the starving, which leads to an ongoing transformation of history and requires behavior to this end, is the fruit of the gratuitous love of the God in whom the psalmist believes and hopes. This accounts for his self-surrender and praise toward the end of the poem [vv. 22–23, 27–28].

Jesus did not compose this psalm; he inherited it. It had its origin in the suffering of a believer, perhaps someone who in some way represented his people. The important thing is that Jesus made it his own and, while nailed to the cross, offered to the Father the suffering and abandonment of all humankind. This radical communion with the suffering of human beings brought him down to the deepest level of history at the very moment when his life was ending.

But in adopting this psalm Jesus also gave expression to his hope in the liberating God who with predilection defends the poor and the dispossessed. Luke could therefore put on the lips of Jesus not the cry of abandonment but words of confident self-surrender: "Father, into thy hands I commit my spirit!" (23:46; see Ps. 31:5). He who has been "abandoned" abandons himself in turn into the hands of the Father. He confronts the forces of evil and sin when, in communion with the hopes of the human race, he asserts that life, not death, has the final say. All this is part of the redemptive experience of the cross. It is there that Jesus experiences and proclaims the resurrection and true, unending life, and becomes "the source of eternal salvation," [as] the Letter to the Hebrews presents the salvific value of Jesus' death (5:7–10).

Communion in suffering and in hope, in the abandonment of loneliness and in trusting self-surrender in death as in life: this is the message of the cross, which is "folly to those who are perishing, but to us who are being saved it is the power of God" (1 Cor. 1:18). Because it is "folly" it can pass unnoticed by those who have eyes only for wonders and manifestations of might. Paradoxically, this power of God is at the same time "weakness" (1 Cor. 1:25). It inspires the language of the cross, which is a synthesis of the prophetic and the contemplative and the only appropriate way of talking about the God of Jesus Christ.

By using this language one engages in a "dangerous remembrance" of him who was publicly crucified at the crossroads and whom the Father raised to life. This kind of talk—which the wise and understanding of this world regard as madness—calls all human beings together via the privileged choice of the weak and despised of human history (see 1 Cor. 1:26–29).

At the same time, however, if we are to use the language of the cross we must have made our own the meaning of the crucifixion. Only within the following of Jesus is it possible to talk of God. From the cross Jesus calls us to follow in his steps, "for," he tells us, "my yoke is easy, and my burden light" (Matt. 11:30). This invitation to follow him completes the passage on the revelation to the simple [Matt. 11:25–26]—the message of the gratuitousness of God's love. It is in the context of gratuitousness that the way of the cross to which Jesus invites us must be set.

All these considerations do not eliminate the element of protest from the final words of Jesus; they are rather an attempt to situate it properly. Even in his lament Jesus "spoke well of God." His cry on the cross renders more audible and more penetrating the cries of all the Jobs, individual and collective, of human history. To adopt a comparison that Bonhoeffer uses in another context, the cry of Jesus is the *cantus firmus*, the leading voice to which all the voices of those who suffer unjustly are joined.

"I WILL NOT RESTRAIN MY TONGUE"

This cry cannot be silenced. Those who suffer unjustly have a right to complain and protest. Their cry expresses both their bewilderment and their faith. It is not possible to do theology in Latin America without taking into account the situation of the most downtrodden of history; this means in turn that at some point the theologian must cry out, as Jesus did, "My God, my God, why hast thou forsaken me?"

This kind of communion in suffering demands watchfulness and solidarity. "Jesus will be in agony until the end of the world. There must be no sleeping during that time. Commitment to the alleviation of human suffering, and especially to the removal of its causes as far as possible, is an obligation for the followers of Jesus, who took upon himself his own "easy yoke and light burden." Such a commitment presupposes genuine human compassion, as well as a measure of understanding of human history and the factors that condition it (consider the effort made in the documents of Medellín and Puebla to understand

317

the causes of the present situation of injustice in which Latin America is living). It also requires a firm and stubborn determination to be present, regardless of the consequences, wherever the unjust abuse the innocent.

Human suffering, whatever its causes—social, personal, or other—is a major question for theological reflection. J. B. Metz has, with refined human and historical sensitivity, called the attention of contemporary theologians, those of Europe in particular, to what it means to talk about God after Auschwitz. For the terrible holocaust of millions of Jews is an inescapable challenge to the Christian conscience and an unappealable reproach to the silence of many Christians in the face of that dreadful event. We must therefore ask: How can we talk about God without referring to our own age? More than that: How can we do it without taking into account situations like the holocaust in which God seems to be absent from immense human suffering?

It needs to be realized, however, that for us Latin Americans the question is not precisely "How are we to do theology after Auschwitz?" The reason is that in Latin America we are still experiencing every day the violation of human rights, murder, and the torture that we find so blameworthy in the Jewish holocaust of World War II. Our task here is to find the words with which to talk about God in the midst of the starvation of millions, the humiliation of races regarded as inferior, discrimination against women, especially women who are poor, systematic social injustice, a persistent high rate of infant mortality, those who simply "disappear" or are deprived of their freedom, the sufferings of peoples who are struggling for their right to live, the exiles and the refugees, terrorism of every kind, and the corpse-filled common graves of Ayacucho [a scene of civil strife in Peru]. What we must deal with is not the past but, unfortunately, a cruel present and a dark tunnel with no apparent end.

In Peru, therefore—but the question is perhaps symbolic of all Latin America—we must ask: How are we to do theology *while Ayacucho lasts*? How are we to speak of the God of life when cruel murder on a massive scale goes on in "the corner of the dead" [the meaning of the word "Ayacucho" in Quechua, language of the indigenous people of the region and of the Inca empire]? How are we to preach the love of God amid such profound contempt for human life? How are we to proclaim the resurrection of the Lord where death reigns, and especially the death of children, women, the poor, indigenes, and the "unimportant" members of our society?

These are our questions, and this is our challenge. Job shows us a way with his vigorous protest, his discovery of concrete commitment to the poor and all who suffer unjustly, his facing up to God, and his acknowledgment of the gratuitousness that characterizes God's plan for human history. It is for us to find our own route amid the present sufferings and hopes of the poor of Latin America, to analyze its course with the requisite historical effectiveness, and, above all, to compare it anew with the Word of God. This is what has been done by those, for example, who in recent years have been murdered for their witness of faith and solidarity with the poorest and most helpless, those now known as "the Latin American martyrs."

"That is why I cannot keep quiet: in my anguish of spirit I shall speak, in my bitterness of soul I shall complain" (Job 7:11). Nor can the poor and oppressed of Latin America remain silent. For them "day comes like a lamentation arising from the depths of the heart." What the poor and oppressed have to say may sound harsh and unpleasant to some. It is possible that they may be scandalized at hearing a frank avowal of the human and religious experience of the poor, and at seeing their clumsy attempts to relate their lives to the God in whom they have such deep faith. Perhaps those who live, and try to express, their faith and hope amid unjust suffering will some day have to say humbly, with Job, "I spoke without understanding marvels that are beyond my grasp," and put aside their harsh language. Yet who knows but that the Lord may tell them, to the surprise of some: "You have spoken correctly about me."

The prophet Isaiah announces that "the Lord God will wipe away tears from all faces, and the reproach of his people he will take away from all the earth" (25:8). Woe to those whom the Lord finds dry-eyed because they could not bring themselves to solidarity with the poor and suffering of this world! If we are to receive from God the tender consolation promised by the prophet, we must make our own the needs of the oppressed; our hearts must be moved at seeing a wounded person by the wayside, be attuned to the sufferings of others, and be more sensitive to persons in conflict and confusion than to "the order of the day."

Only if we know how to be silent and involve ourselves in the suffering of the poor will we be able to speak out of their hope. Only if we take seriously the suffering of the innocent and live the mystery of the cross amid that suffering, but in the light of Easter, can we prevent our theology from being "empty words" (Job 16:3). But if we do, then we shall not deserve to hear from the poor the reproach that Job threw in the faces of his friends: "What sorry comforters you are!" (16:2).

In sending his Son, the Father "wagered" on the possibility of a faith and behavior characterized by gratuitousness and by a response to the demand that justice be established. When history's "losers"—persons like Job—follow in the steps of Jesus, they are seeing to it that the Lord wins his wager. The risks accepted in talking about God with the suffering of the innocent in view are great. But, again like Job, we cannot keep quiet; we must humbly allow the cry of Jesus on the cross to echo through history and nourish our theological efforts. As St. Gregory the Great says in his commentary on Job, the cry of Jesus will not be heard "if our tongues keep silent about what our souls believe. But lest his cry be stifled in us, let each of us make known to those who approach him the mystery by which he lives!"

This mystery is the one proclaimed by the dead and risen Son of God. It is the mystery that we come to know when his Spirit impels us to say "Abba! Father!" (Gal. 4:6).

45. JOHN OF THE CROSS: A LATIN AMERICAN VIEW

In 1991 Gutiérrez was invited to address the Congreso Internacional Sanjuanista (the International St. John of the Cross Congress) in Avila, Spain, on the four-hundredth anniversary of the birth of John of the Cross. There can be no doubt that spirituality has always been at the center of Gutiérrez's concerns as a Christian believer, pastor, and as a professional theologian. Furthermore, in We Drink from Our Own Wells *(1983) Gutiérrez had demonstrated his keen interest in John of the Cross. Yet on this occasion he felt the need to make crystal clear the reasons why the sixteenth-century Spanish saint's "Ascent of Mount Carmel" with its "dark nights, purifications, and betrothals with God" is not alien to the struggle against extreme poverty and injustice in Latin America today. Indeed, as Gutiérrez shows, it is through his "titanic effort" to understand the heart of Christian revelation that John of the Cross "questions"—and thus "helps"—those in Latin America who would be followers of Jesus Christ today.*

Gutiérrez's address "Juan de la Cruz desde América Latina" was published in Páginas *116 (1992): 27–38 and is here published in English translation (by the present editor) for the first time.*

Before trying to express the reason for my interest in a person like John of the Cross, it seems right to present, from the beginning, the difficulty—apparent or real—that arises for one who has had the experience as a citizen and as a Christian of a reality like that of Latin America. I come from a continent in which more than 60 percent of the population lives in a situation which experts call "poverty" or "extreme poverty" or destitution. This means that persons do not manage to satisfy their basic needs and, in the case of the destitute, lack the most elemental things. I come from a continent where in the past twenty years more than 100 sisters, brothers, priests, and bishops have been assassinated and where hundreds of common people, catechists, and members of Christian communities have also been assassinated.

FROM LATIN AMERICA

I come from a country in which about 60 percent (more than the average in Latin America) of the population finds itself in a situation of poverty (13 million people in a population of 22 million) and 25 percent (or 5 million people) live in extreme poverty. A country where 120 of every 1000 children die before reaching five years of age; a country where two of every 1000 people suffer from tuberculosis, a disease which has already been eliminated by medicine; a country where cholera has this year affected 300,000 people, of whom 3000 have died. This disease is a disease of the poor because it is caused by a very fragile virus which dies at a temperature of 60 degrees. But the poor suffer from it because they lack the economic means to boil water or to prepare food in sanitary conditions. I come from a country in which approximately 25,000 people have died as victims of different kinds of violence and where eight priests and religious have been assassinated, three of them in recent weeks. They all worked in poor regions of my country.

I am one of those Christians who in Latin America believe that poverty is contrary to the will of God. We believe that solidarity with the poor person and the fight for justice are unavoidable Christian demands. For this reason I am one of those Christians who are frequently asked about our fidelity to the church and about our orthodoxy or heterodoxy. We are asked—with suspicion—where our place is in this church in which we were born, with which we receive communion, and from which we try to understand the situation of our continent.

Given these realities and these difficulties, of what interest could the saint of the "Ascent of Mount Carmel" be to us? Do not the dark nights, the purifications, the betrothals with God seem very far from daily life? This saint for whom themes such as social justice seem foreign, who never commented on nor even cited Luke 4:16 or Matthew 25:31 —of what interest can he be for us? These are important texts in the lived experience of Christians in Latin America and in my own reflections. How can we be drawn to this great Christian whom we may admire but who seems far from our concerns?

HOW TO SAY THAT GOD LOVES US?

It would be tempting and fun to play what-might-have-been. For example, we might imagine John of the Cross in Mexico (where he was supposed to go, sent into a kind of exile) living his faith on a continent which in previous decades had lost perhaps 80 percent of its population. But circumstances determined that John of the Cross would go to what he delightfully called the "Minor Indies," to an encounter with the Father. It would be tempting also, and a bit more serious, to recall his familiarity with poverty as a religious and the persecution he suffered due to his concern for reform. Perhaps along this path we could find a bridge which links us to him. We could also poke through his writings and find texts such as the one in which he condemns the satisfied who are repulsed by the poor—which, says the saint, is contrary to the will of God.

But I honestly do not believe that the main reason John of the Cross is of interest to the present reality of Latin America is to be found in such approaches. I think that we need to look for it elsewhere, not because what I have said is not important but because it is not exactly for these reasons that his witness and work are relevant for us.

There are persons who are universal due to the extent of their knowledge, their direct influence on their times, or the diversity and number of their disciples. Erasmus might be an example of this type of universality in the sixteenth century. But there are also those who are universal because of the intensity of their lives and their thought. More than traversing the world with their ideas, they go to the very center of it and thus find themselves equidistant from everything that happens on the surface. John of the Cross is one of them, universal because of his singularity—of a concrete universality, Hegel would say. If this is the case, if John of the Cross is a universal man for these reasons, he would not be alien to what is happening in Latin America today. And he is not.

On our continent we pose for ourselves a lacerating question: How to say to the poor person, to the oppressed person, to the insignificant person—God loves you? Indeed, the daily life of the poor seems to be the result of the denial of love. The absence of love is, in the final analysis of faith, the cause of social injustice. The question of how to tell the poor person "God loves you" is much greater than our capacity to answer it. Its breadth, to use a phrase very dear to John of the Cross, makes our answers very small. But the question is there, unavoidable, demanding, challenging. Is not the work of John of the Cross a titanic effort to tell us that God loves us? Is our interest (as Latin Americans) in his witness and work not to be found right there, in the very heart of Christian revelation? Was John of the Cross not someone who made an immense effort to tell us that when everything is over, our "care" will remain "forgotten among white lilies"? Our concern about how to tell the poor person that God is love?

AN EXPERIENCE OF FAITH

I will try to point out several features of his writings which question us and help us and thus why we read them. However, before entering into these matters I want to say that we Christians in Latin America are convinced that what is at stake in our people's efforts to achieve an all-encompassing and complex, multi-faceted liberation is our way of being Christians, our very faith, our hope, and our love. We have always had the conviction that this commitment is not to be limited to the field of social justice, though this is of primary importance, but that we do not see a different way of being followers of the Lord, of being disciples of Jesus. Our being Christian is at stake: here John of the Cross reappears, and powerfully, because for him too what is at stake is a way of being Christian. In Latin America we try to live what we call—using a formula which today has become universal—the option for the poor, the preferential option for the poor person, as a spiritual experience, that is, as an experience of the Lord. This is very clear in the Christian communities throughout the continent. In this spiritual experience, how—in what way and for what reasons—does the witness of John of the Cross become relevant and important for us? I will present five points, among others, in an attempt to answer this question.

1. Gratuitousness. Something profoundly biblical appears in his witness and work: the gratuitousness of God's love. Now there is nothing more demanding than gratuitousness. Duty has a ceiling, it goes up to a certain point and is satisfied when an obligation is fulfilled. This is not the case with the gratuitousness of love because love has no border. When Paul tells Philemon (in a letter widely overlooked by Christians) "I know that you will do more than I ask you," it is a suggestion completely open to permanent creativity. There is nothing which is more demanding than gratuitous love. John of the Cross has reminded us that to be a believer is to think that God is enough. The night of the senses and the spiritual night ought to strip us, and finally liberate us, from idolatries. In the Bible idolatry is a danger to every believer. Idolatry means trusting in something or someone other than God, giving our lives over to what we have made with our own hands. We frequently offer victims to such an idol, which is why the prophets link idolatry and murder so often.

Saint John of the Cross helps us to discover a faith which does not rest on idols, on mediations. This is why the biblical figure Job is so important to him. It is not strange that he would call Job a prophet. He is right; Job was a prophet. A study of the vocabulary of the Book of Job places him closer to the prophetic books than to the wisdom books. . . .

We in Latin America are also convinced—and John of the Cross helps us to understand this—that in the liberation process we are capable of creating our own idols for ourselves. For example, the idol of justice: it might seem strange to say this but justice can become an idol it is not placed in the context of gratuity, if there is no real friendship with the poor person nor daily commitment with him or her. Gratuity is the framework for justice and gives it meaning in history. Social justice, no matter how important it is—and it is—can also be an idol and we have to purify ourselves of this to affirm very clearly that only God suffices and to give justice itself the fullness of its meaning.

In the same way the poor person to whom we wish to commit ourselves and with whom we wish to live in solidarity can become an idol. An example of this is the idealization of the poor person by some in Latin America as if they had to demonstrate to themselves and to others that every poor person is good, generous, religious, and for that reason we have to be committed to him or her. . . . I would also like to make clear—because I say this with great conviction—that another idol can be our own theology, the theology we are trying to formulate in Latin America beginning with the reality of suffering and of hope found in our people. . . . Once again, with the scalpel of his experience and poetry, John of the Cross eliminates what is infected, what blurs our vision of God. Furthermore, in one of his texts, John of the Cross reminds us of a fundamental biblical datum: our love for God grows to the degree that our love of neighbor grows. And vice versa.

To finish this point, which I consider the most important, I would like to read a very brief verse by a Spanish priest assassinated in Bolivia, Luis Espinal: "Lord of the night and of the void, we yearned to know how to sink softly into your impalpable lap confidently, with the security of children." This is what we mean by liberation process. I have always thought this.

2. The journey. This is a particularly expressive and telling theme in John of the Cross. It takes up a fertile biblical image. A journey presupposes time and history, and this time and this history have a very peculiar meaning in John of the Cross, so much so that they can pass unseen. In his work there is movement, displacement, advance, yet there he is, in the same place. There is great mobility and a very profound sense of history or of time and simultaneously a fixation on God. . . . In Deuteronomy we have an explanation for an apparently banal question which Christians sometimes do not ask themselves but which was important to the Jews: why did the Jewish people take forty years to cross the desert from Egypt to Palestine? Even crawling on your knees it would not take forty years. . . .

In Deuteronomy the explanation has to do with a twofold knowledge: so that the people can come to know God and God (anthropomorphically speaking) can come to know the people. This explains the long crossing. And this, it seems to me, is what we also find in John of the Cross. On the journey there is a twofold knowing. As he says, we leave in order to arrive; we don't leave in order to journey, but we journey in order to arrive. We leave one place in order to get to another. This knowledge comes in a dialogue with God.

We in Latin America are seeking to understand the liberation process as a journey not only to social freedom (which is very important) but equally and above all toward full friendship with God and among ourselves. This is, once again, what we understand by the formula "preferential option for the poor." This is the journey and we believe that it implies time. . . . In the final analysis, the option for the poor is a theocentric option, a life centered on God—just as John of the Cross desired.

3. Freedom. The famous phrase, "There is no way through here," does not denote the easiest stretch of the ascent but the most difficult. Up to this point it was possible to follow a marked path; from this point one must continue creatively and with steadiness. John of the Cross lived out this freedom when he chose to be a discalced Carmelite, when he refused to give in to pressures to renounce that condition, when he escaped from prison. We can call it freedom, but there is another way to name this attitude: stubbornness. John was pigheaded—like all saints (which does not mean that all hard-headed people are saints). It is a spiritual attitude: "Where the Spirit is there is freedom," according to the famous phrase of Saint Paul.

In Latin America we understand freedom as the goal of liberation; liberation is not our end but a process, the journey and not the point of arrival. We have also experienced during this time that this journey toward freedom is not something marked out beforehand. . . . "Free to love" is a formula we frequently use to speak of our way of understanding what it means to be a Christian. . . . This is the freedom which matters to us and that is why John of the Cross, like every spiritual person, is a free man and thus is often so dangerous. That is how many of his contemporaries saw him. That is how many Christians in Latin America are seen.

4. Joy. Saint John of the Cross spoke of joy. It is very present in the songs, in the Spiritual Canticle, where the image of the love of a human couple—a profound experience of joy—allows him to speak of the joy of the encounter with the Lord. At the same time this is a joy lived out in the midst of difficulty, ascending the slope of a mountain in the midst of suffering. I do not know (though there are outstanding scholars here who could comment on this with a competence that I do not have). But I think that the experience of poverty of John of Yepes, the fact of having been poor, must have marked him with a profound feeling of pain. Indeed, the experience of the poor person is that of being insignificant and marginal. To have seen his mother begging, to have begged for alms himself, are very profound experiences. Our contact today with the poor makes us see that their lives remain marked not by sadness but by a profound pain. And this is why they appreciate more than others the reasons for being happy. Perhaps his experience of prison, in which he even feared losing his life, is part of this suffering. His joy therefore is, to put it in Christian terms, paschal, an overcoming of suffering, a passage to joy. I would say that at present in Latin America there is no way to be close to the poor without entering into communion with their pain and with their reasons for joy. As Christians we feel loved by God, the fundamental reason for our joy.

But as I said a moment ago, suffering does not necessarily signify sadness. . . . Sadness is the turning in on oneself which is located on the border of bitterness; suffering, on the contrary, can create in us a space of solitude, a space for gaining personal depth. Solitude is another important theme in John of the Cross, solitude as the condition of an authentic communion. After all, Jesus' cry "My God, why have you abandoned me?" was shouted forth on the eve of the greatest communion in history, that of the resurrection, that of the life that conquers death. Solitude is, then, a requirement for communion.

5. Language. John of the Cross affirms that he is trying to approach the themes mentioned here by beginning with experience, science, and equally—as he nicely puts it—by "cuddling up with Scripture." The result is poetry in verse or in prose. And poetry is doubtless the greatest human gift a person can receive. How can we speak of love without poetry? Love is the thing that has always given rise to poetry. From this continent marked by unjust and premature death, we also think that experience is the necessary condition to be able to speak about God and to say to the poor person: God loves you. Experience of the mystery of God.

I have always admired those philosophers and theologians who speak about what God thinks and wants as if they had breakfast with God every day. John of the Cross reminds us, however, that this is impossible, that we can only speak of God and the love of God with great respect, aware of what his master Thomas Aquinas said: "What we don't know about God is much greater than what we know." Without being about to understand things well but convinced that he must love, the Peruvian poet and a dear friend Gonzalo Rose said, "Why should I have loved the rose and justice? Yet this is what we are called to do in Latin America: to love justice and beauty. God is the source of both. Our language about God, that is, our theology, must take both of these aspects into account."

I began by saying that I come from a continent marked by death, but I also want to say that I come from a continent in which a people is undergoing an exceedingly profound experience of life. This is expressed when people organize so that their most elementary rights will be respected; it is also expressed in their rich religious life. From this experience the poor of our continent—without using the word "mystical"—express a profound sense of God. This lived experience does not contradict their poverty or their suffering. And I want to tell you that I come from a continent (this may sound excessively optimistic) where there is great holiness and generous and anonymous self-giving. There are many people who live in extremely difficult areas, who risk their physical life between the two kinds of gunfire that today kill people in my country—hunger and cruel, brutal terrorism.

Just a year ago today they killed Sister of the Good Shepherd, María Agustina Rivas, called "Aguchita," a 70-year old woman. A little before going to work in the place where she was assassinated, which was jokingly called "Florida," this woman wrote a letter in which she said, "I want to go work with the poor of Florida because I do not want to present myself to the Lord with empty hands." If she presented herself with full hands, it is because she humbly believed that they were empty.

Finally, I would like to say that there is something which is being lived out today with great intensity in Latin America: the value of life. Ignacio Ellacuría often said, "Here in El Salvador life is worthless." He was wrong; his own example gives the lie to his affirmation. The life of Salvadorans had to be worth a lot to him to make him and his companions remain in El Salvador. These were people of great intellectual gifts and at the same time committed to that country to the point of risking their lives. The lives of Salvadorans had to be worth a lot in order for them to do this.

We are more and more convinced that death is not the last word of history; life is. This is why Christian celebrations always mock death: "Death, where is your victory?" Every feast is an Easter. Perhaps this is why in the Hispanic tradition we call all the feasts "easter" (*pascua*). We are the only people in the world who say "Happy Easter" ("*Felices pascuas*") at Christmas—and at Epiphany. (Pentecost used to be an "Easter" too.) Every Christian feast is an easter, a passover, because we celebrate the defeat of death.

Let me conclude in what is perhaps not an academic way. I would like to ask you to keep in your prayers and your thoughts this people which resists accepting early and unjust death. We Christians must say, with that great Spaniard Bartolomé de Las Casas, "of the smallest and most forgotten God has a very fresh and living memory." This fresh and living memory permits them to keep their hopes high. I ask you to keep in mind those of my continent who can say with that great Peruvian poet César Vallejo, "I have nothing but death with which to express my life." This is the situation of many Christians, and this is why John of the Cross—he of the nights, he of the solitude, he of the journey, he of the encounter with God—is not foreign to us. Thank you.

46. PASTOR AND WITNESS

For Gutiérrez, discipleship and friendship have often converged as numerous remembrances written to honor deceased mentors, colleagues, friends, and fellow Christians testify. On March 24, 1995, the fifteenth anniversary of the assassination of Archbishop Oscar Romero of El Salvador, Gutiérrez preached the homily during a memorial mass for Latin America's best-known martyr in the chapel of the Universidad Centroamericana there. Speaking for himself, he acknowledged the grief and proclaimed the hope felt by all who love "a people which does not stop fighting for its life." The text of his remarks was published in Páginas *133 (1995), 78–80. The following English translation is by the present editor.*

We have been assembled this afternoon by the physical absence of someone whose presence has flooded hearts and minds the length and width of this continent—and beyond. Someone who knew how to give life generously, someone who was the pastor of this diocese and whose death and resurrection have converted him into a pastor of the universal church, has called us together.

We have just heard the text of the Gospel of John, in which Jesus presents himself as a shepherd, the Good Shepherd (John 10:1–18). This image, as so often occurs in the Gospels, is a rural image which is taken from Jesus' world. Those who heard these words immediately understood the central idea: the shepherd cares for his sheep and gives his life for them. Like Monseñor Romero whose life was not taken from him but who gave it up. And this extraordinary freedom is precisely what marks us today.

Solitary, and in solidarity, Monseñor Romero moved toward death. Solitary—not because his friends were not near or did not express their affection and friendship, but because in the face of death we are always, in some way, alone. We are surrounded by affection but we know that in the final analysis a personal decision is being made. This is why I say that he moved toward death alone but also in solidarity. He would not have taken one step in this surrender of his life if it had not been for his solidarity with others. This is because other people mattered to him, those of his own sheepfold, those of his own "classroom" (as the gospel says), and beyond—those of other sheepfolds and other classrooms—he was in solidarity with all of them too. This made him sure-footed, but not because he *sought* martyrdom. To seek martyrdom is not Christian—it would mean that we want there to be executioners. As Christians, we cannot wish for the existence of assassins. Martyrdom is not sought; it is found.

Jesus himself did not want them to kill him, but he was convinced that his preaching—the proclamation of God's reign, universal love, and preference for the poorest (the love for God's sheep)—challenged the powerful of the day. As in the last part of Monseñor Romero's sermon which we have just heard, in which he directed his attention to the conscience of each soldier, that is, to the people at the bottom of the military, and made them see that conscience is above any order that might be received. One who dares to do something like this knows what awaits him. He knew it and feared it, as any human being would. Yet he surrendered his life. Monseñor Romero said, as we well remember, "If they kill me, I will rise again with my people." If we are here this afternoon, it is because we truly believe that he has risen with Jesus. And we could almost say that he is more and more alive. If on March 24, 1980, his death was bad news, his life will continue being good news. The years he lived among us, the message he left us—his word, always alive and attentive to what was happening daily: "we cannot segregate," to quote him almost verbatim, "the Word of God from the present of a people"—all this makes us see that neither can we separate his witness to life from the Salvadoran people.

In doing so, Monseñor reminded us of what is, in fact, the good news. His martyrdom and that of his friends and Jesuit brothers of this house and that of so many others—a long list in this country and a long list in Latin America, too—also remind us of the good news: the good news of God's love. A martyr, as we all know, wishes to be a witness, and a witness is someone who sees something and testifies to it, communicates it, shares it. And what these martyr-friends of ours shared is the love of God. This is what they were witnesses to. That is why, despite the terrible theme of unjust and murderous death in which our people still find themselves—a crucified people as Ignacio Ellacuría liked to call them—in spite of this, we are here to give thanks. In this Eucharist we remember a death, but we also know that for a Christian—and Romero and so many others told us so with utter clarity—death is not the last word of human existence. Life is.

We are here because we celebrate life. If we are in this chapel and under this roof, it is because someone once told us, "Christ is risen!" This is why we are here: we believed it and we became Christians. The martyrs remind us of this resurrection and thus remind us of the center of our faith and hope. For a people like ours, the people of Latin America, it is important to remind them and repeat to them—always *alongside* them—that death does not put an end to their hopes and joys, that life is the heart of the Christian message. We are here in this

Eucharist to give thanks for Romero and for so many others who have risen with Jesus and who will continue to do so.

As a thanksgiving, the Eucharist is always a moment of joy. It seems strange to speak of joy when we are alluding to blood, unjust death, and murderous bullets. Yet that is what we are doing. Beyond the pain, beyond death, stands the affirmation of the lives of those we have mentioned and of many others. It is because of their lives, and because they are still alive, that we give thanks, and no one is going to stop us from doing so—no one. They will be able to silence voices but they will not be able—and here I am thinking of Monseñor Romero's words—"to make the voice of hope and joy be still." True, it is a paschal joy which passes through death.

The resurrection of Jesus is never called a miracle in the Bible. It is too much for that. The resurrection of Jesus, if you will allow me to express it this way, is the death of death. This is what we are celebrating this afternoon: the death of Monseñor Romero's death, the death of so many others' deaths, the victory of life. Filled with anguish we certainly are and our hearts are oppressed, yet we breathe deeply, in a communion of hope with a people which does not stop fighting for its life. We are here to give thanks to the God of life: this is what calls us together this afternoon.

NOTES TO THE INTRODUCTION

1. Gustavo Gutiérrez, *The God of Life* (Maryknoll, N.Y.: Orbis, 1991), 165.

2. Much of the biographical information in this section is drawn from interviews given by Gutiérrez. See also Mario Campos, "Gustavo Gutiérrez: Defender la vida es subversivo," in *La República* (20 April 1984), 13–21; Mev Puleo, "An Interview with Gustavo Gutiérrez," in *St. Anthony Messenger* (February 1989), 8–16.

3. See Marc Ellis and Otto Maduro, eds., *The Future of Liberation Theology: Essays in Honor of Gustavo Gutiérrez* (Maryknoll, N.Y.: Orbis, 1989) for evidence of his worldwide significance.

4 Gustavo Gutiérrez, *The Power of the Poor in History* (Maryknoll, N.Y.: Orbis), 191.

5. The notes of this course were edited and published three years later as an essay, "Pobreza evangélica: solidaridad y protesta" (Lima: CEP, 1970).

6. The text of his talk "Toward a Theology of Liberation" is included in chapter 1 of this volume. In North America James H. Cone published *A Black Theology of Liberation* in 1970. In 1970 the Brazilian Rubém Alves published *Teología de la liberacion: una evaluación prospectiva* in Montevideo, though in fact the book proposes a "theology of revolution."

7. Interview with present editor, 14 July 1995.

8. This may easily be verified by consulting the footnotes in any of his works.

9. See, for example, *On Job: God-Talk and the Suffering of the Innocent* (Maryknoll, N.Y.: Orbis, 1987); *The God of Life*; and "God's Revelation and Proclamation in History" (more accurately translated "The Revelation and Proclamation of God in History") (1975) in *Power of the Poor*, 3–22. See also the lengthy "Index of Biblical References" in *Theology of Liberation*, 257–60, for the range of scriptural study in his classic work as well as the "Index of Scriptural References" in Gustavo Gutiérrez, *We Drink from Our Own Wells: The Spiritual Journey of a People* (Maryknoll, N.Y.: Orbis, 1984). See also Jeffrey S. Siker's study, "Uses of the Bible in the Theology of Gustavo Gutiérrez: Liberating Scriptures of the Poor," *Biblical Interpretation* 4 (1996): 40–71. Teaching at Lyon were Jean Duplacy, Albert Gelin, A. George, Emmanuel Podechard, and Léon Vaganay.

10. These were a regular feature of *Signos*, published by the Instituto Bartolomé de Las Casas-Rímac, Lima, in the 1980s and covered the three-year cycle of readings in the Catholic lectionary. A collection of these biblical reflections was published in 1995. See *Compartir la palabra a lo largo del año litúrgico* (Lima: Instituto Bartolomé de las Casas–Rímac and CEP). An English translation (*Sharing the Word*) is due from Orbis in 1997.

11. In its first 25 years the "summer course" took an aspect of Scripture or a single book of the Bible as its central theme on numerous occasions and has never failed to include Scripture in some way. Outlines and notes of nearly all the lectures and study sessions from the "summer course" are available at the Pontificia Universidad Católica del Perú, Lima. Tape recordings are also available of some of them

12. Gustavo Gutiérrez, "La teología: una función eclesial" *Páginas* 130 (1994), 11. See "Theology: An Ecclesial Function" below (text no. 38).

13. *God of Life*, xvii.

14. See Gustavo Gutiérrez, *The Truth Shall Make You Free: Confrontations* (Maryknoll, N.Y.: Orbis, 1990), 88, 97, 105, 116, and 141; also Siker, 39.

15. *Truth*, 88.

16. *Power of the Poor*, 4.

17. *God of Life*, xv.

18. Ibid., xvi.

19. *Theology of Liberation*, 9. He has never changed his mind: "[theology is] a vocation which is sustained and exercised in the bosom of the ecclesial community." See "La teología: una función eclesial," 10.

20. See *Power of the Poor*, 111–24.

21. See, e.g., the encyclical letters of John Paul II, *Laborem exercens* (1981), no. 8, and *Sollicitudo rei socialis* (1987), nos. 42–43, *Centesimus annus* (1993), no. 57, and his letter to the bishops of Brazil (1986) published in *Origins* 16/1 (May 22, 1986):13. For its part the Sacred Congregation for the Doctrine of the Faith affirms the preferential option in the introduction to *Libertatis nuntius* (1984) as well as in VI–5, IX–9, and XI–18, and in *Libertatis conscientia* (1986), nos. 46–50, and 66–70. The bishops of the United States take note of the option in their pastoral letter *Economic Justice for All*, no. 87. The bishops of Peru assert it in their message "Liberation and the Gospel," no. 83, published in *Origins* 14, no. 31 (January 17, 1985):509–15.

22. For Gutiérrez, to do theology is to write "a love letter to God, to the church, and to the people to which I belong." *Theology of Liberation*, xlvi.

23. See, for example, Gustavo Gutiérrez, *Las Casas: In Search of the Poor of Jesus Christ* (Maryknoll, N.Y.: Orbis, 1993), 6–8, 117–18, 270.

24. *Truth*, 102. In this position Gutiérrez is in agreement with *Libertatis conscientia*, 70. It is important to note that he does not claim that history can serve as the ultimate theological norm. Rather, as he wrote in 1973, "The great hermeneutical principle of the faith, and hence the basis and foundation of all theological reasoning, is Jesus Christ." *Power of the Poor*, 61.

25. *Truth*, 101. He explicitly excludes "the primacy of praxis [over faith]: praxis that gives rise to truth or becomes the fundamental criterion of truth." See *Truth*, 181, note 45.

26. *Truth*, 103–104.

27. *Power*, 61; repeated in *Truth*, 105.

28. *Truth*, 105.

29. See Roger Haight, S.J., *An Alternative Vision: An Interpretation of Liberation Theology* (New York: Paulist, 1985), for an excellent treatment of this point.

30. See Ellis and Maduro, *The Future of Liberation Theology*, for testimonials to the significance of his life, work, and thought (as of 1988).

31. See Gustavo Gutiérrez, "Expanding the View," the lengthy essay he wrote in 1988 to evaluate the growth of liberation theology during the previous twenty years and to assess the current state of the question. The essay serves as the Introduction to the revised edition of *Theology of Liberation*. See pages xix–xx, xxiii, xxxi, xxxvi.

32. The degree to which Gutiérrez has today succeeded in gaining a hearing in the worldwide theological conversation may be gauged by the fact that few serious theologians after 1975 have failed to take account of his work, either directly or indirectly.

33. *Theology of Liberation*, xxxviii.

34. Ibid., 138–39.

35. Ibid., 87.

36. For accounts of such shifts in consciousness among Latin Americans, see Rigoberta Menchú, *I, Rigoberta Menchú: An Indian Woman in Guatemala* (London: Verso, 1984); Paolo Freire, *Pedagogy of the Oppressed* (New York: Continuum, 1970); and Ernesto Cardenal, *The Gospel in Solentiname*, 4 vols. (Maryknoll, N.Y.: Orbis, 1976). For examples of such a shift among North Americans, see Martin Luther King, Jr., *Stride toward Freedom: The Montgomery Story* (San Francisco: Harper and Row, 1958; and Renny Golden and Michael McConnell, *Sanctuary: The New Underground Railroad* (Maryknoll, N.Y.: Orbis, 1986).

37. For the biblical basis of Gutiérrez's interpretation of the popular movement, see *God of Life*, 182–86.

38. *Truth*, 111.

39. See Karl Rahner, *Foundations of Christian Faith: An Introduction to the Idea of Christianity* (New York: Crossroad, 1984), 79.

40. See Gustavo Gutiérrez, "The Irruption of the Poor in Latin America and the Christian Communities of the Common People," chapter 10 in Sergio Torres and John Eagleson, eds., *The Challenge of Basic Christian Communities* (Maryknoll, N.Y.: Orbis, 1981), 118 (emphasis added).

41. See *Theology of Liberation*, 123–30; *Truth*, 7, 51–52, 106–16; and his 1979 essay "The Limitations of Modern Theology: On a Letter of Dietrich Bonhoeffer" in *Power of the Poor*, 222–34.

42. *Truth*, 7, 51, 106–16.

43. This view is, not surprisingly, disputed by some Europeans but accepted by others. See the responses of Metz, Moltmann, Schillebeeckx, and Christian Duquoc to the work of Gutiérrez.

44. A sketch is provided by Robert McAfee Brown, *Gustavo Gutiérrez: An Introduction to Liberation Theology* (Maryknoll, N.Y.: Orbis, 1990), 22–41.

45. See *Theology of Liberation*, xxv–xxviii; and *Truth*, 155–56.

46. See note 21 above.

47. See the remarks of Bernard Sesboué to this effect and Gutiérrez's response during the defense of the latter's "thesis" at Lyon in *Truth*, 32–39.

48. See, e.g., *Theology of Liberation*, 108–9, 111–12; *Power of the Poor* (1975), 10–11.

49. See Gustavo Gutiérrez, "Option for the Poor: Review and Challenges" in *Promotio Justitiae* 57 (1994): 13.

50. See "Option for the Poor," *Promotio Justitiae*, 16.

51. The term is Roberto S. Goizueta's. See his account of the preferential option in "The Church and Hispanics in the United States: From Empowerment to Solidarity," in Michael Downey, ed., *That They Might Live: Power, Empowerment, and Leadership in the Church* (New York: Crossroad, 1991), 160–75, at 163.

52. Care must therefore be taken when reading the numerous treatments of the preferential option by both Latin Americans and others, especially critics, to be sure that this distinction is respected. In my opinion "standpoint of the poor" is preferable to either "perspective" or "viewpoint" of the poor, terms which remain ambiguous in English since each can refer to both angle of perception and opinion.

53. See *Theology of Liberation*, xxii–xxiii, xxxi, 182, n.48.

54. See ibid., xx, xxii–xxiii, and xxxvi for his assessment of the women's movement and feminist theology and xxii–xxiii for his treatment of the question of race.

55. Ibid., 176, n.6.

56. See the "Introduction to the Original Edition" of *Theology of Liberation*, xiii.

57. See, for example, chapter 9 of *God of Life*, "Holy Is God's Name," 164–86.

58. See Cecilia Tovar, "UNEC: cincuenta años de camino" *Páginas* 111 (1991): 87–97, at 92.

59. See *Theology of Liberation*, 174 and *Power of the Poor*, 101–102. The "summer course" in theology founded by Gutiérrez and sponsored by the Pontifical Catholic University of Peru is but one example of this commitment. From the beginning he has encouraged in this course (as well as in the workshops and seminars beyond counting he has given on the Bible, the church's teaching, pastoral theology and practice, and Christian discipleship) the participation of poor and/or indigenous men and women.

60. *Theology of Liberation*, xxiii.

61. He was elected to the Academia Peruana de la Lengua Española in 1995, only the third priest to be so honored in this century.

62. See, e.g., Gutiérrez's own summary of his entire theological production in the "Presentation of the Dissertation" at Lyon in which he refers to Arguedas, *Truth*, 3.

63. *God of Life*, 158.

64. *On Job*, xi–xix, especially xiii and xviii. Also *God of Life*, 145–46.

65. *God of Life*, 158, 160.

66. *Power of the Poor*, 19.

67. *Truth*, 3. Gutiérrez finds a parallel between Arguedas's insight and that of Thomas Aquinas: "We cannot know what God is, but only what God is not." Ibid.

68. See Gustavo Gutiérrez, *Entre las calandrias: un ensayo sobre José María Arguedas* (Lima: CEP, 1990), 3–4. All translations from this work are by the present editor.

69. *Entre las calandrias*, 52–53.

70. *Entre las calandrias*, 52. This idea was central in the writings and praxis of Martin Luther King, Jr. See, for example, his *Stride toward Freedom*.

71. This is the thread which joins together the diverse essays collected in *The Power of the Poor in History*.

72. This is expressed in Arguedas' great hymn to the eighteenth-century figure Túpac Amaru, who led a nearly successful indigenous revolt against Spanish colonial authority. See *Entre las calandrias*, 26–28.

73. Here too Gutiérrez is at one with African-American experience and theology. See James H. Cone, *God of the Oppressed* (New York: Seabury, 1975).

74. *Entre las calandrias*, 93.

75. See *Theology of Liberation*, 18–21.

76. For a sympathetic but critical evaluation, see Arthur McGovern, *Liberation Theology and Its Critics: Toward an Assessment* (Maryknoll, N.Y.: Orbis, 1990).

77. It is included in *Truth*, 53–84.

78. Ibid., 61.

79. Ibid., 61.

80. Ibid., 62.

81. Of particular importance in this regard are the papal encyclicals of Pius XI (*Quadragesimo anno*, 1933) and John Paul II (*Laborem exercens*, 1983; *Centesimus annus*, 1993), the conclusions of Medellín ("Peace") and Puebla (nos. 1208–1209), the 1967 "Message of Third World Bishops," and the 1968 statement by the French episcopal commission on the working class. For Gutiérrez's response to this part of the church's social teaching, see *Theology of Liberation*, 156–61; and *Truth*, 72–75.

82. *Truth*, 63. Particularly useful, in Gutiérrez's view, is the 1980 letter on "Marxist Analysis by Christians" written by Pedro Arrupe, Superior General of the Society of Jesus at the time. Gutiérrez is "in full agreement" with the "distinctions, evaluations, warnings, and rejections" set forth by Arrupe (see *Truth*, 63). For Arrupe's famous letter, see *Origins* 10 (April 16, 1981): 689–93.

83. *Truth*, 2–4, 53–58.

84. Ibid., 55–57.

85. Ibid., 65.

86. Ibid., 64–65, 152–53.

87. Ibid., 141.

88. Ibid., 56.

89. Ibid., 172.

90. See, for example, Norbert F. Lohfink, *Option for the Poor: The Basic Principle of Liberation Theology in the Light of the Bible* (Berkeley, Calif.: BIBAL, 1987).

91. See note 21 above. See also the positions of Vatican II in *Lumen gentium* 8 and *Ad gentes* 5; Medellín ("Poverty of the Church," 7); Puebla (1134–65); and Santo Domingo (178–81).

92. *God of Life*, 90.

93. This is precisely what "through Mary to Jesus" means for Gutiérrez. See *God of Life* 164–86.

94. *We Drink*, 46–49.

95. *God of Life*, 187–88.

96. Ibid., 115.

97. Ibid., 114.

98. Ibid., 126.

SELECT BIBLIOGRAPHY

A. MAJOR WORKS OF GUTIÉRREZ IN ENGLISH

A Theology of Liberation: History, Politics and Salvation. Maryknoll, N.Y.: Orbis, 1973. A revised edition was published by Orbis in 1988. (Original: *Teología de la liberación: perspectivas.* Lima: CEP, 1971.)

The Power of the Poor in History. Maryknoll, N.Y.: Orbis, 1983. (Original: *La fuerza histórica de los pobres: selección de trabajos.* Lima: CEP, 1979.)

We Drink from Our Own Wells: The Spiritual Journey of a People. Maryknoll, N.Y.: Orbis, 1984. (Original: *Beber en su propio pozo: en el itinerario espiritual de un pueblo.* Lima: CEP, 1983.)

On Job: God-Talk and the Suffering of the Innocent. Maryknoll, N.Y.: Orbis, 1987. (Original: *Hablar de Dios desde el sufrimiento del inocente: una reflexión sobre el libro de Job.* Lima: Instituto Bartolomé de las Casas-Rímac and CEP, 1986).

The Truth Shall Make You Free: Confrontations. Maryknoll, N.Y.: Orbis, 1990. (Original: *La verdad los hará libres: confrontaciones.* Lima: CEP, 1986).

The God of Life. Maryknoll, N.Y.: Orbis, 1991. (Original: *El Dios de la vida.* Lima: CEP, 1989.)

Las Casas: In Search of the Poor of Jesus Christ. Maryknoll, N.Y.: Orbis, 1993. (Original: *En busca de los pobres de Jesucristo.* Lima: Instituto Bartolomé de las Casas-Rímac and CEP, 1992.)

Sharing the Word. Maryknoll N.Y.: Orbis, forthcoming 1997. (Original *Compartir la palabra a lo largo del año litúrgico.* Lima: Instituto Bartolomé de las Casas-Rímac and CEP, 1995.)

B. WORKS ON GUTIÉRREZ IN ENGLISH

Brown, Robert McAfee. *Gustavo Gutiérrez: An Introduction to Liberation Theology.* Maryknoll, N.Y.: Orbis, 1990.

Cadorette, Curt. *From the Heart of the People: The Theology of Gustavo Gutiérrez.* Oak Park, Ill.: Meyer-Stone, 1988.

Ellis, Marc H. and Otto Maduro, eds. *The Future of Liberation Theology: Essays in Honor of Gustavo Gutiérrez.* Maryknoll, N.Y.: Orbis, 1989.

INDEX

335

0 5 5 1